THE BIG BOOK
OF KNOWLEDGE

THE BIG BOOK
OF KNOWLEDGE

p

This is a Parragon book
This edition published in 2006

Parragon
Queen Street House
4 Queen Street
Bath BA1 1HE, UK

Copyright © Parragon Books Ltd 1999

Produced by Miles Kelly Publishing Ltd

All rights reserved. No part of this publication may be reproduced,
stored in a retrieval system, or transmitted by any means, electronic, mechanical,
photocopying, recording or otherwise, without the prior permission of the copyright holder.

British Library Cataloguing-in-Publication Data

A catalogue record for this book is available from the British Library.

ISBN 1-40548-539-6

Printed in China

Contents

6 MAIN INTRODUCTION

8 How to use this book

10 Amazing Factfinder Introduction

12 People

40 Animals

68 Plants

96 The Universe

124 Planet Earth

152 Science

180 Amazing Questions Introduction

182 Plants

210 Animals

238 People

266 Earth

294 Space

322 Science

350 Key Facts

370 Index

INTRODUCTION

FACTS ARE ALL around us. Sometimes it seems there are too many facts for our brains to absorb. This book helps your brains by making the facts interesting and easy to understand. There are two different ways that the facts are presented: 1. in the first half of the book as facts in panels and 2. in the second half as questions and answers.

Fact Panels

Hundreds of key facts are provided in the fact panels. Each key fact has a bullet (·) to help you find it.

Captions also provide additional vital information.

Questions and Answers

One of the best ways of presenting information, is in the form of asking questions and then giving the answers. This book does this as well as providing short quizzes to test how well you remember the facts.

Categories

The book is also broken down into different categories such as animals, science, plants, space etc. to help you find the information you want quickly.

Superb illustrations throughout the book provide visual information to add to your fact-finding.

How to use this book

THIS BOOK has many features to help you look up things or just enjoy browsing from page to page. There are several illustrations on almost every page.

The Factfinder has helpful introductory text at the beginning of each section.

The Factfinder section is packed with fascinating factboxes like this one.

Planet Earth

THIRD PLANET OUT FROM THE SUN, our Earth looks from a distance like a great round blue jewel hanging in the darkness of space. It is blue because three-quarters of its rocky surface is drowned under blue ocean waters which shimmer in the light of the Sun. No other planet has this much water on its surface. Here and there, its rocky surface pokes up above the water to form half a dozen large continents and thousands of smaller islands. The very ends of the world are glistening white – the permanent polar ice caps.

FACTS: Earth measurements

- **The size of the Earth**
  Modern measurements show the distance round the Earth is 40,024km at the equator. The Earth's diameter at the equator is 12,758km – slightly larger than its diameter pole to pole, by 43km.
- **The weight of the Earth**
  The Earth weighs 6,000 trillion trillion tonnes.
- **The angle of the Earth**
  The Earth tilts over at an angle of 23.45°.

▼ Satellites have allowed the Earth to be measured more accurately then ever before. Satellites can detect movements of the continents of just a few millimetres or small variations in the height of the sea's surface.

▲ The Earth looks round, but it is not a perfect sphere. Because it spins faster at the equator than the poles, it is actually shaped more like a tangerine, bulging slightly at the equator and flattened at the poles. So scientists used to describe its shape as an oblate spheroid (flattened ball). Now satellite measurements have detected other slight irregularities, so they call it a geoid, which simply means Earth-shaped.

There are many photographs throughout the book.

Cutaway diagrams, maps, and beautiful illustrations help you to understand the hundreds of facts in the book.

Quizzes throughout this section will test your knowledge.

Questions are used to attract your attention.

Answers provide brief, but interesting information on the questions.

Answers to quizzes appear upside down.

Amazing Factfinder

This is an atom. It is so tiny that two billion would fit on the dot on the top of this "i."

This is what a silicon chip looks like from 8 inches away. It is about 0.3 inches long.

This is what a butterfly looks like from about 3 feet away. It is about an inch across.

This is what a lion looks like from about 30 feet away. It is about 10 feet long.

INSIDE THIS SECTION there is a huge array of facts about everything from the smallest thing in the Universe to the biggest. The tiniest things in the Universe, like atoms, are so small you can only see them under the most powerful microscopes. The very tiniest are particles called quarks, so small that billions of them would fit inside an atom. The biggest things, like stars and galaxies, are so big you can only see them all when they are very far away. The very biggest is a wall of galaxies in space called the Great Wall, 800 million light-years long. In between come all kinds of things, from insects and the little electronic chips that make computers to larger animals like lions and us humans, and from great mountains and rivers to entire continents and the world.

Measurements
1,000 picometers = 1 nanometer
1,000 nanometers = 1 micrometer
1,000 micrometers = 1 mm
10 mm = 1 cm
100 cm = 1 meter
1,000 m = 1 kilometer
9,46 trillion km = 1 light year

SMALL THINGS & BIG THINGS

SMALL THINGS

• A Caesium atom is just 0.0000005 mm across.
• The smallest living thing is the bacteria Mycoplasma laidlawii, 0.1 micrometers long.

BIG THINGS

• The largest galaxy is at the center of the Abell 2029 galaxy cluster in the constellation of Virgo, thought to be 5.6 million light years across.
• The largest structure made by living things is the coral Great Barrier Reef, off Queensland Australia, more than 1,200 miles long.

This is what our galaxy the Milky Way looks like from two million light-years away–that is, about 32 billion billion miles. It is about 100,000 light-years (about 600 billion miles) across.

This is what the Sun looks like from about 87 million miles away. It is about 800 million miles across.

This is what the Earth looks like from 60,000 miles away. The Earth is around 8,000 miles across.

This is what mountains like the Matterhorn in the Alps look like from about 6 miles away. It is about 10,000 feet high.

12

PEOPLE

14 Heart and blood
16 Lungs
18 Muscles
20 Bones
22 Senses
24 The nerves and brain
26 New life
28 Food and waste
30 The healthy body
32 Sickness and disease
24 What's wrong?
36 Treatments and cures
38 Body repairs

Heart and blood

THE HEART IS ONE OF THE BODY'S MARVELS, pumping blood around the body ceaselessly. Every second of the day, even as you sleep, the heart's powerful muscles are contracting to send a jet of blood shooting through the body's intricate network of blood vessels. Blood flows right around the body and back to the heart, creating a complete circulation to every part of the body. Without it, you would quickly die. Blood carries the oxygen, nutrients, and chemicals that every body cell needs to survive, and washes away all the waste products, including carbon dioxide.

FACTS: About blood

- **What is blood?**
  It is a complex mix of cells and platelets in a clear yellowish fluid called plasma. Washed along in the plasma too are salts, hormones, fats, and sugars.

- **Red blood cells**
  The most numerous blood cells are button-shaped "red" blood cells, which are like rafts that ferry oxygen around the body, held on board by a protein called hemoglobin.

- **White blood cells**
  Big "white" blood cells play a vital role in the body's defense against disease. White blood cells called neutrophils swallow invaders. Lymphocytes help identify them.

- **Platelets**
  Tiny cell fragments called platelets help plug leaks such as cuts.

▶ Blood is a mix of red cells (erythrocytes), white cells (leucocytes), and tiny platelets in plasma.

FACTS: About circulation

- **Arteries**
  Blood flows out from the heart through large blood vessels called arteries, which branch into smaller arterioles and then into tiny capillaries.

- **Veins**
  Blood flows back to the heart through small venules that join to form larger veins. The load of oxygen makes blood redder in the arteries than the veins.

- **Double circulation**
  There two systems of circulation in the body, each pumped by a different half of the heart.

- **Double circulation**
  The left of the heart drives the "systemic" circulation, which carries oxygen-rich blood from the lungs around the body. The right half of the heart drives the "pulmonary" circulation, which drives blood through the lungs to the left side of the heart.

- **Pulse**
  The pumping of the heart sends regular shock waves through the circulation, detectable as a pulse. To feel your pulse, lay two fingers gently on the inside of your wrist. Counting the number of pulses tells you how fast your heart is beating.

Factfinder: People

DATA: Blood & heart

- **RACING BLOOD**
  Blood flows through the arteries at 1m a second.
- **BLOOD VESSELS**
  There are 60,000km of capillaries in the body.
- **HEART RATE**
  The heart beats on average 80 times a minute.

▲ This doctor is checking his patient's risk of suffering from 'coronary heart disease'. In this disease, the supply of blood to the heart muscle is restricted in some way — and may be cut off altogether, causing a heart attack, in which the heart stops beating.

▶ The heart is not just one pump but two, separated by a thick wall of muscle called the septum. Blood from the veins flows into each half of the heart from the top, flooding the 'atrium', the first of the two chambers. This is a small reservoir where blood builds up before entering the second chamber, or 'ventricle'. The ventricle has extra thick, muscular walls which squeeze the blood out and send it shooting through the arteries.

Blood returning from the body floods from the vena cava into the right atrium

Blood from the left ventricle is pushed into the aorta

Blood goes off to the lungs via the pulmonary artery

Oxygenated blood returns from the lungs

Blood returning from the body gathers in the right atrium

Blood from the right ventricle is pushed into the pulmonary artery

Left atrium

Left ventricle

Valves ensure the blood flows only one way

Septum separating the two halves

The body's biggest vein, the inferior vena cava

The body's widest artery, the aorta

15

Lungs

IF YOU STOPPED BREATHING, for more than a minute or two, you would quickly die. Breathing provides your blood with the oxygen from the air that is vital to the survival of every body cell. Just as fire burns only if there is plenty of oxygen, so body cells need oxygen from the blood to break down the food they also get from the blood. Without oxygen, brain cells live only a few minutes—which is why the brain is quickly damaged if the heart stops pumping blood. When cells break down food, oxygen joins with carbon in the food to make carbon dioxide, which you breathe out.

FACTS: About breathing

Bronchiole carrying air to and from the alveoli

Blood vessel carrying carbon dioxide waste

Blood vessel carrying oxygen-rich blood

Alveolus (air sac)

▲ At the end of every airway in the lung, there are clusters of tiny air sacs called alveoli—more than 300 million altogether. This is where oxygen is transferred into the blood. The "blue" blood vessels carry carbon dioxide to the alveoli ready for breathing out. The "red" vessels carry fresh oxygen to the rest of the body.

- **Nose and throat**
  Normally, you breathe air in through your nose—although you can also breathe through your mouth. Air then flows down through your throat through a tube—called the pharynx—at the top, the larynx in the middle, and the trachea at the bottom.

- **Two lungs**
  The trachea pipes air into your lungs, the two spongy grayish-pink bags in your chest. Lungs transfer oxygen from the air into the blood.

- **Airways**
  The lungs are like hollow trees with hundreds of branching airways called bronchioles.

- **Air sacs**
  Around the end of each bronchiole are clusters of air sacs or "alveoli," like bunches of grapes.

- **Air to blood**
  When you breathe in, oxygen from the air passes through the thin walls of the alveoli into the tiny blood vessels wrapped around them.

- **Blood to air**
  Unwanted carbon dioxide passes from the blood through the alveoli walls into the lungs—and so goes out of the body as you breathe out.

Factfinder: People

Bronchioles

The trachea or windpipe funnels air into the lungs

The diaphragm flattens to pull the lungs down and draw air in

◀ Your lungs contain miles of airways to provide a huge area for oxygen to seep through into the blood in the short space of each breath. Breathing out requires no effort, because the spongy, elastic material of the lungs just collapses like a balloon when you "exhale" (breathe out). But to breathe in, muscles in the chest must pull to make the lungs expand. Intercostal muscles between the ribs lift the ribcage (the chest's framework of bone) upward and outward. At the same time, a domed sheet of muscle beneath the lung, called the diaphragm, flattens out, pulling the lungs down and further expanding them.

DATA: Breathing

- **BREATHS IN A LIFETIME**
You take about 600 million breaths during your lifetime.

- **LUNG AREA**
Opened out and laid flat, the lungs would cover an area the size of a tennis court.

- **LUNG CAPACITY**
On average, we breathe in and out roughly 2 pints (900ml) of air every ten seconds or so.

- **LENGTH OF AIRWAYS**
The branching of the bronchioles means that altogether there are probably more than 1,500 miles (2,400km) of airways in the lungs!

FACTS: Respiration

- **What is respiration?**
Respiration not only means breathing but also the conversion of sugar to energy in body cells. This conversion is called burning, because it creates heat.

- **Aerobic respiration**
Aerobic respiration is when muscle cells burn sugar with oxygen. Anaerobic respiration is when they burn sugar without oxygen.

▲ There is not enough time during a sprint to boost the oxygen supply to the muscles, so they work anaerobically. Only on longer runs do they begin to work aerobically.

Muscles

EVERY MOVE YOU MAKE—running, dancing, smiling, and everything else—depends on muscles. You even need muscles to sit still: without them, you would slump like a rag doll. Muscles are bundles of fibers that tense and relax to move different parts of the body, and there are two kinds: muscles that you can control, called voluntary muscles, and muscles that you can't, called involuntary muscles. Most voluntary muscles are "skeletal muscles," muscles that move parts of your body when you want to. Involuntary muscles are muscles like those of your heart and around your gut, which work automatically.

▲ The body is covered with an almost complete sheath of skeletal muscle pairs, making up 40 percent of the body's weight. There are more than 600 all told, the largest of which is the gluteus maximus in the buttock. In theory, you can control each muscle pair individually. But most work in combinations so well established by habit that they always work together.

FACTS: About muscles

- **Muscle pairs**
  Muscles work by getting shorter, pulling two points together, then relaxing. So most muscles come in pairs: one to pull, the other to pull it back. Typically, there is a "flexor" to bend or flex a joint, and an 'extensor' to straighten it again.

- **Muscle fibers**
  Muscles are bundles of fiberlike cells. Some contain just a few hundred, others a quarter of a million or more.

- **Striped strands**
  Most skeletal muscle fibers are made of thin strands called myofibrils. All along the myofibrils are dark and light stripes called striations, which are actually two alternating substances—actin and myosin.

Factfinder: People

FACTS: About muscles and exercise

- **Red muscle and white muscle**
  Slow-twitch "red" muscle fibers are good for prolonged gentle movements. "White" fibers are for short, powerful bursts. Fast-twitch red ones work for both.

  ◀ *A sportsman trains to develop big muscles, big lungs, and a strong heart.*

- **Oxygen boost**
  When muscles work hard they need more oxygen to burn sugar. So when you run your breathing gets faster and deeper, and your heart pumps faster and harder to boost blood supply. Getting in shape develops bigger lungs and a strong heart. If you're not, a long run makes you pant and your heart beat fast.

▼ *In the muscles you use for movement are thousands of long fibers, each made up from hundreds of thinner strands called myofibrils. Alternate bands of actin and myosin filaments in the myofibril give this kind of muscle a stripy or striated look. These filaments interlock and draw together to make the muscle contract.*

Muscle made from bundles of muscle fibers

Myofibril made from alternating bands of actin and myosin filament

Muscle fibers are made up from hundreds of myofibrils

Actin filament

Myosin filaments are equipped with hooks like velcro that pull the actin

▶ *In the upper arm, the biceps at the front is the flexor muscle that contracts (and swells) to bend the arm. The triceps at the back is the extensor that contracts to straighten it out again.*

- **How muscles contract**
  In the muscle fibers, filaments of actin and myosin interlock. When the brain sends the muscle a message to contract, little buds on each myosin filament twist sharply, pulling on actin filaments and contracting.

- **Shortening power**
  There are millions of actin and myosin filaments in each muscle. When they pull together, they can shorten the muscle by almost half its length.

- **Smooth muscle**
  Not all muscles are stripy. Muscles called smooth muscles contract blood vessels to control blood flow to the gut to push food through. The heart is powered by "cardiac" muscle, which beats automatically, although its rate may vary.

Bones

YOUR BODY IS SUPPORTED by a strong frame called the skeleton. The skeleton not only provides an anchor for muscles, but makes a mount for skin and other tissues, and protects the heart, brain, and other organs. It is made of more than 200 bones, linked by a rubbery substance called cartilage. Bones are very tough and light because their outside is made from a mixture of hard minerals such as calcium, and stringy, elastic collagen. Inside the tough, dry casing, there are holes called lacunae full of living cells called osteocytes, which are bathed in blood—just like every other cell in the body.

FACTS: About joints

- **Moving joints**
  Joints allow the bones of the skeleton to move. The shoulder is a ball and socket joint. The knee and elbow are hinges, like a door hinge. The neck is a swiveling joint, allowing the head to rotate.

- **Spinal joints**
  The joints between backbones are "cartilaginous," joined by layers of cartilage which are stiff but allow a little movement.

- **Knee joints**
  Knee joints are lubricated by capsules of oil called synovial fluid, so are called synovial joints.

◀ Skiing and other sporting activities put a tremendous strain on the knee joints, but the joints are protected by a sleeve of tough collagen fibre and lubricated by synovial fluid.

▼ The skeleton is a strong but remarkably mobile framework. It has two main parts. The main or "axial" part of the skeleton is the skull, spine, ribs, and sternum (breastbone). The bones of the "appendicular" skeleton—arms and legs, along with the shoulders and pelvis (hip bone)—hang from the axial skeleton.

Cranium (skull)
Scapula (shoulder blade)
Humerus (upper arm)
Rib
Sternum (breastbone)
Radius (main forearm)
Ulna (lesser forearm)

20

Factfinder: People

FACTS: About bones

- **Fusing bones**
  Babies have more than 300 bones, but many fuse together as they grow, so adults have just 206.

- **Strong bones**
  Weight for weight, bone is five times stronger than steel.

- **Long and short bones**
  The longest, strongest bone is the thigh bone, or femur. The smallest is the stirrup in the middle ear.

- **Bone makeup**
  Bone is made up from a network of collagen (protein) fibers filled with calcium and phosphate.

- **Bone breakers**
  Fresh bone material is constantly being made in cells called osteoblasts. Old bone is broken down by osteoclasts.

- **Bone marrow**
  In the hollow center of the breastbone, ribs, and hips is soft, spongy red "marrow" where red and white blood cells are created. All your bones have this red marrow when you are born, but as you grow older, the marrow of long bones such as the legs and arms turns yellow.

▼ Bones have a surprisingly complex structure. On the outside there is a strong casing of "compact" bone made of tiny tubes called "osteons." Inside this is a layer of spongy bone. Inside this is the marrow.

Covering membrane or "periosteum"

Compact bone made of osteons

Spongy bone forms an inner layer

Spongy red marrow makes blood cells, and yellow marrow stores fat

Patella (kneecap)

Tarsals (ankle bones)

Phalanges (toe bones)

Femur (thigh bone)

Fibula (calf bone)

Tibia (shin bone)

Pelvis (hip bone)

Senses

OUR SENSES TELL US what is going on in the world around us. Even when we are asleep, our senses are picking up sensations, some from inside the body, some from outside, and feeding them to the brain via the nerves, which are like the body's telephone wires. We have five main senses to tell us what is going on in the outside world–sight from our eyes, hearing from our ears, smell from our nose, taste from our tongue, and touch from most of our skin. Besides this, there are internal senses, such as pain, and the balance organs in the ear, which tell you whether you are standing upright, or moving fast.

FACTS: About sight

- The iris controls the size of the pupil, narrowing it in bright light
- Optic nerve
- Muscles for turning eyes
- Retina
- Iris
- The cornea focuses the picture
- The lens keeps the picture sharp
- Tear duct
- The dark "pupil" is the window into the eye

▲ The eyes are two tough little balls filled with a jellylike substance called vitreous humor. Each eye gives you a slightly different view of the world. The brain combines these different views to give you a complete 3D picture.

- **Camera-like eye**
Eyes are a bit like video cameras. A lens at the front projects the picture on to the back of the eye, called the retina, where millions of light-sensitive cells detect the picture, and transmit it to the brain via the "optic" nerve.

- **Lens and cornea**
The eye's main lens is called the cornea, the clear dome in the middle of the eye. The "lens" just behind it changes shape to keep the picture sharp.

- **Rods and cones**
The light-sensitive cells in the retina are called rods and cones. Rods work even in dim light, but cannot distinguish colors. Cones can distinguish colors, but do not work in dim light, which is why we do not see colors well at night.

Factfinder: People

◀ Smell relies on a small patch of "olfactory" nerves inside the top of your nose which react to minute traces of chemicals in the air. Taste is a mixture of sensations, including smell. But your tongue has four different kinds of taste receptors, called taste buds. They react to sweet, salty, bitter, or sour tastes in food.

Labels on tongue: Bitter, Sour, Sweet, Salty

FACTS: About hearing

▼ The flap of skin on the outside of your head is only one part of the ear, called the outer ear. It just funnels sound down a canal called the ear canal into your head. The real workings of the ear are inside your head. Here are the bones of middle ear, and the curly tube of the inner ear.

Labels on ear diagram: Ossicles, Stapes, Cochlea, Incus, Malleus, Eardrum, Ear canal

▼ There are touch receptors all over the body, embedded in the skin. They react to four kinds of feeling—a light touch, steady pressure, heat and cold, and pain. Receptors called Meissner's corpuscles are responsible for light touch. Merkel's disks pick up steady pressure.

Cross-section through the skin

Labels: Merkel's disk, Meissner's corpuscle

- **The middle ear**
  The middle ear is the ear's amplifier. Sound entering the middle ear hits a taut wall of skin called the eardrum, shaking it rapidly. As it shakes, it rattles three tiny bones or "ossicles," called the malleus (hammer), the incus (anvil), and the stapes (stirrup).

- **The inner ear**
  The inner ear is mainly a curly tube full of fluid, called the cochlea. As the ossicles rattle, they knock against this tube, making waves in the fluid. Minute detector hairs waggle in these waves and, as they move, they send signals along nerves to the brain.

- **Two ears**
  Because we have two ears, we can detect where a sound is coming from—by the minute differences in loudness between each ear.

23

The nerves and brain

INSIDE YOUR HEAD IS THE MOST amazingly complex known structure in the universe: the human brain. It looks like a huge, soggy gray walnut with a wrinkled surface. It is split into two halves and weighs on average about 3.3 pounds (1.5kg). But within this soggy mass are literally billions of intricately interconnected nerve cells. The chemical and electrical impulses continually shooting through your brain cells produce all your thoughts, and control nearly all your actions—and record every sensation—by signals sent to and fro along the remarkable network of nerves that link your body to the brain like the wires in a computer.

FACTS: About the brain

- **Brain damage**
  Brain cells depend on oxygen in the blood. If the supply is cut off for even a few seconds, a person loses consciousness. If it is cut off any longer, cells die and the brain becomes damaged.

- **Parts of the brain**
  The layout of the brain reflects the way it evolved. As it grew out from the primitive brain stem at the top of the spine, it became more complex, developing first into the hind brain, then the complicated cerebrum.

- **The center of the brain**
  The core of the brain includes the thalamus and midbrain and controls basic functions such as breathing and heart rate, without your awareness. The hypothalamus here controls hunger and sleeping. Around the thalamus is the limbic system, which makes you angry or upset.

- **The cerebrum**
  The huge wrinkles of the cerebrum wrap around the core of the brain. This is where you think, and complex tasks such as memory, speech, and conscious control of movement go on. All the folds allow a huge number of nerve cells to be squeezed inside the skull.

Cerebrum: thinking, memory, speech, eyesight, hearing, and much more
Limbic system: emotion
Thalamus: relay station
Hypothalamus: hunger, thirst, and sleeping
Pons
Medulla
Brain stem (medulla and pons): heart rate, breathing
Cerebellum: coordination
Spinal cord

▲ Different areas of the brain are associated with different tasks, such as walking or speaking. Some regions, known as sensory areas, receive signals from sense organs. Others, known as motor areas, are the areas that help you to control muscles and enable you to move.

Factfinder: People

FACTS: About nerve cells

▼ Nerve cells receive signals from other nerve cells through tiny branches called dendrites and send them out along along a thin, winding tail, or axon. At the far end of the axon the signal is sent on to other cells across tiny gaps called synapses.

Axon
Synapse
Nucleus
Dendrite
Axon of another nerve cell

- **Nerve cells**
  Nerve cells or "neurons" are long lived, but when they die, they are not replaced by others.

- **Multi link**
  The nervous system is a network of long strings of nerve cells linked together like beads on a string.

- **Neurotransmitters**
  Nerve signals are sent across synapses, the gaps between nerves, by shots of chemicals called neurotransmitters. Different receptors pick up different neurotransmitters.

◀ Brain scans show scientists what is going on inside a living brain, and so they now know a great deal about the way the brain works. This has helped them identify, for instance, which areas are active when you are speaking.

DATA: Nerve facts

- **NERVE SPEED**
  The fastest nerve signals travel at 330 feet (120m) per second.

- **NERVE LENGTH**
  Axons vary from 0.04 inches (1mm) to 40 inches (1m) long.

▶ The network of nerves in the body—called the nervous system—focuses on the Central Nervous System, or CNS. This includes the brain and the spinal cord (the bundle of nerves in the spine). From the CNS, nerves branch out all over the body.

25

New life

LIKE MOST HUMANS, your life probably began when your mother and father made love. Inside your father's body are "reproductive organs" that are always making millions of tiny cells called sperm, which are like tiny tadpoles. Inside your mother's body are reproductive organs that release an egg into her womb at a certain time every month. Your life began when your mother and father made love at the right time, so that one of your father's sperm worked its way into an egg and fertilized it. The fertilized egg grew gradually inside your mother's womb, until, at last, after nine months or so, you were born.

FACTS: About reproductive organs

- **Puberty**
You are born with reproductive or sexual organs, but they only develop in the right way for you to have children once you reach the age of puberty—typically 11-13 years. At puberty, chemicals called sex hormones flood through your body, stimulating the changes that turn boys into men and girls into women.

- **Puberty in boys**
When a boy reaches puberty, his testes grow and begin to produce sperm. At the same time, he begins to grow pubic hair and hair on his chin.

- **Puberty in girls**
When a girl reaches puberty, she begins to grow breasts, and her monthly periods, or menstruation, start. She, too, grows pubic hair.

- **Menstruation**
Menstruation is the monthly cycle of changes in a woman's body that prepares her for having a baby. Every four weeks, her ovary releases an egg so that it slides down the Fallopian tube and into her womb. If the egg is not then fertilized, the lining of the womb breaks down and blood flows out of the woman's vagina.

◀ In a man's reproductive organs, the sperm is made in the two testes or testicles. When making love, the man's erect penis is inserted into a woman's vagina. When the penis is stimulated enough, a liquid called semen carries the sperm from the testes out through the end of the penis into the vagina.

Vas deferens
Testicle
Urethra
Penis

◀ In a woman's reproductive organs, eggs are stored in the two ovaries. One egg is released a month into the womb, or "uterus," via the Fallopian tubes. During love-making, millions of sperm from a man's penis enter the woman's vagina and swim up into the uterus, where only one sperm may penetrate an egg.

Fallopian tube
Ovary
Womb, or uterus
Vagina

Factfinder: People

FACTS: About pregnancy

▲ The moment a sperm enters an egg and fertilizes it is called conception. This is the moment a pregnancy begins. A baby is born about nine months later.

- **Embryo to foetus**
  During the first eight weeks of pregnancy, while internal organs are developing, the new life is called an embryo. After that it is called a fetus (say "feet-us").

- **Lifeline**
  The fetus is supplied with oxygen and food via a tube called the umbilical cord. This links the foetus to the placenta, a spongy organ on the womb lining.

DATA: Ova and embryos

- **FERTILE PERIOD**
  An egg or ovum can only be fertilized in the 12-24 hours after it is released (called ovulation).

- **GROWING LIFE**
  At four weeks, an embryo is no bigger than a grain of rice, but once it becomes a foetus it grows rapidly. At 20 weeks, a fetus is 10 inches (25cm) long.

The umbilical cord carries the blood supply from the mother that gives the fetus oxygen and food

The placenta is shed after the birth and follows the baby out

After nine months, the baby turns head down, ready to be born

Cervix, known together with the vagina as the birth canal

▲ In the safety of the mother's womb, the new human life grows from just a few cells to an embryo, then a fetus, to become a baby in nine months, growing larger and more recognizably human by the day. Throughout this time, it is kept warm and cushioned from the outside world inside a bag or sac of fluid called amniotic fluid. When it is ready to be born, the neck of the womb begins to expand, so that the baby can be pushed out through the vagina and into the world.

27

Food and waste

BEFORE YOUR BODY CAN USE any of the food you eat, it must be broken down into simple chemical molecules. This is called digestion. It begins the moment you put food in your mouth and chew it until soft. It continues as you swallow the food and it is pushed down the long tube through your body called the alimentary canal, or gut. A barrage of chemicals and squeezing muscles assault the food all the way through the gut until most is ready to be absorbed through the gut and carried to the rest of the body in the blood. Food that cannot be digested goes out through the anus.

FACTS: About waste disposal

- **Cleaning the blood**
  Toxic chemicals and excess water often build up. It is the task of the kidneys to filter these out of the blood and concentrate them into urine.

- **Kidney**
  The kidneys are two bean-shaped organs in the middle of the back. As they filter blood, they regulate body fluid and salt levels and control blood acidity. They filter 15 pints (7l) of blood an hour.

- **Ureter and bladder**
  The ureters are the tubes that pipe urine continually from the kidneys to the bladder, a bag where urine builds up until you are able to empty it. The bladder can hold up to a pint (450ml) of urine.

- **Urethra**
  When you urinate, urine from the bladder drains out of the body through the urethra. This is 8 inches (20cm) long in men, but just 1.5 inches (4cm) long in women.

▶ The kidneys, ureters, bladder, and urethra together make up the urinary system, the body's liquid waste disposal system. Urine is all that is left after valuable ingredients are retrieved by the kidneys from the blood.

Factfinder: People

FACTS: About digestion

◁ The digestive system is basically a long tube—the alimentary canal—through which food moves as it is gradually broken down and absorbed.

Mouth
Esophagus
Pancreas secretes stomach acid
Liver
Stomach
Duodenum
Colon
Appendix
Rectum
Small intestine
Large intestine

- **The stomach**
  Food spends about six hours in the stomach. Here it is churned up by the muscles of the stomach wall and attacked by "gastric" juices, including hydrochloric acid and powerful enzymes, secreted by glands in the stomach wall.

- **Stomach gate**
  Food is held in the stomach by a ring of muscle called the pyloric sphincter until it is partly digested.

- **Food names**
  A lump of swallowed food is called a bolus. Once partly digested by the stomach it is called chyme.

- **Small intestine**
  From the stomach, food goes into the tube called the small intestine, where it is absorbed into the blood. Food undigested here passes into the large intestine, or bowel, where waste is turned solid.

- **Rippling muscles**
  Food is moved through the gut by ripples of the muscles in the gut wall. Muscles extend in front of the bolus or chyme and contract behind it to push it along. This is called peristalsis.

- **Liver**
  The liver has many functions, including turning digested food into blood proteins.

DATA: Digestion

- **LONG GUT**
  Your gut is folded over so many times that it is six times as long as you are tall—up to 33 feet (10m).

- **FOOD IN THE BODY**
  Food takes on average 24 hours to pass all the way through the alimentary canal.

The healthy body

THE HUMAN BODY IS REMARKABLY GOOD at taking care of itself, and it has a wide range of mechanisms to help it adjust to different circumstances. But to stay healthy, it needs the right food and regular exercise. Most of the food we eat is fuel burned by the body for energy. But the body also needs small quantities of foods such as proteins which are needed to repair cells and build new ones. It also needs minute traces of chemicals that it cannot make for itself: vitamins and minerals. A healthy diet is one that includes all of these foods in just the right proportion and quantity.

FACTS: About diet

- **Foods**
There are three main kinds of food—carbohydrates, fats, and proteins—as well as vitamins, minerals, water, and fiber.

- **Carbohydrates**
Carbohydrates are foods such as sugars and starches, found in abundance in foods such as bread, rice, potatoes, and sweet things. They are the body's main source of energy along with fats.

◀ You need a balanced diet to get the carbohydrates, fats, and protein you need, plus vitamins and minerals, and the fiber needed to take food through the gut properly. A good diet might include fresh fruit and vegetables, brown bread, fish, eggs, cheese, and liver.

Factfinder: People

◄ *Eating too much carbohydrate-rich and fatty food makes you overweight. To stay in shape and at the right weight, you should eat these foods only in moderate amounts, and exercise regularly to ensure your body is efficient at burning off any excess.*

- **Fats**
Fats are greasy foods that won't dissolve in water. Some are solid, such as meat fat and cheese. Others, such as corn oil, are liquid. Fats are not only used by the body as energy stores but are a source of vitamins D and E.

- **Too much fat**
Too much fat not only makes you fat. Too much "saturated" fat—mainly animal fat such as butter—can boost the risk of heart disease.

- **Essential acids**
The body needs 20 "amino acids" to build into protein to make and repair cells. The body can make 12 of these; the other eight it must get from protein in food. These are the "essential amino acids."

- **Protein**
Protein in fish and meat has all the amino acids the body needs. Fruit and vegetables have only some of them, which is why vegetarians must choose the right mixture.

- **Protein sources**
Beans and nuts are the most protein-rich foods. The protein content in: soybean flour is 40%; peanuts 28%; cheese 25%; raw meat 23%; raw fish 15%; eggs 12%; bread 8%; rice 6%.

FACTS: Vitamins & minerals

- **Vitamins**
Vitamins are chemicals vital for life, found in foods. There are 13 major vitamins: A, C, D, E, K, and 8 varieties of B. Each has a range of tasks in the body. Vitamin C (in citrus fruit) helps fight infection and keep gums and teeth healthy. Vitamin A (found in carrots, green vegetables, and milk) helps keep skin and bones healthy.

- **Essential minerals**
Essential minerals include small amounts of salt, calcium for bones, iron for red blood cells, and tiny traces of minerals such as iodine.

▲ *Vitamins are mostly fairly simple chemicals, such as folic acid (one of the B vitamins), but they are vital for life. This picture shows a vitamin crystal in close-up.*

DATA: Food

- **FOOD NEEDS**
On average people need around 2,000 calories of energy food a day.

- **FOOD INTAKE**
On average, people in the United States eat 3,200 calories a day. In Ethiopia, they survive on less than 500 calories a day.

Sickness and disease

EVERY NOW AND THEN, people succumb to sickness and disease. Most diseases, fortunately, are minor, and the victim usually recovers quickly, thanks to the body's remarkable defense system, called the immune system. Sickness is caused either by an internal failure of one of the body's mechanisms—or by invading microbes or germs. This is where the immune system comes in. The body's immune system not only identifies the germs, but fights them with an array of chemical and biological weapons, including formidable "immune cells." Only the very worst diseases defeat the body's immune system.

FACTS: About the immune system

- **The lymphatic system**
  Lymph is a clear fluid that drains from cells into the bloodstream via a network of capillaries, called the lymph system. Immune cells patrol all through the blood, but are concentrated in the lymph system.

- **Inflame response**
  Some germs set off an inflame response. This attacks all germs the same way, increasing blood flow, and bringing a flood of cells called neutrophils into play.

- **Antibodies**
  Antibodies are labels that attach to germs and show killer cells which cells to kill.

- **Killer cells**
  Among the many kinds of immune cells, two kinds of white blood cell are the most important: killer "T" cells, which engulf germs, and B lymphocytes, which identify invaders and make antibodies.

▲ Invaders are targeted by the body's immune system in a number of ways to ensure they are beaten off.

◀ Vaccination is designed to trigger the body to make antibodies against a disease.

Factfinder: People

FACTS: About germs

◀ People infected with the HIV virus often succumb to the deadly disease AIDS. This virus is deadly because it attacks the body's immune system and renders it ineffective.

- **Infection**
Many germs cause infection, when bacteria, viruses, or fungi multiply within your body. As they multiply they either damage cells directly, as viruses do, or may release harmful toxins.

- **Fever and inflammation**
Infection activates the immune system, and many of the symptoms you feel—fever, weakness, inflammation—are side-effects of the immune system's struggle.

- **Bacteria and viruses**
Viruses are very tiny and can only multiply by entering other cells—such as your body's cells—and taking them over. Bacteria are much bigger, and are tiny one-celled organisms.

DATA: Immune cells

- **ANTIBODY NUMBERS**
There are thousands of different antibodies in the blood, each targeted against a particular "antigen" (invader).

- **GIANT EATER**
A single "macrophage" (giant eater) T cell can eat up to 100 bacteria.

▼ Unlike viruses, bacteria can multiply outside the body and can be grown in dishes of protein to create "cultures." By growing cultures, scientists can test antibiotic drugs on them and see which are the most effective at killing them off.

▲ A common form of allergy is hay fever. In the summer, grasses and other plants release pollen. When this is inhaled, it can cause allergic reactions in some people, such as streaming eyes and sneezing.

33

What's wrong?

BEFORE YOU CAN BE TREATED for any illness or injury, the doctor has to decide just what is wrong. This is called diagnosis. The most important clues for a diagnosis are usually the symptoms–that is, all the signs that something may be wrong–a cough, a rash, a pain in your side, and so on. The doctor may also find clues in the story of events that led up to the illness, called the history. The illness or injury can often be identified from the symptoms and history alone. If not, you may have to undergo various tests, or have pictures taken of your insides with X-rays or scanners.

FACTS: Looking for clues

- **History**
  Most visits to the doctor begin with the history. While you tell the doctor your symptoms, he or she asks you other questions about the course of events, takes notes and begins to form an idea about the nature of the problem.

- **The examination**
  The doctor may then go on to look at and listen to the appropriate parts of your body where he thinks there may be further clues. This is called the physical examination. A doctor may look at your eyes using a device called an opthalmoscope, for instance, or tap on your stomach to hear if the taps vibrate through your internal organs normally. He may also check your temperature or blood pressure.

▼ In the physical examination, the doctor may listen to your chest (right) or check your blood pressure (below).

- **Listening to the chest**
  The doctor can tell a great deal just by listening to your chest using a stethoscope. A stethoscope is a simple listening tube. The tight membrane picks up slight sounds inside your body and the tube transmits them to the doctor's ears. Stethoscopes are particularly important for any problems connected with your breathing or heart.

◄ Athletes continually monitor their bodies—whether they are ill or not—to check that they are achieving peak performance.

Factfinder: People

FACTS: About CT and other scans

- **CT scans**
CT or Computerized Tomography scans use computers to build up a series of pictures showing slices through the body.

- **How CT works**
Inside a CT scanner, an X-ray gun rotates around the patient, firing as it goes. Light detectors on the far side pick up the rays. A computer analyzes what happened to each ray as it passed through the patient's body to build up a detailed picture.

- **MRI scans**
MRI or Magnetic Resonance Imaging uses a powerful magnet to line up all the protons (tiny atomic particles) in a patient's body. A brief pulse of radio waves then knocks them briefly out of alignment. As they snap back into alignment afterward, they send out little radio signals themselves. The scanner picks up all these billions of tiny signals to give a detailed picture of the body inside.

▼ *CT scans are especially good at showing deep inside the brain, and have revolutionized the treatment of head injuries.*

The X-ray gun rotates round the porthole firing low-dose X-ray beams

◄ *For a CT scan, the patient lies on a moving bed and slides into a porthole in the scanner.*

FACTS: About X-rays

- **X-rays**
X-rays are a simple and effective way of taking a black and white picture of the inside of your body.

▶ *This is an X-ray of someone's chest. The ribcage shows up clearly as pale, curved bars.*

- **X-rays**
X-rays are a bit like light, but they are made from waves too short to see—and they can pass straight through certain tissues in your body to turn photographic film black. Tissues that block their path show up white on film.

35

Treatments and cures

YOUR BODY HAS ITS OWN RANGE OF defenses against illness, called the immune system, and it can fight off many diseases unaided if you are in pretty good shape. But doctors have many treatments to help when the immune system cannot cope. Some are so effective that many illnesses that were once inevitably fatal, such as tuberculosis, can often now be treated with drugs. Many diseases can be prevented by vaccination programs, that make the most of the body's immune system. Germs-little organisms such as bacteria and viruses that cause illness-can also be kept at bay by proper hygiene.

FACTS: About drugs

- **Antibiotics**
  Many illnesses that are caused by bacteria can be treated with drugs called antibiotics. These were originally made from molds and fungi, but are now made synthetically. They include penicillin and tetracycline.

- **How drugs are made**
  In the past, drugs mostly came from natural substances. Now most are made in the laboratory or designed on computer. A few drugs are made by manipulating the genes of living organisms so that they produce the drug. Insulin, for instance, is made in the pancreas of pigs or oxen.

� The range of different drugs a doctor has to treat illnesses is now enormous. Most come as pills that can be swallowed, but a few are injected directly into the blood with a needle.

FACTS: About vaccination

▶ This is the germ that causes the terrible disease AIDS, magnified tens of thousands of times. The germ is a virus which attacks the body's immune system. Doctors are looking for a vaccine against it.

▼ Most children have vaccinations at regular intervals as they grow up, against diseases such as diphtheria, whooping cough, and tetanus.

Factfinder: People

▲ Many vaccines are made by genetic engineering—that is, by altering the genes of the germ to make it harmless. These are called live attenuated organisms.

- **Disease protection**
  You can be protected from some diseases by immunization or vaccination.

- **Passive immunization**
  For immediate, short-lived protection from an infection, you might be injected with blood from someone who has already survived the disease. The blood contains tiny proteins called antibodies, which defend your body against the invading germ.

- **Active immunization**
  For long term protection, you may be injected with a killed or mild version of the germ. Your body then makes its own antibodies against the germ, and so is resistant to further infection.

- **Killing diseases**
  Many once common diseases—diphtheria, polio, measles, and whooping cough—are now quite rare thanks to mass vaccination of children. Smallpox is now very rare indeed.

▶ The way ordinary hospitals and doctors treat illnesses is based on science and is called conventional medicine. But there are many alternative approaches. Some are based on traditional methods passed down from generation to generation over thousands of years. Many people in Africa go to a witch doctor (right). Other alternatives include herbal medicine which uses herbs as treatments, and Chinese acupuncture, which uses needle pricks in carefully chosen places.

▼ When people are sick, proper care may be as important as the right medicines. If you are only mildly sick, your family or friends can look after you. In hospital, you may be tended by nurses, who make sure you are taking medicines correctly, and provide the right food and fluids.

37

Body repairs

SOMETIMES, WHEN YOUR BODY cannot heal itself, or when treatment with drugs is inappropriate, the only solution may be to cut it open and physically repair it, just as you would a broken-down automobile. This is called surgery. Surgeons might cut open your body to cut out a diseased or wrongly functioning organ, such as your appendix, or mend a broken bone. They might also, if you are very ill, take out an organ from your body and replace it with a healthy organ from another person (maybe from someone who has died). This is called a transplant.

FACTS: About surgery

- **Local anesthetic**
  A minor operation is generally done under a local anesthetic. This means a drug is wiped on the skin or injected to numb any feeling in just the area being operated on.

- **General anesthetic**
  Major operations are done under a general anesthetic. This means the patient is given a drug by injection, or breathes a gas that sends him or her to sleep for the entire operation. You would need a general anesthetic to have a heart transplant, or to have your appendix out.

▲ In a heart transplant, a diseased heart is cut out and replaced with a healthy heart from someone who has died.

- **Organ transplants**
  All these parts of the body may be transplanted: kidney, cornea of the eye; the heart, heart and lung, and lungs; the liver; and the pancreas.

- **Transplanted organs**
  After a transplant, the body's immune system may reject the new organ as foreign. So the patient is given drugs to suppress the immune system.

◄ Major surgery involves a team of people working together in a specially equipped room called an operating theater. The team is headed by the surgeon but also involves an anesthetist and nurses.

Factfinder: People

FACTS: About implants and prosthetics

- **Implants**
  Sometimes, damaged or diseased parts inside the body such as the hip bone may be replaced by special-purpose parts made of materials such as metal and nylon. These are called implants.

- **Pacemakers**
  People with heart problems, for instance, may be given a pacemaker, a tiny electronic device that sends out electrical signals to the heart muscles to keep the heart beating steadily.

- **Prosthetics**
  Prosthetics are artificial parts attached to the outside of the body. Someone who has lost an arm, for instance, may be given an artificial one, complete with hinged elbow and movable fingers.

▶ *Implants have to be made of tough, noncorrosive material. This illustration shows parts of the body that may be replaced by implants made of the metal titanium—the same tough, shiny metal that is often used in aircraft.*

▼ *Using a microscope, a microsurgeon can carry out operations on a minute scale—to connect fine blood vessels in the eye, or rejoin minute nerves and tendons severed in an injury.*

39

ANIMALS

42 Small mammals

44 Large mammals

46 Big cats

48 Monkeys and apes

50 Pandas, bears, and dogs

52 Sea mammals

54 Pets

56 Farm animals

58 Tropical birds

60 Temperate birds

62 Reptiles

64 Amphibians

66 Insects

Small mammals

MAMMALS COME IN ALL SHAPES AND SIZES and live in a huge variety of places, from the frozen arctic wastes to the hottest desert. Like fish, birds, amphibians, and reptiles, they are "vertebrates"—animals with backbones. This really means they have a bony skeleton inside their bodies, which makes a strong frame for hanging everything on. Besides a backbone, mammals usually have two pairs of limbs, a skull to hold the brain, eyes, ears, and a nose—and then a heart, lungs, and guts inside the ribs.

FACTS: About mammals

- **Warm-blooded**
  Mammals are said to be endothermic (warm-blooded) and reptiles exothermic (cold-blooded). This doesn't mean reptiles' blood is necessarily colder. It just means that mammals are able to keep their blood and bodies equally warm all the time—which is why they can survive in so many different places.

- **Babies**
  All mammals begin life as a tiny egg inside their mother's body. But most young mammals develop inside their mother's body until they are born as babies. Very few baby mammals can cope by themselves when they are born, and most need looking after by their parents for while. Human babies need looking after for many years.

- **Mammals that lay eggs**
  A few mammals living in Australia called monotremes lay eggs rather than have babies. These include the duck-billed platypus.

- **Milk power**
  Unlike other animals, mother mammals feed their babies on milk until they are old enough to cope with solid foods. Milk gives all the fat and protein the baby needs to grow.

- **Milk on tap**
  The more babies a mother mammal tends to have, the more pairs of teats she has. Humans have just one pair, but pigs have seven pairs.

- **Big and small**
  The biggest mammal is the blue whale, 100 feet (30m) long and weighing 330,000 pounds (150,000kg); the smallest is the Etruscan shrew, smaller than your thumb and weighing only 1/16 ounce (1.5gm).

- **Fur coats**
  All mammals have a fur coat, even if it is just made up of a few strands like with humans, rhinos, and whales. Fur keeps the animal warm by trapping a layer of insulating air.

- **Clever creatures**
  Compared to other animals, much more of a mammal's brain is cerebrum, the part of the brain devoted to intelligent behavior. In humans and apes, the proportion is biggest of all.

◀ The badger is one of 4,200 known species of mammal around the world.

Factfinder: Animals

FACTS: About rodents

- **Rodents**
  There are more than 1,700 species of rodent, including rats and mice, rabbits, and guinea pigs.

- **Front teeth**
  All rodents have two pairs of ever-growing, razor-sharp front teeth, or incisors, for gnawing.

▲ Porcupines are small mammals covered in incredibly long spines, which protect them from predators. When threatened, they rustle or rattle their spines—or even run backward into the enemy, spines pointing.

◄ Squirrels have fur-lined cheek pouches which they use for storing food.

▲ Weasels are among the most effective of all small predators—they are both agile and strong.

▶ Beavers are the biggest of all rodents, except for the South American capybara. They live in water and use their sharp teeth to gnaw through trees to get wood to dam streams. They build their homes, called lodges, in the pond created behind this dam.

The inside of the beaver's lodge is above water level, but it is reached by an underwater entrance

Beavers have two very sharp teeth for gnawing

Beavers' big flat tails and webbed back feet make them good swimmers

Large mammals

SOME MAMMALS ARE TINY but the big mammals are the biggest living things in the world. The biggest of all the mammals on land are elephants, which can grow up to 13 feet (4m) tall–twice as tall as a basketball player–and weigh 15,500 pounds (7,000kg), which is as much as a big truck. Not that much smaller are two other creatures of tropical Africa and Asia, the rhinoceros and hippopotamus. All of these big mammals are herbivores, which means they eat plants. So, too, are the many medium-sized herd animals such as buffalos and horses.

FACTS: About elephants

- **Long nose**
  An elephant's most remarkable feature is its long trunk, or "proboscis," which it uses for breathing, smelling, pulling down branches, picking up objects, making trumpeting noises, and for sucking up water.

- **Long life**
  Elephants live longer than all mammals apart from man, surviving up until the age of 80 in captivity.

- **Big ears**
  When an elephant holds its ears back flat, it is either relaxed, or feeling cowed by another. A dominant or aggressive bull (male elephant) often sticks its ears out.

- **Big teeth**
  Elephants have two giant teeth called tusks, which they use for digging or to fend off enemies. Bulls sometimes lock tusks and wrestle with their trunks to see who's strongest.

- **Keeping cool**
  To cool off in the heat elephants stretch out or flap their ears. They also cover themselves with mud or spray themselves with dust or water. Coating their skin like this also helps to condition their skin and provide a protective layer.

- **Herds**
  Elephants live in herds, ranging from four to 30 members, led by a mature cow, or "matriarch." The rest of a herd is generally made up of several females and their young, as well as a few young bulls. Adult males tend to move off and live on their own or in all male groups.

Tusks curve as they grow

▶ Elephants in Africa are much bigger than those found in Asia, with an African bull weighing up to 15,500 pounds (7,000kg).

Factfinder: Animals

FACTS: About herbivores

- **Grazers and browsers**
  Herbivores that eat grasses are called "grazers," while those that eat leaves, bark and the buds of trees and bushes are called "browsers." Some animals only eat one kind of plant, but most will actually eat a variety depending on whatever is available.

- **Steady eating**
  Because plants are not as nutritious as meat, most herbivores need to spend large amounts of time eating—unlike carnivores, which feed only occasionally. An elephant, for example, usually feeds for at least 18 hours every day.

▶ *The takin (right) is a herbivore that lives in Central Asia. It looks a bit like a goat, but with shorter horns and a stockier body, covered in dense brown hair.*

▲ *Rhinos such as this Indian rhinoceros have thick, hairless skin which is arranged like protective armor, folding at the neck, shoulders, and legs to allow movement. Some species of rhino also have one horn; some have two. These horns are actually made of densely compacted hair, or "keratin."*

The African elephant has much bigger ears than an Indian elephant, and a sloping forehead instead of a domed one.

▼ *Horses belong to a group of mammals called ungulates, or hooved mammals. As with pigs, cattle, and camels, claws have been replaced with hooves. Each foot of a horse has one toe with a toenail, which is the hoof. They are very fast runners, using just the tip of this toe as they move.*

DATA: Large mammals

- **THE BIGGEST ANIMALS**
  Rhinos and hippos are the second heaviest land mammals after elephants. An African white rhinoceros weighs up to 10 tons.

- **AN ELEPHANT'S DIET**
  Elephants eat up to 330 pounds (150kg) of food per day. They also drink about 50 gallons (180l) of water a day.

- **HORSE BREEDS**
  There are 150 different breeds of domestic horse.

Big cats

LIONS, TIGERS, JAGUARS, PUMAS, AND LEOPARDS are kinds of big cats, found all over the world except Australasia. Although they have the same basic body structure as pet cats, they are very different in other ways. They vary in size considerably, from the big tiger to the tiny wild cat, but big cats are usually much bigger and stronger than pet cats, and they roar and grunt rather than meow and purr. All are deadly hunters, slinking up on their prey then pouncing on it. Their sharp claws, powerful jaws, and fangs inflict terrible wounds on victims.

FACTS: About tigers

- **Very big cat**
  Tigers are the largest of the big cats, with huge heads and growing 8 feet (2.5m) long. The long tail adds another 3 feet (90cm).

- **Disguising stripes**
  Tigers are instantly recognizable by their stripes. But in the forest areas of southern Asia where they live, their black stripes on a gold background act as camouflage. Their chins and stomachs are snowy white.

- **Head hunter**
  Tigers prey on large animals such as deer, buffalo, antelopes, and wild pigs, hunting mainly at night. But it takes a tiger a lot of effort to make a kill; nine out of ten times, the victim will actually make a getaway.

- **Endangered tigers**
  Hunters killing tigers for their skins, and farmers clearing the forest for land, have decimated tiger numbers, and they are now restricted to special reserves in Asia, mainly in India and Sumatra.

- **Lone males**
  Tigers have their own ranges but a male's may include that of some females. They meet only to mate.

- **Young tigers**
  Two to four tiger cubs are born at a time and live with their mother for 3 years as they learn to survive.

▶ Tigers are solitary creatures, living alone most of their lives. To keep other tigers out of their territory, they leave urine samples and scratch marks on trees.

Factfinder: Animals

FACTS: About lions

◀ *A male can be up to around 10 feet (3m) long from his nose to the tip of his tail. Males also have a mane, which gets darker as they get older. Females have no mane and are also a bit smaller.*

- **King of the beasts**
  Lions are majestic big cats once found all over southern Asia but now found mainly on the grasslands of Africa. They are the only truly social cats, living together in groups called prides. The adult male lion is instantly recognizable by the big mane that covers its head.

- **What lions eat**
  Lions feed on wildebeest, zebras, and antelopes—occasionally giraffes. They have big side teeth and short, strong jaws for eating flesh.

- **Lions on the hunt**
  It is usually the female that hunts, alone or in pairs, although the males are the first to eat once the prey has been caught. The hunting lionesses stealthily approach a victim then make a short dash and pounce on it quickly. If they don't succeed in their short dash, they give up and wait for another opportunity. Only one in four hunts leads to a kill.

- **A quiet life**
  A lion spends 18 hours a day sleeping, since the meat it eats is so nutritious. It eats one solid meal then goes without food for the next few days.

▶ *Among the many smaller big cats is the margay, which lives in the forests of South and Central America and preys on small mammals and birds. The margay is solitary, has good reflexes, keen eyesight, and is an excellent climber. However, it has been hunted for its coat and as a result is now quite rare.*

▶ *With its spotted coat, the jaguar is one of the most beautiful of the big cats. It lives in South American forests, usually near water, and hunts peccaries, capybaras, and fish. It looks a bit like the leopard of Africa and Asia, but these have black blotches or rings, whereas jaguars have spots with rings around them.*

47

Monkeys and apes

HUMANS, APES, MONKEYS, AND LEMURS all belong to a group of animals called primates. Most of them, except humans, live in places where there are trees, and have hands with fingers, and feet with toes for gripping branches. The apes are our closest relatives in the animal world and have similar long arms, and fingers and toes for gripping. Monkeys have long arms too, but they are usually much smaller, and have a tail for helping them to balance as they swing through the trees. The live all over the world in warm regions.

FACTS: About lemurs and langurs

- **What are lemurs?**
  Lemurs are nocturnal animals with big, staring eyes. They have soft, thick fur and bushy tails which they use to intimidate other animals, signal to other lemurs and wave scent around (from glands in their bottoms!).

- **Where lemurs live**
  Nearly all lemurs live in forests on the island of Madagascar off the east coast of Africa. They tend to live mostly in trees.

- **Kinds of lemur**
  There are 21 species of lemur. Some are brightly colored, such as the ring-tailed lemur, which has black and white rings all the way down its tail.

- **Tiny primates**
  Lemurs are all quite small— the biggest is only as big as a large house cat, while the smallest, the lesser mouse lemur, grows to only 5 inches (12.5cm).

- **Langurs**
  Langurs are small monkeys that live in Southeast Asia and mainly eat leaves.

▶ Like other langurs, the Hanuman langur has a strong stomach that can cope with the toughest leaves.

◀ Monkeys are divided into those of the Old World and the New World. Old World monkeys, such as the baboon (left), live in the warmer parts of Africa and Asia. They tend to be larger than New World monkeys but do not have prehensile tails (tails that grip). Their backsides are usually naked and their nostrils are close together.

◀ New World monkeys live in Central and South American forests. Many, such as the spider monkey (left), have prehensile tails to help them climb and to hang from branches, keeping their legs and arms free for holding food. Their noses are also much wider than those of Old World monkeys and their nostrils face outward.

Factfinder: Animals

FACTS: About apes

- **Fellow apes**
  Apes are so closely related to humans that some zoologists divide apes into three kinds—lesser apes (gibbons and siamangs), great apes (orangutans, gorillas, and chimpanzees) and man. None has a tail.

- **Great apes and lesser apes**
  Great apes are almost human-shaped, although they tend to have longer arms, big, protruding jaws—and, of course, are covered in fur. They are often very clever, too, especially chimpanzees. Lesser apes are smaller and less clever, but they can be be very agile climbers.

- **Chimpanzees**
  Chimps are man's closest relative and the brightest of the apes. They communicate with varied vocal sounds, gestures and facial expressions. They also use tools such as sticks to get food.

- **Gibbons**
  Gibbons are agile apes which live in Southeast Asian forests and swing swiftly from branch to branch—up to 10 feet (3m) in a single swing.

- **Orangutan**
  Orangutan is Malay for "old man of the forest." They live in the rain forests of Borneo and Sumatra and look like hairy old men.

▼ Gorillas are the biggest of the apes. A big male can be 68 inches (170cm) tall. They look ferocious, but are among the gentlest of creatures. They eat only berries and leaves, and the male only becomes aggressive when a rival male intrudes on his group—even then he only beats his chest and roars.

Adult males are called silverbacks because they have gray hairs on their backs

The gentle gorilla only roars like this when his family is threatened

49

Pandas, bears, & dogs

ALL BIG CARNIVOROUS (MEAT-EATING) ANIMALS are essentially either cats or dogs. Cats are very obviously cats, but the dogs include bears as well as the more obviously doglike creatures such as wolves, foxes, jackals, and coyotes. To a zoologist, a bear is rather like a big dog without a tail. Both bears and dogs are mostly hunters that eat meat, but unlike cats, bears especially will also eat other things if food is scarce. Surprisingly, although pandas look like bears, they are actually more closely related to raccoons.

FACTS: About wolves, foxes, and jackals

- **Big dogs**
  The dog family is a group of 35 species including wolves, foxes, wild dogs, domestic dogs, jackals, and coyotes. All dogs have long legs, long narrow muzzles, and pointy canine teeth for eating flesh. They all also have a very good sense of smell.

- **Wolf packs**
  To hunt animals bigger than themselves such as moose, deer, caribou, or musk oxen, wolves hunt together in packs. Wolf packs use smell to trace their prey, then try to isolate a weak animal within the herd and run it down.

- **Top dog**
  The eldest male and female in a pack maintain a strict hierarchy. Any wolf that tries to challenge their dominance is subdued or even expelled from the pack altogether. A pack may consist of 7-20 wolves.

◀ The red fox is very adaptable and is often found living in cities, surviving by raiding disposal areas.

Foxes are clever hunters that prowl at night, alone or in pairs. They catch and eat rats, mice, and rabbits, but they will also willingly eat whatever is available, such as fruit, birds, and even human food scraps.

- **Jackal**
  Jackals live in Africa and Asia and look like small wolves. They hunt alone, not in packs, killing rats, mice, and birds. They only meet up when there is a chance of getting in on the leftovers from the kill of a lion or a leopard—their deadliest enemy.

◀ Wolves once lived all over Europe and North America, but they have now been all but exterminated in Europe and live only in remote areas of North America.

Factfinder: Animals

FACTS: About bears

- **Where bears live**
  Bears live mostly in the northern hemisphere, in all kinds of environments. Only the spectacled bear lives in South America.

- **Brown bears**
  Brown bears are called "grizzly" because of the white furs on their shoulders.

- **Polar bears**
  White polar bears live in the Arctic and are the only bears that live on meat alone.

▲ Brown bears such as this Himalayan bear hibernate. They put on weight during the autumn and then retreat to a den for winter.

▼ The giant panda is one of the rarest animals, living only in the mountainous forests of central China, where its food, a certain kind of bamboo, grows. The bamboo is not very nutritious, so pandas spend 10-12 hours a day eating. They rarely have cubs, so the birth of a panda is precious.

Pandas have a pad on their forepaws, called a sixth finger, to help them grip bamboo shoots as they chew

DATA: Pandas, bears and dogs

- **THE BIGGEST BEAR**
  The largest bear is the Kodiak, a type of brown bear from Alaska, which measures up to 8 feet (2.5m) and weighs up to 1,700 pounds (780kg).

- **THE LITTLEST BEAR**
  The smallest of the bears is the sun bear of the Southeast Asian rainforests. It is only about 56 inches (1.4m) tall and 60 pounds (27kg) in weight.

- **WOLF RANGE**
  One wolf pack may inhabit a huge territory-up to 385 square miles (1,000sq km). They also cover great distances when hunting for food.

- **PANDA FOOD**
  Because bamboo has such a low nutritional value, pandas may eat up to 30 pounds (13kg) of stems and leaves in a single day.

Sea mammals

MAMMALS ARE WARM-BLOODED CREATURES that breathe air and nurse their young on milk. Most are land animals, but they are remarkably adaptable and a few kinds spend all their lives in the sea, swimming around with the ease of a fish and only coming up for air occasionally. There are two main kinds of sea mammal. There are seals, sea lions, walruses, and sea cows, which mostly live in cold places and have both fur and a thick layer of fat called blubber to keep them warm. Then there are whales, dolphins, and porpoises, which have no fur, only blubber.

FACTS: About whales, dolphins and porpoises

- **Cetaceans**
  Whales, dolphins, and porpoises are together known as cetaceans. Many are very gentle and intelligent creatures.

- **Breathing**
  Whales can stay hours underwater, but must eventually come up for air and spout out water from a blow hole on top.

- **Schools**
  Dolphins live in groups called schools up to 300 strong.

- **Dolphin talk**
  Dolphins keep in touch by clicks, barks, chattering sounds, screams, and moans, each of which seem to have a meaning that scientists do not understand. They find their way with sounds too high for the human ear to hear.

- **Whale sound**
  Whales "talk" with booming sounds. Finback whales can hear each other 500 miles (850km) apart.

Playful leaps, somersaults and spins help knit groups of dolphins together

▲ Dolphins are very friendly, playful, and intelligent creatures. They form strong social relationships, with close mother-child bonds. Mating pairs seem to stay together for life.

- **Toothed and toothless whales**
  Some whales, such as the sperm and killer whales, have teeth and eat large fish. Others, like the humpback and blue whales have no teeth. Instead, they have special comblike sieves in their mouths called baleens. They feed by straining tiny, shrimplike creatures called krill through the baleen.

Factfinder: Animals

FACTS: About seals, sea lions, and walruses

- **Going ashore**
  Seals, sea lions, and walruses are agile swimmers, but unlike whales and dolphins, they can live on land—although once ashore, they tend to waddle.

- **Breeding grounds**
  In spring and summer, thousands of seals crowd together on the shore to breed in vast colonies.

- Seals and sea lions
  Seals and sea lions look similar, but while seals have only ear openings, sea lions have ear flaps like most land mammals. Sea lions can also move their back flippers under their body to help them move around on land, unlike seals.

- Seal meals
  Seals and sea lions feed mainly on fish, but also eat shellfish. Crabeater seals feed mainly on krill, while bearded seals eat mainly clams.

- Walruses
  Walruses are big creatures a little like overgrown seals, growing up to 10 feet (3m) long, but they have massive tusks and face whiskers.

- Leopard
  The most ferocious seal is the Antarctic leopard, which grows to 13 feet (4m) and feeds on penguins.

Seals spend most of their lives in the sea, but come ashore to give birth. They stay on land for several weeks in colonies called rookeries, feeding their young milk. Every now and then, hunters will cull (kill) the young pups while they are still ashore—both for their fur and to keep down numbers. Many believe this is cruel. Others say it is necessary.

Sea cows—dugongs and manatees—are plant-eating seals that live in warm coastal waters. Dugongs live around Africa and Asia. Manatees live in coastal rivers in the southeast USA, the West Indies, and northern South America. They greet one another with muzzle to muzzle kisses.

Manatee

Pets

PEOPLE HAVE KEPT ANIMALS for many thousands of years—sometimes to help with particular tasks, sometimes as companions, sometimes simply to look at and admire. Dogs were first tamed more than 12,000 years ago to help with hunting, and since then many other animals have been adopted as pets—cats, birds, hamsters, guinea pigs, horses, and many others. There are more pet owners now than ever before, with millions of animals living in people's homes around the world. There are 500 million cats alone.

FACTS: About cats

- **Egyptian cats**
  The Ancient Egyptians tamed wild African bushcats to catch mice 3,500 years ago. Later, the Egyptians thought cats sacred.

- **Rough tongues**
  Cats' tongues are covered in bristles, which help them to lap up liquids and foods and to groom themselves, as with a comb.

- **Catnaps**
  Cats spend a lot of time sleeping — in short naps. But they can be awake and ready for action in an instant.

- **Cat litter**
  Most female cats are ready to be mothers by 10 months old—although many are neutered by their owners to stop them breeding. Female cats are pregnant for 9 weeks and give birth to a litter of 2-5 kittens.

◀ *There are many different breeds of cat, from common tabbies and tortoiseshells to valuable pedigree Siamese and Persian cats.*

Dogs

There are more than 130 different breeds of domestic dog, but all are descended from the wolf, and, even though tame, they retain many wolflike traits—body language, guarding territory, hiding bones, and so on.

▲ *Many pets were originally working dogs, like the collie. Originally from Scotland, collies make wonderful sheepdogs. They are fast runners, quick learners and have an amazing sense of smell. They can even locate a sheep lost in the snow.*

▶ *Some pets were originally hunting dogs, like terriers. Great diggers, with strong teeth and jaws, terriers were once used to dig out rats, rabbits, and badgers from the ground, and their name comes from the Latin* terra, *for earth.*

Factfinder: Animals

▲ Hamsters only live for two or three years. Golden hamsters (above)—the small variety kept as pets—all descend from a single wild litter found in Syria in 1930.

▲ Many pet dogs come from hunters and gun dogs, such as setters, pointers, and retrievers. When a red setter (above) spots a game bird, it crouches slightly and freezes, pointing its nose to the bird for the hunter.

▼ St. Bernards are one of many dogs used to help in emergencies and were once trained at the monastery of the Great St. Bernard Pass in Switzerland to rescue people who got lost in the surrounding mountains.

FACTS: About fish

- **Tropical fish**
  Small tropical fish such as butterfly fish, angel fish, and guppies are kept for their bright colors. But they are used to warm water, so must be kept in heated tanks.

- **Deadly fish**
  Some people like to keep piranhas from the Amazon. They have sharp teeth and are voracious flesh eaters, able to attack in a mass and eat large animals.

▶ Descended from dull colored carp, goldfish were carefully bred by the Chinese and Japanese and are now the most popular of all pet fish.

DATA: Pets

- **BIGGEST DOG**
  The tallest dog of all is the Irish wolfhound—44 inches (110cm) to the shoulder.

- **HEAVIEST DOG**
  The heaviest dog is the St. Bernard—200 pounds (90kg).

- **SMALLEST DOG**
  The smallest dog is the miniature Yorkshire terrier—under 18 ounces (500g).

- **OLD CAT**
  Cats may live up to the age of 20.

- **TINY FISH**
  The smallest pet fish are dwarf gobies, which can be less than half an inch (12mm).

Farm animals

BACON, HAMBURGERS, SHOES, BUTTER, woolen sweaters, milk, and many other things are provided by animals kept on farms-including cattle, sheep, pigs, and hens. All these animals are descended from wild animals, but they were domesticated-made tame-many thousands of years ago to give us a steady supply of meat, milk, eggs, fur, wool, and leather. Since then, farmers have created many hundreds of breeds of each animal, such as Herefordshire cows and Merino sheep to create a more meaty animal, or one that gives better milk or wool.

FACTS: About cows

- **What are cows?**
  Cows or cattle are descended from the wild auroch tamed 9,000 years ago. Male cattle are bulls; females cows; and young cattle calves.

- **Dairy cow**
  Females are kept for milk, butter, and cheese and called dairy cows. They give birth to a calf each year and after the birth provide milk twice a day for 10 months.

- **Beef breeds**
  Male cattle are raised for meat. Cattle also provide leather and glue and droppings for fertilizer. Beef breeds are rounder and heftier than dairy cows.

- **Chewing the cud**
  Cows chew the cud. They have four stomachs and after swallowing food they bring it back up into their mouths for further chewing.

▲ Goats are kept for meat, milk, skins, and wool. Goats' milk is very good for people who are allergic to richer cows' milk, while Angora and Kashmir goats provide very fine wool. Goats are often kept in rocky mountain areas because they are agile and have strong enough jaws and stomachs to live off coarse vegetation.

▼ Pigs are kept for meat—pork, bacon, and ham—and leather. Their hairs are also used to make artists' brushes. The European domestic pig is descended from the European wild boar, which is much hairier and darker than the domestic pig, and also has tusks. Most pigs are now raised on factory farms where they are fed on special diets that help them grow rapidly.

Factfinder: Animals

FACTS: About poultry

◀ *On a few farms, hens may scratch around for insects and seeds in the farmyard and lay their eggs in a small hut called a coop. These are called free-range hens.*

- **Fowl**
  Ducks, geese, turkeys, and chickens are all called poultry, and are bred in captivity to be eaten or to provide eggs, meat, and feathers.

- **Old hens**
  Chickens have been domesticated since the 5th century BC and there are over 100 different varieties. Females are called hens; males are called roosters or cocks.

▶ *Turkeys are a type of pheasant. There are several different species, but they all descend from the native wild turkey of North America.*

- **Egg laying**
  Hens lay one or two eggs a day. To keep them laying, the eggs must be taken everyday. If not, the hens wait until they have a small collection, then sit on them, keeping them warm for about 20 days until chicks hatch.

- **Battery hens**
  Very few hens are free range. In Europe and North America, most are crowded into rows of small boxes called batteries inside a heated building where they are fed and watered, and waste and eggs are collected automatically.

- **Turkey tail**
  Male turkeys have 14-18 feathers in their tails and when courting females they spread these feathers out and raise them above their backs. All species of turkey have a "wattle" of bare, floppy skin that hangs down from their head and neck.

- **Turkish turkeys**
  The name turkey may have come from the mistaken idea that the bird came from Turkey.

◀ *The sheep was one of the first animals to be domesticated, some 10,000 years ago. Wooly sheep such as the Merino have fine wool suitable for clothing or coarse hair for carpets. Hairy sheep are bred for milk and meat. Australia, New Zealand, and South America have the right climate and the right pastures for sheep rearing, and there are vast sheep farms or "stations" here.*

DATA: Farm animals

- **COW BREED**
  There are 200 or so different types of domestic cow.

- **HEAD OF SHEEP**
  There are more than 680 million sheep in the world and 800 different breeds.

- **MILK PRODUCTION**
  Cows produce around 4.5 gallons (16l) of milk a day, or 1,660 gallons (6,000l) a year.

- **TURKEY EGGS**
  Turkey hens lay only about 12 eggs a year.

Tropical birds

THE TROPICS ARE HOME TO some of the world's most beautiful and spectacular birds. In the rain forests in particular there is a huge variety of colorful birds, because color is a real asset in finding a mate. In Indonesia and Australia there are birds of paradise and lyre birds with magnificent tail feathers. In South America there are the brilliantly colored cotingas and huge-beaked toucans. Then there are parrots, such as macaws and budgerigars, and big birds such as flamingoes and hornbills, and tiny birds such as hummingbirds.

FACTS: About weaver birds

- **Home makers**
  Weaver birds are small birds that live in the tropics of Africa and Asia. They get their name because many weave elaborate nests.

- **Nest weaving**
  Using their bills and feet they make pouch-shaped nests from plant fibres, which they suspend from tree branches, away from predators. The entrance is usually a funnel with a hole at the end, just big enough for the weaver but small enough to keep other unfriendly animals out.

- **The biggest bird nests**
  Sociable weaver birds of South Africa build big nests containing enough separate cavities for hundreds of pairs of birds under one communal roof. Each has its own entrance tunnel, complete with grass stems pointing downward over it to help keep enemies out.

▶ The nest of the village weaver is begun by the male bird. When he has found a female willing to move in, she finishes off inside. The male then leaves her to lay her eggs while he goes off to start another nest.

▲ Pelicans are fish-eating birds with special pouched bills which they use to scoop up fish from the water. Their pouches can hold as much as two or three times as their stomachs.

▶ Like all bee-eaters, the carmine bee-eater has a long tail—the streamers are up to 5 inches (12cm). Their long, downward-pointing, curved bills are perfect for catching bees on the wing. They rub the bee against a branch to remove the sting. Carmine bee-eaters of Africa often ride on the backs of other birds such as ostriches and storks, as well as grazing mammals such as antelopes and cattle, in order to pick up insects disturbed by their feet.

Factfinder: Animals

▶ The Paradise whydah lives in Africa, and the male has perhaps the most spectacular tail feathers of any bird, four times as long as its body. When in flight, the whydah holds two short upper tail feathers upright while the longer ones dangle down. To attract females, it flies above her so that the long feathers wave up and down in an attractive way!

The tail feathers of a breeding male can be as long as 11 inches (28cm)

◀ The hoatzin is a large ungainly bird that lives in the forests of northern South America. It is an awkward flier so tends to glide from tree to tree. The young have two hooked claws on their wings to help them move around.

FACTS: About parrots and cockatoos

- **Bill for nuts**
  Parrots are colorful birds of the tropics with curved bills for eating fruit and seeds and cracking nuts.

- **Parrot feet**
  Parrot feet have two toes pointing forward and two backward, allowing them to grip onto branches and hold food.

- **Three species**
  There are three groups of parrots—true parrots, cockatoos, and lories—making 330 different species altogether. The largest is the hyacinth macaw (40 inches /100cm bill to tail). The smallest is the tiny buff-faced pygmy parrot 3.5 inches (8.4cm).

- **Mimic**
  Some parrots, such as the African gray parrot can imitate the human voice.

▲ Like all parrots the scarlet macaw can be incredibly noisy, with a raucous, rasping caw.

◀ Male Andean cock-of-the-rocks are famous for their color and their spectacular courtship routines.

DATA: Tropical birds

- **BIGGEST NEST**
  A South African sociable weaver bird nest can be up to 4m deep and 7.5m long.

- **OLDEST BIRD**
  The longest living captive birds are the sulphur crested cockatoos of Australia - up to 80 years.

Temperate birds

BIRDS IN TEMPERATE REGIONS may not be as colorful and spectacular as those of the tropics, but there is an enormous range and variety. There are town and garden birds such as the sparrow, the bluejay, and the pigeon. There are woodland birds such as the wood pigeon and the nightjar. There are birds that live near water too-freshwater birds such as ducks and swans, waders such as curlews and redshanks, and seabirds such as gulls and puffins. Then there are the magnificent birds of prey such as eagles, kestrels, hawks, and falcons, and the night-hunting owls.

FACTS: About water birds

▶ Like many birds of wetlands, the sandhill crane has become endangered by the destruction of its habitat.

- **Waders**
  Wading birds, such as curlews and plovers, have long legs for wading through the water and long bills for probing around in the mud to look for food.

- **Waterfowl**
  Waterfowl, such as ducks, geese, and swans have webbed feet for swimming and long bendy necks for reaching into the water.

- **Seabirds**
  Many seabirds are very good divers and roam the open sea looking for food. They often lay their eggs in nesting grounds high up on the cliffs so that they are kept safely out of the reach of predators.

▶ Like many birds, the redstart feeds on insects, and has a wide beak for catching them in flight. It was originally a woodland bird, but has adapted well to environmental changes.

◀ The waxwing gets its name from the waxy red tips on some of its wing feathers. Like many seed and fruit-eating birds, it has a short pincer-like beak for cracking seeds.

▲ Common pheasants came originally from Asia, like this Monal pheasant. But they have adapted well to other areas, and are now the most widespread of all game birds.

Factfinder: Animals

DATA: Temperate birds

- **ANCIENT BIRD**
  The oldest known bird was a Siberian red crane that died in 1988, aged 82.
- **SHARPEST EYES**
  The keen-eyed peregrine falcon can spot a pigeon at 5 miles (8km) away.

▲ Jays are seed-eating birds that like acorns, which they bury for winter food. But they sometimes steal nestlings and eggs from the nests of other birds.

▼ The pigeons that swarm over many city squares are all descended from domestic pigeons, which came in turn from the wild rock dove. They are called "feral" because they were once tame and are now wild.

FACTS: About birds of prey

▶ The peregrine falcon can plummet at speeds of 110 mph (175km/h) when diving down on prey.

- **What are birds of prey?**
  Birds of prey are hunting birds that feed on small animals such as birds and rabbits. All have sharp, hooked bills, strong feet with talons and very good eyesight and hearing.

- **Different quarry**
  Different birds specialize in hunting different things: honey buzzards eat bees and have talons shaped for digging out nests; eagles have large talons for snatching up rabbits and squirrels; harriers eat snakes and other reptiles; ospreys specialize in catching fish such as salmon.

- **Birds under threat**
  Many birds of prey have been endangered by hunting, egg collecting, and game keepers who want to stop the birds of prey killing game birds and pigeons.

▶ Owls hunt at night and have large, round eyes to see well in poor light, but their hearing is also so sharp they can catch prey in pitch dark by sound alone.

61

Reptiles

REPTILES ARE SCALY-SKINNED CREATURES such as crocodiles, lizards, and snakes. They are sometimes said to be cold-blooded. But their blood is not cold; it can be as warm as a mammal's. Mammals get their warmth by eating. Reptiles can survive on very little food, but they depend on the sun for warmth and must continually shuttle between warm and cold places to stay at the right temperature. They may spend hours basking in the sun, gaining enough energy to go hunting for food. But they depend on the sun for warmth, so cannot live in cold places.

FACTS: About snakes

- **What are snakes?**
Snakes are thin, limbless reptiles that live mostly in warm regions. They are predators, but with no limbs; they kill their prey with poison or by constricting (squeezing) them to death.

- **Tongue scent**
Snakes have no ears, but sense their prey from sound vibrations on the ground. They also use their tongues to smell with—but only use their eyes when close to as their eyesight is poor.

- **Snakes with bite**
Many snakes are venomous—that is, they have a poisonous bite. Those with fangs in the front of their mouths, such as vipers and rattlesnakes, are more dangerous than back-fanged snakes—because back-fanged snakes must get a victim fully into their mouths to bite.

- **Big squeeze**
Boas and pythons kill large victims by constriction. The snake coils itself around its victim. Each time the trapped animal breathes out the snake tightens its hold until its prey finally suffocates.

▲ The taipan is a large, poisonous snake from Australia that grows up to 10 feet (3m)—large for a poisonous snake. It is from the same family as the cobra—the elapids— all of which have venom in their front fangs.

▼ Like all vipers, the Gaboon viper has long fangs in the front of its mouth, which hinge back into the mouth when not in use. The fangs are hollow and act as "syringes"—injecting venom straight into the victim when the snake bites.

Factfinder: Animals

▲ *Geckos can climb up straight walls and even run across ceilings because they have feet like suction caps. Their toes are flat with pads underneath them and these pads are covered with hundreds of tiny hooks, which can grip onto flat surfaces.*

FACTS: About alligators

- **Crocodiles v. alligators**
  Crocodiles and alligators are large reptiles that live in warm rivers and swamps. Crocodiles have thinner snouts and a fourth tooth on the lower jaw which is visible when the mouth is shut.

- **Floating predators**
  Alligators and crocodiles are predators that lurk under the surface with just their eyes and nostrils above the water and can take prey by surprise by springing out suddenly.

▼ *The alligator of the Florida Everglade swamps is now a protected animal because it was once endangered by hunters wanting its skin.*

▲ *Turtles and tortoises are together known as chelonians and all live inside an armored shell of bony plates. On their back is a domed "carapace," underneath is a flat "plastron." Some can pull their arms, legs, and head right in. They are slow moving, but withdrawing inside their shell protects them.*

▶ *The frilled-necked lizard of Australia may not be very big, but it makes up for its lack of size with its enormous frill. Normally, the frill hangs limp, but it spreads out up to 10 inches (25cm) whenever the lizard is threatened, making it look three times as large and twice as dangerous.*

▼ *Iguanas such as the Madagascan iguana (below) are large, tropical lizards. The marine iguanas of the Galapagos are one of the very few lizards that live in the sea. They can stay under the water for up to an hour.*

63

Amphibians

AMPHIBIANS ARE CREATURES such as frogs, toads, newts, and salamanders that live part of their lives on land and part in the water. Most begin life by hatching in water from big clusters of eggs called spawn. At this stage, they are more like fish. But they soon grow legs and develop lungs for breathing air. Before long they are ready to clamber ashore, where most will spend their adult lives. Even so, they rarely stray far from water. They return to water to lay their eggs because their eggs, unlike those of reptiles, are not waterproof and so would dry out in air.

FACTS: About frogs and toads

- **Skin breathers**
  Most frogs breathe partly through their skin and so need to keep damp all the time. They are very good swimmers and, except for tree frogs, spend most of their time in or near water.

- **High jumpers**
  Neither frogs nor toads have tails as adults, but they have long, strong back legs for jumping.

- **Biggest frog**
  The largest frog is the goliath from West Africa which measures up to 32 inches (80cm) when stretched out and weighs up to 6 pounds (2.7kg). The smallest is a Brazilian frog—1/3 inch (8.5mm).

▲ *Tree frogs of tropical rainforests take advantage of other moisture sources to live in the trees far from water.*

- **Flying frog**
  Flying frogs are tree frogs that can glide through the air. They have sticky disks on their fingers for gripping onto branches and their hands and feet are webbed to act as airbrakes.

- **Warty toad**
  Generally, toads have drier, wartier skin than frogs and have shorter hind legs which are better for walking than jumping, unlike a frog's. Toads are also less active than frogs.

- **Baby swallower**
  The male Darwin's frog of Chile swallows the spawn left by the female and keeps it in his throat until it hatches as little tadpoles.

▲ *Poison arrow frogs of the Amazon are brightly colored to warn that their sweat glands contain a deadly poison—which the Indians used to smear on their arrows.*

Factfinder: Animals

FACTS: About newts and salamanders

- **Lizard lookalikes**
Newts and salamanders look a little like lizards, but they are amphibians, not reptiles like lizards, and begin life in water. Newts live in temperate climates and hibernate during the winter under logs and stones. Salamanders live in warmer areas and so do not need to hibernate.

- **Giant salamander**
The giant salamander grows up to 6 feet (1.8m) long.

- **Colored newts**
Many male newts have bright colors and special markings during their mating season to attract females. The crested newt has a bright orange or yellow belly as well as a bumpy crest down the length of its back.

▶ Newts are the most water-loving of all the amphibians, spending much of their lives in ponds.

- **Egg-wrapping**
To protect their eggs from predators, female newts wrap each egg in a leaf with their feet.

- **Fire salamander**
Fire salamanders got their name because they shelter underneath logs and so when in the past logs were burned on fires, salamanders hiding underneath would come rushing out of the fire.

1. The fertilized eggs of a frog are called spawn. Each of the blobs in spawn is an egg containing an embryo, protected in a bag of jelly

2. The eggs hatch in water after a week or so into fishlike tadpoles which swim around, breathe through gills and grow rapidly

3. After 7 weeks, the tadpole begins to grow hind legs, then front legs. Soon the young froglet begins to breathe through lungs rather than gills

▶ As they grow from eggs to adults, all amphibians, like the frog, go through a series of dramatic changes, called a metamorphosis. Each creature has its own special way of developing. But the sequence shown here for the frog is fairly typical.

4. The froglet's legs go on growing and its tail shortens. After 14 weeks, the frog is an adult and leaves the water

Insects

INSECTS MAY BE TINY but they are by far the most numerous of all creatures. There are more than a million known species, and they are found almost everywhere. Ants scurry along the ground. Bees buzz around hives. Butterflies flutter over flowers. Insects are very varied in look, but all have six legs and a body divided into three sections—head, thorax, and abdomen. They also have two compound eyes with anything from six to 30,000 lenses and a variety of other sensors such as antennae (feelers) which they can use to hear, taste, and smell.

FACTS: About butterflies, moths, and caterpillars

- **Butterflies and moths**
  Butterflies and moths are both part of a big group of insects called Lepidoptera, which means "scaly wings," because their wings are covered in tiny dustlike scales.

- **What's the difference?**
  Butterflies are usually brightly colored and fly during the day. They have thin, hairless bodies and a pair of clubbed antennae. Moths tend to be drabber, because they rest during the day—on trees and dead leaves—and so must be camouflaged. They have plump, hairy bodies and straight antennae.

- **Caterpillars**
  Butterflies and moths begin life as an egg, then hatch as long thin caterpillars, which eat leaves voraciously for a month.

◁ Butterflies like the red admiral can migrate astonishing distances, as far as many birds—even crossing oceans, with the help of the wind.

- **Chrysalis and cocoon**
  When the caterpillar is ready, it spins a cocoon of silk around itself or creates a hard shell called a chrysalis. Inside, it becomes a pupa, grows wings and, amazingly, changes to an adult butterfly before emerging.

- **Nectar seeker**
  Most butterflies feed, if at all, only on nectar, the sweet juice of flowers and so spend their brief lives fluttering from bloom to bloom.

◁ Caterpillars are fat and slow-moving, so are very vulnerable to predators. But the Puss Moth caterpillar can scare smaller enemies by rearing up, waving its tail and squirting formic acid.

Factfinder: Animals

The head consists of mouth parts, eyes, and antennae

The thorax is packed with muscles that move the legs as well as the main body organs

Insects breathe through holes in their sides called spiracles

The abdomen holds all the insect's digestive organs and its sex organs

▲ Insects look very different from other animals. Not only are their bodies split into three sections, but they have no bones. Instead, they have a rigid shell or "exoskeleton," made of a tough substance called chitin.

▲ Termites are insects that live in huge colonies in the tropics. Together, they build huge mounds to live in out of dust and saliva, complete with air conditioning. Some termite mounds can be 30 feet (9m) tall.

FACTS: About bees

- **Beehive**
  Bees live together in large numbers in hives or nests. In each colony there is one queen, many female workers, and a few drones (males).

- **Queen bee**
  Only the queen can lay eggs—up to 1,000 a day. Drones exist only to mate with the queen, after which they die.

- **Worker bee**
  Workers collect pollen and nectar from flowers and bring it to the nest. Pollen is fed to grubs and nectar is used for honey.

▶ A honeybee's main protection is the sting in its tail. Its bright yellow and black stripes are a warning.

◀ Dragonflies are large, fast-flying insects that can dart at up to 35mph (60km/h). Their four wings move independently of one another and make a rattling sound. They can also fly backward.

DATA: Insects

- **LONGEST INSECT**
  The world's longest insect is the giant stick insect of Indonesia, which grows up to 13 inches (33cm) long.

- **SMALLEST INSECT**
  The fairy fly is just 0.008 inches (0.2mm) long.

- **AN ANT'S STRENGTH**
  An ant can lift 50 times its own weight–that is like you lifting a truck!

PLANTS

70 Plants

72 Roots and bulbs

74 Flowers, seeds, and fruits

76 Garden and wildflowers

78 How trees grow

80 Deciduous trees

82 Conifers and cycads

84 Mosses and ferns

86 Fungi and mushrooms

88 Algae

90 Plants for food

92 Herbs and spices

94 Tropical plants

Plants

THERE ARE MORE THAN 250,000 different kinds of plant, ranging from tiny plankton barely visible under a microscope to giant trees hundreds of feet tall, the world's largest living things. They grow almost everywhere on land and in the sea, on plains and on mountaintops, even in deserts and snowy wastes. Indeed, 40 percent of the world's land is covered by trees and grass. What makes plants very different from animals is that they do not move around and have no need of senses (or a brain) because they can make their own food from sunlight.

FACTS: About stems

- **The plant stem**
  The stem supports the plant's flowers and leaves. It is also a pipe to take water, minerals and food up and down between the roots and the leaves. Water goes up from the roots via tubes called xylem. Food goes down from the leaves in tubes called phloem.

- **Woody and herbaceous**
  Many plants have stems that are green and bendy. They are called herbaceous plants, because many are herbs such as parsley. Woody plants such as trees have stiff stems or trunks covered in bark.

▶ *Bamboo is an unusual plant. It is a kind of grass and starts off with a soft, bendy, herbaceous stem. But as it grows, very rapidly, the stem becomes hard, tough, and woody.*

FACTS: About leaves

- **Sun traps**
  Leaves are a plant's solar cells and catch the light to make the food the plant needs to grow. Most are broad and flat to catch as much sun as possible.

- **Stalk and blade**
  Each leaf is attached to the stem by a small stalk called a petiole. The flat part of the leaf is called the blade.

- **Simple and compound**
  Some leaves, such as maple leaves are called simple leaves because they only have one blade. Other leaves, such as those of the walnut and willow, are called compound because they have a number of blades on the same stalk.

- **Biggest leaves**
  The biggest leaves belong to the raffia palm tree, which can grow 65 feet long.

▶ *The lines on leaves are veins which not only provide a frame to support the leaf, but carry water in and the food the leaf makes out.*

Factfinder: Plants

Angiosperm: edelweiss

Gymnosperm: pine tree

◁ The first plants to grow on land were plants such as fungi and lichen which grow from tiny cells called spores. But most plants today grow not from spores but seeds. Unlike the more primitive spore-making plants, seed-making plants have stems, leaves, and often roots and flowers. Seed-making plants are divided into gymnosperms which have cones, and angiosperms which bear flowers.

FACTS: About photosynthesis

◁ Leaves are made up from lots of tiny parcels called cells. The wall is made of a tough material called cellulose. Inside are bundles called chloroplasts, which are the plant's solar energy converters.

When the sun shines, chlorophyll in the leaves soaks up the energy to split water into oxygen and hydrogen

Carbon dioxide is absorbed through pores in the leaves called stomata

In the leaves hydrogen joins with carbon dioxide to make sugar

Water and minerals are drawn up through the stem

The remaining oxygen goes out into the air. This is called respiration

Minerals are drawn from the soil.

Water is drawn up through the roots

- **Food making**
  Plants make their food by absorbing sunlight in a process called photosynthesis. The sun gives the plant energy to change carbon dioxide from the air, and hydrogen from water, into food.

- **Green packages**
  Photosynthesis occurs in tiny packages in leaf cells called chloroplasts. These contain a green substance called chlorophyll, which makes leaves green. It is this that soaks up the sun.

▷ In photosynthesis, chlorophyll in the leaves uses the sun's energy to turn carbon dioxide from the air and hydrogen from water into sugars, which the plant uses as fuel for growth.

71

Roots and bulbs

THE GREEN AND COLORFUL PARTS of a plant are the leaves and flowers you see above the ground-but there is more to a plant beneath the surface. This is where the plant's roots are, growing down into soil or water. Roots not only hold the plant in place, anchoring it in the soil, but also draw up the water and minerals that the plant needs to grow. In some plants, such as beets, the roots also act as a food store. Sometimes, new plants can grow, or plants that die back can regrow, from the parts below ground, which form bulbs, corms, rhizomes, and tubers.

FACTS: About roots

▲ Root vegetables are vegetables that grow underground. But not all of them are really roots. Carrots and beets are true roots, but potatoes are tubers, which are underground stems, and onions are bulbs, which are underground leaves.

- **Growing plant**
  When a plant begins to grow, the seed sends out a single primary root. This quickly branches out into secondary roots. The tips of these are protected by a root cap as they probe out through the soil.

- **Taproots**
  Some plants have just one very large root, with only a few very fine roots sprouting off it. The large root is called a taproot.

- **Fibrous roots**
  Some plants, such as grasses, have lots of fine roots spreading out in a dense mat. These are called fibrous roots. Some rye grasses grow 7,000 miles (12,000km) of roots in one chunk of soil.

- **Root hairs**
  Every root has very fine "root hairs" branching off it. These hairs are very good at soaking up water and minerals from the soil.

- **Parasitic roots**
  Parasitic plants are unable to take up water and minerals from the soil themselves. Instead they draw their food from other plants. Mistletoe, for instance, wraps its roots around apple trees.

- **Climbing roots**
  Some climbing plants, like ivy, don't only have roots underground, but on the stem too. These stem roots serve mainly to hold the plant on to trees, walls and fences.

- **Deepest roots**
  The roots of a wild fig tree in Transvaal, South Africa go down 400 feet (120m) into the ground. An elm tree seen growing in Largs, Scotland, had roots 360 feet (110m) deep.

Factfinder: Plants

FACTS: About bulbs, corms, rhizomes and tubers

- **New from old**
  Some plants only grow once from a seed. But many perennials can die back then grow anew again and again from parts of a root or stem. This is called vegetative propagation.

- **Rhizomes**
  Plants such as irises sprout from thick stems called rhizomes that grow sideways beneath the ground.

- **Tubers**
  Sometimes, the end of a rhizome swells into lumps called tubers. Potatoes are tubers.

- **Corms**
  Flowers such as crocuses grow from the bulbous base to their stem, called a corm.

▲ To survive the winter, many plants die back to leave nothing visible above the ground. But the plant stays alive in the form of a corm, tuber, bulb, or rhizome. All of these are "storage organs," providing food to sustain the plant through the winter and to feed new shoots when they reemerge the following spring.

- **Bulbs**
  Bulbs, such as onions, look like corms, but they are actually made of leaf parts rather than the stem, which is why the onion has layers.

- **Food stores**
  Plants such as lupins grow in a ring around the outside of an old stem as the stem gets older and grows wider.

FACTS: About runners and suckers

◀ Strawberry plants are plants that spread by growing runners—that is, long stems that creep over the ground. Here and there along the stem it puts down new roots and a new plant grows.

Strawberry runners

- **Creeping stems**
  Some plants, such as roses, propagate (grow new plants) not from seeds or bulbs, corms, rhizomes, or tubers, but from long thin stems that creep over the ground (runners) or under it (suckers).

- **Buried leaves**
  With some plants, like begonias, new plants can grow from broken leaves that get embedded in the soil.

73

Flowers, seeds, & fruits

MOST OF THE WORLD'S PLANTS are flowers. Not only garden and wild flowers, but many trees and every herb, shrub, grain, fruit, and vegetable is a flowering plant or "angiosperm." The blooms may not all be as big and beautiful as those of a rose, but all flowering plants have flowers, and all serve a purpose. Flowers are not just for show–they are sexual, just like us, and contain male parts that make the pollen to fertilize the eggs or "ovules" made by female parts. Only when these come together can flowers create the fruits and seeds from which new plants will grow.

FACTS: About seeds and fruits

- **Seeds**
  Seeds are the tiny packages from which new plants grow. A hard shell or "kernel" holds not only the new plant in embryo, but all the food it needs to nourish it.

- **What is a fruit?**
  When scientists talk of fruit they don't just mean apples and pears, but the part of a flower that protects the seed as it ripens and helps spread it. A flower's eggs grow inside its ovaries. Once the eggs are fertilized and turned into seeds, the ovary swells around it into a fruit.

- **Juicy fruits**
  Fruits are often juicy and sweet when ripe so that animals are tempted to eat them. The seeds are then spread in the animals' droppings.

◀ *The pips inside each grape are seeds from which new grape vines might grow.*

◀ *Even though they are often very small, like this bottlebrush of Australia, most trees have flowers.*

- **Plums and cherries**
  Fruits such as plums are called "drupes." They have a fleshy outside and a hard kernel or stone inside protecting the seeds. The stone may be too big for animals to swallow so they eat just the flesh, but the seeds still get spread.

- **False fruits**
  Some fruits are called false fruits because they are made from more than just the ovary of the flower. Apples and pears, for example, have the ovary as their core, but their fleshy parts are actually swollen stalk.

- **Legumes**
  Peas, beans and other legumes are soft, dry fruits held in a case called a pod.

Factfinder: Plants

▶ Poppies are "annuals" and flower, scatter their seeds, and die in just one year. Buds appear in early summer, then open up as it gets warmer, releasing a flower that is fully grown by midsummer. Once pollinated, their petals wither and fall off, leaving a seed capsule. By autumn, the capsule has dried and developed holes, and the ripe seeds can be shaken out by the wind.

1. The fully-formed flower is packed inside a bud, enclosed by the green "sepals"

2. Once the weather is warm enough, the bud begins to open

3. The sepals open wider and the petals grow outward and backward

4. The poppy is now fully grown and ready to attract insects. Poppy flowers always have four petals

5. After pollination, the petals fall away, leaving a seed capsule

6. By autumn, small holes appear at the top of the dry capsule so seeds can be shaken out

FACTS: About spreading plants

▶ Pollen are the male germ cells which must reach the eggs to fertilize them. They are microscopically small and some are spread by sticking to the legs and bodies of insects drawn to the flower's nectar.

- **Scattered far and wide**
  Plants can't move, but they can spread their pollen and seeds over a wide area. Only a few seeds will grow, so plants usually produce large numbers to ensure their survival.

- **Seed spreading**
  Some seeds are so tiny that they are easily carried by the wind. Others have hooks or hairs on them so that they catch on the fur of passing animals.

Garden & wildflowers

ALL FLOWERS WERE WILD ONCE but through history gardeners have adapted them to the garden by selecting seeds and grafting plants together to bring out particular qualities. Their efforts have created a huge range of beautiful new plants, including roses, carnations, chrysanthemums, tulips, and many more. There are now more than a million kinds of garden flower, although wildflowers are becoming rare as human activity restricts the places where they can grow. Many wildflowers, such as the lady's slipper orchid, are now in danger of becoming extinct.

FACTS: Garden flowers

- **Big and bold**
  On the whole, garden flowers have much bigger flowers in bolder colors than their wild cousins. The wild dog rose has tiny pale pink or white blooms. Garden roses have big blooms in strong colors, from deep red to blue.

- **Cut flowers**
  Once cut flowers could only be bought in the right season. Now they are grown in warm places all year round such as Colombia and flown in chilled conditions to bring them fresh to local shops in under two days.

  ▼ An enormous range of cut flowers can now be brought all year round.

FACTS: Wild flowers

▶ The edelweiss survives because it can grow at very high altitude in the Alps, sprouting out from cracks in the rocks. This is because its leaves and blooms are covered in a coat of wooly hairs that protect it from the cold.

- **Meadows and woodlands**
  Every kind of place has its own kind of wild flower. On heathlands, flowers such as bell-heather, gorse and scarlet pimpernel grow. In meadows, tiny buttercups, daisies, and clover grow in the grass. In woodlands, flowers like bluebells, primroses and celandines grow. By the sea, sea campion and thrift grow on the rocks, and birdsfoot trefoil on grassy clifftops.

- **Protected flowers**
  Some wildflowers are now so rare that the few survivors must be protected by law. This is true of many orchids.

Factfinder: Plants

FACTS: About perennials & biennials

- **Annuals**
  Annuals are plants such as delphiniums that grow from seeds, flower, disperse their seeds, and die in a single growing season.

- **Biennials**
  Biennials live for two years. In the first, the plant grows leaves on a bulb or taproot, which sustains it with food through the winter. It flowers in the second summer.

- **Perennials**
  Perennials such as wallflowers and chrysanthemums live several years, surviving through the winter on underground food stores such as bulbs.

- **Ephemerals**
  Ephemerals such as groundsel are short-lived plants that grow from seed, bloom, and die within a few weeks.

▲ The giant sunflower is a perennial. It is a native of Peru but is now grown in many places, both for its big yellow flowers and for its seeds which give cooking oil.

▼ Flowers probably evolved their colorful blooms and beautiful scents to attract the insects they rely on for pollination. But the efforts of gardeners over the centuries have added many new and often spectacular blooms to those created by natural evolution, including roses, tulips, delphiniums, and many more. Many of these new flowers no longer rely on insects for pollination, but are pollinated by humans.

Lupin, Carnation, Rose, Soapwort, Rosebay willowherb, Tulip, Michaelmas daisy, Bluebell, Poppy, Scarlet pimpernel

77

How trees grow

ALTHOUGH SOME DWARF WILLOWS grow just a few inches high, trees are generally the largest of all plants. Indeed the giant redwood tree is the biggest of all living things. Trees can grow big because they don't have soft, green "herbaceous" stems like other plants; they have stiff, brown, woody stems, covered in protective bark, that can grow tall and support an enormous weight of leaves. With most trees, there is a single, thick central stem–the trunk–and leaves and side branches only grow some way off the ground–so they are well out of the reach of most browsing animals.

FACTS: About tree trunks

▲ Slicing through a tree's trunk can reveal a lot about its history—its age, the rate at which it has grown, and the conditions it has faced over the years.

- **Inside the trunk**
  The center of a trunk is the dead "heartwood." The living part is the middle—the "sapwood" and the "cambium." Outside is a protective layer of bark.

- **Tree rings**
  Each ring inside the trunk represents a year's growth. Rings close together indicate slow growth; rings far apart indicate rapid growth.

FACTS: About seeds

- **Seed production**
  Because only a small portion of their seeds survive, most trees produce thousands each year.

- **Seed dispersal**
  The seeds of many trees are dispersed by wind, so are shaped to become airborne easily—maple tree seeds are encased in a pair of flat wings, while willow seeds are shaped like tiny parachutes.

▼ Many trees have seeds that are spread by the wind. The eucalyptus trees of Australia are among the many that have long helicopter-like wings on which they can flutter long distances before they land.

Factfinder: Plants

▶ Timber is either hardwood, from broad-leaved trees (page 76) or softwood, from conifers (page 78). Softwood trees are much faster growing (about 33 feet/10m every 30 years) and are grown in huge numbers on plantations in places like the Rocky Mountains, North America (right). Because they grow faster, these trees provide softer wood. Softwoods are mostly used for making cheap furniture, paper, and for building. Hardwoods are used for more expensive furniture and shipbuilding.

◀ Cedars have smooth, upright cones, which are made up of lots of closely packed scales, each attached to two seeds. Over a few years these scales gradually break off the cones and fall to the ground, taking their seeds with them.

- **Seed cones**
  The seeds of conifers develop inside hard, protective cones until they are ready.

- **Catkins**
  Oak trees produce male flowers called catkins—long clusters that hang from the branches and release pollen into the air. When the pollen lands on the ovaries of female flowers and fertilizes them, the ovaries develop into acorns.

- **Nuts and berries**
  Some trees have seeds growing inside soft, fleshy fruits, such as berries. Others have them growing inside hard shells, such as acorns and walnuts.

DATA: Trees

- **THE BIGGEST TREE**
  In the world is "General Sherman," a giant sequoia in California—272 feet (83m) tall and 82 feet (25m) around.

- **THE FASTEST-GROWING TREE**
  The Albizia falcata is a tropical pea tree and can grow 33 feet (10m) in 13 months.

- **THE LONGEST LIVING TREE**
  The oldest surviving tree was a bristlecone pine in Nevada, which had lived for 5,100 years.

- **THE LONGEST LIVING SPECIES**
  The oldest surviving species of tree is thought to be the maidenhair tree of China, which first appeared more than 160 million years ago.

Deciduous trees

DECIDUOUS TREES are trees that lose their leaves at some time during the year, usually to cut down their need for water. In cool regions, they lose them in winter because water is hard to come by when groundwater is frozen. In warm regions, they lose them in the summer when the soil dries out quickly. All deciduous trees are flowering plants (see page 71) and have broad, flat leaves, which is why they are also known as broad-leaved trees–although there are also evergreen broad-leaved trees. Broad-leaved trees include deciduous trees such as ash and chestnut, evergreen trees such as holly, and palm trees.

FACTS: About palm trees

- **Long leaves**
  Palm trees have thick, tough leaves that help them survive in hot places. There are about 2,800 species, some with leaves as long as 40 feet (12m).

- **No branches**
  Palms have no branches. The leaves grow directly out from the trunk.

▶ The leaves, stems, and fruit of palm trees provide lots of useful products, ranging from baskets, furniture, food and oil. Even soap.

▼ In spring, the buds of new leaves shoot on the trees, and slowly open. Flowers appear on the tree, too, and fruit trees blossom. Because plenty of sunlight can still filter down to the ground through the thin canopy of leaves, woodland flowers such as bluebells bloom beneath the trees.

▼ In summer, the leaves on the trees are fully grown, providing a sheltered home for a wide variety of different animals and plants. The dense foliage keeps the woodland beneath at an even temperature—nights are warmer and days are cooler here than out in the open.

Factfinder: Plants

FACTS: About deciduous trees

- **Tree life**
  Oaks and other trees can live up to 500 years. Some elms that reproduce from suckers never really die at all because the trees are constantly renewing themselves, creating a whole grove of their offshoots.

- **Fallen trees**
  Every now and then, trees die and fall over. As they crash to the floor, they open up the woodland floor to the sky, creating a glade where new trees and other plants thrive.

▲ *Deciduous forests once covered the whole of Europe, but now only fragments of these great forests remain.*

- **Oak trees**
  There are 450 species of oak tree, some deciduous, some evergreen. But all grow from acorns.

- **Dutch elm disease**
  Elm trees were once common in northern Europe, but many have been killed by Dutch elm disease—a fungus whose spores are spread by beetles that live in the bark.

- **Coppicing**
  Many European woodlands have long been managed by foresters. Trees such as willows are cut off at the trunk or "coppiced." The new straight shoots that grow from the top make "withies," good for basketmaking.

▼ *By autumn, the days are getting colder and there is less water available. To survive, the trees must prepare to lose their leaves. The chlorophyll that makes the leaves green starts to break down and sugars in the leaves gradually turn them brown, red, or orange.*

▼ *As winter approaches the trees get ready to close down altogether. The leaves that changed color in the autumn start to drop off, leaving the trees bare and dormant. During this time, though, winter buds develop, containing new leaves which will burst open the following spring.*

Conifers and cycads

CONIFERS, AND THEIR TROPICAL RELATIVES cycads and gingkos, are among the oldest of all kinds of plants. They first appeared more than 300 million years ago, long before the age of dinosaurs. Conifers, cycads, and gingkos are all called gymnosperms, and make their seeds in cones. Conifers are tall, mostly evergreen trees that generally grow in cool and mountainous regions. A few cypresses are the only tropical conifers. Cycads, however, are tropical trees that look like stubby palm trees. Gingkos or maidenhair trees are tall trees with fan-shaped leaves that grow only in eastern China.

FACTS: About coniferous forests

Like all conifers, pine trees have long needles and cones. They also grow tall and fast and are fully grown in under 20 years, which is why they provide three quarters of the world's timber.

- **Cold resistance**
  Conifers are able to survive in cold areas with little water because instead of leaves they have thin waxy needles that shed snow easily and lose very little water. (Water cannot be used by trees when it is frozen). Their tall, narrow shape helps shed snow too.

- **Evergreen**
  Nearly all conifers are evergreen, which means that their leaves stay on all year round. Larches are an exception—their needles fall off in autumn.

- **Plantations**
  In various cold regions of the world conifers are grown in narrowly planted rows on massive plantations to provide timber. They are fast-growing and can also survive on soil that is too poor for other crops.

- **Life in a coniferous forest**
  Coniferous forests are usually quite dense and dark, and so there is much less other plant life beneath the trees than there is in a deciduous forest (see page 76)—usually just fungi, ferns, and lichen.

- **Pine family**
  Pines make up the largest family of conifers. This includes almost 100 different species, such as the Scots pine, Corsican pine, and the white pine.

- **Boreal forest**
  The most extensive coniferous forests are found in the colder, northern parts of the world—mostly North America, Scandinavia, and Siberia.

- **Tree mix**
  Most coniferous forests are made up of conifers like pines, spruces, and firs.

Factfinder: Plants

▲ The giant redwood or sequoia trees of Sierra Nevada in California are the world's largest living things, growing 300 feet (90m) or more tall. Some are among the oldest too. Some redwoods date back to before the days of the Ancient Egyptians, 4,000 years ago.

DATA: Big, old trees

- **THE TALLEST TREE**
  The tallest tree in the world is a coastal redwood in Redwood National Park, California—365 feet (111m).

- **THE OLDEST LIVING TREE**
  Is a 4,700 year old bristlecone pine in California's White Mts.

- **THE BIGGEST FOREST**
  Is in Siberia—6.5 million square miles (17 million sq km).

FACTS: Seeds and cones

- **Cone-bearers**
  Instead of flowers, conifers and cycads have male and female cones that produce and carry seeds.

- **Male cones**
  The smaller male cones grow in clusters and produce pollen grains which travel on the wind to fertilize the female cones.

- **Female cones**
  Once fertilized, female cones may take as long as three years to develop their seeds.

- **Female scales**
  Each scale of the female cone has one or more seeds attached to it. As they develop they are protected within the hard cone. When they are ready, the scales open up and either release the seeds or fall away from the cone, taking the seeds with them.

▲ Cones are very sensitive to changes in the dampness of the air. In dry weather, the scales shrivel and stand out stiffly. When it is damper, they absorb the moisture and close up neatly again.

83

Mosses and ferns

NOT ALL PLANTS GROW FROM SEEDS. The very first plants to grow on land some 400 million years ago grew from tiny, dustlike cells called spores. These ancient plants, including mosses, liverworts, club mosses, horsetails, and ferns, still survive today, although none of them ever grow as big as they did in the time before seed-bearing plants appeared some 200 million years ago. They love damp, shady places, and are often seen carpeting rocks along streams and growing all over trees in moist woodlands and steamy tropical rain forests—sometimes far above the ground.

FACTS: About ferns

- **Roots, leaves, and stems**
  Unlike mosses, ferns are "pteridophytes," or featherplants, and have roots and leaves, and veins to take food and water up and down inside the stem. Fern leaves are called fronds.

- **Tree ferns**
  Tree ferns can grow up to 80 feet (25m) tall, and they are abundant in moist tropical rain forests. They have no branches, and the fronds grow in a crown from the top of the trunk.

- **Passenger plants**
  Some ferns, such as bird's-nest fern and stag's horn fern, grow on other plants without harming them. They get their moisture by collecting dripping rainwater.

- **Horsetails**
  Horsetails are similar to ferns, but they belong to a group called sphenophytes. Although nowadays most are small, these plants grew more than 100 feet (30m) tall in the Carboniferous Period 300-355 million years ago.

▶ Ferns grow from spores made on the underside of their leaves. The spores form a prothallus, which creates the embryo for a new fern to grow from.

Sporangia are where the fern makes spores

In each sori, there are sacs called sporangia

On the underside of leaves are balls called sori

The root and stem grow to form a new fern frond

A new root and stem grow and the prothallus dies away

Factfinder: Plants

FACTS: About moss

- **Moss**
Mosses and liverworts make up a group of their own called bryophytes. They form in thin cushions on walls, rocks, and old logs and have no true roots so they have to draw their moisture from the air through their stems and tiny threads called rhizoids. This is why they like damp places such as riverbanks.

- **Sponges**
Sphagnum moss lives in bogs and can soak up to 25 times its own weight in water. It is the main constituent in peat bogs in Ireland and Scotland.

- **New moss**
Moss spores make male and female cells, which swim together to create the embryo for a new moss.

Spores burst from the sporangia and spread on the wind

Settling in a suitable place, the spore puts out shoots

The shoots form a heart-shaped plant or prothallus, which makes male and female cells

The male cells fertilize the female

When it rains, male cells swim to the female cells

The embryo of a new plant grows in the prothallus.

▲ Ferns are by far the biggest group of spore-bearing plants and there are more than 9,000 different kinds. Unlike all the other spore-bearing plants, they have big leaves called fronds. Fronds can grow to an enormous size. The fronds of the Marattia can grow more than 23 feet (7 m) long. Technically, fronds are called megaphyllous leaves, which just means big spore-bearers.

Fungi and mushrooms

FUNGI AND MUSHROOMS grow in the ground like plants, but they are not plants at all. Fungi and mushrooms, along with toadstools, yeast, mildew, and mold (like the mold on bread), all belong to a special group of organisms called Myceteae. Unlike plants, fungi have no green chlorophyll, so cannot make their own food. So they have to get their food in other ways. Many fungi are parasites, which means they feed off living animals, plants and other organisms. Others are "saprophytes," which means they live off the remains of dead plants and animals.

▶ Fungi are both good and bad for us. Some kinds of fungi, such as mushrooms and cheese mold, are good to eat, but others are deadly poisonous. Some grow on plants and animals and make them ill, such as the aspergillus mold. Others provide antibiotic drugs. Yeast helps bread rise and beer ferment.

Destroying angel

Fly agaric

Honey fungus

Puffball

FACTS: About parasites

▲ Fungi live off other organisms. These fungi are growing on a tree, clinging on with hundreds of cottonlike threads called hyphae, which digest and absorb materials from the tree.

- **Chemical rotters**
Fungi rot the organism they are feeding on by sending out special chemicals called enzymes, which break down plant and animal cells.

- **Food source**
Fungi absorb food from the rotting organism.

- **Blue cheese**
The enzymes released by mold are what give blue cheese its flavor—and make bread mold toxic.

Factfinder: Plants

FACTS: What fungi are made of

- **Spreading threads**
  Fungi are made of cottonlike threads called hyphae which spread out in a tangled mass through the soil—or into the tissues of the plant or animal the fungi are living on.

◀ Sometimes, hyphae (pronounced hi-fi) bundle together to form what are called fruiting bodies—such as mushrooms and toadstools. But they can also make tiny pinheads, such as the mold on rotting fruit.

Shaggy ink cap

Field mushroom

Oyster mushroom

Death cap

FACTS: Poisonous fungi

- **Fly agaric**
  Fly agaric makes the poison muscarine, which causes stomach pains and convulsions, and can occasionally kill. Fly agaric was once taken in small doses for its hallucinatory effect.

- **Death cap**
  The death cap and destroying angel toadstools look quite like harmless mushrooms—but they are deadly. Death cap contains the poisons amanitine and phalloidine, which can kill a human within six hours of eating it, due to kidney and liver failure.

- **False morel**
  False morel makes the poison gyromitrin which can create terrible stomach pains.

▶ Fly agaric announces its deadly poison with its bright color. Eating even small amounts can completely knock you out.

87

Algae

A KIND OF ALGAE was among the first living things to appear on Earth some three billion years ago. There are now many different kinds of algae, and although some are tiny, they are very important. They grow almost everywhere there is water, from the oceans to damp walls. Algae in the oceans not only provide food for creatures such as whales, but maintain the levels of oxygen in the air—and without this we could not breathe. Algae can draw energy from sunlight like most plants, but they have no leaves, stems, roots, or flowers. Indeed, many scientists don't put algae in the plant kingdom at all but in their own kingdom called *Protoctista*.

FACTS: About lichens

◀ Lichens grow on bare rock, and can often be seen on stone walls and old stone buildings. But they are very sensitive to any pollution in the air—especially sulfur dioxide from coal-fired power stations—and will not grow where the air is dirty.

▼ Lichens grow in three kinds of shapes. Crusty or "crustose" lichens grow in disks on stones and walls. Leafy or "foliose" lichens grow on the ground or on trees, and their edges curl up like leaves. Shrubby or "fruticose" lichens look like tiny bushes.

- **Algae and fungi**
  Lichens look like plants. But they are actually a remarkable partnership between algae and fungi. The algae are tiny green balls, and use sunlight to make food for the fungi. The fungi create a protective blanket above and below and act as a water store.

- **Reindeer food**
  The algae-fungi partnership enables lichens to live on bare rock faces and very harsh places such as the Antarctic and on mountaintops. If things get too dry or cold, they simply go into suspended animation, ready for the good times to begin again. Some lichens provide the only food for reindeer in the Arctic.

Crustose lichen

FACTS: About seaweed

- **Large algae**
  Seaweeds are very large algae that grow on seashores, or get washed up on beaches. They are usually brown, red, or green in color. They tend to grow in the shallows because they need sunlight.

- **Brown and red**
  Brown algae such as kelp grow 50-65 feet (15-20m) down. Red algae grow 100-200 feet (30-60m) down.

- **Holding on**
  Seaweeds have a "holdfast," which looks like a mass of roots, but is just the seaweed's suckers for holding on to rocks despite crashing waves. They actually rely on the water to support them.

- **Natural floats**
  Some seaweeds have air-filled bladders to help them float near the surface.

- **Useful weeds**
  In many places, seaweed is gathered from the seashore to put on the land as fertilizer. It is also a valuable source of iodine and some antibiotics. "Alginates" from seaweeds help set ice cream.

Seaweed helps oxygenate the water, and provides grazing for many sea creatures

- **Sea food**
  Seaweed may not look appetizing, but it is popular in Chinese and Japanese cooking. The red seaweed Porphyra is used in Wales to make a kind of pudding called "laver-bread."

▶ Most seaweeds stay submerged all the time, but many have to cope with the tides—and long periods when they are left high and dry out of water. Some can survive almost a day in baking sunshine, drying up, then returning to life when the tide comes in and refreshes them again. In fact, seaweeds are banded in the tide zone according to how long they can live out of water.

FACTS: About algae

- **Plankton**
  In the oceans, the most important plants are "phytoplankton"—tiny organisms that float in in the surface waters of the oceans and grow in huge numbers. These are food for a wide range of sea creatures.

- **Algal bloom**
  Sometimes algae grow in such huge numbers that they choke other life. These "algal blooms" can sometimes be caused in rivers by fertilizer pollution from farms.

Plants for food

PLANTS PROVIDE the "staple" (basic or essential) food for most people around the world, and an area one and a half times the size of the United States is used for growing crops. More than 12,000 species of plant have been used for food at one time or other, but only about 150 or so are regularly grown as crops, including cereals such as wheat, rice, and corn, fruit such as oranges and bananas, root vegetables such as potatoes and yams, green vegetables such as cabbage and kale, and pulses such as soybeans and lentils. Some of these were first cultivated more than 10,000 years ago.

FACTS: Fruit and vegetables

- **Citrus fruits**
  Oranges, lemons, grapefruits, tangerines, and limes are citrus fruits and are grown in huge quantities in places with Mediterranean climates. The fruits are picked in winter and often made into juice.

- **Fruit farms**
  Apples are grown in orchards, oranges are grown in groves, and bananas on plantations.

- **Potato blight**
  Potatoes come originally from South America, but they became the staple for poor Irish farmers in the 19th century. When the potato crop was ruined by a disease called "blight" in the 1840s, millions of Irish people starved.

▶ Bananas are the major export of many countries in Central America, such as El Salvador and Honduras. They are picked while still green and semi-frozen for export by sea.

Millet is grown in dry places such as Africa and is ground to make flour

Sunflower seeds are crushed to produce oil

▶ These are just some of the plants grown for food. Many, including sunflowers, corn, and olives are made into oil. The cereals can be ground to make flour, but rice is usually cooked as whole grains, while corn, millet, and sorghum (as well as oats) are typically made into a kind of porridge. Corn comes in two kinds. One gives the large head with lots of grains, known as sweetcorn or corn on the cob. Smaller-grained, smaller-headed corn is used for corn oil or corn starch.

Olives grow on trees in Mediterranean areas. They are eaten whole or pressed to make oil

Factfinder: Plants

Sorghum is a cereal grown in places such as Egypt and China

Wheat

Corn

Rice

▲ Sugarcane is a tall plant grown in warm places such as the Caribbean. To make sugar, the cane is crushed to make a sugary liquid, which is then boiled and condensed until crystals form. These crystals are white sugar which may then be further refined to make icing sugar and castor sugar, or even compressed to make sugar lumps.

Barley is grown in temperate regions. It is used for food as well as for making alcoholic drinks

FACTS: About cereals

- **What are cereals?**
  Cereals are crops such as wheat, corn, rice, oats, rye, and barley. They are all grasses and we eat the seeds or grain, leaving the stalks and leaves to rot into animal food called silage.

- **Wheat**
  Wheat provides the basic food for over one in three people in the world. Wheat grain is ground to make flour, which is then used to make things such as bread and pasta.

- **Rice**
  Widely grown in southern Asia, rice is the staple food for half the world's population. In China alone, 200 million tons are grown every year. There are more than 14,000 types, including many long-grained rices such as Basmati rice used with Indian curries, medium-grained rices used for Italian risotto, and short-grained rice used for puddings. Brown rice is white rice with the husk on.

- **Paddy fields**
  Rice is the only cereal crop grown in water—in flooded fields called "paddies." Most of the work in producing it is done by hand. There are typically three crops a year.

▶ Before processing, rice grains are enclosed in tough husks. Removing this outer layer makes brown rice; refining the grains even further makes white rice.

Herbs and spices

HERBS AND SPICES HAVE BEEN used to flavor food and to make medicines since prehistoric times. Herbs are small flowering plants, and there are hundreds of different kinds, each with its own special properties. Usually it is the leaves that are valued, but it can be the flowers or the stem. Some, such as basil and oregano, are edible and used in small quantities to flavor food. Others, like feverfew, are valued more for their medicinal qualities. Spices are strongly flavored seeds, roots, and bark that are usually ground into powder to add to food as it is cooked.

FACTS: About tea and coffee

- **Tea**
  Tea is the dried leaves of a small camellia bush that grows on hillsides in subtropical areas, especially in India and Sri Lanka, Japan, and China. The best tea grows slowly at high altitudes (up to 6,600 feet/2,000m in places).

- **Black tea and green tea**
  There are two main kinds of tea: green tea and black tea. Green tea is picked and dried quickly, giving a mild flavor. Green tea is popular in China. Black tea is only partly dried before it is crushed in rolling machines, giving a much stronger flavor. Black tea is preferred in Europe.

- **Coffee**
  Coffee is made from the ground and roasted beans of the coffee bush. The beans are collected and soaked, then the husks are removed and the beans are dried, sorted, and roasted. The longer the roast, the stronger and darker the coffee.

- **Instant coffee**
  Coffee can be made into instant coffee powder by boiling coffee dry, or into instant coffee granules by plunging ground beans into liquid gas to freeze-dry them.

◀ For tea, tea pickers—mainly women—neatly pluck the young tips of the leaves by hand and put them in baskets slung over their shoulders.

◀ Coffee grows in the tropics in places such as Brazil. The best is grown on slopes 2,000-6,000 feet (600-1,800m) up. Coffee beans are not actually beans at all, but a kind of berry, and are bright red when on the bush.

Factfinder: Plants

FACTS: About herbs

- **Herbal drugs**
  Many of today's medicines came originally from plants, including aspirin (from willow trees), morphine (from the seeds of the opium poppy), and quinine (from the bark of the cinchona tree of South America). An extract of the rosy periwinkle, called vincristine, is one of the drugs used against leukemia, a childhood cancer.

- **Herb facts**
  Egyptian pyramid builders ate garlic because they thought it would give them strength...rosemary gets its name from the Latin *ros marinus* which means sea dew...bay leaves were used to crown poets and heroes in Ancient Rome...the Ancient Greeks called basil "King of Herbs"...the Latin name for sage is Salvia, which means healthy, and sage is thought to have healing qualities...mint and the spice cinnamon keep moths away from clothes...oregano is used as a dye as well as a food flavor.

FACTS: About spices

- **Spice facts**
  It takes 182,000 hand-picked crocus flower heads to make one pound (450g) of saffron...ginger is the root of a tall grasslike plant that is harvested after flowering... chilli can actually cool you down because it makes you sweat...cinnamon comes from the bark of a tree...nutmeg is the seed of a tree...star anise takes 15 years to grow.

- **Spice islands**
  Many spices come from the Moluccas in Indonesia, which were once known as the Spice Islands.

Opium poppy flower
Opium poppy seed head
Foxglove
White willow
Periwinkle
Feverfew

◁ *This shows just a few of the many herbs and flowers valued for medicinal purposes. Foxglove in large doses is poisonous, but it yields the drug digitalis, used in small doses to treat heart problems. Feverfew was once thought an effective treatment for fever.*

Tropical plants

The tropics are warm nearly all the time, and in the rain forests there is abundant moisture. The combination creates almost ideal conditions for plant growth, and tropical forests are not only lush but contain an astonishing variety of plants—including some of the world's most spectacular and strange. The rain forests are the world's richest plant habitats, containing more than 40 percent of the world's plant species. No one knows exactly how many different plants there are. But botanists counted more than 180 species of tree alone in one hectare (2.5 acres) of the Malaysian forest.

FACTS: Coping with drought

- **Deep roots**
  When there is no water on the surface, plants can often find moisture deep underground by growing long roots. Mesquite roots often grow as deep as 33 feet (10m), and may be as long as 165 feet (50m).

- **Tough leaves**
  In moist places, plants lose water by evaporation from their leaves. So desert plants usually have tough, waxy leaves that cut moisture loss to a minimum— and have as few leaves as possible.

▲ The baobab of Africa and Australia survives in dry places by retaining moisture in its barrel-shaped trunk, which can be up to 30 feet (9m) thick.

- **Cacti**
  Cacti live in American deserts. They have no leaves and a thick skin, so water loss is cut to a minimum. Their fat stems can hold huge amounts of water, which is why they are called succulents.

- **Prickly plants**
  Lush vegetation is so rare in deserts that animals eat anything. So cacti, prickly pears, and thorn bushes grow prickles to protect themselves.

◄ Cacti have to pollinate, just like every other flowering plant and so every few years they produce big colorful blooms in order to attract insects quickly.

Factfinder: Plants

FACTS: About tropical water plants

- **Amazon lily**
  The world's biggest water plant is the Amazon water lily. Its massive floating leaves grow up to 6 feet (1.8m) across, and can sometimes support the weight of a child.

- **Water hyacinth**
  The water hyacinth is the world's fastest growing water plant—so fast growing that it is thought of as a pest, especially since it chokes waterways and encourages mosquitoes.

Rafflesia has no stem—just a huge flower that sits on the ground

◀ The Rafflesia of Southeast Asia is the world's biggest flower. A single bloom can be up to 3 feet (90 cm) across. It smells like rotting meat—perhaps to attract the flies it needs to help it pollinate.

95

THE UNIVERSE

98 Planet Earth
100 The Moon
102 The Sun
104 Inner planets
106 Giant planets
108 Outer planets
110 Comets and meteorites
112 Stars
114 Galaxies and nebulae
116 Black holes
118 How far to the stars?
120 Space travel
122 History of the Universe

Planet Earth

THIRD PLANET OUT FROM THE SUN, our Earth looks from a distance like a great round blue jewel hanging in the darkness of space. It is blue because three quarters of its rocky surface is drowned under blue ocean waters, which shimmer in the light of the Sun. No other planet has this much water on its surface. Here and there, its rocky surface pokes up above the water to form half a dozen large continents and thousands of smaller islands. The very ends of the world are glistening white—the permanent polar ice caps.

FACTS: Earth measurements

- **The size of the Earth**
  The distance around the Earth is 24,815 miles (40,024km) at the equator. It's diameter at the equator is 7,910 miles (12,758km)—larger than its diameter pole to pole, by 27 miles (43km).

- **The weight of the Earth**
  The Earth weighs 6,000 trillion trillion tons.

- **The angle of the Earth**
  The Earth tilts over at an angle of 23.45°.

▼ *Satellites have allowed the Earth to be measured more accurately then ever before. Satellites can detect movements of the continents of just a fingernail's width or small variations in the height of the sea's surface.*

▲ *The Earth looks round, but it is not a perfect sphere. Because it spins faster at the equator than the poles, it is actually shaped more like a tangerine, bulging slightly at the equator and flattened at the poles. So scientists used to describe its shape as an oblate spheroid (flattened ball). Now satellite measurements have detected other slight irregularities, so they call it a geoid, which simply means Earth-shaped.*

Factfinder: The Universe

FACTS: Inside the Earth

- **Probing the Earth**
  Scientists have worked out what the Earth's interior is like from vibrations from earthquakes and underground explosions.

- **Crust**
  The Earth has a thin shell of solid rock called the crust, which varies from 3-7 miles (6-11km) under the oceans to 18-42 miles (30-70km) under the continents.

- **Mantle**
  Beneath the crust is a layer almost 2,000 miles (3,200km) deep, called the mantle. It is so hot here that the rock flows very, very slowly.

- **Core**
  Below the mantle is a core of metal, mostly iron and nickel.

- **Outer core**
  The outer portion of the core is so ferociously hot that the metal is always molten.

- **Inner core**
  The Earth's inner core is even hotter—up to 12,600°F (7,000°C)—but the metal here is solid because pressures here are so great that metal simply cannot melt.

Inner core   Outer core   Mantle   Crust

Lunar eclipse

Solar eclipse

▲ Earth has several different layers because the materials it is made of have separated out over billions of years. Dense metals such as iron sank to the center to form the core, while lighter rock-forming materials floated to the top to form the crust.

◀ Every now and then, the Earth and Moon get in between each other and the Sun. This is called an eclipse because the planet in between "eclipses," or blocks out, the Sun. A lunar eclipse is when the Moon goes round behind the Earth into its shadow. A solar eclipse is when the Moon comes in between the Sun and the Earth, casting a shadow a few miles wide on the Earth.

The Moon

Earthrise on the Moon

THE MOON IS THE BIGGEST, BRIGHTEST object in the night sky. It seems to shine almost like a pale sun. But it does not give out any light itself. It is just a big, cold ball of rock and shines only because it reflects sunlight. The Moon is the Earth's companion in space, and circles round it continuously, just as the Earth circles the Sun. The Moon is about a quarter of the Earth's size and was probably formed shortly after the Earth, perhaps from hot splashes flung out as a small planet collided with the Earth.

FACTS: About the Moon

- **Pitted surface**
  The Moon's surface is pitted with craters—dents created by the impact of huge rocks early in its history.

- **Seas on the Moon**
  All over the Moon's surface are dark patches that people once believed were seas. In fact, they are not seas at all, but vast plains formed by lava flowing from volcanoes that erupted early in the Moon's history.

- **"Moonths"**
  The word month comes from the Moon, and the time it takes to go once round the Earth. It takes the Moon 27.3 days to circle the Earth, but it actually takes 29.53 days from one full moon to the next, because the Earth moves as well, and the Moon falls a little behind. This 29.53 days cycle is called a lunar month. However, the length of our calendar months was decided a few centuries ago by the Pope.

- **Watery Moon**
  In 1998, X-ray cameras on a NASA space probe revealed that there are huge quantities of water on the Moon, in the form of ice under the Moon's surface.

The moon's rocky mantle is cool and solid, unlike the Earth's mantle

The Moon's outer core is probably solid metal

The Moon has a small inner core of molten metal

▲ The Moon's surface is very dead compared with the Earth. It has no atmosphere. The surface is just fine white dust, pitted with craters. Also, its rocky interior is cool, not hot like the Earth's, and the volcanic activity that constantly changes the Earth's surface has long since died out on the Moon.

100

Factfinder: The Universe

FACTS: On the Moon

- **Men on the Moon**
  The first men to land on the Moon were Neil Armstrong and Buzz Aldrin—in July 1969. The most recent was Eugene Cernan in 1972.

- **High jumping**
  The Moon's gravity is only a sixth of the Earth's, so everything is very light. Moon astronauts can jump easily—even in heavy space suits.

- **Footprints forever**
  Because there is no air, the sky on the Moon is inky black even in daytime, and there is no wind to ruffle the dust. So the footprints left by the first men on the Moon will be there forever.

- **Day and night**
  Each day on the Moon lasts 360 hours, and the temperature reaches 260°F (127°C)—but the night is just as long and temperatures plunge to -260°F (-162°C).

▲ *The Moon is the only world beyond ours that people have visited. When Neil Armstrong set foot on it on July 21, 1969, he said famously, "That's one small step for man, one giant leap for mankind."*

The phases of the Moon

Only the part of the Moon lit by the Sun is bright enough for us to see. But as it circles the Earth, the Sun shines on the Moon from changing angles, and we see more or less of the moon at different times—and so the Moon appears to change shape over the course of a month as it circles the Earth. These changes are called phases.

▼ *During the first half of the month, the Moon grows from a crescent shaped new Moon, to a half-circle shaped half Moon, to a full Moon. This is called waxing. In the second half, it gets smaller or "wanes" through a half Moon back to a crescent-shaped old Moon— curving the opposite way from the new Moon.*

The Sun

THE SUN IS OUR LOCAL STAR, a vast fiery spinning ball of hot gases–three quarters hydrogen and a quarter helium. It is well over a million times as big as the Earth. The gigantic mass of the Sun creates immense pressures in its core. Such huge pressures fuse hydrogen atoms together in a continual nuclear reaction that boosts temperatures to 27 billion°F (15 billion°C). This heat turns the outer surface of the Sun into a raging inferno that burns so brightly that it completely floodlights the Earth, more than 900,000 miles (1.5 million km) away.

FACTS: Inside the sun

- **A bomb in the heart**
  Pressures in the Sun's core are 2 trillion times the pressure of the Earth's atmosphere. These fuse so many hydrogen atoms together that it is as if 100 billion nuclear bombs were going off each second.

- **All down to Einstein**
  We owe our understanding of how the Sun produces heat and light to the famous scientist Albert Einstein (1897-1955), who showed how mass can be changed into energy.

- **Surface layers**
  The visible surface layer of the Sun is the photosphere. Above this lies the chromosphere and the corona.

- **Hot surface**
  Temperatures at the surface of the Sun are a phenomenal 10,800°F (6,000°C), enough to melt almost anything. This unimaginable heat accounts for the Sun's brightness.

- **The Sun's age**
  The Sun probably formed about five billion years ago, just a little before the Earth, which formed from the debris left over. It will burn out in about five billion years' time.

- **The Solar wind**
  Streaming out from the Sun every second are a million tons of electrically charged particles. Earth is protected from this lethal stream, called the solar wind, by its magnetic field.

- **SOHO**
  The SOHO space observatory sits in space between Earth and Sun and monitors the Sun continually.

◄ *The Sun's energy is generated by nuclear reactions in its core and makes its way to the surface over millions of years.*

Factfinder: The Universe

▲ Every now and then, the Moon swings between the Sun and the Earth, blocking out the Sun and creating a shadow a few hundred miles wide on the Earth. This is called a solar eclipse. Sometimes, the Sun glints through a valley on the Moon's surface, as in this picture, creating an effect like a jewel on a ring.

DATA: The Sun

- **DIAMETER**
  The Sun is a medium-sized star 865,000 miles (1,392,000km) across–10 times the diameter of the Earth.

- **MASS**
  The Sun's weight is more than 300,000 times that of the weight of the Earth.

- **ENERGY CONSUMPTION**
  The Sun burns up four million tons of hydrogen fuel every second.

- **ENERGY PRODUCTION**
  The Sun's energy production each second could keep the USA supplied with electricity for 50 million years.

- **CORONAL TEMPERATURE**
  The temperature of the Sun's outer ring or corona is 2.7 million°F (1.5 million°C).

▶ The heat from the Sun's core erupts on the surface in patches called granules. Here and there, giant flamelike tongues of hot hydrogen, called solar prominences, loop 60,000 miles (100,000km) out into space. Every now and then, too, huge five-minute eruptions of energy called solar flares burst from the surface. There are dark blotches on the Sun's surface, called sunspots, some fifty times the size of Africa. They are dark because they are slightly less hot than the rest of the surface. The number of spots seems to peak every 11 years, and some scientists believe these peaks are linked to spells of stormier weather on Earth.

103

Inner planets

Mercury

THE INNER PLANETS are the four planets in the solar system that are nearest the Sun. Nearest the Sun is little Mercury, then comes Mars, Earth, and Venus. All four are made of rock, unlike the big planets farther out, which are made mainly of gas. Because they are made of rock, they have a hard surface which a spaceship could land on, and they are sometimes called terrestrial (earthlike) planets. They all have an atmosphere of gas above the rocky surface-although Mercury's is very thin-but each is very different.

FACTS: About Mercury

◄ Mercury's atmosphere of sodium is so thin that there is nothing to stop meteors smashing into its surface—and nothing to smooth out any dents. So its surface is more deeply pitted with the scars of meteor impacts than the Moon's. All you'd see on a voyage across the surface would be vast empty basins, cliffs, and endless views of yellow dust.

- Hot and cold
  Temperatures on Mercury veer from one extreme to the other because its atmosphere is too thin to provide any insulation. In the day, temperatures soar to 800°F (425°C), but at night they plunge to -300°F (-170°C).

- Mercury's brief year
  Mercury is so near the Sun that its orbit is very short. It gets round in just 88 days, compared with 365 days for Earth. On the other hand, it takes a long time to turn around—58.6 days. So its day lasts 58.6 Earth days.

- Burning cold
  Mercury has small ice caps at each pole—but the ice is made from acid, not water.

DATA: The inner planets

MERCURY
- Mercury ranges from 28.5 million miles (45.9 million km) to 43.2 million miles (69.7 million km) from the Sun.
- Mercury's diameter is 3,024 miles (4,878km) and its mass is barely a twentieth of Earth's.

VENUS
- Venus is 66.6 million miles (107.4 million km) to 67.6 million miles (109 million km) from the Sun.
- Venus's diameter is 7,503 miles (12,102km) and its mass is about four-fifths that of Earth's.

MARS
- Mars is 141.3 million miles (227.9 million km) from the Sun.
- Mars's diameter is 4,207 miles (6,786km) and its mass is just over a tenth of Earth's.

Factfinder: The Universe

FACTS: About Venus

▲ Venus is the hottest planet in the solar system, and its surface is as barren as any desert on Earth. The buildup of carbon dioxide gas in its atmosphere has created a runaway "greenhouse effect," trapping so much of the Sun's heat that temperatures reach a scorching 875°F (470°C).

- **Evening star**
  Venus reflects sunlight so well off its thick atmosphere that it shines like a star. But because it is quite close to the Sun, we can only see it in the evening just after the sun has gone down, which is why it is sometimes called the evening star. We can also see it just before sunrise.

- **Thick air**
  Venus's atmosphere would be deadly to humans. It is very deep and thick, so pressure on the surface is enormous. It is also made mainly of poisonous carbon dioxide and filled with clouds of sulfuric acid gas belched out by the volcanoes on its surface.

FACTS: About Mars

- **High and deep**
  Mars has the biggest volcano in the solar system, called Olympus Mons, 9 miles (15km) high, three times higher than Mt. Everest. It also has a canyon called Valles Marineris, which is 6,400 miles (4,000km) long and four times as deep as the Grand Canyon.

- **The red planet**
  None of the space missions to Mars so far have found even the remotest trace of life. But in 1996, NASA scientists found what they though might be the fossil of a microscopic organism in a rock from Mars in the Arctic. So the search is on.

▶ Mars is sometimes called the red planet because it is rusty red. The surface contains a high proportion of iron dust, and this has been oxidized (rusted) in its carbon dioxide-rich atmosphere. It has small ice caps.

Giant planets

Saturn

OUT BEYOND MARS THERE are two planets far bigger than any others in the solar system. Jupiter and Saturn, the fifth and sixth planets out from the Sun, are gigantic. Jupiter is twice as heavy as all the other planets put together and 1,300 times as big as Earth. Saturn is not that much smaller. Unlike the inner planets, though, they are both made mostly of gas, and only their very core is rocky. This doesn't mean they are vast cloud balls. The huge pressure of gravity means the gas is squeezed until it becomes liquid or even solid.

Great Red Spot

Galilean moon

FACTS: About Jupiter

◀ Jupiter's surface is covered in a thin layer of swirling clouds of ammonia, indicating powerful storms. One storm called the Great Red Spot is 25,000 miles (40,000km) across and has lasted at least 330 years.

- **Mighty magnet**
Jupiter's bulk and its fast spin churn up the metal insides of the planet so much that the planet becomes a giant dynamo creating a magnetic field ten times as strong as Earth's.

- **Many moons**
Jupiter has 16 moons. There are four big ones discovered by Galileo as long ago as 1610, which is why they are called the Galilean moons. Then there are 12 smaller ones.

▼ The power of Jupiter's gravity drags volcanoes of sulfur from the surface of its moon Io.

- **Fast spinner**
Jupiter spins faster than any other planet. Despite its vast size, it turns right around in just 9.8 hours, so the surface is moving at 27,900mph (45,000km/h)!

- **Hydrogen deeps**
Jupiter is made mostly of hydrogen and helium gas, but this is squeezed so hard by the planet's gravity that it turns to liquid. Beneath Jupiter's thin atmosphere of ammonia, there is an ocean of liquid hydrogen 15,500 miles (25,000km) deep.

Factfinder: The Universe

FACTS: About Saturn

▸ Saturn is the most beautiful of all the planets, with its pale butterscotch surface of ammonia gases and its huge halo of rings.

- **Saturn's rings**
  Saturn's rings are countless billions of tiny chips of ice and dust. The rings are thin—no more than 160 feet (49m) deep—yet stretch 46,000 miles (74,200km) out into space.

▾ Saturn's rings have definite bands, named with the letters A to G.

- **Light planet**
  Saturn may be big, but it is surprisingly light, weighing 600 billion trillion tons. If you had a large enough bathtub, it would float.

- **Most moons**
  Saturn has more moons than any other planet—at least 19. Iapetus is black on one side and white on the other. Enceladus is covered in shimmering balls of ice. Tethys was once almost split in half by a giant meteor, which left a giant crater. Titan is the only moon with an atmosphere.

- **Windy planet**
  The surface winds on Saturn are faster than those on Jupiter, roaring around at 1,100 mph (1,800km/h).

DATA: About the giant planets

JUPITER
- Jupiter ranges from 459.4 million miles (740.9 million km) to 505.7 million miles (815.7 million km) from the Sun.
- Jupiter's diameter is 88,650 miles (142,984km) and its mass is 318 times that of Earth's.
- It takes 11.86 years to orbit the Sun.
- Its surface temperature is -238°F (-150°C).

SATURN
- Saturn ranges from 835 million miles (1.35 billion km) to 934 million miles (1.51 billion km).
- Saturn's diameter is 74,732 miles (120,536km) and its mass is more than 95 times that of Earth's.
- It takes 29.46 years to orbit the Sun.
- Its surface temperature is -290°F (-180°C).

Outer planets

Neptune

OUT BEYOND SATURN are the seventh, eight, and ninth planets of the solar system: Uranus, Neptune, and Pluto, along with Pluto's companion Charon. Unlike the other planets, these were unknown to ancient astronomers. They are so far away and so faint that Uranus was only discovered in 1781, Neptune in 1846, Pluto in 1930, and Charon as recently as 1978. Uranus and Neptune are giant gas planets like Saturn and Jupiter. Pluto and Charon are rocky planets and may have been asteroids trapped by the Sun's gravity in the outer reaches of the solar system.

FACTS: About Uranus

- **Rollover planet**
  Unlike any of the other planets, Uranus does not spin at a slight angle. Instead it is tilted right over, and rolls around the Sun like a giant bowling ball. In summer, the Sun does not set for 20 years.

- **Blue planet**
  Uranus has an atmosphere of hydrogen and helium, but beneath that are oceans of liquid methane, and it is this that gives the planet its beautiful blue-green color.

◁ Uranus is so far from the Sun that temperatures drop to -340°F (-210°C). Winds whistle through its atmosphere whipping up huge waves in the icy oceans of methane below.

FACTS: About Neptune

◁ Neptune has its own thin set of rings, like Saturn.

- **Blue planet**
  Like Uranus, Neptune has a thin atmosphere of hydrogen and helium, but is mostly deep oceans of liquid methane. The methane makes Neptune a beautiful cobalt blue.

- **Long year**
  Neptune is so far from the Sun that its orbit takes 164.79 years.

- **Discovering Neptune**
  Neptune's moon Triton is the only moon to orbit backward. It is the coldest place in the solar system -390°F (-236°C) and looks like a green melon with pink ice cream on the ends—ice caps of frozen nitrogen. Its volcanoes erupt ice.

Factfinder: The Universe

DATA: The outer planets

URANUS
- Uranus ranges from 1.7 billion miles (2.7 billion km) to 1.86 billion miles (3 billion km) from the Sun.
- Uranus's diameter is 31,693 miles (51,118km) and its mass is over 14 times that of Earth's.

NEPTUNE
- Neptune ranges from 2.76 billion miles (4.46 billion km) to 2.81 billion miles (4.53 billion km) from the Sun.
- Neptune's diameter is 30,707 miles (49,528km) and its mass is over 17 times that of Earth's.

PLUTO
- Pluto ranges from 2.93 billion miles (4.73 billion km) to 4.57 billion miles (7.37 billion km) from the Sun.
- Pluto's diameter is 1,760 miles (2,840km) and its mass is just a fiftieth of Earth's.

- **Discovering Neptune**
Neptune was discovered because in the 1840s two young mathematicians, John Couch Adams in England and Urbain le Verrier in France predicted where it should be from the way its gravity made a slight difference to Uranus's orbit. The planet was actually spotted by John Galle from the Berlin observatory on September 23, 1846.

▼ This is a view of Neptune and its moon Triton taken by the Voyager space mission, which reached the planet in 1989.

FACTS: About Pluto

▶ *Pluto and Charon are so far away from the Sun that the Sun looks little bigger in their sky than a star, and shines as palely as the Moon on Earth. So surface temperatures plunge to -365°F (-220°C).*

- **Pluto**
Pluto is very, very small, which is why it took so long to spot. Indeed some people say it should not be called a planet at all. It is five times smaller than the Earth and 500 times lighter.

- **Charon**
Pluto is only twice as big as its companion moon Charon. So they circle round each other locked in space like a pair of weightlifter's dumbbells. If you stood on Pluto's surface, you would see Charon in the sky, three times as big as our Moon, but never moving.

- **In and out**
Pluto has an elliptical orbit that every now and then swings it closer to the Sun than Neptune.

Comets and meteorites

PLANETS AND MOONS are not the only things whirling around the Sun. Along with the Earth and its companions are thousands upon thousands of tiny bits and pieces of rock and ice of all shapes and sizes. Some are smaller than a car. Others are several hundred miles across. These lumps of space debris are called asteroids. Every now and then, a very large lump of debris swings in from the outer limits of the solar system, creating a comet in the night sky. And all the time, lumps of this debris cannon into the Earth as meteors, some penetrating right through to the ground as meteorites.

FACTS: About asteroids

- **The asteroid belt**
  Asteroids are little chunks of debris that never clumped together to make a planet when the solar system was young. There are probably a million or more lying in a belt circling the Sun between Mars and Jupiter.

- **Ceres**
  The first of the asteroids to be spotted—and the biggest—is Ceres, as big as Maine. The brightest is called Vesta, the only asteroid that can be seen with the naked eye.

- **The Trojan asteroids**
  The Trojans are two small groups of asteroids that circle the Sun on the same orbit as Jupiter.

▼ Asteroids were first discovered in 1801, after a group of astronomers, calling themselves the Celestial Police, began hunting for a missing planet they were certain lay somewhere between Mars and Jupiter. Nowadays, new asteroids are discovered frequently. Each is given an identification number, and is named by the discoverer. Names vary from Greek goddesses to calculators.

▲ Every day, tons and tons of space debris rain down on the Earth, sometimes in such great concentrations that they make a golden rain in the night sky—called a meteor shower—as they hit the Earth's atmosphere and burn up. Meteors are space dust and lumps so small that they burn up long before they hit the ground. Meteorites are big enough to plunge right through the atmosphere and hit the ground. Most of these fall harmlessly into the oceans, and vary in size from lumps the size of shoes, to the meteorite the size of a car that hit Namibia, Africa, in 1920, creating an enormous crater.

Factfinder: The Universe

FACTS: About comets

▼ As it swings round the Sun, a comet's tail changes direction. It contains so little solid matter that it is blown out easily by the solar wind, the stream of charged particles flowing from the Sun— and so always points away from the Sun.

At the heart of a comet is a tiny nucleus of dust and ice

A tail of ionized atoms is blown out millions of miles behind the comet by the solar wind

- **Dirty snowballs**
  Comets with their flaming tails are the most spectacular sights in the night sky. But they are actually just dirty balls of ice, only a few miles across.

- **Visitors from afar**
  Many comets circle the Sun like the planets, but they have very long, stretched out orbits, and spend most of their time in the far reaches of the solar system. We see them only when their orbit brings them, for a few weeks, close to the Sun.

- **Glowing tails**
  The comet's tail is created as the comet hurtles towards the Sun and begins to melt. A vast plume of gas, millions of miles across, is blown out behind it by the solar wind, and this is what we see shining in the night as it catches the sunlight.

- **Periodics**
  Some comets, called Periodics, appear at regular intervals. Encke's comet comes every 1,206 days. Halley's Comet comes every 76 years.

- **Speeding comets**
  Comets speed up as they near the Sun, sometimes reaching speeds of up 1.2 million mph (2 million km/h). But far away from the Sun they slow down to speeds of little more than 600 mph (1,000km/h), which is why they stay away for so long.

▲ Halley's comet, discovered by Edmund Halley (1656-1742), appeared before the Battle of Hastings in 1066, and some say it was the star of Bethlehem.

Stars

A star in close-up: our Sun

THE FEW THOUSAND STARS you see twinkling in the night sky are just a tiny fraction of the trillions scattered through the Universe. Like our Sun, they are huge fiery balls of hot gas. They shine because they are burning. Deep inside, atoms of gas fuse together in nuclear reactions that boost temperatures to millions of degrees, making their surfaces glow. A star goes on glowing, sending out light, heat, radio waves and radiation, until its nuclear fuel—mainly hydrogen gas—is used up.

FACTS: About giants and dwarfs

- **Giant stars**
  Most stars are much the same size as our Sun—about 800,000 miles (1.4 million km) across. But some are giants 100 times as big, or supergiants some 300 times as big.

- **Dwarf stars**
  Dwarf stars are actually very small—smaller than the Earth. Very old stars can shrink under the power of their own gravity to even tinier neutron stars—no bigger than a major city, but so dense that they are as heavy as the Sun!

- **Starlight**
  The color of starlight tells us what the star is made of, and how hot it is.

▲ The color of a star depends on how bright it is. The Herzsprung-Russell diagram shows how the hotter and whiter stars glow, the brighter they are; the redder and cooler they glow, the dimmer they are. All medium-sized stars behave like this and form a band, called the Main Sequence stars, across the middle of the graph. Giants, dwarfs and neutron stars fall outside this band.

◄ Stars vary in brightness or "magnitude." The Herzsprung-Russell diagram shows how we expect stars of a certain color to be a certain brightness, their Absolute Magnitude. But if a star is far away, it looks dimmer than expected. This is its Relative Magnitude.

Factfinder: The Universe

FACTS: About constellations

- **Patterns in the stars**
  Ancient astronomers found their way around the heavens by looking for patterns of stars in the night sky. These patterns are called constellations. Astronomers now identify 88 of them, such as the Great Bear and Orion.

- **The Big Dipper**
  The Big Dipper, also known as the Great Bear or Ursa Major, is one of the best known constellations in the northern sky. It points toward the Pole Star, indicating north.

- **Alpha and beta**
  The stars in each constellation are named after letters in the Greek alphabet. The brightest star in each constellation is called Alpha, the next brightest Beta and so on. So Alpha Pegasi is the brightest star in Pegasus, the Flying Horse.

▲ Stars are being born and dying all over the Universe. The bigger the star, the shorter its life. The biggest stars end their lives in gigantic explosions called "supernovas," which are, briefly, the brightest things in the night sky as incredibly hot gas billows away.

DATA: Stars

- **THE BRIGHTEST-LOOKING STAR**
  Sirius, the Dog Star, is the brightest star in the night sky. But it is quite nearby (8.6 light-years) so its brightness is only relative.

- **THE BRIGHTEST STAR**
  Deneb burns as bright as 60,000 Suns, but because it is 1,800 light-years away, it looks dimmer than Sirius.

- **THE BIGGEST STAR**
  No one knows what the biggest star is, but Antares is very big, 700 times as big as our Sun.

- **STARS WITH PLANETS LIKE THE SUN**
  At least nine other stars, including 51 Pegasi, are now known to have planets, like our Sun has.

▲ Without constellations to help us, it would be hard to locate stars in the sky, but there is no real link between the stars in a constellation—they are completely imaginary patterns.

113

Galaxies and nebulae

OUR SUN IS JUST ONE OF A MASSIVE collection of two billion stars arranged in a shape like a spinning fried egg. This gigantic collection of stars is called the Galaxy. It gets its name from the Greek for milky, because we see it as a milky white band across the night sky-called the Milky Way. But the Galaxy is just one of many millions of similar giant groups of stars, also called galaxies (with a small "g"), scattered throughout the Universe.

FACTS: About galaxies

▶ Spiral galaxies are spinning, Catherine wheel-shaped galaxies, like the Milky Way and Andromeda galaxies. They have a dense core of stars, surrounded by long whirling arms.

▶ Barred spiral galaxies are variations on spiral galaxies with a central bar from which arms of stars trail like water from a spinning garden sprinkler.

▶ Elliptical galaxies are huge egg-shaped galaxies sometimes containing a trillion stars. They are the oldest galaxies of all, some over 12 billion years old.

▶ Irregular galaxies are different from the others in that they have no obvious shape at all, and may have formed from the debris of colliding galaxies.

▲ On a clear night, fuzzy patches of light can be seen among the stars. Some of these patches are distant galaxies. But others are huge clouds of dust called nebulae, many times bigger than any star. Only a few, called glowing nebulae, actually glow themselves; most are bright because the dust reflects starlight, just as clouds on Earth reflect sunlight. This picture show the famous Horsehead nebulae in the constellation of Orion, so-called because it is shaped a little like a horse's head.

▶ Stars start life in giant clouds of dust and gas called nebulae. Stars are born in these clouds as gravity pulls the dust into clumps—so ferociously that the pressure makes them glow.

- **Visible galaxies**
  Only three galaxies apart from the Milky Way can be seen with naked eye: the Large and Small Magellanic Clouds and the Andromeda galaxy.

- **Far lights**
  Galaxies contain many millions of stars, each as big as our Sun. But they are so far away that even with a reasonably good telescope, most look like blurs in the night sky. Andromeda, one of the nearest galaxies beyond the Milky Way, is more than three million light-years away!

- **The size of galaxies**
  Galaxies are absolutely gigantic. Although they contain millions or even trillions of stars, they are mostly empty space, for the stars are far apart. If each star was a person, the nearest neighbor would be almost as far away as the Moon.

- **How many galaxies?**
  Astronomers estimate that there are something like 20 trillion galaxies in the Universe.

- **Spiral galaxies**
  Just as the planets spin around the Sun, so spiral galaxies seem to be spinning too, which is why they have trailing arms.

- **Groups**
  Galaxies are often clustered in Groups of 30 or more. The Milky Way is part of the Local Group.

▶ The band of stars across the night sky called the Milky Way is an edge-on view of our own Galaxy, a vast cluster of stars 100,000 light-years across. It is a spiral galaxy, and our Sun is just one of millions of stars on one of the trailing arms. As it whirls round, it sweeps the Sun (and with it the Earth) in a huge circle 60 million miles (100 million km) every hour. The Sun travels more than 100,000 light-years to go around once—and it will get round in 200 million years. So the dinosaurs had just appeared on Earth last time it was where it is now.

The Milky Way is 100,000 light-years across and 1,000 light-years thick.

Black holes

GRAVITY IS THE FORCE that holds the Universe together. It is the force that keeps the Earth in one piece, keeps us on the ground, and keeps planets circling the Sun and the stars together in galaxies. Yet it can also be so powerfully destructive that it can squeeze stars to nothing and suck galaxies into oblivion. When some giant stars burn out, there is nothing to hold them up and they start to collapse under the force of their own gravity. As they shrink, they get denser and denser, and their gravity becomes even stronger... and so they get denser and denser, and their gravity becomes stronger still. Eventually, they shrink to nothing... and if one goes on shrinking, it may create a hole in space, called a black hole.

FACTS: About gravity and orbits

- **Orbits**
  Things stay in orbit when their forward momentum exactly balances the pull of gravity.

- **Earth's orbit**
  Earth stays on the same path around the Sun because it is bowling through space too fast to be drawn in by the pull of the Sun—yet not so fast that it can overcome the Sun's pull altogether and hurtle off into space.

- **Satellites**
  Satellites seem to hang in space because they are moving too fast to fall into the Earth.

Launched too slow, the satellite falls back to Earth

Launched too fast, the satellite hurtles off into space

Launched at the right speed, the satellite goes into orbit

◀ A satellite has to be launched at exactly the right speed and on exactly the right trajectory (path) to be placed successfully in orbit. The lower the orbit is to be, the faster it must go if it is to avoid being pulled down by gravity. For an orbit 23,000 miles (35,800km) above the ground, the satellite has to be going fast enough to complete an orbit in exactly 24 hours—the same time it takes the Earth to spin. So a satellite placed in this orbit stays in the same place above the Earth.

◀ The destructive power of gravity can be seen on Jupiter's moon Io. The giant planet Jupiter is so massive that its gravity alternately pulls and sucks so powerfully on Io as it revolves that the insides of the moon get incredibly hot— so hot that volcanoes burst onto the surface.

Factfinder: The Universe

FACTS: About the search for black holes

- **Do black holes exist?**
No one has ever seen a black hole. Indeed, we cannot be sure they actually exist. But the bright radiation from quasars (see below)—and from the centre of our galaxy may be signs that black holes do exist.

- **Where are black holes found?**
Some scientists think there is a giant black hole at the center of each spiral galaxy. Some believe there are tiny ones everywhere.

◀ *This bright galaxy may have a black core.*

As matter is sucked into the hole, it is ripped apart and jets of radiation are sent out

Matter whirls around the black hole like water around a plug hole

◀ *Black holes are places where gravity is so strong that it sucks everything in, even light. This is why they are called black holes. They form when a star or galaxy collapses to the stage where it is so dense that its gravity sucks it all into an impossibly small point called a singularity. Gravity around the singularity is so ferociously powerful that it not only sucks in light, but even bends space and time. The brightest objects in the Universe, called quasars, may be like the screams of mangled stars—the intense radiation from matter being ripped to shreds as it is sucked into a black hole.*

117

How far to the stars?

THE UNIVERSE IS VERY, VERY BIG and the distances between the stars are so huge that astronomers don't measure them in miles or kilometres, but in light-years–which is how far light travels in a year. Light is the fastest thing in the Universe and travels at about 186,000 miles (300,000km) per second, so a light-year is 5.86 billion miles (9,46 billion km). The nearest star is 4.3 light-years away. The most distant objects so far discovered are more than 13 billion light years away. That means that light takes more than 13 billion years to reach us–so astronomers are looking at them as they were 13 billion years ago!

DATA: Distances in space

- **THE NEAREST PLANET**
  The nearest planet to Earth is Venus, which is more than 24 million miles (40 million km) away.

- **THE FURTHEST PLANET**
  The farthest planet from Earth in the solar system is Pluto, which is nearly 3.7 billion miles (6 billion km) away.

- **THE NEAREST STAR**
  The nearest star is Proxima Centauri, in the constellation of the Centaur, which is 4.3 light-years away.

- **THE NEAREST OUTSIDE GALAXY**
  The nearest galaxy outside our own is the Andromeda galaxy, which is some 2.5 million light-years away.

- **THE FURTHEST GALAXY**
  The farthest galaxy–a quasar–yet seen is more than 13 billion light-years away across the Universe.

- **DISTANCE TO THE MOON**
  The Moon varies from 220,274 miles (356,410km) to 252,152 miles (406,697km) from Earth.

- **DISTANCE TO THE SUN**
  The Sun is between 91 million miles (147 million km) and 94 million miles (152 million km) away.

- **PARSECS**
  Astronomers may measure large distances in parsecs. A parsec is 3.26 light-years. Parsec distances are worked out by using the geometry of "parallaxes"–the way a star seems to shift slightly in position in the night sky as the Earth moves around the Sun.

Distances in space are vast

Factfinder: The Universe

◀ The distance to the Moon is measured to within a few yards by bouncing laser beams off mirrors left on the Moon by astronauts.

FACTS: Galactic distances

- **Standard candles**
  To find the distance of a nearby galaxy, astronomers look for stars within it whose brightness they are sure of. These include stars called "cepheid variables," "supergiant stars," and giant exploding stars called "supernova."

- **Very distant galaxies**
  Astronomers cannot pick out individual stars in very distant galaxies, so they estimate the distance by tricks such as the Tully-Fisher technique, based on how it appears to be spinning. The faster it spins, the brighter it should be. So if it is dim, it must be far away.

- **Red shift**
  The redder a distant galaxy looks, the faster it is moving away from us.

▶ The distance to the Sun and nearby planets is measured by bouncing radar beams off them. Space probes help with planets farther away.

▶ Distances to the nearer stars are generally worked out either by the parallax method (see parsecs) or by estimating their brightness. Astronomers can guess how bright a star should look compared to other stars from its color. If it actually looks brighter than it should, it must be nearby; if it looks dimmer, it must be farther away.

▼ Distances to the galaxies are worked out by looking for "standard candles," stars whose brightness we can be sure of. Really far off galaxies call for even more ingenious methods.

Working out distances

The method astronomers use to work out the distance of an object in space depends on how far away it is. For nearby objects such as the Sun and the planets, they can use radar beams, and estimates can be accurate within a few thousand miles. They measure distances to nearby stars by gauging their brightness, and estimates are accurate only to within a few billion miles. Distances to far galaxies are accurate only to within a few billion light-years!

119

Space travel

THE AGE OF SPACE EXPLORATION began in 1957, when powerful rocket engines boosted the Russian satellite Sputnik 1 free of Earth's gravity. This was the start of an extraordinary series of adventures for mankind which has seen scores of satellites put in space, man's first steps on the Moon, live broadcasts from Mars and space probes venturing past the outer planets of the solar system. These probes have not only beamed back the first pictures of new previously unknown moons but have also provided remarkable insights into the nature of the Universe.

FACTS: About spacecraft

- **Rocket power**
  Very powerful rockets are needed to push a spacecraft clear of Earth's gravity—but once clear, such power is no longer needed. So rockets are made in separate stages, each of which falls away when its fuel is spent.

- **The space shuttle**
  In the early days, manned spacecraft could only be used once, with just a tiny capsule holding the astronauts falling back to Earth at the end of the mission. The US space shuttle was the first spacecraft that could be reused, landing back on Earth like an airplane. The boosters that launch it into space are recovered.

- **Space probes**
  Unmanned space probes, guided by computer, have now visited all the planets but Pluto, the smallest and most distant, and probes have actually landed on Mars and Venus. Late in 1997, the Mars Pathfinder beamed back live pictures from the surface of Mars.

- **Slingshot effect**
  Space probes voyaging to the planets use gravity to help them travel huge distances on very little fuel. As they pass each planet, their gravity pulls them in and hurls them onward on a slightly different course, like a slingshot.

▲ The space shuttle is launched with solid fuel booster rockets that fall away but are then recovered. Typical shuttle missions include launching and repairing satellites and performing scientific experiments.

Factfinder: The Universe

FACTS: About satellites and probes

- **Staying in orbit**
  Satellites stay in space because they are circling, or "orbiting," the Earth just too fast to be pulled down by Earth's gravity—but not so fast that they fly off into space.

- **Staying still**
  An orbit 22,000 miles (35,800km) above the ground takes exactly 24 hours—the same time it takes the Earth to spin once. So satellites on this orbit stay in exactly the same place above the Earth. This is called a geostationary orbit.

- **Hubble Space Telescope**
  Satellites not only give a clear view of the Earth from space, but a better view of space too, because they are free from Earth's atmosphere. The Hubble Space Telescope, launched in 1990, gives extraordinary pictures of distant objects in space.

▲ *Spacecraft can be remarkably ungainly looking objects. Once they are free of the Earth's atmosphere, there is no need for streamlining, and aerials and dishes stick out in all directions. This is the Galileo launched in 1989 to explore Jupiter.*

DATA: Milestones in Space Exploration

- **THE FIRST LIVING CREATURE IN SPACE**
  Laika the dog was launched in the Russian *Sputnik 2* in November 1957. Sadly she could not be brought back.

- **THE FIRST MAN IN SPACE**
  The first man in space was the Russian cosmonaut Yuri Gagarin, in April 1961.

- **THE FIRST SPACE WALK**
  In 1965, Russian cosmonaut Alexei Leonov was the first man to walk in space.

- **THE FIRST MEN ON THE MOON**
  The American *Apollo* astronauts Neil Armstrong and Buzz Aldrin stepped on the Moon on July 21, 1969.

- **REACHING VENUS**
  In 1970, the Soviet Union's *Venera 7* landed on Venus.

- **PASSING SATURN**
  In 1969, the US *Pioneer II* probe reached Saturn and discovered new moons.

- **REACHING NEPTUNE**
  In 1989, the US *Voyager 2* reached the planet Neptune.

- **MARS LANDING**
  In 1997, the Mars Pathfinder roved the surface of Mars, beaming back pictures.

History of the Universe

THE UNIVERSE PROBABLY BEGAN about 13 billion years ago. One moment there was nothing. The next there was a minute, unimaginably hot ball—and suddenly the Universe burst into existence with the biggest explosion of all time, called the Big Bang, swelling at a totally astonishing rate. This explosion was so big that everything is still hurtling away from it still, which is why the Universe is expanding. Even now, 13 billion years on, astronomers can still detect the faint afterglow, called the cosmic microwave background radiation, spread throughout the night sky.

FACTS: Expanding universe

- **Receding galaxies**
  As astronomers observe space, they can see galaxies zooming away from us in all directions at astonishing speeds. The farther they are away, the faster they seem to be moving. This can only mean the Universe is expanding.

- **The Big Crunch?**
  Some scientists think the Universe will go on expanding forever. This is called the "open universe" idea. Others think gravity will put a break on its expansion. If there is a great deal of dark matter—matter we can't detect—it may be enough to make it all start to shrink again. Then it may end in a Big Crunch.

▶ We know how fast galaxies are receding because of the color of light from them. The faster they are receding, the more light waves from them get stretched out. When light waves are stretched they look redder. This is called red shift. The redder the light, the faster the galaxy is moving away.

Factfinder: The Universe

FACTS: About how the solar system was born

- **Swirling cloud**
4.6 billion years ago, the solar system did not exist. There was just a hot, dark cloud of gases swirling around the Sun. The planets began to form as the cloud cooled and droplets began to clump together.

- **The birth of the Earth**
The Earth probably formed as gravity began to pull together clumps of star dust from around the Sun. But this early Earth was a molten ball.

▼ No one knows where the material that formed the solar system came from. Some think it was the remnants of an exploded star, others the result of a collision between stars.

◄ Scientists have worked out how the Universe began by mathematical calculations and experiments with huge machines called particle accelerators, which hurl atoms together. It started with a tiny hot ball which cooled to many billions of degrees as it grew to the size of a football. In a split second, it swelled to create a space bigger than a galaxy in a period called inflation. Within this space, all the matter and energy and forces began to take the form we know in the Universe today. At first, it was a dense chaotic soup of particles and energy. But then atoms began to form, and the atoms formed clouds, and the clouds galaxies.

123

124

PLANET EARTH

126 Home planet
128 Earth's atmosphere
130 Weather
132 Wind
134 Structure of the Earth
136 History of the Earth
138 Rocks
140 Minerals
142 Volcanoes
144 Earthquakes
146 Mountains
148 Rivers
150 Oceans

Home planet

THE EARTH MAY SEEM QUITE STILL but it is actually spinning around like a top at more than 500 miles per hour (800km/h)-faster than most jet planes. It is also hurtling through the dark on its orbit around the Sun at over 60,000 miles per hour (100,000km/h)! Every year it covers 582,729,560 miles (939,886,400km) in its orbit around the Sun. The Earth's entire journey around the Sun takes exactly 365.242 days, which is why there are 365 days in our year. We make up the extra 0.242 days in our calendar by an extra day every fourth year, called a leap year-then miss out a leap three centuries out of four.

FACTS: About latitude and longitude

▲ Lines of latitude are called parallels because they form rings around the Earth parallel to the equator, which is latitude 0°. The North Pole is latitude 90°N.

▲ Lines of longitude or meridians run around the Earth from pole to pole, dividing the world up like the segments of an orange.

- **Lines of latitude**
Every place on the Earth's surface can be pinpointed by two figures: its latitude and longitude. Lines of equal latitude (called parallels) form rings around the Earth parallel to the equator. A place's latitude is given in degrees North or South of the equator.

- **Lines of longitude**
Lines of longitude (called meridians) run around the Earth from North to South. A place's longitude is given as degrees West or East of the Prime Meridian which runs through Greenwich in London, England.

Factfinder: Planet Earth

In spring, north and south get equal sun

When the north is tilted away from the Sun, it is winter here, but summer in the south

When the north is tilted toward from the Sun, it is summer here, but winter in the south

In autumn, north and south get equal sun

▲ We get seasons because the Earth is always tilted over in the same direction. So when the Earth is on one side of the Sun, the northern hemisphere (the world north of the equator) is tilted toward the Sun, bringing summer here. At this time, the southern hemisphere is tilted away, and so gets winter. When the Earth is on the other side of the Sun, the northern hemisphere is tilted away, bringing winter, while the south gets summer.

DATA: Our Home Planet

- **DISTANCE OF THE EARTH FROM THE SUN**
  The Earth is 92.7 million (149.6 million km) from the Sun. At its nearest, it is 91,200,636 miles (147,097,800km) away. At its furthest it is 94,300,884 miles (152,098,200km) away.

- **SPIN TIME**
  The Earth spins round once every 23 hours, 56 mins and 4.09 seconds. The Sun appears to comes back to the same place in the sky once every 24 hours.

FACTS: About the time of day

- **Time zones**
  As the Earth spins, the Sun is always rising in one place and setting in another. So the time of day varies around the world. When it's dawn where you live, it's sunset on the other side of the world. To make it easier to set clocks, the world is split into 24 time zones, one for each hour of the day. As you go east around the world, you put clocks forward by one hour for each zone—until you reach a line called the International Date Line. If you carry on across the Date line, you carry on adding hours, but put the calendar a day back.

▲ Half the world is facing the Sun and is brightly lit; the other half is facing away and in darkness. As the Earth spins round on its axis, the dark and sunlit halves move around, bringing day and night around the world. Because the Earth is turning eastward, the Sun appears from the ground to come up in the east and sink again in the west. The Earth turns once every 24 hours, which is why days are 24 hours long.

127

Earth's atmosphere

WRAPPED AROUND the Earth is a thin blanket of gases called the atmosphere. This blanket is no thicker on the Earth than the peel on an apple. Yet without it, the Earth would be as lifeless as the Moon. It gives us the air we need to breathe. It gives us clean water to drink. And it keeps us warm by trapping the Sun's heat-yet at the same time shielding us from the most harmful of its rays. It gives us weather, too, for everything we call weather is the churning of the atmosphere's lowest layer, next to the ground, as it is stirred by the Sun's warmth.

FACTS: About water in the air

- **Water cycle**
  All the water on Earth is forever being recycled in a process called the water cycle (see below).

- **Watery planet**
  Over 70 percent of the Earth's surface is covered by water. At any one time, though, just one percent is in the atmosphere. 97 percent is in the oceans. The rest is in lakes and rivers or frozen as ice.

- **Humidity**
  The air is full of invisible water vapor. The amount of water vapor in the air at any one time is known as its humidity.

- **Relative humidity**
  The total amount of moisture in the air is its "absolute" humidity. But the warmer air is, the more water it can hold, so meteorologists look at "relative" humidity, or rh, which is the percentage of moisture actually in the air relative to the maximum it could hold at that temperature.

- **Turning to water**
  As air cools, its rh must go up, because cool air can hold less moisture. Eventually, the rh reaches 100 percent and the vapor condenses into drops of water. This is called the dew point.

Clouds drop rain and snow on the land

Water falling on the land runs in rivers back to the sea

Water evaporated from the oceans forms clouds

◀ The Sun's heat makes water evaporate from the oceans and rise into the air. As it rises, it cools off and condenses into tiny drops of water, forming clouds. When the drops get big enough, they fall as rain or snow back into the oceans—or onto the land where the water runs in rivers back to the sea.

Factfinder: Planet Earth

▶ The atmosphere all looks like thin air, but scientists have shown that it has five or more layers or "spheres," each with its own characteristics. We live in the lowest layer, called the troposphere. This layer is just 7 miles (12km) thick, but 75 percent of the atmosphere's gases sink into this layer. As you go higher and higher, the gases get more and more spread out until by the time you are about 600 miles (1,000km) up, the gases are so thin or "rarefied" that the atmosphere fades off into space.

FACTS: About air pressure

▲ Air pressure can be measured on a device called a barometer. Barometers help tell you if a storm is on its way, because storms are linked to low pressure. If the pressure drops sharply, you can be sure rain and wind are on their way.

- **Atmospheric pressure**
  At sea level, the atmosphere is so dense that there is a crush of air molecules. This crush creates enormous pressure in the air, called atmospheric or air pressure.

- **Wind and pressure**
  Air pressure varies from time to time and place to place. High pressure pushes air toward zones of low pressure, and this is what creates winds—air moving from high pressure to low pressure zones. The sharper the pressure difference, the stronger the wind.

Eventually the atmosphere fades into the vacuum of space

Satellite

Exosphere (up to 440 miles/700km: the gases are very rarefied

Thermosphere (to 190 miles/300km): is even thinner in gases, but is heated by the Sun to over 3,600°F (2,000°C)

Higher level aurora

Comet

Lower level aurora

Mesosphere (up to 50 miles /80km): is too thin in gases to soak up much heat so it is very cold

Radio waves bounce off ionosphere

Stratosphere (up to 30 miles /50km): gets hotter higher up. Airliners cruise in the still air

Ultraviolet rays

Troposphere (up to 7 miles/ 12km): 70% of the gases and all the weather is here.

800km
700km
600km
500km
400km
300km
200km
100km
80km
50km
12km
0km

Weather

THERE ARE MANY DIFFERENT KINDS OF WEATHER—rain, snow, sun, wind, fog, mist, frost. But all of them are simply changes in the air caused by the varying effect of the Sun's warmth. Winds blow up, for instance, when the Sun heats some places more than others, setting the air moving. Rain falls when air warmed by the Sun lifts moisture high enough for it to form big drops of water when it condenses. Frost and snow occur when the power of the Sun is reduced. All weather comes down to three factors: the way the air moves (wind), its moisture content (humidity), and its temperature (warmth).

FACTS: About thunderstorms

- **Thunder clouds**
  Huge thunderclouds are built up by strong updrafts on a hot day or along a cold front. Eddies in the cloud hurl water drops and ice together so hard they become charged with static electricity (see p151). Positive particles clustering at the top of the cloud and negative particles at the bottom, create a charge difference. Soon the charge difference builds up so much that lightning flashes from positive to negative.

▼ Fork lightning flashes from cloud to ground. Sheet lightning flashes within the cloud. Lightning heats the air so much it bursts in a clap of thunder.

Fronts
The stormiest weather in many places is linked to depressions (low pressure regions). A wedge of warm air intrudes into the heart of depressions, and the worst weather occurs along the edges of this wedge, called fronts, where the warm air meets the cold. As the depression moves over, the fronts bring a distinct sequence of weather.

Cold front

▲ Once the warm front has passed, the weather becomes milder and clearer for a while. But after a few hours, a buildup of thunderclouds and gusts of wind warn that the trailing edge of the wedge, called the cold front, is on its way. As the cold front passes over, the thunderclouds unleash short but heavy rain showers, and even thunderstorms, before calm returns.

Factfinder: Planet Earth

FACTS: About clouds and rain

- **Making clouds**
Clouds form when water vapor rises with warm air then condenses as the air cools in the upper air. It rains when the water drops in clouds get too heavy to float on the air.

- **Icy rain**
Most rain comes from water droplets freezing into ice particles in a cloud. The particles grow into snowflakes, then melt into raindrops as they fall—or stay as snow if the air is cold.

- **Tropical rain**
In the tropics, raindrops form inside tall clouds as small raindrops join up to make bigger drops heavy enough to fall as rain.

◀ *Rain clouds are gray because they are so thick with large drops of water that they block out the sunlight.*

▼ *Natural snowflakes are six-sided and consist of crystals that are mostly flat plates, but can be needles or columns. But under a magnifying glass, you can see that no two snowflakes are ever the same.*

▲ *First to arrive is the leading edge of the wedge of warm air, or warm front, where warm air slides over cold air. As it rises it forms banks of clouds along the front. So the coming of the warm front is heralded by feathery 'cirrus' clouds high in the sky. Soon the clouds thicken until the sky is full of slate-grey 'nimbostratus' clouds, which bring long periods of steady rain.*

DATA: Weather

- **WETTEST**
The wettest place in the world is Tutunendo in Colombia which gets 460 inches (1,170cm) of rain anually-18 times as much as New York.

- **THE COLDEST AND HOTTEST**
The coldest place is Vostok in Antarctica, where it averages -72°F (-57.8°C). The hottest is Dallol in Ethiopia, where it averages 93°F (34°C) in the shade, and can get much hotter.

Wind

ALL WIND IS SIMPLY AIR MOVING. Strong winds are air moving fast. Gentle breezes are air moving slowly. Air moves because the Sun warms some places more than others, creating differences in air pressure which push the air about. Warmth makes the air expand and rise, lowering air pressure. But where the air is cold and heavy, air pressure is high. Winds blow from areas where pressure is high, called anticyclones, to areas where pressure is low, called cyclones or depressions. The sharper the difference in pressure, the stronger the wind is.

FACTS: About hurricanes

◀ Every summer, nine or so hurricanes develop in the eastern Atlantic and spiral westwards to the Gulf of Mexico, tracked all the way by satellite. Here a hurricane's distinctive spiral of clouds is seen hitting the coast of Texas.

▶ Hurricanes are shaped like huge spiral cakes. Winds spiralling in towards the low pressure centre, or eye, help line the thunderclouds into great walls of cloud towering into the sky.

- **Hurricanes and typhoons**
  Hurricanes are the Atlantic version of the cyclone storms that batter eastern coasts in the tropics. In the Pacific they are known as typhoons.

- **What a hurricane does**
  When a hurricane strikes, trees can be ripped up and buildings flattened by winds gusting up to 220 mph (360km/h). Vast areas can be battered and swamped by torrential rain, and coasts can be overwhelmed by the "storm surge"—the mound of seawater that builds up in the storm center.

- **Hurricane year**
  There are on average 103 typhoons and other tropical storms and 45 hurricanes every year.

- **How hurricanes start**
  Hurricanes begin in the eastern Atlantic as thunderstorms set off by moist air rising over the warm ocean. If the water is warm enough, they pile up together, then begin to spiral westward across the ocean, growing bigger all the time.

- **Gaining power**
  By the time the hurricane has crossed the Atlantic, it is spiraling tighter round its centre or "eye." The eye shrinks to just 30 miles (50km) across and winds howl round it at over 70 mph (120kmh).

Factfinder: Planet Earth

FACTS: About tornadoes

- **Twisters**
  Tornadoes are tiny spirals of wind that sweep past in less than 15 minutes—but 180 mph (300km/h) winds and a low pressure center that sucks like a giant vacuum cleaner can toss people, cars, and buildings high in the air like toys. They are common from March to July in "Tornado Alley" in the Midwest.

- **Supercells**
  Tornadoes are set off by giant thunderclouds called supercells. Winds whipping through the clouds set updrafts spinning. As they spin, they create a vortex which hangs from the cloud base down to the ground, like an elephant's trunk.

Dry air sinks in the eye

Warm, moist air spirals around the eye

Air rises, building up huge thunderclouds

Calm eye of storm, where winds drop and pressure is very low

Air drawn in toward the low pressure at the center of the storm

▲ Often it is the torrential rain and the storm surge of ocean water that do most of the damage in a hurricane, but the ferocious winds can also wreak havoc, blowing down trees and buildings.

- **The eye**
  The air in the dead center or eye of the hurricane is at very low pressure, and is very calm. As the eye passes over, the winds may drop altogether and a small circle of blue sky may often be seen. But the lull is short-lived, for the rain and wind are at their strongest either side of the eye.

- **Big wind**
  A hurricane can be 500 miles (800km) across, and it can take 18 hours to pass over.

- **Hurricane warning.**
  Each hurricane is given a name and tracked by satellite to help give people plenty of warning that one is on its way.

133

Structure of the Earth

THE EARTH IS NOT QUITE THE SOLID BALL it seems. Using sensitive equipment to detect the pattern of vibrations from earthquakes and big explosions, scientists have shown it has quite a complicated structure. Only a very thin shell, called the crust, is completely solid. Inside are a number of different layers, some solid, but some soft like molasses, while some of the core is molten metal. Atomic reactions in the core mean the Earth gets hotter and hotter as you go deeper toward the center, reaching over 12,600°F (7,000°C) in the center—hotter than the surface of the Sun.

FACTS: Inside the Earth

- **Thin crust**
  The Earth's crust of rock is on average 25 miles (40km) thick under the continents and just 3.5 miles (6km) beneath the oceans.

- **Soft mantle**
  Beneath the crust is the mantle, nearly 2,000 miles (3,000km) thick and made of rock so warm it flows like molasses, only very slowly.

- **Metal core**
  In the center of the Earth is a core of metal (iron with a little nickel). The outer core is so hot it is molten. The inner core is even hotter, but pressures are so great the metal stays solid.

- **Crust edge**
  The boundary between the crust and mantle is called the Mohorovicic discontinuity.

- **Rigid top**
  The very top of the mantle is stiff and attached to the crust, so that they move as one—so scientists sometimes talk of the "lithosphere," which is the crust and the outer 60 miles (100km) of the mantle.

- **Soft underneath**
  Beneath the lithosphere in the upper mantle is the softer "asthenosphere" down to 120 miles (200km), where rock circulates very slowly.

▲ *The world is a bit like a partly boiled egg, with a hard shell or crust, a white of semisoft rock called the mantle, and a yolk or core of molten and solid metal.*

- **Lower down**
  Below the asthenosphere is a third, stiffer layer within the upper mantle, called the mesosphere.

- **Mesophere**
  Heat makes the whole of the mantle churn very slowly, over millions of years. Sometimes big hot blobs rise right up from the core to the crust. These "superplumes" may create huge volcanoes.

Factfinder: Planet Earth

▲ The pulling apart of tectonic plates creates giant cracks in the Earth's surface. Usually, these cracks are hidden underwater on the ocean bed. But in Iceland, the crack that runs right down the middle of the Atlantic ocean bed comes to the surface. Each side of this valley is a different plate, and they are slowly pulling apart.

▼ The giant plates that make up the Earth's hard shell or lithosphere are always moving, although very, very slowly. In some places, plates are crunching together, and one of the plates—typically a continent—rides over the other and forces it down into the Earth's interior. This process is called subduction. In other places—usually in mid-ocean on the seabed—plates are pulling apart. But even as they pull apart, so they gain new material as hot molten rock wells up through the gap and solidifies on the exposed edges. This is called mid-ocean spreading.

FACTS: Moving plates

- **Tectonic plates**
  The Earth's rocky crust is broken into 20 or so huge fragments called tectonic plates. As these move slowly about, they set off earthquakes and volcanoes, and pile up mountain ranges.

- **Continental drift**
  As tectonic plates move, they carry the continents slowly about the world.

▼ The Earth's crust is broken in 20 or so plates which carry continents as they move. Africa and South America were once joined. Europe is drifting slowly further from America.

In the middle of the ocean, where plates are pulling apart, new molten rock wells up to create a series of ridges under the sea

Deep trench in the ocean where a plate is subducted

Ocean

Subducted plate pushed into the Earth's interior

In "subduction zones" plates are pushing together, pushing one plate beneath the other

Rock from the melting plate burns up to erupt through as volcanoes

Continent

Molten rock from the mantle

Plates pulling apart

Lithosphere

Asthenosphere

Plates pushing together

Subducted plate melting

History of the Earth

THE EARTH probably formed about 4.6 billion years ago from debris spinning around the Sun. At first, it was a molten ball, but it gradually cooled and a thin crust formed around the outside. The first signs of life—probably bacteria—appeared nearly four billion years ago. But the first animals with shells and bones easily preserved as fossils did not appear until less than 600 million years ago. It is mainly with the help of such fossils that geologists have built up a picture of Earth's history since then. Very little is known about the four billion years before this, called Precambrian time.

Earth formed 4.55 billion years ago

Archean 4,600-2,500 million years ago (m.y.a.)

▲ This spiral shows some events in Earth's history, starting with its origin at the center of the spiral and the coming of humans at the end. The scale is distorted because so little is known about what happened in the first 85 percent of Earth's history—so the last 15 percent is given much more space. If Earth's history were crammed into a day, humans would appear only at the end, just two seconds before midnight.

FACTS: Geological time

- **Units of time**
  Just as the day is divided into hours, minutes and seconds, so geologists divide the Earth's history into time periods. The longest are Eons, billions of years long; the shortest are Chrons, a few thousand years long. In between come Eras, Periods, Epochs, and Ages.

- **Fossil time**
  Because different plants and animals lived at different times in Earth's past, geologists can tell how long ago rocks formed from the fossils in them. Using fossils, they have divided the Earth's history since Precambrian times into 11 Periods.

- **Geological column**
  Layers of rock form one on top of the other, so the oldest is usually at the bottom, unless they have been disturbed. The sequence of layers from top to bottom is called the geological column.

FACTS: About dating

- **Fossil dating**
  By looking for certain key fossils, geologists can tell whether one layer of rock is older than another so they can then place it within the geological column. This is called 'biostratigraphy'.

- **Absolute date**
  Fossils can only show if a rock is older or younger, not give a date in years—and many rocks don't contain fossils. To give an "absolute" date, geologists often use radioactivity.

- **Radioactive dating**
  After certain substances such as uranium and rubidium form, their atoms slowly break down into different atoms, sending out rays as they do so. The rays are called radioactivity. By assessing how many atoms in a rock have changed, geologists can tell how old it is.

Factfinder: Planet Earth

Precambrian time: The first life forms (bacteria) appear, and give the air oxygen

Cambrian Period: No life on land, but shellfish flourish in the oceans

Ordovician Period: Early fishlike vertebrates appear. The Sahara is glaciated

Silurian Period: First land plants. Fish with jaws and freshwater fish

Devonian Period: First insects and amphibians. Ferns and mosses as big as trees

Carboniferous Period: Vast warm swamps of fern forests, which form coal. First reptiles

Permian Period: Conifers replace ferns as big trees. Deserts widespread

Triassic Period: First mammals. Seed-bearing plants spread. Europe in the tropics

Jurassic Period: Dinosaurs widespread. Archaeopertyx, earliest known bird

Cretaceous Period: First flowering plants. The dinosaurs die out

Tertiary Period: First large mammals. Birds flourish. Widespread grasslands

Quaternary Period: Many mammals die out in Ice Ages. Humans evolve

Proterozoic 2,500-590 m.y.a.

590 m.y.a.
505 m.y.a.
438 m.y.a.
408 m.y.a.
360 m.y.a.
286 m.y.a.
248 m.y.a.
213 m.y.a.
144 m.y.a.
65 m.y.a.
2 m.y.a.
Today

Precambrian
Cambrian Period
Ordovician Period
Silurian Period
Devonian Period
Carboniferous Period
Permian Period
Triassic Period
Jurassic Period
Cretaceous Period
Tertiary Period
Quaternary Period

Palaeozoic Era
Mesozoic Era
Cenozoic Era

Key to lifeforms
1. Jellyfish
2. Trilobite
3. Acanthodian (jawed fish)
4. Cooksonia (early land plant)
5. Ichthyostega (early amphibian)
6. Dimetrodon (early mammal-like reptile)
7. Anteosaurus
8. Herrerasaurus (early dinosaur).
9. Pterandon (early flying reptile)
10. Cephalopod (squidlike shellfish)
11. Brachiosaurus (dinosaur)
12. Crusafontia (small mammal)
13. Merychippus (early horse)
14. Proconsul (great ape)
15. Homo sapiens (early man)

137

Rocks

ROCKS ARE THE HARD MASS the ground is made of. You can only see bare rock exposed on the surface in a few places–cliffs, mountain crags, and quarries. But it is there everywhere, not far beneath the city streets or the thin covering of soil or vegetation. Some rocks are just a few million years old; some are almost as old as the Earth. But they all tend to be very tough solids made of tiny crystals or "grains" of naturally occurring chemicals called minerals. All these minerals came originally from the Earth's hot interior, but at the surface they form three kinds of rock: igneous, sedimentary, and metamorphic.

FACTS: About igneous, sedimentary and metamorphic rock

▲ 90 percent of the Earth's crust is made from igneous rocks, like this granite, which is an intrusive rock and formed underground.

▲ Although most surface rock is igneous, 75 percent of the land surface is covered by thin layers of sedimentary rock like this limestone.

▲ Metamorphic rock such as this hornfels is rock made when other rock is altered by extreme heat or pressure.

- **Igneous rock**
  Igneous rock is formed from red hot magma (molten rock) that wells up from the Earth's interior. Some erupts on the surface through volcanoes and cools to form "volcanic" or "extrusive" igneous rock. Some is pushed up under the surface, forming "intrusive" igneous rock.

- **Acid and basic igneous rock**
  There are many different kinds of rock. Some, like granite, are generally light in color and are made from quite acidic magma (rich in silica). Others, like basalt, are darker and made from basic magma.

- **Sedimentary rock**
  Sedimentary rock forms in thin layers from debris that settles mainly on the seabed and is then squeezed and cemented over millions of years into solid rocks. Some, like limestone, are made mainly from plant and animal remains. Most are made from fragments of rock worn away by the weather.

- **Metamorphic rock**
  Metamorphic rock is made when other rocks are crushed by movements of the Earth's crust or scorched by magma—and changed so much that they form a new kind of rock, such as marble or slate.

FACTS: About coal and oil

▼ In the Carboniferous Period, there were huge tropical swamps filled with giant, treelike ferns. It is these that most coal formed from, as the remains of the plants were buried and squeezed.

1. Remains of swamp plants were first buried and squeezed to make peat
2. As they became buried deeper, heat and pressure changed the peat to brown coal
3. Further pressure changed brown coal to black bituminous coal and finally anthracite

- **Fossil fuels**
  Coal, oil, and natural gas are fossil fuels, which means they formed over millions of years from the remains of plants and small creatures.

- **Carboniferous swamps**
  Most coal formed from the remains of plants that grew in huge, warm swamps in the Carboniferous Period, 300 million years ago.

- **Oil bearing rocks**
  Oil formed from the remains of tiny plants and animals that lived in warm seas. As they died, they were buried and squeezed into oil, then collected in porous (sponge-like) layers of rock.

- **Crude oil**
  Oil usually comes up from the ground as thick, black "crude" oil and must be refined for use.

1. Igneous rocks form from magma forced up from the Earth's interior

2. Weather wears away the rock and fragments are washed into the sea, then settle on the seabed

▼ The materials rocks are made of is continually recycled to make new rocks in a process called the rock cycle. Magma from the interior cools to form igneous rock which is gradually worn away by the weather. The fragments are washed down into the sea and settle on the seabed to form sedimentary rock. Both sedimentary and igneous rock may be altered into metamorphic rock—and all three are eventually broken down so that they too can be formed into new sedimentary rocks.

3. Sediments buried under the seabed are cemented into layers of rock, then lifted up above the sea to be worn away again

Minerals

MINERALS ARE THE natural chemicals from which the Earth's crust is made. A few are powdery or resinous, but most are crystals. Usually, minerals occur as a mass of tiny crystals or grains. Occasionally, though, crystals grow as big as flagpoles. Geologists identify minerals by various factors including the color and shape of the crystal. There are 2,000 or so different minerals, but fewer than a hundred are common. A handful of minerals are pure chemical elements that occur naturally, such as gold or silver. Most are compounds, of which by far the most common are silicates.

FACTS: Gems

- **Gems**
  Gems are especially rare and beautiful mineral crystals such as rubies and emeralds.

- **Veins and geodes**
  Many precious gems form either in veins, where hot volcanic fluid forces its way into a crack in the rock, or in gas pockets in cooling volcanic rock called geodes.

▲ *Gems are rare because they only form naturally under very special conditions—usually deep within volcanic rocks. A few can now be made artificially, but these are not so precious.*

- **Diamonds**
  Diamonds are very hard, very rare—and very old. They were probably made by the mighty collision of continents during subduction (see page 131) and taken deep into the Earth. They are only found because volcanoes bring them near the surface again after billions of years.

- **Colored gems**
  Many gems get their vivid colors from tiny traces of chemicals within them. Traces of iron turn common clear quartz into purple amethyst. Manganese turns quartz pink.

FACTS: About crystals

- **What are crystals**
  Crystals are glassy-looking, brittle solids that form in regular shapes, with sharp corners and flat sides.

- **Crystal shapes**
  Crystals are regular and there are only a certain number of possible basic regular shapes, called systems—cubic, pyramid, and so on. The crystals of each mineral fit into one of these systems.

▶ *Minerals only rarely form in large, distinct crystals like these. Most of the time they form much smaller grains, and are mixed in with other minerals in rocks. Granite, for instance, is made of the minerals feldspar, quartz, and mica, along with small amounts of other minerals. Quartz is a silicate mineral—the most common silicate mineral of all—but over 99 percent of it is actually mixed in with other minerals in granite and other rocks, such as sandstone.*

140

Factfinder: Planet Earth

FACTS: Elements & silicates

- **Native elements**
Native elements are minerals that occur naturally as pure chemical elements, including all those shown on this page.

- **Silicates**
Silicates are minerals that form when the chemical elements silicon and oxygen—two of the most common elements on Earth—combine with a metal. There are over 500 of them, including quartz, olivine and pyroxene.

▼ *Gold is rare but almost always found in pure form because it just won't mix with any other mineral.*

Twists of silver

Bismuth rarely occurs in pure form in nature. It is usually mixed with sulfur

Silver rarely looks silvery in nature because exposure to air tarnishes the surface black

Copper only rarely occurs in pure form. Normally it is linked into minerals such as chalcopyrite

Yellow fluorite is a rare mineral made of calcium and fluorine

The green crystals are uraninite, chemically uranium oxide, the main source of the metal uranium

Yellow crystals of sulfur are often found around the smoking vents of volcanoes

141

Volcanoes

VOLCANOES ARE PLACES where hot molten rock or "magma" from the Earth's interior erupts on the surface. With some volcanoes, it oozes out gently and flows overground as lava-red hot liquid rock. Others get clogged up with thick plugs of magma and then suddenly burst through in a mighty explosion that sends up jets of steam and hurls scorching fragments of debris from under the plugs thousands of feet in the air. Most volcanoes occur near the cracks between the giant tectonic plates that make up the Earth's surface (page 131), but a few occur at "hot spots" where plumes of hot magma rise under the crust.

FACTS: Types of volcanoes

- **Thick and thin magma**
  Volcanoes take many forms, but the most explosive volcanoes occur near subduction zones where the collision of tectonic plates creates a very thick, sticky "acid" magma that clogs up the volcano easily. Where plates are pulling apart, the magma is less acid and runs freely.

- **Cinder volcanoes**
  Most volcanoes are made of solidified lava, but some are mounds of ash.

◀ When the lava is quite runny, it floods out far and wide, creating a broad, gently sloping "shield" volcano.

◀ The thick lava from explosive volcanoes piles up steeply around the volcano, creating a cone.

◀ In "strato" volcanoes, alternate layers of ash and lava build up as ash falls on the lava flow from each eruption.

▶ The biggest eruptions are powered by a combination of steam and bubbles of carbon dioxide gas. Extreme pressure normally keeps them dissolved in the magma, but as the eruption begins the pressure drops and bubbles begin to form in the magma and swell rapidly. The eruption sends out three kinds of material apart from steam and gas—clouds of ash, solid fragments of the volcanic plug called tephra or volcanic bombs, and lava. Sometimes, lethal clouds of glowing ash hurtle down the slope.

▼ It is very hard to tell exactly when a volcano is going to erupt. But vulcanologists can get an idea by keeping a very careful watch on the slopes of the volcano, using laser rangefinders for accuracy. Any very slight change in slope might be the magma bulging up underneath, indicating an imminent eruption.

Eruptions begin with a build up in pressure in the "magma chamber" beneath the volcano

Factfinder: Planet Earth

▲ Water heated under pressure underground by hot magma can burst onto the surface in a ferocious jet of steam and hot water called a geyser. The biggest geysers are hundreds of feet high.

Big eruptions can send so much ash into the upper air that they blot out the sun and turns the world cool

Tephra vary in size from tiny "lapilli" to volcanic "bombs," which can measure up to 3 feet (90cm) across

Lava flows look spectacular, but it is ash that is really deadly

FACTS: Famous eruptions

▲ The eruption of Mt. St. Helens in Washington state in 1980 was one of the biggest to rock North America this century. The eruption blew away the top of the mountain and blanketed the forest far around with ash.

- **Big bang**
  The eruption of Krakatoa, near Java, in 1883 was so loud that people heard it in North America.

- **Grey skies**
  The eruption of Mt. Tambora in Java in 1815 sent up so much dust that the sun was blocked out right around the globe, causing two years of poor summers.

- **Roman remains**
  When Mt. Vesuvius in Italy erupted in AD79, the people of the Roman town of Pompeii were buried instantly. The remains of the city, almost perfectly preserved under the ash, were discovered in the 18th century.

- **Biggest in human history**
  There was a giant eruption 20,000 years ago of Sumatra's Mt. Toba, which covered the entire island in ash 1,000 feet (300m) deep.

- **Biggest ever**
  One of the biggest-ever eruptions covered nearly all of India in lava 65 million years ago.

Earthquakes

EVEN A PASSING TRUCK can make the ground tremble, but most earthquakes are the ground shuddering as the huge tectonic plates that make up the Earth's surface (see page 131) grind past each other. Most of the time the plates slide past each other quietly. But they sometimes jam. Then pressure builds up until they suddenly lurch on again, sending shock waves radiating in all directions. The nearer a place is to where the earthquake began—called the epicenter on the surface—the more severe the earthquake is. The worst earthquakes can bring down mountains and destroy cities.

FACTS: Earthquake zones

▲ Earthquake zones—places that suffer earthquakes repeatedly—are near plate edges, such as SE Europe and the Pacific coast.

- **San Andreas**
  The San Andreas fault in California is where two great plates slide past each other, often setting off earthquakes, such as the one that destroyed San Francisco in 1906.

- **Predicting earthquakes**
  Earthquakes are hard to predict, but they are most likely to occur in earthquake zones—especially when there has not been one for some time. Seismologists use satellites and laser beams to detect slight movements, and look for changes in the magnetism of rocks.

DATA: The worst earthquakes

- **856**: 200,000 people killed in Damghan, Iran.
- **1138**: 230,000 people killed in Aleppo, Syria.
- **1556**: 830,000 people killed in Shansi, China.
- **1737**: 300,000 people killed in Calcutta, India.
- **1908**: 100,000 people killed in Messina, Italy.
- **1920**: 200,000 people killed in Gansu, China.
- **1923**: 144,000 people killed in Kwanto, Japan.
- **1976**: 255,000 people killed in Tangshan, China.
- **1995**: The earthquake in Kobe, Japan, killed 5,200 people, destroyed 190,000 buildings, and left 300,000 people homeless.
- **1999**: 40,000 people killed in northwestern Turkey

Raised freeways are very vulnerable to earthquake damage

Factfinder: Planet Earth

FACTS: About earthquake measurement

▲ Seismometers detect tremors in the ground and display them on a seismograph. The strong vibrations of big earthquakes show as dramatic zigzags.

- **Richter scale**
  The severity of an earthquake, measured on a machine called a seismometer, is usually assessed on the Richter scale, which goes from 1 (slight tremor) to over 9 (severe earthquake).

- **Mercalli scale**
  The Richter scale gives the absolute magnitude (size) of an earthquake, but no idea of its effects. These are sometimes assessed on the Mercalli scale, which rates the damage done on a scale of 1 (barely noticeable) to 12 (total destruction).

Earthquakes usually last only a few minutes, but their effects can be devastating

Tall buildings are especially prone to earthquake damage

▼ This picture shows the destruction that occurs when buildings lie directly over a fault in the Earth's crust. But the shock waves—called seismic waves—can be devastating even tens of miles from the epicenter. A great deal of damage is done by an earthquake itself, as the tremors shake buildings to pieces and snap roadways. But they can also fracture gas pipes and electricity cables and set off terrible fires.

This earthquake is set off by the two edges of a fault sliding past each other

145

Mountains

MOUNTAINS LOOK FAIRLY PERMANENT but they are continually being created and destroyed. Most of the biggest mountains are actually quite young in geological terms. The Himalayas of Asia, for instance, include the world's highest peaks, yet they were first raised less than 40 million years ago–and they are still growing today. Mountains are created in one of a number of ways. Most are created by the folding of rock layers as the huge tectonic plates that make up the Earth's surface crunch together. Others are created as crustal movements lift up huge blocks. Others are created by volcanic eruptions.

FACTS: About fold mountains

- **Fold ranges**
  Most of the world's greatest mountain ranges—the Himalayas, the Andes, the Rockies, the Caucasus, and the Alps—are created by the crumpling edges of colliding tectonic plates. This is why they often form long narrow ranges along the edges of continents. The Himalayas were created by the collision of India with Asia.

- **Runny mountains**
  The rock in mountains is not completely rigid. It flows a bit like very stiff molasses. So ranges such as the Himalayas are flowing out and getting flatter at the edges, at the same time as they are being pushed up.

- **Dip and strike**
  The angle at which folded rock layers are tilted is the "dip." This can be anything from a few degrees to over 90°. The direction of the fold is the "strike."

- **Upfold and downfold**
  Downfolds (like a dish) are called synclines; upfolds (like an arch) are called anticlines.

- **Overturned folds**
  Sometimes a fold may fold right over. This is called an "overturned" fold. If it folds so far that it rests on the next fold it is said to be "recumbent."

▲ *If tectonic plates go on pushing together, the folding may go well beyond a simple fold (top). First it overturns and the layers begin to snap (middle). Finally the layers snap altogether, creating a "nappe."*

146

Factfinder: Planet Earth

▲ The Alps were created by folding, but the dramatic shape of the Matterhorn, one of the highest Alpine peaks was created by glaciers.

DATA: The highest mountains

- The world: Everest in the Himalayas 29,021 feet (8,848m).
- South America: Aconcagua 22,829 feet (6,960m).
- North America: Mt. McKinley 20,316 feet (6,194m).
- Africa: Kilimanjaro 19,336 feet (5,895m).
- Europe: El'brus in Russia 18,506 feet (5,642m).
- Australasia: Papua New Guinea's Mt. Wilhelm 16,020 feet (4,884m).

FACTS: Faults & blocks

▶ As the tectonic plates of the Earth's crust jostle together, they may put rocks under such strain that they fracture, creating cracks or "faults" in the rock. Large blocks of rock may then be thrown up to create mountains.

A fault scarp is a cliff, exposed as a massive block of rock is thrown up or down

- **Where faults occur**
  Faults occur mainly in areas that are called "fault zones." These lie mostly along the edges of tectonic plates.

- **Normal fault**
  In most faults, the cracking of the Earth's crust as tectonic plates pull apart allows a block of rock to slip straight down. In a "wrench" fault, however, blocks slip sideways past each other. In a "reverse" fault, one block slides up over another as plates crunch together.

- **Horsts and rifts**
  If a block of rock is thrown down between two faults it may create a deep, steep-sided "rift" valley. If the block is thrown upward, it creates a high plateau called a horst.

▼ No mountain range lasts forever. Sooner or later they are worn down by the weather. Frost, for instance, may shatter rocks on mountain peaks, leaving the lower slopes littered with fragments known as scree.

147

Rivers

RIVERS RUN DOWN to the sea or lakes wherever there is enough rain or melting snow to keep them flowing. Even when it is not raining, most rivers in moist regions are kept flowing by water from underground. This is because a lot of rain does not flow directly over the land, but seeps into the ground—only to bubble up lower down, in places called springs. Most rivers are very tiny as they start high up in the hills, tumbling over rocks and rapids. But they get bigger further down as they are joined by tributaries (side rivers). As they near the sea, they run in broad, smooth-flowing curves called meanders.

Heavy rainfall and melting snow high up starts a river with plenty of water

High up, the river tumbles over rocks and rapids in steep, narrow valleys

FACTS: About river valleys

◀ The Grand Canyon in Arizona is one of the world's deepest river valleys, carved by the Colorado River over millions of years. The area is so dry that there is little rain to wear away the valley sides so these sides are often steep cliffs.

- **River power**
Rivers continually batter their banks and beds with running water, sand and pebbles. Over thousands of years, rivers can carve huge valleys out of solid rock.

- **Valley to plain**
To start with, river valleys are narrow, steep-sided, and winding—and they are usually like this near their source in the hills. But, with time, they carve out broader, flatter valleys, and they meander over a wide "floodplain"—a flat area liable to flooding when heavy rain or melting snow makes the river full.

Factfinder: Planet Earth

▲ Every river has a natural tendency to wind—especially in the lower reaches, where it is wide and deep and flows across a broad plain. Here, giant horseshoe-shaped meanders develop as the river wears away the outside bank of each curve and washes up sediment on the inside.

In the lower reaches, the river is broad and deep and flows through smooth channels of sediment, washed down from higher up

Where it meets the sea, the river may split into several branches, forming a "delta"

▲ A river changes dramatically in character as it runs down toward the sea. High up, it is a small stream, tumbling over rocks because it is too small to wash them out of the way. Near the sea it flows through a smooth channel of silt and mud washed down by the river from higher up, over tens of thousands of years.

FACTS: About waterfalls

- **Where falls form**
  Waterfalls typically form where a river flows over a band of hard rock, as the water wears away the soft rock below.

- **"The smoke that thunders"**
  So much water flows over Victoria Falls in Zimbabwe—33,000 cubic feet (935 cu m) every second—that the roar can be heard 25 miles (40km) away.

▼ The Angel Falls in Venezuela—named after an American pilot, Jimmy Angel—is the highest waterfall in the world, plunging 3,211 feet (979m).

DATA: The longest rivers

- The Nile in Africa is 4,137 miles (6,673km) long.
- The Amazon in S. America is 4,073 miles (6,570km) long.
- The Yangtze in Asia is 3,891 miles (6,276km) long.
- The Mississippi-Missouri is 3,732 miles (6,019km) long.
- The Danube in Europe is 1,771 miles (2,857km) long.

Oceans

ALMOST THREE QUARTERS of the world is under water. There are five great oceans: the Pacific, the Atlantic, and Indian–which all merge into the Southern Ocean around Antarctica–and the smaller Arctic Ocean. Then there are many smaller stretches of water called seas, including the Mediterranean, the Baltic, and the Red seas. Yet until quite recently, the bottom of the oceans were as mysterious and unknown as the surface of Mars. Modern ocean surveys have now begun to reveal that the landscape of the ocean bed is as varied as that of the continents, with high mountains, vast plains and deep valleys.

FACTS: About coasts

- **Eroded coasts**
  In some places, especially on headlands, coasts are worn away by waves crashing on bare rock. Hills are cut back to sheer cliffs, leaving behind platforms of rock washed over by the waves and, occasionally, isolated stacks of rock.

- **Sandy coasts**
  In other places, especially bays, material worn away is deposited as sandy and pebbly beaches and bars across river mouths.

- **Tides**
  In most places, the sea rises then falls back again twice daily. These "tides" are created by the pull of the Moon's gravity which creates a tidal bulge of raised water on opposite sides of the world. As the Earth turns beneath the Moon during the day, so the tidal bulge moves around the world.

▼ *Constant battering by waves and salty water gives coastlines their own unique range of landforms, including cliffs, headlands, and sandy bays.*

Beach
Sand bar
Estuary
Stack
Groyne to stop sand being washed along the beach
Headland

Factfinder: Planet Earth

FACTS: About the ocean bed

- **Ocean floor revealed**
  In the last 30 years, surveys using sound equipment and robot submarines have allowed oceanographers to lift away the ocean waters to create detailed maps of the ocean floor (right).

- **Shallow margin**
  Around the edge of each ocean is a shelf of shallow water called the continental shelf. At the edge of this shelf, the ocean floor plunges to the deep ocean floor or "abyssal plain."

- **Seamounts**
  The abyssal plain is not completely flat but dotted, especially in the Pacific, with huge mountains known as seamounts, often thousands of feet high. In places, there are flat-topped seamounts called guyots, which may once have projected above the surface and been worn flat there.

◀ *In this map of the ocean floor, the light blue is the continental shelf, the dark blue is the abyssal plain.*

▲ *Sonar systems map the ocean floor by sending out high-frequency pulses of sound. The time it takes for the sound pulse to echo back from the ocean floor indicates how deep the ocean is.*

DATA: The oceans

- **SEA AREA**
  The seas cover more than 139 million square miles (361 million square km) of the Earth's surface. The biggest ocean is the Pacific, over 63 million square miles (165 million square km), more than a third of the Earth's surface.

- **WATER VOLUME**
  There is 322 million cubic miles (1.35 billion cubic km) of water in the oceans.

- **DEEPEST WATER**
  The deepest point on the Earth's surface is the Challenger Deep in the Marianas trench in the west Pacific, which is 35,818 feet (10,920m) deep.

SCIENCE

154 Electricity

156 Magnetism

158 Electronics

160 Radiation

162 Light

164 Levers and machines

166 Force and motion

168 Energy

170 Heat

172 Solids, liquids, and gases

174 Matter

176 The elements

178 Chemicals and compounds

Electricity

ELECTRICITY IS THE ENERGY that makes everything from toasters to tube trains work. It is also linked with magnetism. Together they form one of the basic forces that holds the universe together–electromagnetism. Electricity starts with atoms and tiny parts of each atom called electrons. Just as magnets are drawn together, so electrons are drawn to the centre of the atom. This attraction is called "electric charge." Electrons have a "negative" charge; atomic centers a "positive" one. It is the combined attraction of billions of tiny electrons to billions of tiny atom centers that creates electricity.

▶ Electricity is generated in power stations and sent across the country along big cables carried on towers called pylons, or along cables buried underground. The electricity is sent down these cables at very high voltage (high pressure) to make sure they reach their destination.

▲ If a coil of wire is wrapped around a bar of iron, switching on the current turns the bar into a very powerful magnet, called an electromagnet, or solenoid. The gray curves show lines of magnetic force.

FACTS: Electromagnetism

- **Making electricity**
  When a coil of electric wire is moved near a magnet—or a magnet is moved near a coil—the magnetism draws electrons through the wire, creating an electric current.

- **Power stations and generators**
  Power stations make electricity using generators. In generators, turbines (like fan blades) are turned by running water or by steam heated by burning oil or coal, or by nuclear energy. The turning of the turbines turns banks of electric coils round magnets.

- **Electric motors**
  Just as moving magnets create electricity, so an electric current can make a magnet move. In electric motors, an electric current is sent through a coil wrapped round a magnet. The surge of electricity through the coil makes the magnet turn.

Factfinder: Science

◀ Electric light bulbs rely on the fact that when an electric current reaches a restriction in a wire—called resistance—the wire gets hot. Inside a light bulb, there is a very thin wire called a filament which glows white hot when you switch the current on. The bulb is filled with a nonreactive gas, such as argon, to ensure the filament doesn't burn up.

FACTS: Static electricity

▶ Lightning is the release of the huge charge of static electricity made as raindrops bash together in a thundercloud.

- **Static charge**
Static electricity is what makes dry hair go frizzy when you comb it and a nylon sweater tingle if you pull it off too fast. It is called static because it doesn't move, like electricity in a circuit. It is made when surfaces rub together. Electrons rub off one surface and on to the other. The extra electrons give it a negative electric charge. This attracts surfaces which have lost electrons and so are positively charged.

FACTS: About electric currents

- **Currents and circuits**
Electric currents can move through certain materials in a continuous flow. But for the current to flow, there must be a complete loop or circuit.

- **Free electrons**
Electric currents work like a row of marbles—flicking one jolts marbles down the row. The marbles are "free" electrons—electrons not attached to atoms.

- **Conductors**
Materials that have many free electrons, such as copper, make good conductors of electricity.

▲ Batteries use chemical reactions to create electricity. Each cell (part) has a positive and negative electrode. In a car battery, the electrodes are metal (usually lead) plates dipped in acid.

▲ Car batteries are called wet cell batteries. Flashlight batteries are "dry cells." They often have electrodes of zinc and graphite (ground carbon).

155

Magnetism

MAGNETISM IS THE INVISIBLE FORCE between magnetic materials such as iron and nickel. It affects only a certain area around each magnet, called its "field." It is strongest at the two ends, or "poles," of the magnet, and gets steadily weaker farther away. Magnetism sometimes attracts magnetic materials to each other; sometimes it repels them. Magnetism works in opposite ways at each of a magnet's poles, and whether two magnets snap together or spring apart depends on which poles meet. If the same poles of each magnet meet, they push each other away. If opposite poles meet, they pull together.

FACTS: About Earth's magnetic field

- **Magnet Earth**
  The Earth is a giant magnet—it behaves almost like there was a giant iron bar magnet running through its middle from pole to pole.

- **Spinning core**
  The Earth gets its magnetism from its core of iron and nickel. Because the outer core is liquid and the inner core solid they rotate at different rates. The circulating currents this sets up turns it into a giant solenoid (p150).

- **Magnetosphere**
  Earth's magnetism not only affects magnets on the surface, but also electrically charged particles 37,000 miles (60,000km) out in space. The vast region of space affected is called the "magnetosphere." Without its protection, Earth would be exposed to the "solar wind," the lethal stream of charged particles whizzing from the Sun.

- **Why magnets point north**
  If you hold a magnet so that it can rotate freely, it always ends up pointing the same way, with one end pointing to the Earth's North Pole and the other to the South Pole. This is how compasses work.

- **Magnetic North**
  The Earth's magnetic field is slightly tilted, so compasses do not point to the Earth's true North Pole, but to a little way off northern Canada. This is called Magnetic North.

- **Magnetic dip**
  Magnets not only swivel to point north but also point down. This is called magnetic dip.

Lines of magnetic force created by Earth's magnetism

▲ There is not actually a giant bar magnet inside the Earth, but it is almost as if there was. The Earth's field, though, constantly varies from place to place and from time to time. Scientists can work out changes that happened in the distant past from magnetic particles, frozen in rocks as they formed. This is called "paleomagnetism."

Factfinder: Science

FACTS: Magnets

◄ *The effects of magnetic attraction are transmitted between objects affected by magnetism. So a magnet can pick up a string of paper clips.*

- **North and South Pole**
  Every magnet has two ends: a North (north-seeking) Pole and a South (south-seeking) Pole.

- **Magnetic domains**
  Cut a magnet in half and you get two little magnets, each with North and South Poles. You can go on dividing magnets into new magnets virtually down to atoms. This is because magnetic materials are made of tiny groups of atoms called domains, which are like mini-magnets.

- **Curie temperature**
  Iron loses its magnetic properties above 1,400°F (760°C), called the Curie temperature after Pierre Curie, the scientist who discovered this.

▼ *Lines of magnetic force may be invisible, but they are real. Around a bar magnet, they form a hamburger shape. They crowd close together around the poles, where the field is strongest.*

▲ *Auroras are spectacular curtains of light that ripple through the night sky above the poles. The northern lights or Aurora Borealis is seen over the North Pole and the southern lights or Aurora Australis over the South Pole. Auroras occur because there is a gaping hole in Earth's magnetic field over the poles, where lines of magnetic force funnel in toward them. Every now and then, charged particles from the Sun stream in through the hole and cannon into air molecules at tremendous speed. The violent collisions make all the air molecules glow so brightly they light up the sky.*

► *The Ancient Chinese were probably the first to make magnetic compasses, for telling fortunes as well as finding directions. But sailors everywhere have been using compasses to navigate for more than a thousand years.*

Electronics

ELECTRONICS ARE AT THE HEART of a huge range of modern technologies, from hi-fis to rocket control systems. All work by using electricity to send signals. Inside every electronic device there are lots of small electric circuits continually switching on and off telling the device what to do. But electronic switches are not like electric light switches on the wall; they work automatically. The most basic switches are "transistors," which are made using special materials called semiconductors that change their ability to conduct electricity. Electronic systems work by linking lots of transistors together into "integrated circuits," "chips" and "microprocessors."

FACTS: About chips and microprocessors

- **Silicon chips**
  In most integrated circuits, dozens or even thousands of tiny transistors are joined together in circuits that are packed inside a single tiny slice of silicon. This is called a silicon chip.

- **Minichips**
  Chips are getting smaller and more sophisticated by the year. This is why even complex devices like powerful computers can be made pocket-sized.

- **Computer chips**
  The most complicated silicon chips are "microprocessors" containing a million or more transistors. These are the brains in computers.

▲ The biggest things in a silicon chip are not all its circuits and switches—the tiny patch in the center. The connectors that send its instructions to the rest of the machine—the teeth along the side of the chip—are much bigger.

▶ Televisions work by controlling a beam electronically. Inside is a "gun" that fires a nonstop stream of electrically charged particles at the screen. Where it hits, it makes the screen glow by heating up its coating of phosphor. The picture is made of thousands of these glowing spots. Electronics control just where the gun hits the screen, makes it glow and so creates the picture.

Each gun hits the right color dot–blue, red, green–and makes it glow

Colors are made with three guns–one for blue, one for green, and one for red

A mask with small holes ensures each gun can only hit the right color dot on the screen

Factfinder: Science

FACTS: About computers

- **Binary code**
Computers work electronically. Since electronic circuits can only be on or off, computers work by using a "binary" system. This codes all data as strings of 1's or 0's—ons or offs.

- **Bits and bytes**
Each 1 or 0 in a computer is called a "bit" and bits are grouped together into bytes. This is why a computer's memory is measured in bytes. A kilo byte is 1,000 bytes. A megabyte is 1,000,000 bytes.

- **RAM and ROM**
Some of a computer's memory, called the ROM (read-only memory) is built into its microchips. The RAM (random-access memory) takes new data and instructions whenever needed. Data can also be stored on magnetic patterns on removable discs, or on the laser-guided bumps on a CD.

▲ Many of the world's billions of computers are now linked down phone lines via the Internet, a system that controls all the links.

▼ Inside a computer are a number of microchips. At the heart is the Central Processing Unit (CPU). The CPU is what works things out, within guidelines set by the ROM, and processes and controls all the programs by sending data to the right place in the RAM.

▶ Computers are often controlled by a "mouse." Inside the mouse is a ball, which turns as the operator glides the mouse over the table. The movement of the ball moves a pointer, or "cursor," on the screen.

RAM CPU (inside) where all data is processed Slot for disk drive Power transformer

Solar panels provide electric power for both electronic devices and motorized tasks, such as adjusting stabilizers

▶ Satellite and space technology depends on the sophisticated and compact control provided by electronic systems. Every spacecraft has its own onboard computers, and electronic circuits allow probes to be guided through elaborate tasks over millions of miles of space.

Radiation

RADIATION IS BASICALLY energy shot out by atoms at very high speeds. Some kinds of radiation are tiny particles splitting off from the atom. This is called radioactivity. But most radiation is tiny bursts of vibration or "waves" such as X-rays, microwaves, radio waves, and light. Light is the only form of radiation you can see; all the rest are invisible. Radiation that comes in waves is called electromagnetic radiation because it is linked to electricity and magnetism. But the length of the waves varies. The waves in gamma rays are very short, but they pack in a lot of energy, which is why they can be dangerous. Radio waves are very long and low in energy, which is why they are used for radio broadcasts. The rest come in between.

FACTS: About radioactivity and nuclear energy

- **Radioactivity.**
Radioactivity is when an atom breaks down or "decays," sending out radiation: lethal gamma rays (invisible electromagnetic waves) and two kinds of particle: "alpha" particles and "beta" particles.

- **Nuclear radiation**
Nuclear bombs and energy both create radioactive material. Radioactivity from bombs is huge, controlled and dangerous, causing death and radiation sickness and deforming unborn babies.

- **Nuclear fission and fusion**
In nuclear power stations, huge amounts of energy are released as heat from the nuclei of atoms by splitting them. This is called nuclear fission. Inside stars and in nuclear bombs, on the other hand, vast amounts of energy are unleashed when atomic nuclei are pushed together. This is called nuclear fusion.

▲ Nuclear fission relies on a chain reaction between atomic nuclei. Tiny alpha particles called neutrons are fired at uranium nuclei, splitting them. This not only creates heat but sets free more neutrons, which shoot away and split up more uranium nuclei, releasing more neutrons, which split more uranium nuclei and so on. Control rods in the power plant absorb neutrons and prevent the chain reaction getting out of hand.

▶ Nuclear bombs are the most devastatingly powerful bombs of all. They release so much energy so quickly that anything nearby is turned to dust, which billows up in a huge mushroom-shaped cloud.

Factfinder: Science

FACTS: Scans and X-rays

▼ CT scans create a 3D picture of the inside of the body by making a complete circuit of the body along a particular "slice" with X-rays. A computer then constructs the X-ray slices into a 3D picture.

The waves are scattered around the oven by a fan

Microwaves are created by a device called a magnetron

The patient is fed through the scanner as the X-ray gun rotates around her

▲ Microwave ovens work by bombarding food with invisible microwaves. It is because they are electromagnetic that microwaves heat food so quickly. Molecules of water in the food are like magnets and they are turned to and fro so quickly by the electromagnetic vibrations that they get very hot very quickly.

◀ SQUID scans pick up the tiny radiation from firing nerve cells, and so show the brain working in detail.

- **X-rays**
X-rays can be picked up on photos just like light, even though we can't see them. They have enough energy to pass clean through skin, but are stopped by muscle and bone. So muscle and bone show up in silhouette on an X-ray photo, giving doctors a vital view inside the body to help reveal problems.

- **PET scans**
PET (Positron Emission Tomography) scans detect particles called positrons to show blood moving.

DATA: Radiation

- **SPEED**
All electromagnetic radiation moves at the speed of light, 186,000 miles (300,000km) per second.

- **RADIOACTIVE MATERIALS**
50 radioactive materials occur naturally, including uranium. 2000, like plutonium, are made artificially.

- **HALF LIFE**
Half the atoms in a bit of strontium decay radioactively in just 9 mins. In uranium it takes 4.5 billion years.

Light

LIGHT IS JUST ONE OF THE FORMS of electromagnetic radiation, but it is vital to us. It is the only form we can see—and without it we could see nothing. Plants grow by soaking up light, too, and changing it into food. And light from the sun provides most of our warmth and energy. Yet although we are surrounded by light during the day, very few things give out light. The Sun, the stars, electric lights, and other things that glow are sources of light. But most things you see only because they reflect light from light sources. If they do not send out or reflect light, they are invisible like air.

FACTS: About reflection and refraction

- **See-through**
  When light rays hit something, they bounce off, are absorbed or pass through. Anything that lets light through like glass is "transparent." If it jumbles it on the way, like frosted glass, it is "translucent." If it stops light altogether it is "opaque."

- **Reflection**
  When light strikes a surface, some or all is reflected. From most surfaces it scatters in all directions. But from mirrors and shiny surfaces, it bounces off in the same pattern it arrived, giving a mirror image.

- **Refraction**
  When light goes into something transparent like glass or water, the rays are bent or "refracted." This happens because light travels slightly slower in glass or water.

◀ The refraction (bending) of light by water makes a straw in water look as if it is bent up in the middle. Of course, it is completely straight.

▲ When light is reflected off a mirror, it is reflected at just the same angle. The angle it hits, called the "angle of incidence," is the same as the "angle of reflection."

▲ Glass lenses are shaped so that light is refracted in certain ways. Concave lenses (above) spread them out. Convex (below) lenses focus them (bring them together).

▲ Combinations of lenses in binoculars and telescopes gather light rays together to make things look bigger and closer.

Factfinder: Science

FACTS: About light waves

▲ Most light contains a jumbled mixture of wavelengths. This is called "incoherent" light. But in laser light, all the waves are the same length and travel in step. This is called "coherent" light.

- **Light waves**
  Light travels in waves, like ripples on a pond. The waves are tiny—2,000 would fit across a pinhead.

- **Light packets**
  A light beam is made up of millions of tiny packets of energy called photons.

- **Wavelength**
  Every photon has its own distinctive wavelength. The color we see depends on the wavelengths of the photons.

- **Light from atoms**
  All light comes from atoms. When an atom is energized by, say, an electric spark or by heat, it becomes "excited" and its electrons are moved. As they settle back to their normal position, they let fire a photon.

FACTS: About color

- **Color**
  When we see different colors, we are seeing different wavelengths of light. Light that contains an equal mix of all colors, like sunlight, appears white.

- **Red apples**
  The colors of objects depends on what wavelengths they soak up and what they reflect. A red apple is red because it soaks up every color but red, and only bounces red back to your eyes.

- **Primary colors**
  You can make any color of light by mixing red, green, and blue light. You can make any color of paint by mixing cyan (a bluish color), magenta (a reddish color), and yellow paint.

▲ Different colors are refracted different amounts. So white light splits into all the colors of the rainbow when it passes through a prism (a triangular block of glass).

163

Levers & machines

IN EVERYDAY LIFE we take advantage of all kinds of machines, from toasters to TVs. But for a scientist, a machine is a device that makes life easier by reducing the effort needed to move something. There are always two forces involved in such a machine: a Load that is the force the machine is designed to overcome; and the Effort, which is the force used to move the load. The amount a machine cuts the effort you need to move a load is called the Mechanical Advantage. The mechanical advantage tells you how effective any machine is, whether it is a set of gears or a lever or a crane.

FACTS: About gears

- **How gears work**
  Gears can reduce work by spreading the Effort over a greater distance. This can make it easier to cycle uphill or for a car to accelerate from a standstill. They are pairs of wheels of different sizes that turn one another. They often have interlocking teeth to avoid slipping.

- **Gear ratio**
  The number of times the wheel that is driving turns the wheel that is driven is called the gear ratio. With a ratio of 5:1, the driving wheel turns five times for every time the driven wheel turns.

▶ Inside a transmission, there are four or five pairs of gear wheels. Changing gear means selecting the right pair for the best combination of speed and force to be transmitted from the engine to the wheels.

▼ The pedal wheel and cogs on a bicycle wheel don't actually touch, but they are gears too, for the chain connects them just like the teeth on gear wheels.

- **Increasing force**
  With a big gear ratio, the driven wheel turns slower relative to the driving wheel. But although it turns slowly, it turns with more force. This is why you select a big gear ratio to ride a bicycle uphill. Although you have to pedal much faster, pedaling is less effort.

- **Increasing speed**
  With a small gear ratio, the driven wheel turns with less force, but turns faster. This is why you select a smaller gear ratio for riding along a level road.

Factfinder: Science

Effort Fulcrum Load

Some levers have the fulcrum between the load and the effort, like crowbars

Some levers have the load between the effort and the fulcrum, like wheelbarrows and screwdrivers

Some levers have the effort between the load and the fulcrum, like tweezers

▲ A lever is a simple machine that makes it easier to move a load. If a rod is fixed at one point, but is free to swivel, it is a lever. The fixed point is called the fulcrum, and if you push on one end of the rod, your effort can be used to move a load on the other. This is called a turning effect. The farther away from the fulcrum you apply your effort, and the nearer the load is, the more your efforts will be multiplied.

FACTS: About machines

- **Spreading the load**
Machines do not give anything for nothing. The amount of effort to move a particular load is always the same. They make a load easier to move by spreading the effort over a greater distance.

- **Velocity ratio**
The distance moved by the effort you apply divided by the distance moved by the load is called the velocity ratio. If the velocity ratio is greater than 1, the effort moves farther than the load. So you need less effort to move the load, but you have to apply it for longer.

- **Work**
The sum of the efforts you put in to move something is called the "work." Work is basically the force you apply multiplied by the distance the load moves. Moving a load of 10 pounds (4.5kg) over 10 feet (3m) always requires the same amount of work.

▼ A mechanical digger uses powerful hydraulic (fluid-filled) systems to move its digging arms, but the same mechanical principles apply. The arms are levers and give the same mechanical advantage.

Force & motion

A FORCE IS SIMPLY SOMETHING that pushes or pulls. Without forces, nothing in the universe would happen. Every object in the universe has its own "inertia"–that is, it will not move unless it is forced to. So if something is moving, you can be sure it has been pushed or pulled. Similarly, once it is moving, it will go on moving forever, at the same rate and in the same direction, unless some force slows it down or speeds it up or pushes or pulls it off course. This is called "momentum." It is because heavy, fast moving objects have a great deal of momentum that car crashes do so much damage.

FACTS: About gravity

- **Universal pull**
  Gravity is the force of attraction that holds us all on the ground and holds the universe together. In fact, every bit of matter in the universe has its own gravitational pull and attracts every other bit of matter. The strength of the pull depends on how massive things are and how far they are apart. Massive objects nearby exert a strong gravitational pull. Light objects far away exert little pull.

▼ When you kick a ball, at first the power of your kick overcomes air resistance and gravity and the ball climbs. But after a while, air resistance slows the ball, and gravity pulls the ball down to the ground. So it loops through the air.

Gravity   Air resistance

At this point the pull of gravity exceeds the remaining force of the kick

If two balls are kicked together with equal force...

...they will bounce back with equal force

▶ A tightrope walker can balance on the high wire when gravity pulls down equally on each side. This happens when the exact middle of his weight, called the "center of gravity" is directly over the wire.

▶ Space probes rely on gravity to pull them in toward planets. But for a safe landing, they must slow down their descent with a parachute. But this only works for small planets; the gravitational pull of massive planets such as Jupiter is too great for a parachute to have much effect.

Factfinder: Science

▶ When you measure the weight of an apple on a spring balance—or any other way—you are simply measuring the pull of gravity. The heavier the apple is—that is, the more mass it has—the more strongly it is pulled by the Earth's gravity, and so the farther it stretches the spring on the spring balance that indicates its weight.

- **Mass and weight**
  When an object is heavy, we talk of its weight. But scientists use the word "mass." Mass is how much matter it contains. They use weight only for the force of gravity—that is, how strongly an object pulls or is pulled by gravity.

- **Acceleration by gravity**
  Like all forces, gravity makes things accelerate. Falling objects gain speed as they go down. On Earth they get faster at 32.1 feet (9.8m) per sec.

- **Terminal velocity**
  As objects fall faster, the resistance of the air has more effect. Eventually, air resistance equals the pull of gravity and the object can fall no faster. It then falls at a steady speed. This speed is called the object's "terminal velocity."

FACTS: Newton's Laws

▶ The great English scientist Isaac Newton (1642-1727) showed the link between force and motion in three Laws of Motion. He also discovered that the same force, gravity, made things fall and kept planets orbiting the Sun.

- **Newton's First Law of Motion**
  Newton's First Law is about how an object accelerates (or decelerates) only when a force is applied.

- **Newton's Second Law of Motion**
  The Second Law is that the acceleration depends on the size of the force and the object's mass.

- **Newton's Third Law of Motion**
  The Third Law is that when a force pushes or acts one way, an equal force pushes in the opposite direction.

- **Dynamics and statics**
  The study of the way objects move when acted upon by forces is called dynamics. The study of things that do not move is called statics.

▼ Newton's laws work for everything larger than an atom that moves in the universe, from an opening bud to a speeding truck.

Energy

FOR ANYTHING TO HAPPEN, for things to move or even change–for chocolate to melt or a rocket to fly–you need energy. Scientists say energy is "the capacity to do work," and by this they simply mean energy makes things happen. It comes in many forms, from the chemical energy locked in sugar to the mechanical energy in a moving truck. But it always works in two ways: transfer or conversion. Energy transfer simply means it is moving from one place to another, like heat going up a chimney or a ball being kicked. Energy conversion is when it changes from one form to another–from the steam-powered turbines to electric power in power stations, for instance.

FACTS: About solar energy

- **Solar power**
  Energy that arrives as light from the Sun gives us virtually all our energy, either directly by its warmth or indirectly by, for instance, providing the energy to grow plants which are eventually converted into coal for burning.

- **Solar panels and cells**
  Solar panels provide heat as water, sandwiched between sheets of glass, is heated by the Sun. Solar cells are light-sensitive chemicals which generate an electric current when hit by light.

▶ Each solar cell generates only a tiny electric current, but connecting hundreds together can create a significant amount of electricity.

▼ Honda's record-breaking experimental solar-powered car show just what could be done with a car run entirely on sunlight.

▼ Less than half the Sun's energy striking the Earth reaches the ground. 53 percent of it is absorbed or reflected on the way down through the atmosphere. 16 percent of this is soaked up by water vapor and dust in the air; 7 percent is scattered by the air; 3 percent is soaked up by clouds; 23 percent is reflected off clouds; and 4 percent is reflected by the land and oceans.

Almost a quarter of the sunlight reaching Earth is reflected away off clouds

Factfinder: Science

FACTS: Renewable energy

▲ To build up water pressure to turn the turbines and to even the flow, most hydroelectric power stations are built inside big dams.

- **Alternative energy**
Fossil fuels are irreplaceable and pollute the air, so there is a search for clean, renewable alternatives, including electricity generated by winds, the sun (solar power), the tides, or waves.

- **Hydroelectric power (HEP)**
HEP is electricity generated by turbines turned by water. It is the only major alternative energy source.

FACTS: Energy sources

- **Fossil fuels**
90 percent of our energy comes from fossil fuels (page 135). About 40 percent comes from oil, 27 percent from coal and 21 percent from natural gas. These sources are nonrenewable, since they took millions of years to make. So all the world's fossil fuels will eventually be used up.

- **Nuclear energy**
Nuclear energy is also nonrenewable but it uses fuel such as uranium so slowly that it will not run out in the near future. Unfortunately it leaves a dangerous radioactive waste.

▲ When cars burn gasoline, they not only use up a nonrenewable source of energy, they also fill the air with polluting exhaust fumes such as nitrous oxides.

Just 47 percent of sunlight is absorbed by the ground

◀ Flowers and other plants get their energy directly from sunlight in a process called photosynthesis. This allows them to use carbon dioxide in the air to create the energy-rich chemical sugars they need for growth. Humans, like animals, have to get their energy indirectly, by eating plants—or by eating animals that have themselves eaten plants.

Heat

HEAT IS NOT JUST THE WARMTH of the Sun or a fire; it is a form of energy, the energy of molecules moving. The faster molecules move, the hotter things are. When you feel the heat of a fire, you are simply being battered by millions of fast-moving air molecules—hurried up by millions of even faster-moving molecules in the fire. The fire heats the air because heat always spreads out, and something hot always makes its surroundings warm too as it itself loses heat and cools down. We measure how hot something is by its temperature. But temperature is just a measure of how fast the molecules are moving; heat is the total energy of all the moving molecules.

FACTS: About conduction, radiation, and convection

- **Convection**
Convection is when warm air rises through cool air, like a hot-air balloon. It rises because the warmth makes it expand and so it becomes less dense and lighter than the cooler air around.

◄ *Infra-red radiation from the intense heat caused by silicon crystal meltdown.*

▼ *The heat of a candle flame heats up a nearby thermometer mainly by radiation, which travels in waves, just like light.*

- **Spreading heat**
Heat spreads in three ways: conduction, radiation, and convection.

- **Conduction**
Conduction is the spread of heat through substances by direct contact—a bit like a relay race, as vibrating molecules cannon into their neighbors and set them moving too. Good conducting materials like metals feel cool because they carry heat away quickly.

- **Radiation**
Radiation is the spread of heat as heat rays—invisible "infrared" electromagnetic radiation (page 156). Radiation moves through space spreading heat without direct contact.

Factfinder: Science

◀ Heat makes things expand. So thermometers can measure temperature by showing how much a liquid such as coloured alcohol expands and rises up a tube. Everyday temperatures are measured in degrees—Fahrenheit (°F) or Celsius (°C). Water freezes at 32°F which is also 0°C. Water boils at 212°F (100°C). The temperature of the surface of the Sun is 10,800°F (6,000°C). Scientists, however, would say the Sun's temperature is 6,000K, because they use a scale called the Kelvin Scale which starts at -459°F (-273°C).

FACTS: Pressure and heat

◀ If air is squeezed, it gets warmer as the pressure rises. You can see this for yourself if you pump up a bicycle tire quickly. After a few pumps, it will feel quite warm. The pump works by squeezing air down through the tube with a plunger as you push down. On the upstroke, a one-way valve lets more air in.

- **What is pressure?**
  Pressure is the way water and air push against their surroundings. Molecules in air and water are always zooming about, and the pushing is actually all the molecules smashing into their surroundings.

- **Rising pressure**
  When air is squeezed, its pressure rises in proportion, because more molecules are squeezed into a smaller space. This is Boyle's Law.

- **Heat and pressure**
  If air cannot expand, heating it up boosts its pressure in proportion, because heat makes the molecules zoom about faster and smash harder into their surroundings. But if it can expand, it swells in proportion instead. This is Charles's Law.

DATA: Temperatures

- **LOWEST TEMPERATURE**
  The lowest possible temperature is Absolute Zero -459.67°F (-273.15°C), when all molecules stop moving. The lowest recorded on Earth was -128°F (-89°C).

- **HIGHEST TEMPERATURE**
  The temperature may reach 36 million°F (20 million°C) in the heart of stars. The highest on Earth was 138°F (59°C).

171

Solids, liquids, & gases

NEARLY EVERY SUBSTANCE IN THE UNIVERSE is either a solid, a liquid, or a gas. These are said to be the three states of matter. They seem very different, but every substance can change from one to the other and back again, providing the temperature and pressure are right. Just as ice melts to water and water turns to steam when it gets hot, so every substance changes from solid to liquid to gas at certain temperatures. The temperature at which a substance melts from solid to liquid is called its melting point. The highest temperature a liquid can reach before turning to a gas is its boiling point.

FACTS: Three states of matter

Gas: water vapor

Liquid: rainwater

Solid: ice

◀ A gas, like air, does not have any shape, strength, or fixed volume. This is because its molecules are moving fast enough to break the bonds that try to hold them together.

◀ A liquid flows and takes up the shape of any container it is poured into. This is because although bonds hold the molecules together, they are loose enough to fall over each other like dry sand.

◀ A solid has strength and a definite shape. This is because its molecules are bonded together firmly in a regular structure, and simply vibrate on the spot. The hotter it gets, the more they vibrate.

- **Melting**
In a solid, molecules are held together tightly by bonds and simply vibrate on the spot. Heat makes them vibrate faster, until the bonds loosen. Eventually they become so loose that the neat structure breaks down, and the substance melts and flows all over the place.

- **Boiling**
If the temperature goes on rising, the heat makes molecules zoom all over the place, until they move so fast that the molecules break away altogether. More and more molecules start shooting away from the surface as gas or steam. Eventually, all the liquid turns to gas.

Factfinder: Science

◀ *The more firmly molecules are bonded together, the stronger and tougher solid they make. Diamond is the hardest solid of all, because all its molecules are bonded together in an incredibly strong structure.*

FACTS: About solutions

- **Special mixtures**
  Water often contains traces of other substances mixed in. If they're mixed so well that they are indistinguishable, the mixture is called a solution. Seawater is a solution of salts dissolved in water. Solutions play a vital part in our body chemistry.

- **Saturated solutions**
  When solids dissolve in a liquid, the solution becomes stronger and stronger until it becomes "saturated" and no more dissolves. If it is heated, however, more will dissolve before it becomes saturated.

Stalactite

▶ *Some substances turn water acid—and acids are very good at dissolving things. Rain is a mild acid and can dissolve limestone rocks—then leave the minerals it dissolves as "stalactites" in caves as it seeps through the ground.*

◀ *Sugar dissolved in tea is a solution. If you go on piling sugar in, it will eventually become saturated—as the sugar molecules fill the spaces between the water molecules.*

- **Evaporation**
  As a liquid heats up, more and more of its molecules break away from the surface, turning it to gas. This is called evaporation. When clothes dry, it is because water evaporates from them.

- **Condensation**
  When a gas cools, molecules slow down until bonds form between them, forming drops of liquid. This is called condensation. Water condensing from the air is called dew.

- **Ice, water, and water vapor**
  Water is the only substance commonly found in all three states: solid ice, liquid water, and gas. Water is called water vapor when it is a gas. Steam is actually lots of tiny drops of liquid water in air. Only when these drops evaporate does it turn to water vapor.

- **Space saving**
  Substances get smaller when they freeze as molecules pack tighter—except water. Water expands when it freezes, which is why ice bursts water pipes. It is also why ice floats, as it is less dense than water.

Stalagmite

173

Matter

MATTER IS EVERY SUBSTANCE in the universe, from the tiniest speck of dust to the largest star—everything that is not simply empty space. Surprisingly, though, even the most solid-looking matter is mostly empty space too, for matter is made from tiny pieces called atoms. You cannot see them, or the space between them, because they are amazingly small. You could fit two billion atoms on the period at the end of this sentence. Scientists once thought they were the smallest things in the universe—and that they were like tiny balls that could never be split or destroyed. But they are more like clouds of energy, and they too are mostly empty space, dotted with even tinier "subatomic particles."

FACTS: About atoms and sub-atomic particles

- **The atomic nucleus**
  The core of an atom is a cluster or "nucleus" of two kinds of particle: protons and neutrons. Protons have a positive electrical charge. Neutrons have none.

- **Electrons**
  Whizzing around the nucleus as fast as the speed of light are even lighter particles called electrons. Electrons are negatively charged.

- **Atoms and ions**
  Most atoms have identical numbers of protons and electrons, so the electrical charges balance. An ion is an atom that has either lost or gained electrons, so it may be either positively or negatively charged.

- **Short-lived particles**
  By smashing atoms together at high speeds, scientists have found more than 200 subatomic particles besides electrons, protons, and neutrons, but most of these last only a fraction of a second.

- **Quarks and leptons**
  Scientists believe that all particles are made from just two basic kinds: quarks and leptons. Electrons are leptons. Protons and neutrons are made from different "flavors" of quark.

◀ Protons are made from clusters of three quarks, held together by gluons. There are actually six different kinds of quark but only two— "up" quarks and "down" quarks—are long-lived, and this is what protons are made of.

▶ Atoms are not really like this. All the particles are really just clusters of energy that probably only occur in certain places. But it is a good way to imagine them, with electrons whizzing around the nucleus.

- **Atomic forces**
  Atoms can be split, but are usually held together by three forces—the electrical attraction between negative electrons and positive protons, and the "strong" and "weak" nuclear forces that bind together the particles of the nucleus. These forces, together with gravity, are the basic forces that hold the universe together.

Factfinder: Science

FACTS: About crystals

- **Crystal shapes**
  Crystals are hard, shiny solids formed in regular geometric shapes. Grains of salt, sugar, and sand are all crystals. So are diamonds. Each is made from a very regular structure of atoms, ions, or molecules.

- **Crystallization**
  When melted substances turn solid or dissolved substances leave solutions, they form crystals. This is called crystallization.

- **Crystallography**
  Crystallography is the study of crystals, usually using X-rays (p156).

▲ Most hard substances are crystals. A powerful microscope reveals the regular structure of crystals of sulfur. The colors are computerized.

Water molecule

◀ Atoms rarely exist alone. Usually they join up in small groups called molecules. Hydrogen atoms, for instance, exist in pairs or joined to other atoms. A molecule of hydrogen gas is a pair of hydrogen atoms. A water molecule is a pair of hydrogen atoms joined to an oxygen atom.

▶ The study of matter is called chemistry. In the past most chemistry was done in laboratories—boiling and mixing chemicals in flasks and test tubes. Now a great deal of chemistry is done on computer, constructing molecules in cyberspace. In this way chemists have been able to create entirely new chemicals.

Nucleus of protons and atoms

Around the nucleus whirl clouds of tiny negatively charged electrons

175

The elements

ALL THE SUBSTANCES IN THE UNIVERSE are made up from 100 or so basic chemicals or "elements," such as gold and oxygen. Each element has its own unique character–and its own special atoms. Each element has a different number of protons and electrons in its atoms, from hydrogen with one of each to lawrencium with 103. The number of protons and electrons in their atoms is really the only difference between the elements, but this difference has a huge effect on their nature. Nitrogen gas atoms, for instance, have seven protons and carbon have six, just one less, but they are totally unlike.

FACTS: Groups and Periods

- **Rows and columns**
  The Periodic Table of elements is laid out in rows called Periods and columns called Groups.

- **Electron shells**
  Electrons spin around atoms in up to 7 layers or "shells." There is a limit to how many electrons that can fit in each shell. Only 2 fit in the first shell, closest to the nucleus, 8 in the second, and 8 in the third. After that it gets complicated, but the outer shell never holds more than 8.

- **Shells and Periods**
  The number of electron shells an atom has increases down each Group. So every atom in each Period has the same number of electron shells. What varies is the number of electrons.

- **Electrons and Groups**
  Each Group is for elements with a certain number of electrons in their outer shells—and this is what determines an element's chemical properties. Every element in the same Group has similar properties.

- **Reactive to stable**
  Each Period starts on the left with a highly reactive "alkali metal" which has one electron in its outer shell. It ends on the right with a stable "noble gas," such as argon, which has eight electrons in its outer shell.

▼ All the elements can be displayed in order on a chart called the Periodic Table. The number of protons an element has in each of its atoms is called its Atomic Number, and the chart lists elements in Atomic Number order, starting with hydrogen at 1.

Above the name for each element is its abbreviation, or "formula"; below is the Atomic Number

The block of elements in the middle (yellow) is called the Transition metals

This Group is called Alkali metals

This is the Alkaline-Earth Group

This row, called the lanthanides or rare earths, fits into Group 3

176

Factfinder: Science

FACTS: About atomic mass and formulae

- **Atomic mass**
  Atomic mass is the "weight" of an atom of an element and corresponds to the average number of protons and neutrons in the nucleus.

- **Formula**
  Every element has a short name, or formula. Carbon is C, Hydrogen is H, Copper Cu, and so on.

▲ Atoms of gold have 79 protons in their nuclei, and, on average, 118 neutrons. So its (relative) atomic mass is 197. The formula for gold is Au.

As the Atomic Numbers increase by one along each period, so the chemical properties change

These elements (purple) are called non-metals

These elements (blue) are called poor metals

The final Group on the right is the noble gases

This row, called the actinides, fits into Group 3

FACTS: About metals

- **Metals**
  Metals are hard, dense, shiny solids. They conduct heat well. They are also good conductors of electricity because they are electropositive, which means electrons easily become "free" (page 151).

- **Transition metals**
  Transition metals are metals in the middle of the Table like gold—shiny and tough, but easily shaped.

- **Lanthanides or rare earths**
  These silvery metals are called rare earths because they were once thought too reactive to stay in the ground unmixed with other elements for long.

FACTS: About noble gases

- **Nobly aloof**
  Group 0 is the far right group called the noble gases. The outer shells of their atoms are full up, so they do not react with other elements. They are sometimes called inert gases.

- **Bulb gases**
  Noble gases like argon and krypton are used in lightbulbs because they are unreactive.

Chemicals & compounds

SOME SUBSTANCES, like gold, are made of just one element. Most are made of two or more elements joined together to make what is called a compound. Table salt, for instance, is a compound of the two elements sodium and chlorine. A compound is usually very different in nature from the two elements that make it up. Sodium, for instance, is a metal that fizzes and gets hot when dropped in water; chlorine is a thick, green gas.

◀ One of the most remarkable molecules is this molecule built from carbon atoms called a buckyball. It was constructed by scientists as an experiment but may well have practical uses in the future.

FACTS: About chemical bonds

Atomic nucleus • Electrons in their shells • Shared electrons

Sodium atom gives up an electron

Mutual electric attraction

Chlorine atom gains an electron

▲ Atoms are only stable when they have a full set of 8 electrons in their outer shells. Atoms that have too many or too few can get a full set by sharing electrons with other atoms. This makes a covalent bond.

- **Valency**
  Each atom joins only with a certain number of others—as if each only has so many hooks it can hang others on. This number is called its "valency."

- **Chemical bonds**
  There are two main ways elements can combine: by sharing electrons in what are called "covalent bonds," or by losing or gaining them in "ionic bonds." "Metallic bonds" occur between huge numbers of atoms in a giant metallic lattice.

- **Ionic bonds**
  Ionic bonds occur when atoms with just a few electrons in their outer shells (page 172) donate them

▲ In ionic bonds, one atom donates an electron to another and so becomes negatively charged. The atoms are then bonded by mutual electrical attraction. This is what joins sodium atoms to chlorine atoms in salt.

to atoms with just a few missing from theirs. This makes the atom losing electrons positively charged and the other negatively charged (page 170)—so they stick together by electrical attraction.

- **Covalent bonds**
  In covalent bonds, atoms share electrons. In water, two hydrogen atoms share electrons with one oxygen.

Factfinder: Science

▲ Some substances make acids when they dissolve in water. Weak acids, like lemon juice or vinegar, taste tart. Strong ones, like sulfuric acids, are highly corrosive, burning, stinging and even dissolving metals. The opposites of acids are bases, known as alkalis when dissolved in water. Weak bases such as baking soda taste bitter and feel soapy. Strong ones, like caustic soda, are as corrosive as acids. Chemists use "indicators" such as litmus paper to test for acidity. Acids turn the paper red. Alkalis turn it blue.

▼ Strong acids are dangerous, but they can be useful in many ways. Sulfuric acid is used to make everything from fertilizers to paints. Crystals of salicylic acid (below), which occur naturally in willow trees, are used to make aspirin.

FACTS: About water

▶ Water molecules are made from two hydrogen atoms and an oxygen atom arranged in a V-shape. This is why the chemical formula is H_2O.

- **Water poles**
Water molecules are special. In sharing electrons with an oxygen atom, the electrons on each hydrogen atom are tugged to the side nearest the oxygen—leaving the far side "bare," and exposing the positively charged nucleus. This gives water molecules a + (positive) and a - (negative) end, and so they are called polar molecules.

- **Hydrogen bonds**
Pairs of water molecules bind together as + ends are drawn to - ends. These "hydrogen" bonds keep water liquid to 212°F (100°C), at which heat most similar substances are gases.

The sequence of chemicals that make DNA's are coded instructions

▲ The element carbon forms thousands of different compounds. Indeed, most of the "organic" compounds on which life depends are carbon compounds. The most remarkable of these is deoxyribonucleic acid or DNA. DNA forms long molecules shaped like a twisted rope ladder. In the pattern of its rungs, DNA carries complete coded instructions for life—for everything from how a plant is to grow, to what color your eyes should be.

179

AMAZING QUESTIONS

1. How many chambers has the heart?

Why questions?

THE WORLD IS A WONDERFUL AND FASCINATING PLACE yet all too often we are told not what we want to know about–what makes us curious–but what someone wants to tell us about. In this book, we pose the kind of questions that you might

2. What is the world's biggest flower?

180

3. What's the smallest planet?

4. What's the Earth's core made of?

5. What's the smallest bit of an element?

ask if you had the chance—and answer these. On every spread too, there is a series of questions that we ask you—to give you a chance to test your general knowledge—or to challenge your friends and family. Here are some to get you going.

6. What is the world's biggest reptile?

Answers
1. Four 2. Rafflesia
3. Pluto 4. Iron and nickel 5. An atom
6. Alligator

181

How did scabious get its name?

There are exploding cucumbers in the jungle: true or false?

What tree is the national symbol of Canada?

Can plants cure cancer?

What plant has two different flowers?

Where does chocolate come from?

Which woodland plant is good for a kiss?

What plant amputates its own branches?

Plants

184 Plants of all kinds
186 Flowering plants
188 Trees and shrubs
190 Plants for food
192 Plants for health
194 Plants for materials
196 Woodland plants
198 Tropical plants
200 Water plants
202 Grassland plants
204 Desert plants
206 Mountain plants
208 Arctic plants

What plants have their own water tanks?

What is the strongest rope in the jungle?

Why don't all trees lose their leaves?

What is the world's biggest flower?

Plants of all kinds

What are plants?

THERE ARE MORE THAN 270,000 KINDS of plant around the world, ranging from tiny single-celled organisms to giant trees, the largest living things. Most have green leaves and can make their own food from sunlight, which is why most don't need to move around like animals. But some microscopic plants can move like animals, even though they can make their own food, while others cannot move, but steal food off other plants.

Elm tree
Sunflower
Tulip
Palm tree
Larch
Fern
Liverwort
Seaweed
Grass
Moss

Flowering plants: monocotyledons
Flowering plants: dicotyledons
Conifers and cycads
Ferns
Mosses and liverworts
Algae

▲ **The plant kingdom**
The plant kingdom is split into: mosses and liverworts, ferns, and their relatives, conifers, and flowering plants. Lichens and algae are not true plants.

Life all around: Plants

▶ **Flowering tree**
Deciduous trees like this bottlebrush are among more than 240,000 species of flowering plant.

What is a flowering plant?
Flowering plants are plants that have flowers to make the seeds and fruits from which new plants will eventually grow. This doesn't only mean garden and wild flowers, but every herb, grass, fruit, shrub, and vegetable—all of which have tiny flowers. Another name for flowering plants is angiosperms.

Are any big plants not flowering plants?
Yes. Plants that make their seeds in cones, rather than in flowers. These cone-bearing plants or conifers are also known as gymnosperms. They include trees such as pines.

What are monocotyledons?
Flowering plants are either monocotyledons or dicotyledons. Monocotyledons begin from seeds with just a single leaf. They also tend to have longer, narrower leaves, like grasses, tulips, and daffodils. Dicotyledons start with two or more leaves from their seeds. Most flowering plants are dicotyledons.

Do all plants grow from seeds?
No, only flowering plants and conifers do. Ferns and mosses grow from tiny cells called spores, which can be seen only under a microscope.

Why are plants green?
Plants are green because they contain a green substance called chlorophyll. This plays a vital role in photosynthesis, the process by which plants make their food by absorbing sunlight. In photosynthesis, the plant changes carbon dioxide from the air, and hydrogen from water, into energy-giving sugars.

What is the stem?
A plant's stem not only supports the flowers and leaves; it is also a pipe to take water, minerals, and food up and down between the leaves and the roots. Water goes up through tubes called xylem. Food goes down to the roots through tubes called phloem. In herbaceous plants, the stem is soft and green. In woody plants like trees it is stiff, and often covered in bark.

◀ **Conifer**
Conifers like pines are among the oldest of all plants, appearing 275 million years ago.

QUIZ

1. What are the biggest plants?
2. Seaweeds are a kind of algae: true or false?
3. How do plants get water?
4. Some plants eat meat: true or false?
5. Plants that take their food from other plants are called a) felons b) parasites c) clingers?
6. Some ferns can grow as big as trees, more than 80 feet (25m) tall: true or false?
7. Plant spores can survive in outer space: true or false?
8. The oldest known plant is a creosote plant in California. It is thought to be: a) 250 years old, b) 1,260 years old c) 11,700 years old?

Answers
1. Trees 2. True 3. Through their roots 4. True 5. b) 6. True 7. True 8. c)

185

Flowering plants

What are flowering plants?

FLOWERING PLANTS are not just garden flowers and wild flowers with pretty blooms, but every herb, grass, shrub, tree, fruit, and vegetable too. Indeed, nearly every plant except ferns, mosses, lichens, and fungi is a flowering plant. The flowers may not be obvious but all have flowers that create the seeds and fruits from which new plants will grow.

How do flowers make seeds?

Just as there are male and female animals, so a flower has male parts, known as stamens, and female parts, known as pistils. Seeds for new plants are made when pollen from the stamens meets eggs in the pistils.

Where are a flower's sex organs?

The female parts or pistil, containing the ovaries where eggs are made, is the thick, short stalk in the middle of the flower. The male parts, or stamens, which make pollen, are the spindly stalks round it.

▲ **The largest seeds**
The largest seeds are double coconuts, weighing up to 40 pounds (18kg).

Can flowers pollinate themselves?

Many flowers have both male and female parts. So some flowers can indeed pollinate themselves, and the pollen moves from the stamens to the pistil on the same plant. This is called self-pollination. Most flowers, however, are cross-pollinating. This means the pollen must be carried from the stamens of one plant to the pistil of another plant of the same kind.

Why are flowers such pretty colors?

Pollen from some flowers spreads on the wind. But others rely on insects such as bees and butterflies, or even birds and bats to help them spread their pollen. Bright colors draw the bees to the flower's sweet juice or nectar. As they sip it, they brush the stamens and pick up pollen which they carry to the next flower they sip.

▲ **Parts of a flower**
Pollen is made in the "anthers" on top of the stamens, the male parts of the flower. The female part or pistil is topped by a sticky "stigma," which traps the pollen. A long tube or "style" takes it down to the ovary where it meets the eggs to create the seeds.

Labels: Petal; Filament (male); Stigma (female); Style (female); Ovary (female) where eggs are fertilized by pollen to make seeds; Sepal; Anther (male)

Life all around: Plants

◀ Seed spreaders
Some seeds are spread by the wind in feathery seed cases. But many are spread by insects, birds and other animals. Birds such as these eat fruits, drawn by their color. They digest the flesh, but the hard seed passes through the bird and emerges ready for germination.

Waxwing

Jay

Are fruits seeds?
No, they develop from the flower's ovary—and the hard pips inside are the seeds. Juicy fruits such as berries are called "true fruits" because they are made from the flower's ovaries alone. Apples and pears are "false" fruits because only the core is made from the ovary. Plums and cherries are "drupes" meaning there are no pips, but the seed is held in a hard shell.

Are any vegetables fruits?
Potatoes and other root vegetables are plant roots, not seeds. But peas, beans, and other "legumes" are actually fruit and the seeds are the peas and beans inside the pod.

How do seeds grow?
Each seed is the germ (start) of a new plant and contains the food it needs to help it germinate (grow into a plant). Growth starts with just a single root or radicle, which grows down into the soil, and a single green shoot, or plumule, which grows up toward the sun. Then the plant's seed leaves—its first leaves, like baby teeth—appear. Soon after, the main stem begins to grow, and true leaves sprout from this.

▶ Date palm
The sweet, sticky fruit of the date palm looks a little like a plum, but it is not a drupe. The stone of a date is actually the seed for a new tree, not the seed container like the plum stone.

QUIZ

1. How many pollen grains can a single American ragweed make in a day: a) 18 b) 1,800 c) 18 billion?
2. The flowers of the baobab tree are pollinated by bushbabies: true or false?
3. How many seeds can a single flower of the trumpet tree of the Amazon rain forest make: a) 900 b) 900,000 c) 9 million?
4. Are any seeds poisonous?
5. Do any flowers bloom just for a day?
6. What are the smallest seeds?
7. What are the world's oldest flowers?

Answers
1. c) 2. True 3. b) 4. Yes, to save them being eaten by birds 5. Yes, like morning glory and the day lily 6. Orchids 7. Magnolias

187

Trees and shrubs

What are trees?

ALTHOUGH SOME DWARF WILLOWS are just a few inches high, most trees are much bigger; trees are the biggest of all plants. The biggest trees are the world's biggest living things, as tall as a skyscraper. They can grow big because they have huge numbers of leaves and hard, woody stems covered in a protective layer of bark.

What are conifers?
Conifers, are among the oldest of all plants, first appearing more than 275 million years ago. They get their name from the fact that they rely on cones rather than flowers to make the seeds for new trees. They usually grow tall and straight with hardly any big side branches and, unlike "broad-leaved" trees, they tend to have narrow, needle-like leaves.

What is an evergreen?
An evergreen is a tree that keeps its leaves all the year round. Each leaf lasts for years, and is usually a dark, waxy green. The leaves of trees that lose their leaves each year, called deciduous trees, are a lighter, yellow green.

▶ Going red
As days grow shorter and colder in autumn, the chlorophyll which makes leaves green breaks down in deciduous trees like the maple. This allows other colours – yellows, reds, browns and golds – to shine through, giving the trees their beautiful autumn hues.

Why do some trees lose their leaves every year?
Deciduous trees such as oaks, ashes, and elms shed their leaves to cut down on moisture loss in seasons when water is harder to come by. In the tropics, they lose their leaves at the start of the dry season. In temperate regions, between the tropics and the poles, they lose them in autumn because water is much harder to come by in winter.

Why don't all trees lose their leaves?
In warm, moist places, like tropical rain forests, moisture is available all year round, so even broad-leaved trees can keep their leaves all year round. Conifers, too, can keep their leaves, because their narrow needles do not lose moisture nearly as quickly as the big leaves of broad-leaved trees, so they can survive through the winter when water is short.

What are tree rings?
If a tree is cut across the trunk, you can see the trunk is marked by a series of rings called growth rings. These show how the tree has grown each year. The edge of the ring marks where growth ceased in winter. By counting the rings, you can tell how old a tree is. You can also tell whether a summer was good or bad for tree growth from just how wide each of the rings is.

What is heartwood?
Heartwood is the dark, dense dead wood found in the center of a tree trunk. It is surrounded by lighter, living "sapwood," which carries all the tubes that feed moisture and nourishment to the tree's leaves.

Jay

▶ **Life in a tree**
An oak tree like this is home to countless animals and plants. Birds nest on branches and in holes, insects feed on the leaves and burrow in the bark, and fungi and ivy grow on the trunk.

Tawny owl

Woodpecker

Stag beetle

Ivy

Bracket fungi

Quiz

1 The giant sequoia tree in California is the world's biggest living thing. Is it a) 138 feet (42m) b) 272 feet (83m) c) 505 feet (154m)?

2 Every tree can be identified by its leaves: true or false?

3 What tree is the national symbol of Canada?

4 What is the seed of the oak tree called?

5 Can trees warn other trees of caterpillar attacks?

6 Is the eucalyptus of Tasmania commonly known as a a) gum tree b) oil tree c) glue tree?

7 Are the pipes that carry a tree's sap called a) reeds b) xylem c) xylophones?

Answers
1. b) 2. True 3. Maple 4. Acorn 5. Yes; willows and alders send out airborne chemicals 6. a) 7. b)

189

Plants for food

What food do plants give?

PLANTS GIVE most of the world's people their "staple" food, the basic food they need for survival—whether it is bread, or cereal or soybeans. Fruit and vegetables provide us with most of the vitamins we need to keep us healthy. They also make some of the most delicious foods and drinks, from apple pies to orange juice.

Why do we eat grass?
Cereals are the world's most important foods—including wheat, rice, corn, barley, oats, and rye—and they are all grasses. We usually eat their seeds, or "grain," leaving the stalks and leaves to rot to make silage to feed animals.

What is wheat?
Wheat is the most important of the cereals. It was first cultivated in the Middle East 12,000 years ago from the wild grass emmer. Now it provides the basic food for more than a third of the world's population. Wheat grain is usually ground into flour to make bread and pasta and many other things.

What was the Green Revolution?
40 years ago, farmers in North America and Europe began growing special "high-yield" varieties of wheat, rice, and corn. These grow so fast and big they give bumper harvests—sometimes more than twice a year. Soon, the idea was adopted in India and elsewhere.

What's wrong with the Green Revolution?
High-yield crops only give big harvests if the land is well watered and the farmer uses a lot of fertilizer, pesticides, and machines—farmers now need to apply ten times as much nitrogen fertilizer to keep the soil fertile as they did 40 years ago. This not only poses much greater strains on the environment, but means small farmers may be put in debt to the suppliers of fertilizers, pesticides, and seeds.

What are root crops?
Root crops are plants cultivated mainly for their big, solid roots, such as potatoes, yams, cassava and manioc. These roots are rich in carbohydrates, the food we need for energy.

▶ Paddy fields
In Asia, most people's basic food is rice, grown in flooded fields called paddies, where they can grow up to three crops a year. To keep the fields flooded on steep hillsides, farmers often have to build row upon row of terraces.

▲ Corn fed
Corn is usually grown on large farms. It comes in two main forms. One has a big head with big grains and gives us corn on the cob and sweetcorn (above). The other has a small head and small grains and gives corn oil and corn starch.

Life all around: Plants

Where does chocolate come from?

Chocolate is made with cocoa powder, ground up from the roasted and fermented beans of cacao pods. The pods are the fruit of the cacao tree, which came originally from the Andes mountains in South America, but is now grown mainly in West Africa and the Caribbean.

How many plants can be eaten?

There are more than 12,000 species of edible plant, but fewer than 100 are usually grown as crops.

Which plants give sugar

Most sugar came originally from the sweet sap of sugarcane, a tall grass that grows in the tropics, especially the Caribbean. Now as much comes from the sweet, thick roots of sugarbeet, a plant that grows well in cooler places.

Most paddy rice is still planted and picked by hand

▲ **Prickly pear**
Different crops grow well in different places. In the hottest, driest parts of India, farmers often grow this cactus, called a prickly pear, which yields a sweet fruit.

Some rice terraces, like these in the Philippines, are thousands of years old

QUIZ

1. Is a fallow: a) an old Irishman b) a kind of fruit c) a period in which soil is allowed to rest and recover?

2. Is a cash crop: a) an expensive haircut b) a banker's whip c) a crop a farmer grows to sell for money, not to eat?

3. What is a combine harvester?

4. Where did potatoes come from originally: a) Ireland b) South America c) India?

5. What plant gives most of our wine?

6. Japanese farmers use 65 times as much fertilizer per acre on their grains as farmers in Nigeria: true or false?

Answers
1. c) 2. c) 3. A machine which both cuts the wheat from the ground and separates the grain from the stalks 4. b) 5. The grape vine 6. True

Plants for health

Can plants heal?

YES. PLANTS HAVE BEEN USED as medicines since prehistoric times, and the effectiveness of some is beyond doubt. Many of today's most important drugs, such as aspirin, morphine, and quinine, came originally from plants. In some countries such as China, herbal remedies are still among the most widely used of all medicines, although not all are equally effective.

▲ **Poppy power**
The opium poppy is the source of opium, which oozes from the unripe seed head when cut with a knife. Opium is the source of the powerful drug morphine, used to help ease extreme pain. It is the basis too for the milder painkiller codeine, used in cough medicines. Opium can also be turned into the dangerously addictive drug heroin, which is why it is sometimes grown in secret in Southeast Asia.

How can a willow cure a headache?
People used to chew willow bark to ease pain. In the last century, scientists discovered this worked because willow contains a certain chemical, also found in meadowsweet. This chemical was later used to make aspirin.

Why might a foxglove stop your heart?
Foxglove in large doses is highly poisonous. But it also yields the drug digitalis, used in small doses to treat heart problems.

Can plants cure cancer?
No drug yet known can cure cancer. But an extract of the rosy periwinkle, vincristine, is very effective against leukemia, the childhood cancer.

▶ **Plants for health: key**
1. Periwinkle
2. Feverfew
3. White willow
4. Opium poppy
5. Foxglove

Life all around: Plants

Why might a gin and tonic help cure malaria?
The tropical disease malaria once killed millions of people. Then it was discovered that it could be treated with quinine, extracted from the bark of South America's cinchona tree. Quinine also gives the bitter flavor in tonic water.

How did feverfew get its name?
"Feverfew" comes from the plant's Latin name *febrifuga*, which means driving away fever, and it was once thought an effective treatment of fever. It is still used to alleviate headaches today.

What is ginseng?
Ginseng is a plant related to ivy, prized in China for 5,000 years. Its powdered root helps relieve tiredness, and is said to relieve kidney disease and headaches.

Why did women put deadly nightshade in their eyes?
Deadly nightshade has poisonous, red berries. The juice of these berries is used to make the drug atropine, which makes the pupil bigger for eye examinations. In the Middle Ages, women put this juice in their eyes to make their pupils wider and more attractive, which is why the plant is also called "belladonna," from the Italian for beautiful woman.

◀ **Medicinal plants**
In the past many herbs were grown for their medicinal properties, and scholars wrote huge books listing the healing qualities of thousands of plants. One of the most famous was "The Complete Herbal" of Englishman Nicholas Culpeper (1616-1654). Today, doctors are more skeptical about the value of all these herbs. But many important drugs are based on plants, and scientists are discovering more and more all the time.

QUIZ

1. Oranges are good for preventing colds: true or false?
2. The coca in Coca-Cola is the same coca plant that the dangerous drug cocaine comes from: true or false?
3. Coffee beans contain the stimulating drug caffeine: true or false?
4. Is someone who studies plant medicine: a) a vegetarian b) a herbalist c) a plantain?
5. The wild yam–a bit like a turnip–helps with birth control: true or false?
6. Poison ivy is a type of clover: true or false?
7. Rubbing beet on the skin cures acne: true or false?
8. Lungwort gets its name because it is good for lung problems: true or false?

Answers
1. True 2. True; Coca-cola originally contained coca and cola, a nut that contains the pick-me-up caffeine 3. True 4. b) 5. True 6. False 7. False – but it makes all your face equally red! 8. True

193

Plants for materials

What kinds of materials can plants be used for?

PLANTS PROVIDE A HUGE range of materials, used for all kinds of purposes. The most important is wood for building and paper, perhaps, but there is also cotton for clothes, cork for wine bottles, oils, rubber, dyes, rope and string, and much more besides.

▲ Cotton head
Many of our clothes are made from cotton—or cotton mixed with man-made fibers. Cotton is a natural fiber that comes from the cotton flower, a plant that grows in warm regions. Its seed pods or "bolls" hold a dense mass of fluffy fibers, which can be separated into strands of cotton "lint." It is the lint from which cotton cloth is woven.

What plants make paper?
Most paper is made from wood pulped into a soft white mush. Many conifers are planted especially for paper. But natural forests are also a source. The main trees are spruce and pine, but aspen, poplar, and eucalyptus are used too. In south Asia, paper may be made from bamboo. Paper can also be made from grasses, straw, and sugarcane.

What trees make wood?
All trees are woody, but we call wood for making things from timber. Timber is either softwood or hardwood. Softwood comes from fast-growing conifers like pine, larch, fir, and spruce, which grow in colder places. Hardwood is from slow-growing, broad-leaved trees such as oak. It also comes from tropical trees like mahogany.

▲ Reed hut
In the past, people made the most of plants that were available locally. Some of the first boats and houses were made from reeds pulled from marshes. The Ancient Egyptians and South Americans made boats of weed. The Marsh Arabs of southern Iraq still do.

▶ Wooden houses
When most European people still lived in the countryside, before the Industrial Revolution of 200 years ago, only the houses of the very rich were built mainly of brick or stone. Most ordinary houses were built with timber frames and even walls, and were often roofed by thatches made from reeds and straw.

Life all around: Plants

▶ **Plant carrier**
When tankers carry oil, the fuel we use to run cars and fire power stations, they are in fact carrying the ancient remains of plants and animals.

What are fossil fuels?

Fossil fuels are fuels such as coal, oil, and natural gas, made mainly from the remains of plants that died long ago. The remains were buried underground and gradually squeezed and concentrated into fuels over millions of years. Coal was made from giant ferns that grew in huge swamps 300 million years ago; oil from tiny plants and animals that lived in warm seas.

How do plants warm houses and run cars?

Plants provide 80% of all our fuels—for running cars, keeping houses, warm and generating power. In developing countries, most people cook and keep warm by burning wood they gather from forests and shrubs. In Brazil, they run cars not on gasoline but on a fuel like diesel, tapped from the copaiba tree. In North America and many other places in the world, the main fuels are fossil fuel—that is, coal, oil, and natural gas.

Quiz

1 How do plants give plastics?
2 Where does mahogany come from?
3 What plant is sunflower oil made from?
4 Cork comes from the sea: true or false?
5 Does ivory come from a plant or an animal?
6 What connects bicycle wheels with tropical plants?
7 What color dye did Ancient Britons make from the leaves of the yellow flower woad?
8 Why does a madder plant make you redder?

Answers
1. Most plastics are made from either oil or coal. 2. Tropical rain forests. 3. The seeds of the sunflower. 4. False; cork comes from the bark of the cork-oak tree. 5. Animal; the elephant. 6. The tires are made of rubber which comes originally from the sap of the rubber tree. 7. Blue. 8. Madder is a flower which gives a red dye.

195

Woodland plants

What are woodland plants?

WOODLANDS are the home for plants that prefer the shady conditions under trees to full sunlight. There are spring flowers such as bluebells and primroses, summer flowers such as foxgloves and rosebay willowherb, shrubs such as brambles and hawthorn, as well as ferns, mosses, and fungi.

▼ Woodland plants
This picture shows just some of the many wildflowers and other plants that grow on the woodland floor. Although all the flowers are shown in bloom here, they do not all bloom at the same time. Each has its season, keeping the floor alive with color for many months of the year.

Why do primroses bloom in spring?

Like many flowers of deciduous woodlands, primroses bloom in spring before the leaves have grown thick on the trees, so that they get plenty of sunshine. Many other woodland flowers bloom in spring for the same reason, including wood anemones, oxlips, daffodils, lesser celandines, bluebells, early purple orchids, and dog's mercury. It is flowers like these that give the woodland floor a colorful carpet every spring.

196

Life all around: Plants

Why are dead trees good news?
When big trees die and come crashing down through the branches, they creating a clearing in the wood called a glade. Here sunlight can reach the woodland floor again, allowing all kinds of plants to sprout anew, including flowers such as foxgloves and rosebay willowherb and all kinds of fungi, such as fly agaric, which thrive on the rotting wood.

What plant has two different flowers?
Wood sorrel has a big spring flower to attract the bees that spread its pollen, and another smaller flower in summer to make seeds.

Which woodland plant is good for a kiss?
At Christmas, many people still hang up a sprig of mistletoe and kiss beneath it. Mistletoe is a parasitic plant with white berries which clings to trees such as apples, hawthorns, poplars, and willows and puts its roots into them. The custom goes back to the druids, the white-robed priests of Ancient Britain more than 2,000 years ago, who used to cut down mistletoe with a golden sickle to use in their sacred rites.

What is a coppice?
Since early times, people living in woodland areas have cut down trees to allow new, straight shoots to grow through. This is called coppicing, and ensured a good supply of straight poles for fencing and making tools.

Are fruits seeds?
No, they develop from the flower's ovary—and the hard pips inside are the seeds. Juicy fruits such as berries are called "true fruits" because they are made from the flower's ovaries alone. Apples and pears are "false" fruits because only the core is made from the ovary. Plums and cherries are "drupes" in which there are no pips, but the seed is held in a hard shell.

◀ **Woodland plants: key**
1. Lords and ladies
2. Wood anemones
3. Honeysuckle
4. Fly agaric
5. Wood Blewit
6. Bluebells
7. Orchid
8. Primrose
9. Rhododendron

QUIZ

1. What poison do foxgloves contain a) arsenic b) cyanide c) digitalis?
2. What trees are used to make baseball bats?
3. King Alfred's cake fungus gets its name because it looks like burned buns: true or false?
4. What is a bloody cranesbill?
5. Fungus sharpens knives: true or false?
6. In spring, the faint ringing of bluebells can be heard in woods: true or false?
7. Elizabethan lords used lords and ladies for a) cooking b) stiffening their collars c) smoking?
8. Ferns are the world's oldest trees: true or false?

Answers
1. c) 2. Hickory 3. True 4. A crimson flower 5. True; the razor strop fungus was used to sharpen razors 6. False 7. b) 8. True; there were forests of ferns 300 million years ago

Tropical plants

What makes tropical plants different?

THE TROPICS ARE WARM nearly all the time, and in the rain forests there is abundant moisture. The combination creates almost ideal conditions for plant growth, and the forests are not only lush but contain an astonishing variety of plants—including some of the world's most spectacular and strange.

▲ The Rafflesia has no leaves, and the only part of the plant above ground is the huge, blotchy red and white bloom. It is a parasite, and beneath the ground is a tangle of thread-like roots growing inside the roots of lianas and gaining nourishment from them.

What is the world's biggest flower?

A single bloom of the Rafflesia of Southeast Asia can be 3 feet (90cm) across and weigh 15 pounds (7kg) or more. The titan arum is 10 feet (3m) tall, but is made of many small flowers, not a single bloom like Rafflesia.

What is the world's worst smelling flower?

The Rafflesia may not only be the world's biggest flower; it may also be the foulest smelling. Some people call it the stinking corpse lily and say it smells like rotting meat. The stench is said to draw the flies it needs to pollinate.

How many plants are there in the rain forest?

The rain forests are the world's richest habitats, containing over 40 percent of all plant species. No one knows exactly how many different plants there are, but botanists counted more than 180 species of tree alone in one hectare (2.4 acres) of the Malaysian forest.

Do plants grow on trees?

The forest is so dense that to get nearer sunlight, small plants called epiphytes wrap their roots around high branches and grow there. The most common epiphytes are bromeliads.

What is the strongest rope in the jungle?

The liana is a vine or creeper that dangles down from trees in the rain forest. It is so strong that monkeys and other forest animals can use lianas to swing through the trees. The vine is actually a very long stem. The liana's roots are in the ground and its leaves are in the sun above the trees.

What are the world's largest leaves?

Palm tree leaves can be very big. The leaves of raffia palms and the Amazonian bamboo palm can grow up to 65 feet (20m) long.

▶ What makes the rain forest so rich in plant life is that plants don't just grow in the soil. Trees are festooned not only with dangling creepers and vines, but many plants that actually grow in the tree, including bromeliads, orchids, ferns, and mosses—and "air plants," which get enough moisture from the air alone.

What plants have their own water tanks?

Some bromeliads grow high up on trees and their roots cannot reach water from the ground. Instead, they grow a tight cluster of leaves which traps a pond of rainwater.

What are the layers in a tropical forest?

The top layer is the "emergent" layer—a few trees, towering above the rest, up to 200 feet (60m) tall. Beneath them, 100-150 feet (30-50m) above the ground, is the dense "canopy" of leaves and branches of big trees. In the gloom beneath is the "understory" where small trees and shrubs grow.

Why are rain forests threatened?

Every year an area of rain forest the size of Belgium is burned or cut down to make way for grazing land—or simply for the wood. Once cut down, it takes centuries to grow again—if it ever does—because the forest's richness lies not in the soil, which is easily washed away once exposed, but in the trees themselves.

QUIZ

1. Is the world's biggest rain forest in a) Brazil b) India c) Australia?
2. The world's fastest growing plant is Burma's giant bamboo. In a day, it can grow a) 1 inch (2.5cm) b) 7 inches (17cm) c) 18 inches (46cm)?
3. Flowers grow on tree trunks in the jungle: true or false?
4. There is a plant in the jungle that eats frogs: true or false?
5. There is a plant in the jungle that strangles trees: true or false?
6. There are exploding cucumbers in the jungle: true or false?
7. Lianas can strangle monkeys: true or false?

Answers
1. a) 2. c) 3. True 4. True; the venus flytrap does 5. True; the strangler fig does 6. True; the squirting cucumber shoots seeds up to 26 feet (8m) 7. False; except by accident

199

Water plants

What plants grow in water?

The very first plants developed in water, then gradually colonized the land as they evolved. Since then many new plants–called aquatic plants–have learned to live in water, including flowers like water lilies, water hyacinths, and grass-like plants such as reeds, rushes, and papyrus.

Do plants float?

Yes, the leaves of flowers like the water lily and hyacinth float on the surface. But the leaves are on long, flexible stalks that reach down to the lake or riverbed, and the roots are firmly anchored in the mud. Even so, they cannot survive in fast-moving water.

Why don't floating plants sink?

Because some plants have air sacks in their stems and leaves. Others, like the water lily, have leaves that turn up at the edges so that they float like boats.

What is the world's biggest water plant?

The leaves of the giant lily of the Amazon in South America grow 6 feet (1.8m) across and can bear the weight of a child.

What water plant did the Pharaohs write on?

The papyrus is a giant reed that grows along the River Nile. The Ancient Egyptians discovered 5,000 years ago that the pith of papyrus stems could be used to make paper. Although paper is now made from wood pulp, we owe the word to the papyrus reed.

Why are water hyacinths a nuisance?

The purple flowers of the floating water hyacinth are attractive, but the plants can spread rapidly, choking waterways and blocking the path of boats.

Life all around: Plants

How do river plants cope with the current?
To survive in anything but the very slowest-flowing rivers, water plants have to anchor themselves with firm roots to save themselves from being washed away, and their leaves must be feathery, like those of the fanwort, to avoid offering resistance to the water. The river water crowfoot can survive in quite fast-flowing streams because its leaves are streamlined.

What water plant eats bugs?
The bladderwort is a plant of swamps that develops underwater bladders on its stem. When an insect such as a water flea touches a trigger on one of these bladders, the bladder springs open and sucks in the flea with the inrushing water.

Why don't all lakes have plants?
Because the chemical composition of the water varies. Lakes filled by water draining from lime-rich soils tend to to be rich in plant life. Those near acid soil are more sterile.

▼ **Water life**
Slow-flowing rivers and shallows in lakes are often densely packed with all kinds of water plants. Most plants are rooted to the bed, but a few get all the nutrients they need directly from the water. Some plants are hidden underwater. Some float on the surface. Plants such as rushes and reeds are called emergents because they grow up out of the water.
Key: 1. Bulrushes 2. Frogbit 3. Water crowfoot 4. Water lily 5. Yellow flag iris 6. Water plantain

QUIZ

1 What water flower was adopted as a symbol by French and English kings?
2 What important food crop is grown in water in China?
3 Do lakes last forever?
4 How do water plants keep out the rain in parts of England?
5 The Amazonian Indians make cartwheels out of water-lily leaves: true or false?
6 What water plants did the Egyptians make boats from?
7 What water plants was Moses found among?
8 The pollen of most water plants spreads by floating on the water: true or false?

Answers
1. The yellow flag iris or fleur-de-lys 2. Rice 3. No, most are eventually choked by plants and silt 4. Sedges are used for thatching rooves 5. False 6. Reed 7. Bulrushes, though the famous Victorian painting by Alma-Tadema wrongly shows reedmace 8. True

Grassland plants

Are grasslands all grass?

AT FIRST GLANCE grasslands look as uniform and unvaried as a lawn–just mile upon mile of green grass. But a closer look reveals that there are, for a start, many types of grass, including tussock grass, marram grass, meadow grass, blue grass, and many more–and mixed in with the grasses are a rich variety of herbs and flowers.

▲ **Rokerboom**
There is too little water for most ordinary trees in tropical grasslands like the veld of South Africa. So, like the baobab of the savanna, the rokerboom tree has developed a huge swollen trunk that acts as a water store to help it survive through dry periods.

▼ **South American pampas**
The pampas stretches across Argentina, Uruguay, and southeastern Brazil, forming the largest area of temperate grassland in the southern hemisphere. Many parts of the pampas are dominated by tussock grasses like those seen in the foreground.

Do grasslands have any other name?
They have special names in every continent. In North America they are called prairies. In South America, they are called pampas. In northern Asia, they are the steppes. In South Africa, they are the veld. In Australia, the bush. In Britain, grasslands occur mostly on chalk hills and are called downs.

Where do grasslands occur?
Grasslands occur all over the world where there is only moderate rainfall—mostly in the heart of continents, far from the sea—or where the ground is so dry and well-drained that only grass will grow.

Why don't trees grow in grasslands?
Because trees need a lot of water. Grasslands are too dry. The few trees that do grow in grasslands, such as the baobab and the rokerboom, have immensely thick trunks that are very good at retaining moisture.

What is meadow grass?
Meadow grass is the most common of all grasses, found in grasslands all over the world. This is the grass that people use in lawns. It is almost always green because although each plant lasts only a few years, they continually produce fresh seeds, so new grass is springing up all the time.

Life all around: Plants

▶ **Acacias**
Acacia trees, sometimes known as thorn trees because of their prickly thorns, are the most widespread trees of the African savanna, and their flat tops are a distinctive part of the savanna landscape. Their partnership with ants helps them survive. The acacia's leaf stalks secrete a nectar, which attracts ants. In return, the ants attack any animal that tries to browse on the leaves. They also help to spread the acacia's seeds.

Why do farmers like rye grass?
Rye grass is the grass that many farmers grow for cows to graze on, and to make hay for feeding livestock from. Typically, new pastures are sown with either pure rye grass or mixed rye and clover.

What wild flowers grow on grasslands?
Vetches, trefoils, worts, orchids, and various herbs are among the many flowers native to grasslands.

Which garden flowers come from grasslands?
Flowers from the prairies of North America include the coneflower, the sunflower, and the blazing star. From the grasslands of Europe and Asia come flowers such as adonis, anemones, delphiniums, and scabious.

How did scabious get its name?
The juice was said to cure scabies and other skin diseases.

QUIZ

1. What animals are raised on the pampas?
2. What large animal used to roam the prairies?
3. What animals are raised on Australian grasslands?
4. Which U.S. state is famous for its bluegrass a) California b) South Carolina c) Kentucky?
5. What is a billabong?
6. What color is prairie soil a) brown b) black c) yellow?
7. On which continent would you find a gaucho?
8. What is a big cattle farm on the prairies called?
9. What was a prairie schooner?
10. What grass would you find on sand dunes a) sedge grass b) rye grass c) marram grass?

Answers
1. Cattle 2. Bison 3. Sheep 4. c) 5. A lake in Australia 6. b) 7. On the pampas in South America; a gaucho is a cowboy 8. A ranch 9. A settler's covered wagon 10. c)

203

Desert plants

Do any plants grow in the desert?

A DESERT IS A PLACE where very little rain falls–but only rarely is there no rain at all, and wherever there is a little moisture, some especially adapted hardy plants, such as cacti, will survive.

How do plants find water in the desert?

When there is no water on the surface, plants can often find moisture deep underground by growing long roots. Mesquite roots grow as deep as 30 feet (9m), and may be 150 feet (43m) deep.

How do plants save water?

Wherever water is short, plants have developed ways of saving water. Other plants lose a great deal of water by evaporation from their leaves. So desert plants usually have tough, waxy leaves—and plants that live in extreme conditions cut down their leaves to a minimum.

▶ **Saguaro**
The saguaro of the southwest states and Mexico is the biggest cactus, growing up to 60 feet (18m) tall and 2 feet (60cm) thick.

What plant amputates its own branches?

The branches and trunk of the quiver tree are filled with a soft fiber that can store water. But in severe drought, it seals off branches to save moisture loss through the leaves. The branch end looks like an amputated limb.

Life all around: Plants

▼ **Cactus in flower**
Cacti have to pollinate just like every other flowering plant and so every few years they produce big colourful blooms in order to attract insects quickly.

What is a window plant?
Some plants, such as pebble plants, escape the drying heat of the desert by growing partly underground. But the window plant grows almost entirely underground. It is like a cigar poked down into the ground. All that is visible on the surface is the end, a little green button—the plant's window to the sun.

▲ **Oasis**
In places in the Sahara desert in Africa, water-bearing rocks are exposed at the surface, creating an oasis where moisture-loving plants such as palm trees can flourish.

How do cacti survive in Death Valley?
Cacti are the most impressive of all desert survivors. They are remarkable plants that live in American deserts. They have no leaves and a very thick skin, so water loss is cut to a minimum. Their fat stems are able to hold huge quantities of water, which is why they are called succulents.

Why is cactus prickly?
Lush vegetation is so rare in the desert that animals eat anything available. So plants such as cacti, prickly pears, and thorn bushes, grow prickles to protect themselves from being eaten.

◄ **Blooms in the desert**
When it rains in the desert, seeds that have lain dormant during the long drought suddenly burst into brief bloom.
Key: 1. Saguaro 2. Evening primrose 3. Prickly pear

QUIZ

1 Is a half-man a) a mythical camel b) a desert monkey c) a prickly desert plant?

2 How much does the Joshua tree of the Mojave Desert grow in a year: a) 0.5 inch (1cm) b) 4 inches (10cm) c) 40 inches (100cm)?

3 What happens to the shriveled brown leaves of a resurrection tree after it rains?

4 Where do some owls live in the deserts?

5 What is the hottest desert?

6 How often does it rain in Chile's Atacama desert– every a) 5 years b) 20 years c) 400 years?

Answers
1. c) 2. b) 3. The leaves turn green 4. In holes in cacti 5. The Sahara, where it often gets to 110°F (43°C) 6. c)

205

Mountain plants

What plants live on mountains?

THE WEATHER GETS COLDER, windier, and wetter the higher you go up a mountain. Some mountaintops are even permanently covered with snow. So the plants that grow on mountains have to be hardy, and they usually get smaller the higher you go, varying from big trees such as conifers on the lower slopes to tiny flowers, low grasses, and mosses higher up.

▼ Alpine flowers: key
1. Alpine bluebell 2. Alpine gentian
3. Mountain avens 4. Edelweiss
5. Purple saxifrage

What is the timber line?

Above a certain height, it gets too cold for trees to grow well. This is the timber line. It varies according to local conditions, but gets lower toward the poles. It is about 9,200 feet (2,800m) in the Alps.

Can plants survive on rock faces?

The purple saxifrage and starry saxifrage have tough, penetrating roots that exploit cracks and crevices, enabling them to colonize the narrowest rocky ledges. Their roots anchor so firmly that they were once thought to be able to actually crack the rock. The word saxifrage means "stone breaker."

Why do some alpine flowers have big blooms?

There are few insects to pollinate flowers high up on the mountainside, so flowers such as purple saxifrage and the snow gentian produce big colorful blooms to ensure that insects don't waste time searching for them.

Life all around: Plants

▶ **Edelweiss**
The edelweiss can grow at very high altitudes in the Alps, sprouting out from cracks in the rocks, because its blooms and leaves are covered in a coat of wooly hairs that protect it from the cold.

How do alpine flowers cope with a short summer?
High up near the snowline, the time available for growing after the snow melts in spring is very short. So the alpine snowbell makes the most of each summer by developing its flowerbuds the previous summer. They lie dormant through the winter under a protective blanket of snow, ready to burst through at the first thaw.

How do plants survive in the cold?
Plants have evolved various different ways of coping with the cold. Some cover themselves with a coat of wooly hairs, like edelweiss, or have thick, waxy leaves. The Himalayan saussurea is almost all wool. Others, such as the daisies of Tasmania, pack their stems into a tight padded cushion.

Can plants freeze?
Few plants can survive being frozen, but many can thrive under the snow. Snow acts like a blanket, keeping ice and wind at bay, and saves the plant from being frozen to death. Alpine grasses stay alive and green under the snow, ready to grow again as soon as it melts.

Where are there dandelions as big as trees?
On Mt. Kenya in Africa, baking daytime sun and icy nights have created giant groundsels. Elsewhere, groundsel is a small plant similar to dandelions—but on Mt. Kenya it grows more than 30 feet (9m) tall! The European lobelia is a tiny plant too—but on Mt. Kenya, lobelias grow huge.

◀ **Alpine flowers**
Above the timber line, many small flowers thrive, including cinquefoil, stonecrop, and campion, besides those shown.

QUIZ

1. What is the snow-line?
2. It gets 48°F (9°C) colder for every 150m you climb: true or false?
3. Do fir trees lose their leaves in winter?
4. In the Alps, which side of the mountain is warmest: the north or the south?
5. Where might you find alpine flowers in an ordinary garden?
6. Is gentian violet a) an antiseptic b) an artist's colour c) a uniform?
7. In Switzerland, is edelweiss a symbol of a) good luck b) spring c) purity?
8. Edelweiss means in German a) lazy good-for-nothing b) snow bell c) noble white?
9. Is Mt Kenya in the tropics?
10. Which berries grow on mountains a) gooseberries b) blueberries c) bilberries d) strawberries e) crowberries?

Answers
1. The lower limit of permanent snow 2. False; 34°F (1°C) 3. No 4. The south, because it faces the sun 5. A rockery 6. a) 7. c) 8. c) 9. Yes 10. b), c) and e)

Arctic plants

Do plants grow in the Arctic?

FOR NINE MONTHS of the year, the Arctic is bitterly cold and dark. But for a few months in summer, it is daylight most of the time, and in this brief respite from the worst of Arctic weather, a surprising variety of plants–more than 900 species–spring up.

Why does it never get dark in the Arctic summer?
In summer, the sun sets for only a few hours in the middle of the night. This happens because the Earth is tilted over. As the Earth makes its year-long journey round the Sun, the part of the Earth tilted toward the Sun gradually shifts north, then south. In the Arctic summer, the Earth has reached the point in its journey where the North Pole is tilting most toward the Sun.

Why are trees shorter than daisies?
Willow trees grow in the Arctic, but because of the fierce Arctic wind, they never grow more than 4 inches (10cm) tall. Instead, they spread out along the ground.

Why do Arctic plants like skulls?
Nutriment is so scarce in the Arctic that plants take what there is. So when an animal such as a musk ox dies, seeds make the most of its corpse, and Arctic flowers often spring up inside the skull.

How do some plants melt snow?
Some plants have dark leaves and stems. When the sun shines, their dark color soaks up the sun's warmth and melts the snow.

▶ Arctic bloom: key
1. Saxifrage
2. Snowbell
3. Avens
4. Willowherb
5. Saxifrage
6. Stonecrop
7. Arctic poppy

Life all around: Plants

How do plants cope without bees to pollinate them?
There are so few bees and butterflies in the Arctic that many Arctic flowers find other ways of spreading their pollen. Some flowers, like mustard, rely on the wind. Others rely on flies, and so only put out yellow or white flowers, since flies are color blind.

What is the tundra?
Tundra is a region so cold that no large trees grow—only dwarf trees, shrubs such as heathers, grasses, and other small plants. There is a vast area of tundra stretching through the north of Canada, Siberia, and Scandinavia and into Greenland. There is tundra on high mountains too.

Why are many Arctic plants evergreen?
Leaves grown the previous summer are ready to make the most of the brief summer. Over the winter, they are protected by dead leaves.

Do plants grow in Antarctica?
Most of Antarctica is covered in snow and ice all year round, so very few plants can survive here, unlike the Arctic. Yet there are fungi and lichen growing within 300 miles (500km) of the South Pole, and two species of flowering plant are native to Antarctica.

Why is snow pink in Antarctica?
Some algae live in the snow, just below the surface, but the UV rays from the sun are so bright in snow that the algae must protect itself with red pigment. The red algae turns the snow pink.

◀ **Arctic bloom**
Full-size trees will not grow in the Arctic tundra, but the brief summer sees it bursting into life. Grasses and sedges, mosses and lichens thrive, along with various small flowers such as saxifrages, avens, and Arctic poppies, especially adapted to survive the cold.

QUIZ

1. Gentian is used to make a bitter tonic for stomach complaints—true or false?
2. Which flower blooms nearest the North Pole a) snowdrop b) bluebell c) Arctic poppy?
3. Lichen growing in Antarctica may be the world's oldest living things. Are they a) 1,000 years old b) 10,000 years old c) 100,000 years old?
4. In Antarctica, the temperature can drop to a) 5°F (-15°C) b) -128°F (-89°C) c) -423°F (-253°C)?
5. Is the North Pole in the Arctic or Antarctic?

Answers
1. True 2. c) 3. b) 4. b) 5. The Arctic

What creature turns green with rage?

Why do elephants have trunks?

How do seals keep warm?

Why does a woodpecker peck wood?

Why does a beaver slap its tail on the water?

Which bird never sees the sunset?

What's the noisiest creature in the Amazon jungle?

What frog makes Indian arrows deadly?

Why is a flamingo pink?

What bird has a beak as big as its body?

Animals

212 Rain-forest animals
214 Woodland animals
216 Cold forest animals
218 Animals of cold seas
220 African animals
222 Wetland animals
224 Mountain animals
226 Desert animals
228 Seashore life
230 Australian animals
232 Freshwater animals
234 Grassland animals
236 Deep sea animals

Do bears hug?

How does a giraffe drink?

What is a female deer called?

Rain-forest animals

What animals live in rain forests?

THE LUSH, WARM RAIN FORESTS of the tropics are home to more species of animal than any other habitat in the world. Huge numbers of small, tree-dwelling creatures especially live here—scores of different reptiles such as snakes and lizards, hundreds of different kinds of bird, and perhaps more than a million different insects.

What creature turns green with rage?

The chameleon is a strange tree lizard with swivelling eyes, a long tail that coils up and an amazingly long sticky tongue that darts out to catch flies. But what is strangest of all is that the chameleon can change its skin color, either when it is in a certain mood—in a rage, for instance—or to camouflage itself by blending in perfectly with its background.

What frog makes Indian arrows deadly?

The sweat of the poison-arrow tree frogs of Central and South America is deadly to humans. Local Indians collect the poison by holding the frogs over a fire to make them sweat, then scraping the sweat off into a jar. If they want their arrows to kill, they dip the tips in the poison jar.

▲ Toucan
The toucan uses its big beak to fight rival males and to eat fruit and birds' eggs. But no one knows just why it is so colorful.

◄ Poisonous frog
Some tree frogs like the kokoi and the poison-arrow have a poison much more deadly than any snake. Their bright colors act as a warning.

Life all around: Animals

What is the slowest creature in the jungle?
Hanging upside down in the trees, the three-toed tree sloth takes a minute to lope just 10 feet (3m). On the ground, it can manage only 6 feet (1.8m).

What's the noisiest creature in the Amazon jungle?
Howler monkeys have a sound box in their throats that resonates very loudly. When a small group howls together, the noise can be heard over 2 miles (3km) away.

What's a prehensile tail?
Monkeys in the New World—the Americas—often have prehensile tails. Monkeys in the Old World—Asia and Africa—don't. They are muscular tails that can curl to grip things like a hand, which is very useful for swinging through trees.

What's a jaguar?
A jaguar is the biggest cat in the Americas. It looks like a leopard, but it is larger and has a shorter tail. Its spot pattern is also slightly different.

▼ **The reticulated python**
This python, which lives in the forests of Asia, grows up to 33 feet (10m) long, and can swallow a goat whole—then not eat for a month.

▲ **Three-toed sloth**
Sloths live in the jungles of South America. They live in trees, climbing and hanging upside down, using their long claws as hooks.

What bird has a beak as big as its body?
The toco toucan has a huge, brightly colored beak 9 inches (23cm) long—longer than its body. It doesn't overbalance because the beak is full of holes inside and so is very lightweight.

What snakes squeeze victims to death?
"Constrictor" snakes like pythons wrap their coils around a victim and squeeze until they suffocate.

QUIZ

1. The sloth moves so slowly that plants grow on it: true or false?
2. What is the world's smallest bird?
3. What is the world's loudest bird a) the great bittern b) the golden eagle c) the Indian peacock?
4. How much poison from the kokoi frog's sweat does it take to kill a man: a) 1 fluid oz. (27ml) b) 1 pint (450ml) c) 0.00001 oz. (0.0003 gm)
5. Cockatoos have been heard talking to each other in English: true or false?
6. Victorians used blue morpho butterflies as broaches: true or false?

Answers
1. True; algae grows in its fur, making it look green. 2. The bee hummingbird is just 2.1 inches (57mm) long 3. c) 4. c) 5. False; they can mimic a few words but not converse 6. True

213

Woodland animals

What creatures live in woods?

MANY DIFFERENT ANIMALS live in woodlands in the temperate zone, in between the tropics and the poles. The leaf litter beneath the trees teems with tiny creatures—worms, millipedes, ants, and other insects—all of which draw predators such as spiders, shrews, and mice. The trees themselves provide a haven for many insects, birds, and small mammals.

Why does a woodpecker peck wood?

A woodpecker clings to tree trunks, propped up by its stiff tail, and rapidly hammers its long, powerful beak against the trunk. The idea is to bore a hole for nesting or to get at insects and grubs, which the woodpecker licks out with its long, wormlike tongue. The tip of the tongue is barbed so that the bird can harpoon tiny insects deep inside narrow tunnels.

Where do badgers live?

Badgers live in families in extensive burrows called setts, which they dig out with their broad, powerful forepaws. American badgers live in the dry scrub of southwestern states. The smaller European badgers have their setts in woodlands, but they may also be in fields or even dumps.

What do foxes eat?

Foxes eat all kinds of food. They often hunt at night for small animals such as voles and rabbits. But they also eat beetles, worms and berries. They are scavengers too, and in recent years, foxes have been seen in towns going through trashcans for scraps. Occasionally, when food is scarce they kill farmers' chickens.

Why are foxes cunning?

Foxes are intelligent hunters with very keen senses of smell, sight, and hearing. These senses warn foxes about threats, helping them to escape from attackers. Farmers whose chickens have been stolen are the first to call them cunning as they cleverly elude capture.

◄ **Red fox**
The fox is rather like a small dog, but the red fox, with its russet coat, large ears, bright amber eyes, and big, bushy tail, is unmistakable.

Life all around: Animals

▶ **Fallow deer**
Herds of wild fallow deer have lived for centuries in the English royal forests such as the New Forest, where only the king and his courtiers could hunt them.

What are antlers?
Antlers are the hard, spiky branches of bone on a deer's head. They are used as weapons like horns, but antlers are different from horns and only male deer have them. Horns are permanent bony growths covered in horn, but antlers are covered in a hairy skin called velvet, and grow then drop off once a year.

What happens in the woods at night?
Many small mammals, such as shrews, moles, squirrels, mice, weasels, stoats, ferrets, and foxes, go hunting. So too do night-flying birds such as the nightjar, which sleeps camouflaged on the ground by day. And so does the tawny owl, which preys on the small mammals.

What are the smallest woodland carnivores?
Weasels, mink and wolverines are very fierce, despite their small size, and are able to kill animals such as rabbits that are much larger.

▶ **Wood mouse**
Like many woodland mammals, wood mice go into a sleepy stage, almost like hibernation, in winter. This helps them save energy when food is scarce.

QUIZ

1 What is a female fox called?
2 What is the biggest woodland creature?
3 Do chipmunks build nests in trees?
4 What is the special long winter sleep of animals called?
5 What animal leaves tracks in the snow seeming to come down from a tree?
6 What is the smallest woodland mammal?
7 What is a female deer called?
8 An opossum is what type of mammal?
9 What is the wood mouse's most deadly enemy?

Answers
1. Vixen 2. Red deer 3. No—under twigs and stones 4. Hibernation 5. Squirrel 6. Pygmy shrew 7. Doe 8. Marsupial 9. Weasel

215

Cold forest animals

What animals live in cold forests?

THE FOREST TREES OF THE COLD NORTH are mainly conifers like pines and many of the woodland creatures feed on pine leaves and cones, including chipmunks, crossbills, and insects such as pine-shoot moths, and animals that prey on them, such as pine martens, owls, wolves, and bears.

What do bears eat?
Brown bears eat almost anything. Fruits and berries, honey straight from bees' nests, fish, and carrion (carcasses left by other animals). They also hunt small mammals. They can even catch fish by scooping them out of the river with their paw. The technical name for such wide-ranging eaters is omnivore.

Do bears hug?
The idea that bears hug their victims to death is an old wives' tale. They usually kill any animals they hunt with a swift blow or "cuff" from their huge, strong forepaws—or with a bite from their sharp teeth.

◀ **Big and brown**
Bears usually move around on all fours. But they can often stand up to reach berries in trees. A standing male brown bear is a full seven feet tall—quite a bit taller than a man.

▲ **Raccoon**
Raccoons live near water because they often feed on frogs, crabs, water snails, and small fish.

What is the woodland bandit?
The raccoon of the forests of North America looks like a bandit because of the distinctive black eye mask across its white face. Equally distinctive is its big, bushy black and white striped tale.

Do pine martens live in pines?
Pine martens are small creatures like weasels. They don't actually live in pine trees, but they are incredibly agile climbers—one of the few predators that can catch a squirrel in a tree.

Life all around: Animals

What's a moose yard?
In deep snow, a moose can easily be overcome by a marauding puma. So when herds of moose get together in winter, they trample out big flat areas of snow called "yards." Here they can get a good enough footing to give them a fighting chance of using their antlers and hooves on an attacker.

Why does a beaver slap it's tail on the water?
To warn other beavers of approaching danger.

Do reindeer pull sleighs?
Reindeer are one of the longest domesticated of all creatures. The people of Siberia were using them to pull sleighs and for riding more than 7,000 years ago.

◀ **The winter trek**
In winter, when the weather in the cold north gets bitter and forage gets poor, reindeer begin a long trek to the south. In the past, they used to migrate in herds a quarter of a million strong.

▶ **Big feller**
Beavers can bring down literally scores of small trees to build dams and their homes on the river, gnawing through them with their two razor-sharp front teeth.

QUIZ

1. What do they call a pine marten in Russia?
2. What's the difference between a reindeer and a caribou?
3. What's a beaver's home called?
4. Which animal has the biggest horns?
5. Why's a grizzly bear grizzly?
6. What's the difference between a moose and an elk?
7. What is a lynx?
8. Does a wolf really howl at the moon?

Answers
1. A sable 2. None; a caribou is the North American name for a reindeer 3. A lodge 4. A moose 5. It has grey hairs among the black 6. None; moose is the North American name for an elk 7. A small wild cat 8. No, but they do howl at night to communicate with the rest of the pack

217

Animals of cold seas

Big bird
The albatross is the world's largest seabird, more than 10 feet (3m) from wingtip to wingtip.

What animals live in the Arctic?

THE WEATHER GETS SO BITTERLY COLD in the Arctic that it is hard to imagine how any creatures can live there, yet a surprising number do–in the sea, including seals and whales; in the air, such as the Arctic tern; and on land, such as the polar bear, the Arctic fox, and the Arctic hare.

Which bird never sees the sunset?

The Arctic tern lives in the Arctic only during the summer when the sun never completely sets. At the end of the summer, it makes an incredible 12,000-mile (20,000-km) flight to the other end of the world to catch the summer in Antarctica, where it remains daylight for months on end too.

How does the snowshoe hare get its name?

The snowshoe hare, which goes white as snow in winter, gets its name from its huge feet, which act like snowshoes when it bounds easily across the softest snow. Long hair grows between the toes, both to stop the toes sinking into the snow, and to keep the hare's feet warm.

Are seals fish or mammals?

Despite their streamlined, fishlike shape, seals are warm-blooded mammals. Just like other mammals, they have babies that feed on their mother's milk.

How do seals keep warm?

On land, mammals rely on the air trapped in thick fur to keep them warm, but this is no good in the water. Seals have only a thin layer of fur, but they have, instead, a layer of fatty blubber under their skins up to 4 inches (10cm) thick.

Harp seal

Life all around: Animals

◀ **Ice birds**
Penguins are Antarctica's most distinctive inhabitants. Penguins can't fly, and they waddle ungainly on land, but they are agile swimmers, using their wings as flippers.

How do Emperor penguins keep their eggs warm?
Emperor penguins are the only birds to lay their eggs in the bitter Antarctic winter. They keep them warm by resting them on their feet, tucked under their belly.

Do all penguins live in the Antarctic?
All 18 species of penguin live in the southern hemisphere, and most live in or near Antarctica.

▼ **Seals and sea lions**
Seals and sea lions are different. Only sea lions have external ears and also back flippers that they can use to move about on land.

What is the biggest creature of cold seas?
The Blue whale, the biggest creature in the world, which grows more than 100 feet (30m) long and weighs from 90 to 180 tons.

How do whales communicate?
By clicks, whistles and low-pitch rumbles which echo hundreds of kilometres through the water. The humpback whale sings like this.

Sea lion

QUIZ

1 What is the biggest penguin?
2 What bird makes the longest migration?
3 What sea mammals have two long tusks?
4 What color do Arctic foxes go in winter?
5 What do seals eat?
6 How many kinds of animals breed in the Antarctic: a) 1 b) 8 c) 49?
7 What ox lives in the Arctic?
8 How do whales breathe out?
9 Which is the largest meat-eater in the Arctic?

Answers
1. Emperor penguin 2. Arctic Tern 3. Walrus 4. White 5. Mainly fish 6. b), four kinds of seal, two kinds of penguin, the southern skua, and the snow petrel 7. Musk ox 8. Through the blowhole on top of their heads 9. Polar bear

African animals

▲ Amboseli, Kenya
Many of Africa's most spectacular animals have been reduced almost to extinction by hunters who call them "Big Game." Now many animals are protected inside safari parks such as the Amboseli in the shadow of Mount Kilimanjaro.

How do lions hunt?
Although they sometimes attack young giraffes or weak buffaloes, lions' main prey is antelopes. Lions hunt silently, usually in small groups—lying in wait for the antelopes at waterholes or creeping stealthily through the grass. When they near their prey, they make a sudden sprint, then pounce, sinking their sharp fangs into their victim's neck. Meat is so nutritious that one kill is usually enough to last a lion for days.

What animals live in Africa?

AFRICA IS HOME TO SOME of the world's most spectacular animals. The tropical forest in the center is home to many different kinds of monkeys as well as apes such as the gorilla. In the bush country or savanna beyond live such magnificent creatures as elephants, lions, giraffes, rhinos, hippos, zebras, and many more.

Why do elephants have trunks?
An elephant uses its trunk for all kinds of different tasks. The trunk is used mainly for feeding and the elephant pulls off grasses and leaves with it and stuffs them in its mouth. But the elephant also uses the trunk to suck up water, which it then drinks or uses to spray itself clean. The trunk is the elephant's nose too, and an elephant may often put its trunk in the air to sniff the wind. The trunk is even used for caressing baby elephants.

▶ Big bird
Africa is home not only to the largest land mammal, the elephant, but the largest bird too—the ostrich. Ostriches can reach 8 feet (2.5m) tall. They can't fly, but they can run fast, and their long legs can inflict a hefty kick.

◀ Deadly huntress
Male lions with their big manes may look impressive, but it is the females, called lionesses, that do most of the hunting.

How can you tell an African elephant from an Asian elephant?
African elephants are generally bigger than Asian elephants. African elephants have much bigger ears and much longer tusks. The Asian elephant also has a slightly humped back and just one fingerlike lip on the end of its trunk, while the African has two. The African elephant lives on hot, dry plains, while the Asian lives in shady forests.

How tall is a giraffe?
A male giraffe can grow up to 18 feet (5.5m) tall, taller than any other animal. Its legs are long, and its neck is even longer. With such a long neck a giraffe can feed on leaves high in the trees that other animals can't reach.

How does a giraffe drink?
Its long legs and neck mean a giraffe has a long way to bend for a drink. So it has to either spread its front legs very wide or kneel right down—making it vulnerable to attack by lions.

◀ **Tall order**
Giraffes reach high branches with their long necks, but the leaves they eat aren't soft and succulent. Giraffes eat branches of thorn trees—prickles and all.

Can hippos swim?
A hippo spends most of its day in or near water, only coming out at night to feed on plants. Yet it cannot really swim. Instead it walks or runs along the riverbed, often at amazing speeds, only coming up for air occasionally.

What is a gnu?
A gnu or wildebeest is a large African antelope that migrates across the plains between waterholes in huge herds.

Why do zebras have stripes?
Zebras' stripes seem hard to miss. But in the shimmering heat of Africa, they act as camouflage, blurring the zebra's outline, like shadows of grass, especially when the zebra is moving slowly.

How many kinds of zebra are there?
Three: the common, the mountain, and Grevy's zebra. The Grevy is the biggest, and brays like an ass.

QUIZ

1. What's the world's fastest runner?
2. How fast can an ostrich fly?
3. What's a group of lions called?
4. What's the world's biggest mammal?
5. What animal has a horn on the end of its snout?
6. How can you tell a male lion from a female?
7. What's an okapi?
8. What are elephant's tusks made of?
9. Do zebras neigh like horses?

Answers
1. The cheetah, reaching speeds of up to 66 mph (110kp/h) 2. An ostrich can't fly at all 3. A pride 4. The Blue whale 5. A rhinoceros 6. An adult male has a big mane; a lioness has not 7. A relative of the giraffe 8. Ivory 9. No, they bark or bray.

Wetland animals

▲ **Cool crocodile**
Crocodiles adjust their lives to the weather, basking on the bank to warm up, but slipping into the water when it gets too hot.

What animals live in wetlands?

WETLANDS ARE AMONG THE WORLD'S most precious animal habitats, havens for many wild creatures. Not only are there big animals like crocodiles and alligators, but smaller creatures like coypus and voles, and numerous birds, insects and, of course, fish.

What's the difference between a crocodile and an alligator?

Alligators are generally rounder and fatter, with short, blunt snouts. Crocodiles are slightly thinner, and their snouts are longer and thinner. Crocodiles also have a fourth tooth on the lower jaw that can be seen when their mouths are shut.

Are crocodiles like dinosaurs?

Crocodiles may be the nearest thing to dinosaurs alive today. Many dinosaurs may have had the same scaly skin and creatures very like crocodiles lived in the early Triassic Period, 200 million years ago, when the dinosaurs first appeared. But dinosaur's legs were underneath, not sticking out to the side like a crocodile's. Some people believe that dinosaurs' nearest living relatives are birds.

Are there any other creatures like crocodiles?

Crocodiles belong to a group of animals called the crocodilians. Besides various species of crocodiles and alligators, the group includes smaller crocodile-like animals called caimans and gharials. Caimans have bony plates on their bellies. The gharial has a distinctive long, thin snout.

▼ **Wetland hunter**
Crocodiles live in the rivers and swamps of the tropics. They are fearsome hunters, with massive, snapping jaws—yet it is their tail that is most lethal. Crocodiles lie in wait in the shallows, looking for all the world like a log, until animals come to drink at the water. Then they make a sudden lunge at their victim, drag it into the water, and stun it with a blow from its tail, and drown it.

Why is a flamingo pink?

For a long while, flamingos in zoos kept losing their delicate pink color and fading to white. Then keepers realized the problem was due to their diet. Flamingos feed on a certain kind of algae and these algae contain chemicals called cartenoids that are responsible for the pink. If a flamingo does not get these algae, it does not get the cartenoids, and its color fades.

The eyes and nostrils stick out of the water even when the crocodile is submerged

A crocodile's teeth do not overlap when the jaw is closed, unlike an alligator's

222

Life all around: Animals

◀ **Spoon bill**
A spoonbill is a large wading bird that paddles through swamps in the tropics dragging its long spoon-shaped bill through the water from side to side. It is searching for shrimps and other small water creatures and when it finds a meal, it snaps the bill shut on its victim like a pair of spring-loaded sugar tongs.

What's special about Okavango?

The Okavango Delta in Botswana is one of the world's largest wetlands, swelling to 8,500 square miles (22,000 sq km) in the wet season. A continual outflow and inflow of water keeps the water fresh and turns it into an astonishingly rich habitat—home to hippos, crocodiles, and elephants, as well as antelopes and countless birds and fish. But the Delta is coming under increasing threat from human activities.

The crocodile's tail is immensely powerful

Many crocodiles have been killed for their shiny, scaly skin

QUIZ

1. What's so remarkable about the mudskipper?
2. What gives the proboscis monkey of Borneo its name?
3. Where would you find a terrapin?
4. What is the Everglade kite?
5. Is it true that a mother crocodile carries her babies between her teeth?
6. Can crocodiles climb trees?
7. Are leeches good for you?

Answers
1. It can survive out of water 2. Its big red nose 3. In a swamp 4. A rare bird of prey that lives in the swamps of Florida 5. Yes 6. Yes 7. Yes; they can be used to reduce blood clotting

223

Mountain animals

What animals live on mountains?

COLD AND WINDY, mountaintops are among the harshest environments in the world, but surprisingly many animals can survive here, including hunting animals such as pumas and snow leopards as well as sure-footed grazers, such as mountain goats, chamois, ibex, and yaks.

▲ **Lammergeier**
The huge lammergeier is one of the few birds that can survive in the high mountain peaks. They are superb gliders, floating over the slopes looking for carcasses for hours, seemingly without effort.

▼ **Himalayan Snowcock**
The Himalayan Snowcock is one of the highest living of all birds, nesting more than 13,000 feet (3,900m) up in the Himalayan mountains. Its gray and white plumage blends perfectly with the landscape of gray rock and snow.

Why does the lammergeier drop its dinner?

The lammergeier is a kind of vulture found in Africa and southern Europe. Food is scarce in the mountains, so the lammergeier has learned to feed on the toughest hide and bones in a carcass, too tough for other animals. But some bones are too tough even for the lammergeier. So it drops the bones again and again from a great height on to its own chosen rock (called an ossuary)—until the bone smashes and the bird can get at the soft marrow inside.

What is the world's biggest bird of prey?

The condors of California and the South American Andes are the world's biggest birds of prey with huge wings more than 10 feet (3m) across. They are actually vultures, feeding on carcasses, and soaring for hours on the buffeting winds that howl through the peaks while they wait for an animal to die.

▲ **Yak pack**
In Tibet, the docile yak has been domesticated and is used as a pack animal, as well as for milk and meat, and for its wooly coat.

What is highest living mammal?

The yak is a remarkable ox with huge curved horns and a very shaggy coat that lives in the Himalayan mountains of Tibet, the world's highest mountains. Protected from the cold by its coat and able to eat the toughest grass, it can survive over 20,000 feet (6,000m) up among the peaks.

Life all around: Animals

▶ Snow cat
The snow leopard is a big cat that lives in the Himalayan mountains. It has a beautiful pale coat with dark markings, which has sadly made it a target for fur poachers.

How do mountain goats climb?
Mountain goats are incredibly nimble climbers, able to get up the steepest slopes and leap from crag to crag with amazing agility. Their secret lies not only in their sense of balance but in their hooves. A mountain goat's hooves have sharp edges which dig into rock crevices. They also have slightly hollow soles, which act almost like suction pads.

What is a chamois?
A chamois is a tiny animal that leaps around the highest peaks in Europe. It is a kind of goat-antelope, with the face and horns of an antelope and the mountaineering abilities (and smell) of a goat.

What dogs live in mountains?
The timber wolf looks rather like a German shepherd dog. It has been driven from lowland forests in North America, but many still survive high in the mountains, hunting their prey in packs.

What animal can jump highest?
The puma, also known as the cougar or mountain lion, can jump an astonishing 18 feet (5.5m) into the air to get into a tree or jump up on a ledge. This is the equivalent of jumping up to an upstairs bedroom window—and much higher than any kangaroo, which can only jump 10 feet (3m).

What was the highest climbing cat?
In September 1950, a four-month old kitten belonging to a little Swiss girl named Josephine Aufdenblatten began following a group of climbers. It followed them all the way to the top of the famous Alpine peak, the 14,688-foot (4,478-m) high Matterhorn!

What happens in winter to a mountain hare's coat?
Like the coat of many animals in snowy places, the mountain hare's coat, or "pelage," turns white so that it is much harder for predators to spot against the white of the snow.

QUIZ

1. What big cat lives in the steamy Amazon jungle and the icy peaks of the Rocky Mountains?
2. Which of these animals is in the camel family: a) llama b) alpaca c) guanaco d) vicuna?
3. What is the biggest British bird of prey?
4. How do you say ptarmigan?
5. The lynx is a big cat that lives on mountains. Is it bigger than a dog?
6. What are an eagle's claws called?
7. What is an ibex?

Answers
1. Puma 2. All four 3. Golden eagle 4. TAR-mig-un 5. It is bigger than a dog but smaller than a wolf 6. Talons 7. A kind of mountain goat

225

Desert animals

Do animals live in the desert?

DESERTS ARE HARD PLACES FOR ANIMALS to live. They are very dry and often very hot too. Many insects, spiders and scorpions, as well as lizards and snakes have adapted to life under these harsh conditions, but mammals such as the camel survive here too.

▲ **Sand cat**
The desert even has its own predatory cat—the sand cat. It is quite small, and by hunting only at night, it can survive in hot deserts.

How do kangaroo rats save water?

The kangaroo rat gets its name from its big hind legs. It can survive even in California's Death Valley because it gets its water from fats in its food and saves water by eating its own droppings.

What antelope lives in the desert?

The Sahara desert has its own large antelope, the addax. It never needs a waterhole, because it gets all its water from its food.

How do camels cope with the desert sand?

Camel's feet have just two joined toes to stop their feet sinking into soft sand or snow, in the case of the Bactrian camel of central Asia. They also have nostril's that close up completely to block out the sand, and double rows of eyelashes to protect their eyes from both sand and the sun's glare.

A camel has a huge stomach for taking in lots of grass and water when it is available

Heavy eyebrows protect the camel's eyes in desert sandstorms

◀ **Ship of the desert**
The camel is perhaps the desert's most distinctive animal, with its long neck and the big hump on its back for storing water.

A camel's skin has no sweat glands to cut down on moisture loss

What does a camel have a hump for?

The camel's hump is made of fat, not water as some people insist. But the fat can be broken down within the body and converted to both energy and water, whenever food and water is scarce.

▶ **Bearded vultures**
Vultures gather to feed around the carcasses of dead animals. Here the vultures are bearded vultures which get their name from the clump of black bristles under their beaks; the carcass is an antelope.

Life all around: Animals

Desert hedgehog

Fennec fox

Jerboa

▲ **The burrowers**
A number of small animals cope with the desert heat by resting in burrows or sheltering under stones in the day, and only coming out to feed in the cool of the night. The fennec fox also has big ears to help it keep cool by radiating heat.

Do birds live in the desert?

Although many birds, like vultures, live in fairly dry parts of the world, only a few live in true deserts. Among these is the sand grouse. It rests under bushes during the day, then flies hundreds of miles at night to watering places. It soaks up water in breast feathers to help protect its young from the sun.

Do vultures hunt?

No. Vultures are mainly scavengers, which means they feed on animals that have died already, or been killed by other animals such as lions. Their strong claws and beaks are for tearing carcasses apart. Each species feeds on a different bit of the carcass. So small Egyptian vultures wait until big lappet-faced vultures have finished before diving in.

Quiz

1 What is a gila monster?
2 How many humps does a camel have?
3 What is a dromedary?
4 Where is a scorpion's sting?
5 How do lizards survive the desert heat?
6 What is the biggest desert in the world?
7 What continent does the kangaroo rat live on?
8 What is the biggest animal in the desert?

Answers
1. A Mexican desert lizard with a poisonous bite 2. The Asian or Bactrian has two; the Arabian, one 3. An Arabian camel for racing 4. The tip of its tail 5. By sheltering under rocks during the hottest part of the day 6. The Sahara 7. North America 8. The camel

227

Seashore life

Common gull

What makes the seashore special?

WATER IS CONTINUALLY moving up and down the seashore as waves roll up and down, and as the tide rises and falls. So creatures that live on the seashore have to be well adapted to surviving long periods out of water-or long periods in salt water. The seashore, then, has its own special creatures, including crabs, anemones, and a range of shellfish such as barnacles and limpets.

▼ **Rock pool**
Rock pools are seashore aquariums full of all kinds of sea life.
Key:
1. Mussels
2. Starfish
3. Cladophora
4. Gem anemone
5. Common prawn
6. Bladder wrack
7. Common goby
8. Dog whelk
9. Barnacles
10. Sugar weed
11. Cockle
12. Limpet

▶ **Crab**
Crabs have a hard shell, eight legs, and two powerful pincers for grabbing prey. They scuttle along the beach or the seabed sideways.

Life all around: Animals

▶ Puffin and guillemot
A huge number of birds live by the sea, feeding on the seashore or diving for fish in the sea. Most have webbed feet for swimming, waterproof plumage and sharp bills for gripping fish. The puffin's big colourful beak can hold up to 11 fish at once. Puffins live in burrows on clifftops. Guillemots nest in big, closely-packed colonies on narrow cliff ledges.

Guillemot

Puffin

What lives in rock pools?
Rock pools are pools of seawater left behind on seashore rocks as the tide goes out. They can get so warm and salty in the sunshine that they have their own special range of creatures, including shrimps, hermit crabs, fish such as blennies and gobies, anemones, and sea slugs.

What creature looks like a blob of jelly?
The beadlet anemone looks just like a blob of purple jelly stuck on the rocks when half uncovered by the tide. But when they are completely submerged, they open to reveal a ring of tentacles which they use to trap the small creatures they feed on. They look a bit like flowers, which is how they get their name, but even though they never move, they are in fact carnivorous animals.

What is a mollusk?
Mollusks are a huge group of creatures including slugs and snails, clams and oysters, octopuses and squids that live mostly in water or damp places. They are mostly soft, squidgy creatures, but octopuses and squids are protected by stinging tentacles and shellfish and snails by shells.

What creatures live on beaches?
Sandy shores often look completely lifeless, but just below the surface are often all kinds of creatures burrowing in the sand to escape from the drying wind and sun, and also from hungry predators. They include razor clams, lugworms, sea cucumbers, small crabs, and burrowing sea anemones. Some filter food from seawater; others eat tiny particles from the sand. Along the hightide line you might see sandhoppers which look like tiny yellow woodlice, feeding on rotting seaweed.

QUIZ

1. Puffins talk to each other by growling: true or false?
2. What does a sea urchin use its spikes for?
3. How many legs do barnacles have?
4. Why do fiddler crabs waggle their pincers a) to attract a mate b) to swim c) to frighten prey?
5. What color are lobsters?
6. The sooty tern can fly nonstop for 10 years: true or false?
7. Kittiwakes get their name because they dive toward sleeping cats: true or false?
8. The common gull feeds on dumps in big cities: true or false?

Answers
1. True 2. Walking 3. 10 4. a) 5. Blue; they only go red when cooked 6. True 7. False 8. True

Australian animals

▲ **Dingo**
The dingo is Australia's own wild dog, the only large carnivore. But it is a scavenger, not a hunter.

▲ **Wombat**
Wombats look a little like bears, but they behave more like rabbits, living in burrows and feeding on bark, roots, and grass.

▶ **Kangaroo**
The kangaroo is the biggest of the marsupials. But a newborn kangaroo is smaller than a thumb—and blind and deaf—when it makes its amazing way up through its mother's fur from the birth opening, up through her belly fur and into the pouch.

What's strange about Australian animals?

AUSTRALIA HAS ANIMALS LIKE NOWHERE else in the world. The land links to Asia were cut off millions of years ago, and a unique set of pouched animals called marsupials developed, along with many other unusual creatures.

What are marsupials?
Babies of ordinary mammals grow fully inside their mother before they're born. Marsupial babies grow only partially, and are born so tiny they can't survive in the open. After they're born, they crawl into a pouch on their mother's belly and stay there until they're big enough to climb out.

Can marsupials fly?
No, but squirrel-like creatures called gliders come close. They have big flaps of skin stretched between their legs, so when they leap from tree to tree, they can glide long distances. The best flier is the great gliding possum.

Is the koala a bear?
No. It looks just like a big teddy bear, but the koala is not related to any bear. It is a marsupial belonging to a group of animals called phalangers, which includes the possum. When born, a baby koala crawls into its mother's pouch. After six months, it climbs round on to her back and rides piggyback.

What bird sounds like a chainsaw?
The male lyre bird is one of the world's weirdest sounding birds. To attract a female, it imitates any sound it hears—including machines. It mimics a chainsaw starting up and hacking through wood, for instance, so well that people are fooled into thinking they're hearing the real thing.

What's a Tasmanian devil?
A fierce little marsupial that lives in Tasmania and looks like a cross between a black rat and a dog. It eats rats, wallabies, and birds—not to mention sheep, chickens, and poisonous snakes.

Life all around: Animals

QUIZ

1. What is a baby kangaroo called?
2. What is a wallaby?
3. Is a wallaby bigger than a kangaroo?
4. What do bandicoots eat?
5. Is a cuscus: a) an Arabian meal b) a possum c) a very awkward man?
6. What does "playing possum" mean?
7. Is a quoll or dasyure a kind of: a) rat b) bat c) cat?
8. How does the kookaburra get its name?
9. What is a thorny devil and is it dangerous?

▲ **Koala and baby**
Koalas eat only the leaves and bark of certain eucalyptus, or "gum," trees. So they live only in a small area where these trees grow in eastern Australia.

▼ **Marsupial mole**
Many creatures in the rest of the world have their marsupial equivalent in Australia—even the humble mole.

How far can a 'roo jump?
Kangaroos' huge back legs help them jump huge distances. They can bound along at nearly 30 mph (50km/h), covering 30 feet (9m) or so at every single leap.

What's a duck-billed platypus?
The duck-billed platypus is a mammal with four legs and fur — but with webbed feet and a beak like a duck's. What's more, it is a "monotreme" which means it is one of the few mammals that lays eggs.

Answers
1. A Joey 2. A small kangaroo-like animal 3. No 4. Insect grubs 5. b) 6. Playing dead, as a possum does to escape predators 7. c) 8. From its rippling call 9. A harmless thorny lizard

231

Freshwater animals

What animals live close to rivers and lakes?

THE RIVERS AND LAKES of the world teem with all kinds of small creatures—small mammals such as voles, water rats, and otters, birds such as kingfishers and herons, insects such as dragonflies and water boatmen and, of course, many freshwater fish such as trout.

Why do some birds have long thin legs?
Birds that have long thin legs are generally wading birds, such redshanks, avocets, and herons. They need their long legs for wading through the water to look for insects and worms. The biggest wading birds are herons, storks, and flamingoes.

Why do ducks have bills?
Ducks have broad, flat bills because they feed on insects that live in the water. The broad bill enables them to scoop up a big gulp of water and filter out the insects. "Dabbling" ducks such as mallards and widgeons simply upend in shallow water. "Diving ducks" such as scoters dive to the bottom.

How does a kingfisher catch fish?
By sitting on a perch above the water silently watching for fish. When it sees a minnow or a trout, the kingfisher dives into the water in a flash, then flies back to its perch, tosses the fish in the air and swallows it.

Why do frogs have long legs?
To help them jump huge distances to escape predators. A small frog can jump several yards—the equivalent of a human jumping the length of a football field. Frogs also have strong front legs to withstand the shock of landing.

What's a tadpole?
A tadpole is a young frog, soon after it emerges from its egg. A tadpole looks like a little black fish, but after seven weeks or so it will grow two back legs and get a frog face. After 10 weeks, its legs are quite long and it has front legs as well. By 12-14 weeks, the tail is gone, and it emerges from the water as a frog.

▲ **Otter**
Otters live close to rivers and lakes in North America, Europe, and Asia. Their lithe, powerful bodies make them strong swimmers, and they can dive for five minutes at a time.

▲ **Barheaded goose**
Geese, ducks, and swans are all water fowl, with webbed feet and long, supple necks for reaching down into the water.

◄ **Common frog**
Frogs have two big swiveling eyes to help them judge distances when jumping and catching flies.

Life all around: Animals

How do young otters spend their day?
Otters are mainly nocturnal animals, coming out of their dens in the riverbanks at night to hunt for fish in the river. But young otters are among the most playful of all animals, and they can often be seen during the day tumbling and rolling happily around on the bank, sliding down mud chutes, and leaping in and out of the water.

What's a coypu?
A coypu is a large water rat, more than 3 feet (90cm) long and related to the guinea pig. It comes originally from South America, but was brought to North America and Europe by fur farmers and has thrived in rivers and marshes.

Is a water vole a rat?
No, though people sometimes call them water rats. The vole prefers clean water, unlike the rat. The water vole is now becoming very rare, partly due to mink predation.

Bream

Rainbow trout

Why don't fish sink?
Because they have a special air bag inside their bodies called a swim bladder. This acts like the air in a lifejacket, keeping the fish afloat. Without it, the fish would have to swim continuously

Why don't fish drown?
Fish breathe through gills, not lungs. Gills are rows of feathery brushes under flaps on the fish's head. The fish gulps in water through its mouth, and lets it out through the gill covers. As the water passes over the feathery surfaces of the gill, they absorb oxygen from the water just as our lungs do from the air.

What is the main predator in European rivers?
The pike can grow to over 65 pounds (30kg). Long and sleek, with a large mouth full of sharp teeth, the pike is a deadly hunter that lurks among the weeds waiting for fish, or even rats and birds, waiting to pounce. This is why it prefers deep ponds and slow rivers.

◀ **Fish**
Bream is a common freshwater fish that was once the staple diet of poor people in Europe. Rainbow trout is a native of North American rivers and fast-flowing streams.

QUIZ

1 Do water voles eat any meat?
2 What bird is famous for its boom?
3 What is a water boatman?
4 What is an amphibian?
5 What is a young eel called?
6 What is the real name for an otter's den ?
7 What fish leaps up waterfalls?
8 What is a young dragonfly called?
9 How many legs does a crayfish have?
10 What is the jelly called frog spawn?

Answers
1. No, voles eat only waterside plants 2. The bittern 3. A water bug with legs that drive it through the water like oars 4. An animal that is born in water but lives on land 5. An elver 6. A holt 7. Salmon 8. Nymph 9. 10; it is a kind of lobster 10. The eggs of a frog

Grassland animals

What animals live on grasslands?

SOME GRASSLANDS ARE HOT. Some are quite cool. But they are all home to large herds of grazing animals such as antelopes, buffalo, and horses, and the animals that prey upon them, such as big cats like lions and cheetahs.

Wildebeest

Why do antelopes have long legs?
There is nowhere for a large animal to hide in open grasslands, so nearly all grassland animals are fast runners with long legs.

How fast can an antelope run?
Cheetahs can reach 66 mph (110km/h) when chasing antelopes, but only for a short distance. The pronghorn antelope has been timed at 41 mph (67km/h) for well over 10 miles (16km) but has a top speed of more than 60 mph (98km/h).

Are all antelope horns the same?
There are more than 60 species of antelope living in Africa and southern Asia—and each has different-shaped horns.

▲ **Grazing herds**
Grasslands in the tropics are the home of vast herds of antelopes of various kinds. In the last century, herds of 10 million springboks, hundreds of miles long, were sometimes seen in South Africa.

▲ **Cheetah**
The fastest runner in the world, the cheetah shows an astonishing turn of speed over a short distance to catch gazelles—a kind of antelope.

Which is the biggest antelope?
The biggest antelope is the giant eland of Africa, which has now become very rare. It stands over 6 feet (1.8m) tall at the shoulder, and weighs about a ton. The smallest is the royal antelope, which is very tiny—no bigger than a hare.

What's odd about cheetahs?
Cheetahs are not like other big cats. In fact, some scientists think they are not that closely related. They have a much longer, flatter head than other cats. They also have permanently extended claws on the end of very long legs.

Life all around: Animals

Males have blue skin on their heads

Emus reach up to 6 feet (1.8m) tall

Emus have no need of flight feathers, so their plumage is entirely for display

◀ **Emu**
The emu is a giant bird that lives in Australia. It has virtually no wings and can't fly but, like ostriches and cassowaries, it can run very fast on its long, powerful legs. Emus are rather inquisitive birds. They feed on fruit and insects but may often steal coins and keys.

What's the difference between a buffalo and a bison?

Buffalos are huge cowlike animals that live in Africa and southern Asia, recognizable by their gigantic curved horns. But North American bisons may be called "buffaloes." Bison are very different creatures with huge, low slung heads, a big hump and a shaggy coat. They were once common in both Europe and North America.

Do horses have toes?

Yes. All the big grazing animals have toes, even hooved animals. They are divided in two big groups. Ungulates, including horses, rhinos, and tapirs, have an even number of toes on each foot. Artiodactyls, such as pigs, cows, and camels, have an odd number of toes.

What are the world's biggest birds?

The world's biggest birds are all flightless birds, including the ostrich and the cassowary, with very long legs for running and long necks. The biggest, the North African ostrich, lives on the fringes of the Sahara desert and grows up to 9 feet (2.7m) tall.

What was the biggest bird ever?

Bones found in New Zealand show that until 1,000 years ago, there was a bird called the moa, which was as tall as an elephant. When the first bone was found in 1839 some people thought that it did indeed belong to an elephant. It was the eminent Victorian naturalist Richard Owen who worked out what the bone really belonged to.

QUIZ

1. How do cows 'chew the cud'?
2. What is an animal that eats plants called?
3. What animal has the longest horns of all?
4. How fast can an ostrich run:
   a) 12 mph (20km/h)
   b) 24 mph (40km/h)
   c) 36 mph (60km/h)?
5. What is an oryx?
6. What are prairie dogs?
7. Is it true that prairie dogs kiss each other when they meet?
8. How does a springbok get its name?
9. Were horses' ancestors bigger or smaller?

Answers
1. By rechewing partially digested food 2. A herbivore 3. Buffaloes 4. c) 5. A kind of antelope 6. A large, hamster-like creature that lives in big burrows beneath the prairies 7. Yes 8. By springing up to 10 feet (3m) straight up 9. Smaller

Deep sea animals

What creatures live in the sea?

LIFE BEGAN IN THE OCEANS and now a huge range of creatures live there. There are thousands of kinds of fish, from tiny gobies to giant whale sharks. There are also many shellfish, including mollusks such as clams and squids, and crustaceans such as shrimp and lobsters-not mention echinoderms such as sea urchins and sea cucumbers. Then there are various reptiles like sea snakes, amphibians such as turtles, and even a few a mammals such as seals and whales.

▼ **The great white shark**
Sharks have powerful jaws and double rows of razor sharp teeth. When the outer row wears out or breaks, the inner row moves forward to replace them.

How big are whales?
Most full-grown whales are quite big, but the biggest of all—the Blue whale—is absolutely gigantic. It is the largest creature that has ever lived. An average Blue whale is over 100 feet (30m) and weighs some 90 tons. Some can grow twice as heavy. The biggest ever caught weighed 190 tons.

Are dolphins and whales related?
Yes. Dolphins are a kind of whale. In fact, the biggest of the 37 kinds of dolphin is called the killer whale. Together, whales, dolphins, and porpoises are known as cetaceans.

▲ **Giant turtle**
The leatherback, the world's biggest turtle, grows 10 feet (3m) long and can weigh 2.5 tons.

What is the fiercest shark?
The great white shark is one of the biggest and most fearsome of the sharks. Attacks by sharks on humans are quite rare, but most of the time it is great whites that are the culprits. They live all around the world in warm waters, and can grow up to 23 feet (7m) long. Their double rows of razor-sharp teeth can rip through sheet steel.

Life all around: Animals

▶ **Different levels in the sea**
Different creatures live at different levels in the sea.
1. Dolphin
2. Jellyfish
3. Plant plankton
4. Zoo (animal) plankton
5. Tuna
6. Turtle
7. Whale
8. Squid
9. Deep sea fish, including angler fish and gulper eel.

How do fish stay afloat?
Fish stay afloat because they have a special air bag inside their bodies called a swim bladder. Without this, they would have to swim all the time. As a fish swims deeper, the extra pressure of water squeezes more gas made in the blood into the bladder. As the fish swims up again, this extra gas is let out, so the fish floats easily.

Are any fish poisonous?
Quite a few, such as the pufferfish. The most poisonous is the stonefish, whose fins have spines containing a deadly neurotoxin, which can kill in minutes.

How do fish breath underwater?
Fish get oxygen from the water just as we get oxygen from the air. But they absorb the oxygen through gills, which are feathery brushes under flaps on the side of the fish's head. To take oxygen in, the fish gulps water through its mouth, swashes it over the gills and lets it out through the gill flaps.

QUIZ

1 What shark has a head shaped like a mallet?

2 Some fish can fly 500 yards (450m) over the water; true or false?

3 What fish has a long lancelike nose?

4 Some fish can survive many days out of water: true of false?

5 The catfish makes a noise like a bagpipe with its swim bladder: true or false

6 Parrot fish get their name because they eat nuts like parrots: true or false?

7 What whale is famous for its singing?

8 What fish can blow itself up to three times its normal size?

Answers
1. The hammerhead shark 2. True, flying fish can 3. Swordfish 4. True 5. True 6. False 7. The humpback whale 8. The pufferfish

237

What was the Stone Age?

Who were the first farmers?

Who built the first roof gardens?

Who first wore trousers?

Why does vomit taste sour?

What food makes you grow?

How long are your guts?

Why is blood red?

238

What's a brain?

How do you smell?

People

Why do ears pop?

240 Human origins
242 Peoples of the world
244 The first farms
246 The first cities
248 Clothes and costumes
250 Eating
252 Breathing & circulation
254 Moving
256 Seeing
258 Hearing
260 Taste, smell, and touch
262 Thinking
264 Growing

How many muscles has a football player?

Why do we have two eyes?

239

Human origins

▲ **Cave painting of a horse**
Both Neanderthal Man and early humans often lived in caves and left behind extraordinary paintings on the wall—mainly of the animals they hunted.

When did the first humans live?

THE FIRST TRUE HUMANS lived about 30,000 years ago, but there were humanlike creatures millions of years earlier. Scientists call these humanlike creatures hominids, and there were many different kinds. The earliest hominids were very like apes, with long arms and a big jaw, but over time they evolved (changed) to become more and more like humans. Hominids and apes probably had the same ancestor—an orangutan-like creature that lived in Africa six million years ago.

Who were the first hominids?

Some of the oldest remains of hominids date from around four million years ago and belong to a group of creatures called Australopithecus. Australopithecus means "southern ape." Most southern apes walked upright like humans but were little more than 3 feet (90cm) tall. They had a smallish brain, jutting apelike jaws and hairy bodies, and lived on fruit and vegetables.

Who first used tools?

Humans are not the only creatures to use tools. So do many animals such as sea otters. All early hominids probably did. But the first hominid to use tools with skill was *Homo habilis*, or "Handy Man," who appeared about two million years ago. Handy Man was the first really humanlike creature. He had a large brain and used tools to cut hides to make clothes and food for eating.

Where did hominids live?

All early hominids lived in Africa, and only began to spread out further two million years ago. The first humans may have come from Africa too.

◀ **Making fire**
Learning to make fire was one of Homo Erectus's greatest achievements. It not only kept him warm in winter, allowing him to live in cold places. It also meant he could cook food, and so eat meat.

▲ **Ancient home**
Early humans were usually nomadic and lived in tents made of hide, bones and sticks rather than permanent houses.

Homo habilis (Handy Man)

Australopithecus (Southern Ape)

Life all around: People

Who were the first hunters?

The earliest hominids were vegetarians like apes. But about 1.5-2 million years ago, a kind of hominid called *Homo erectus*, or Upright Man, began to hunt and eat meat. Upright Man could light fires, cook food, and hunt with wooden spears. Upright Man was also the first hominid to spread out of Africa, and remains have been found as far away as Russia and Indonesia.

Who was Neanderthal Man?

We humans belong to a group of creatures called *Homo sapiens*, or Wise Man, and Neanderthal Man was the first Wise Man, appearing about 100,000 years ago. He had a bigger brain than ours and a rugged body, and no one knows why he died out.

Prehistoric flint spear head

What was the Stone Age?

Until humans discovered how to make tools from bronze about 6,000 years ago, humans made their tools from stone. So all of human history, from the time Upright Man appeared two million years ago until the beginning of the Bronze Age 6,000 years ago, is called the Stone Age. The Stone Age is divided into three periods: the Paleolithic or Old Stone Age from two million to 12,000 years ago; the Mesolithic from 12,000 to 9,000 years ago, and the Neolithic or New Stone Age from 9,000 to 6,000 years ago.

Homo erectus (Upright Man)

Homo sapiens neanderthalis (Neanderthal Man)

Homo sapiens sapiens (Human)

▸ **Evolution of humans**
This series shows some of our ancestors, beginning with Australopithecus on the far left and ending with us humans, called by scientists Homo sapiens sapiens, on the right. The first human was called Cro-Magnon Man and lived about 30,000 years ago.

QUIZ

1. Early hominids made clothes from wool?
2. Early humans hunted dinosaurs: true or false?
3. Place the following ages of prehistory in the right order: the Iron Age, the Stone Age, the Bronze Age.
4. The first hominids lived in northern Canada: true or false?
5. Which of these is the most ancient: a) Java Man b) Neanderthal Man c) Cro-Magnon Man?
6. The oldest almost complete skeleton of a hominid is a) Bill b) Methusalah c) Lucy?

Answers
1. No; if they wore clothes at all they wore hide. 2. False; dinosaurs died out long before 3. Stone, Bronze then Iron 4. False 5. b) 6. c)

Peoples of the world

What are ethnic groups?

ETHNIC GROUPS ARE GROUPS of people who belong to the same race, nationality, religion, or culture. Irish people, for instance, come from the nation of Ireland or have ancestors who do. Jews are people descended from the ancient Hebrews of the Middle East and follow the Jewish religion. African Americans are descended from the West African peoples who were taken to the Americas as slaves in the 17th, 18th, and 19th centuries.

African American

▲ Easter Island
Huge and strange stone statues on Easter Island in the Pacific were made by Polynesian peoples thousands of years ago.

Who are Afro-Caribbeans?

Afro-Caribbeans are descended from African slaves taken to work in the Caribbean. In the 1950s, many moved to Britain, France, and the Americas. So some British people have Afro-Caribbean parents.

Who are Caucasians?

Police use the word Caucasian to describe white people whose ancestors came from Europe. The word comes from the Caucasus Mountains in southern Russia.

◀ Masai warrior
The Masai are nomadic people of East Africa. Many have given up the nomadic life and now live in towns.

Who lives in Africa?

In the north, in countries like Egypt, most people are Arabic. But south of the Sahara are 800 ethnic groups of black African, each with its own lifestyle and culture. Descendants of European colonists live here, too.

Who are nomads?

Nomads are people like the Bedouins of the Sahara, Mongols of Asia, and the Masai of Africa who move around the country taking their shelters with them.

▶ Maoris
Maoris are the people who first settled in New Zealand 1,000 years ago, coming over the Pacific from the Polynesian islands in large sailing canoes.

Life all around: People

▲▶ Ethnic clothes
In the past, people from different ethnic groups could be recognized by their traditional way of dressing, like the Polish woman in traditional costume on the right. But now most people wear modern European style like the Aboriginal children above.

Who lives in S. America?
In the country, some small groups of Native American peoples still survive. But in cities, there is a mix, including people descended from: Spanish settlers who came in the 1500s; marriages between Spanish settlers and Native Americans; African slaves brought here in the 18th century; and more recent European immigrants.

▶ Oaxaca woman weaving
The Oaxaca of Mexico are among the few Native American peoples who survived after the Spanish arrived in the 1500s. They are famous for their woven cloth.

Who lives in North America?
North America was originally inhabited by Native Americans. But now most people are descended from Europeans who have come here over the centuries, from immigrants from South and Central America, to African Americans.

Do peoples move about?
In history, whole peoples have migrated or moved huge distances. The Polynesians spread across the Pacific from South America, thousands of years ago. Asian peoples crossed into Alaska from Siberia 11,000 years ago and spread south to become Native Americans. The Anglo-Saxons of England came originally from northern Europe.

QUIZ

1. How many people were there in the world in 1999: a) 600 million b) 1.2 billion c) 6 billion?

2. How many babies are born every minute in the world a) 2 b) 167 c) 15,000?

3. Are mestizos a) sausages b) shoes c) offspring of marriages between Native South Americans and Spanish settlers?

4. Which country has the most people: a) Russia b) India c) China?

5. What is the world's most crowded large country a) Australia b) Bangladesh c) Italy?

6. Is a kimono a) a Japanese silk gown b) a Chinese fruit c) a large lizard?

Answers
1. c) 2. b) 3. c) 4. c), China has more than 1.4 billion people 5. b) 6. a)

The first farms

Who were the first farmers?

EARLY PEOPLES mostly lived in small bands and moved around hunting animals and gathering food from wild plants. Then about 12,000 years ago, some people learned to herd animals such as sheep and goats to provide a ready supply of food. Others learned to sow the seeds of wild plants to grow crops. This happened at different times in different parts of the world. The earliest farms were created by the people of the Middle East around 11,000 years ago. But there were farms long ago in China, India, and Central America too.

▼ Ancient Egyptian farmers
The development of farms led to the creation of the world's first great civilizations—including that of Ancient Egypt, where the pyramids were built. Egypt's farms were alongside the River Nile, which not only provided water, but brought rich silt soil in its floods to an area that would otherwise be desert.

What were the first crops?

The first crops were grown from the seeds of wild grasses which gave wheat and barley. One of the oldest known kinds of wheat is one called emmer. Vegetables such as peas were also grown on early farms.

How did farming change people's lives forever?

For the first time, people had no need to move around looking for food. They could settle in one place and build first villages and then towns. At Jarmo in Iraq, there are the remains of 24 mud huts where 150 people lived around 11,000 years ago.

Life all around: People

What new skills did people learn?

To begin with farming was mixed with hunting, but the extra food meant people were free to do other tasks. Soon some people became skilled in things such as building houses and food stores, weaving cloth and making pots. They also learned how to use metals—first bronze in the Bronze Age and then iron in the Iron Age.

What were the first inventions?

Once they were settled in farms, people began to invent all kinds of things to make life easier. They learned how to make pots from clay around 9,000 years ago. At about the same time, they learned how to grind grain into flour in shallow bowls called mortars using clublike stone pestles.

How did they plant seeds?

At first, farmers planted seeds simply by dropping them in holes made with a stick. Then someone learned that you could get better results if you turned over the soil a bit and carved out long furrows to put the seeds in with a blade called a plough.

When was the wheel invented?

Sometime before the wheel was invented, people may have moved heavy loads using tree trunks as rollers. The first wheels were probably slices of tree trunk with a rod or axle pushed through. A platform could rest on the axle to make a cart. By about 5,200 years ago, solid wheels made of short planks of wood bolted together were being used in Mesopotamia in the Middle East.

QUIZ

1 Is a sickle a a) bout of feigned illness b) small black fruit c) curved blade for cutting the ears off grain?

2 What did early farmers make from wheat and barley?

3 Why did early farmers drive cattle over their grain harvest?

4 Was the farming area by the Middle East's Tigris and Euphrates rivers called the a) Grain Belt b) Fertile Crescent c) Golden Triangle?

5 5,000 years ago is a) AD 3,000 b) 7,000 BC c) 3,000 BC?

6 Is crop rotation a) spinning a horsewhip b) turning grains to face the sun c) using fields for different crops each year to preserve the soil?

Answers
1. c 2. Bread and beer 3. To "thresh" the grains from the stalks 4. b 5. c 6. c

245

The first cities

What were the first cities?

ONCE EARLY PEOPLE BEGAN to settle in one place in the Middle East around 11,000 years ago, families soon grew, and villages grew into cities. They were places where those who governed the land lived, craftsmen made things, and people came to buy and sell things—not only food grown in the countryside around, but metal goods, cloth, jewels, spices and much more besides.

What's the world's oldest city?

No one knows for certain. One of the oldest is Jericho in Israel. The ruins of some of the city walls date back over 11,000 years. They were massive stone structures perhaps 23 feet (7m) tall. There were also many other cities in the Middle East at least 7,000 years ago.

Were there any early cities in China?

Chinese civilization began more than 7,000 years ago when the Yang-Shao people built the first villages on the land between the Hwang-Ho and Wei-Ho rivers.

Walls and roof covered in white plaster to reflect away the sun's heat

Rush mats

Front door

Ladder for getting into the house through the roof

▲ Çatal Hüyük, Turkey
One of the world's oldest cities is Çatal Hüyük in Anatolia in Turkey. No one knows quite how old it is, but some of the surviving remains date back to 6250 BC. What is remarkable about the city is that people got into their houses through holes in the flat roof.

Life all around: People

Who built the first roof gardens?
6,000 years ago the civilization of Sumer began to flourish on the fertile land between the Tigris and Euphrates rivers in modern Iraq. Here they built the great cities of Ur and Eridu. One of the centerpieces of Ur was the ziggurat, a temple built like a step-sided pyramid—with trees and lush gardens on top.

Where did writing begin?
Writing did not begin in any one place, but in the Middle East in Sumeria, in China and in Central America independently. The first written symbols were probably used by rulers to show their power and by city officials to record and label food and other things. One of the earliest systems of writing is "cuneiform," used in Sumer and Babylon, which used wedge-shaped marks on clay tablets.

What were the hanging gardens of Babylon?
Babylon was first built 3,800 years ago. But it reached its height under King Nebuchadnezzar II in the 6th century BC. Its beautiful hanging gardens were one of the wonders of the world. They were planted high on a ziggurat (see left) to remind Nebuchadnezzar's queen of her mountain home.

Who were the pharaohs?
The pharaohs were the kings of the civilization of Ancient Egypt on the banks of the River Nile. The pharaohs ruled for nearly 3,000 years, from 2920 BC, and left behind astonishing monuments to their power and wealth—not only the great pyramids and statues in the desert, but fabulous treasures in their tombs, including mummies, writing, and beautiful gold and jeweled objects.

What is civilization?
The word civilization comes from the Latin word for city-dweller. It is the highly organized, settled way of life—complete with rules and laws, as well as writing—that came with the creation of the first cities.

Holes filled with daub (mud and straw)

Walls built with mud bricks

Framework built from wooden posts and beams

QUIZ

1. What ancient city was carved from desert stone a) Stonehenge b) Ur c) Petra in Jordan?
2. Pyramids were built in Mexico 2,800 years ago: true or false?
3. What ancient civilization was based in Crete: a) Aztec b) Minoan c) Persian?
4. What was a chariot?
5. What would you ask a scribe to do?
6. What did the Ancient Egyptians write on?
7. Are the ruins of the ancient city of Mohenjo-Daro in a) Pakistan b) Arizona c) Turkey?

Answers
1. c) 2. True 3. b) 4. A two-wheeled horse-drawn wagon used in battle 5. Write 6. Paper made from papyrus reed 7. a)

Clothes and costumes

When did people first wear clothes?

NO ONE CAN BE SURE WHEN people stopped going naked. But the first clothes were probably animal skins people wrapped round themselves to keep off the cold. It was when people began to farm and settle in villages that the earliest proper clothes were worn. At first, these were just skirts and shawls built up from twisted tufts of wool and flax. But by about 6,000 years ago, people had learned to spin and weave cloth, and sew it to make attractive clothes.

Who were the first fashion followers?

Over 5,000 years ago, the women of Ancient Sumeria wore beautiful coloured clothes, along with fancy headdresses, and gold and silver ear-rings and necklaces, studded with jewels such as lapis-lazuli and carnelian.

Who first wore cosmetics?

It may have been the women of Ancient Egypt, who had elaborate makeup, including eyeliner, skin powder, and lipstick. They mixed ground malachite (copper ore) and galena (lead ore) with oil to make kohl to line eyes. They made lipstick and rouge from red ocher, and also painted their nails with henna.

▼ **All kinds of clothes?**
Today, fewer and fewer people wear distinctive traditional clothes. Instead, people everywhere wear the shirt, pants, skirt, and jacket made popular in North America and Europe.

Muslim girls often wear a veil called an aba or chador covering their whole body and head

Sari, a traditional Indian dress made of silk or artificial material

Traditional turban from central Asia

Jelaba, a traditional smock worn in northern Africa.

Smocks are common in China

Baseball cap

Life all around: People

▲ **Warm skins**
Animal skins have provided clothes for many tens of thousands of years, especially in very cold places where wool and cotton are too thin. The Inuits and Saami people of the far north traditionally dress in skins.

Who invented silk?
The Chinese discovered how to make silk thread from the cocoon of the Silk moth caterpillar almost 5,000 years ago. According to legend, it was the Princess Si-ling-chi who found that the cocoon could be separated into threads in hot water. She was known thereafter as the Silk Goddess, Seine Than.

Who first wore platform shoes?
Chopines were worn by women in Italy in the Renaissance in the 1400s. The biggest belonged to prostitutes in Venice, whose soles were built up to a height of 32 inches (80 cm) as a high as a chair.

Who wore togas?
Togas were wraps of beautiful light cloth often worn by men in Ancient Rome over their tunics. The early togas were simple, and worn with both ends thrown over the shoulder. But in later years, they became more elaborate. Officials had togas edged in a special purple dye.

Who first wore trousers?
The Ancient Celts of Britain wore trousers over 2,000 years ago, and so did the Chinese. Dutch and English sailors revived them in Europe in the 16th century. But it took French Revolutionaries of the 1790s to make them popular.

What is a crinoline?
The underskirt of steel hoops Victorian ladies wore to make their dresses fuller.

QUIZ

1. Is a jerkin a) a pickled cucumber b) a violent tennis shot c) a medieval vest?
2. The word "dungarees" comes from Indian: true or false?
3. What kind of cloth came from De Nîmes in France?
4. Where were parkas invented?
5. What do British people call a derby hat?
6. What is a tartan?
7. Some crinolines were so large, ladies had to go through double doors sideways: true or false?
8. Who wears the most armor today?

Answers
1. c) 2. True 3. Denim, the blue material used to make blue jeans 4. In the Arctic by Inuits 5. A bowler 6. A pattern of clothing linked to a Scottish clan 7. True 8. Ice hockey players

249

Eating

Why do we eat?

MOST OF THE FOOD YOU EAT is fuel, burned by your body for energy to keep you going. It gets this mainly from substances in food called carbohydrates and fats. But you also need to eat small amounts of food such as proteins to help repair and build body cells, and tiny traces of chemicals called vitamins and minerals the body cannot make itself.

Epiglottis
Esophagus
Liver
Stomach
Bile duct
Small intestine
Appendix
Large intestine
Anus

Where does food go when you eat it?
Your food goes down through your body in a long tube called the alimentary canal. When you swallow, food slides down your gullet or esphagus into the stomach, where it churns around for a few hours. Then it is squeezed into a long, coiled tube called the small intestine where nourishing parts of the food are absorbed into the blood. The rest then passes on into a larger tube called the large intestine, and the waste or faeces is pushed out through the anus.

How long are your guts?
Your guts or intestine are so coiled that if you unwound them, they would be more than three times as long as your body.

◀ **Digestive system**
If you could see your digestive system through your body, this is what you would see. Most of the system is the alimentary canal, the long tube that takes food through your body.

How is food broken down?
Food is broken into the small molecules the body needs by a process called digestion in two ways. First, food is broken up mechanically by chewing and by the squeezing muscles of your gut. Second, it is attacked chemically by acids, such as the bile and hydrochloric acid in your stomach, and by biological chemicals called enzymes, mixed in with your saliva and stomach juices.

What are carbohydrates?
Carbohydrates are foods made of kinds of sugar like glucose and starch. Foods such as bread, rice, potatoes, and pasta, as well as sweet things, are rich in carbohydrates.

What is fat?
Fats are greasy foods that won't dissolve in water. Some are solid, like cheese and meat fat. Others are oils. Fats are usually stored by the body as energy reserves, rather than burned up at once like carbohydrates.

Life all around: People

◀ A healthy diet
A healthy diet contains just the right amount of each kind of food your body needs, and no more. The bulk of your diet must be solid food like carbohydrates, but it must also contain enough fat, plenty of protein, and the right vitamins and minerals.

What food makes you grow?
To grow, your body needs proteins, the natural substances from which cells are built. Proteins are made from 20 basic chemicals called "amino acids." The body can make 12 of these. The other eight you must get by eating protein-rich food such as milk, fish, meat, eggs, and beans.

Why are teeth different?
Different teeth do different jobs. The flat "incisors" at the front have sharp edges for slicing through food. The pointed "canine" teeth just behind are good for ripping chewy food. The big flat-topped "premolars" and "molars" toward the back of your mouth are good for grinding food into a small, mushy ball ready to be swallowed.

Dentine
Pulp
Enamel
Blood vessel

▶ Inside a tooth
To chew food every day, your teeth must be incredibly hard-wearing. The outside of a tooth is made from enamel, the hardest substance in your body. Inside that is dentine, a material as hard as bone. In the centre is a pulpy mass of blood and bones.

QUIZ

1. How many teeth do most grown-ups have: a) 12 b) 32 c) 64?
2. Why does vomit taste sour? Is it because a) you've eaten sour food b) your stomach is full of acid c) vomit gets rid of body poisons?
3. Vitamin C helps your body fight infection. What foods do you get it in?
4. What is another name for the teeth you had as a baby?
5. How long can you survive without eating: a) 2 days b) 20 days c) 300 days?
6. How long can you survive without drinking: a) 2 days b) 20 days c) 300 days?
7. What kind of food is meat mostly: a) carbohydrate b) fat c) protein and fat?

Answers
1. b) 2. b) 3. Fresh fruit, especially oranges, plus green vegetables 4. Milk teeth 5. b) 6. a) 7. c)

251

Breathing & circulation

Why do we breathe?

JUST AS A FIRE NEEDS air to burn, so every cell in your body needs a continuous supply of oxygen to burn up the food it gets in the blood. They get their oxygen from the air you breathe in. Without oxygen your body cells quickly die–and brain cells die quickest of all. If you stopped breathing for very long, you would soon lose consciousness, your brain would be damaged and eventually you would die.

▲ **Blood vessels**
Arteries rich in oxygen carry bright red blood. Veins which return carbon dioxide to the lungs are bluer.

How does your body get oxygen?

Every time you breathe in air through your nose or mouth, the air rushes down your windpipe into your lungs. Your lungs are spongey bags inside your chest, filled with millions of minute branching airways. At the end of each airway is an airsac or alveolus with walls so thin that oxygen can seep through into the tiny blood vessels wrapped around it.

What do you breathe out?

Most of your outbreath is the air you breathed in, minus a little less oxygen. But it also contains a little waste carbon dioxide brought to the lungs from your body cells in the blood.

How does oxygen get to each body cell?

This is what your blood circulation is for. Driven by the pumping of the heart, blood circulates through an intricate network of blood vessels all the way round the body again and again, every 90 seconds or so. As it passes through the lungs, it picks up oxygen as it washes around the airsacs. The heart then pumps this oxygen-rich blood on round the body. As the blood returns to the lungs, it carries with it the waste carbon dioxide from the cells.

Why does the heart have two sides?

Your heart has two sides because your body has two blood circulations. The left side of the heart pumps blood through the lungs to pick up oxygen, and take it to the right of the heart. This is called pulmonary circulation. The right side pumps oxygen-rich blood around the body and back to the left of the heart. This is called the systemic circulation.

Artery taking oxygen-poor blood to the lungs

Veins bringing oxygen-rich blood back from the lungs

Right atrium, where blood is held ready to be pumped

Right ventricle, the heart's pumping chamber

Life all around: People

How does your heart pump?
Your heart has walls of muscle that contract automatically once a second or more. As they contract, they squeeze blood into the blood vessels. The entrances of each of the heart's two pumping chambers or ventricles have little flaps, or valves, to ensure blood can only enter and leave one way.

Why is blood red?
Blood is ferried through the blood inside red blood cells. Red blood cells can carry oxygen because they contain a remarkable substance called hemoglobin. Hemoglobin glows bright red when it is carrying oxygen but fades to dull purple when it loses oxygen.

Vena cava—the body's main vein bringing blood from the body

Artery taking oxygen-poor blood to the lungs

Veins bringing oxygen-rich blood back from the lungs

Left atrium where blood is held ready to be pumped

Left ventricle, the heart's pumping chamber

Aorta—the body's main artery

◀ **Heart**
This artwork shows the heart sliced in half to reveal its two halves. Each half has two chambers—an atrium where blood builds up and a ventricle or pumping chamber.

QUIZ

1 There are 1,500 miles (2,400 km) of airways in your lung: true or false?
2 Your heart is in the middle of your chest, slightly to the right: true or false?
3 Blood carries food as well as oxygen to the body cells: true or false?
4 Your pulse–the rate your heart beats–is normally 300 beats a minute: true or false?
5 What are the major blood vessels that carry blood away from the heart called?
6 Are the tiniest blood vessels called: a) filigrees b) venioles c) capillaries?
7 Smoking damages which body tissue?

Answers
1. True 2. False: it is slightly to the left 3. True 4. False; it is about 90 a minute 5. Arteries 6. c) 7. Lung

Moving

Why do you have bones in your body?

WITHOUT BONES, YOU WOULD FLOP on the floor like jelly. Your bones make the strong, rigid framework called the skeleton that supports your body. It not only provides an anchor for your muscles, but supports your skin and and other tissues. It also provides a protective casing for your heart, brain, and other organs.

How many bones do you have?
A baby's skeleton has more than 300 bones, but some fuse together as it grows. You probably have 213 bones—though some people have extra bones in their back.

What's inside a bone?
The very center of many bones is a core of soft, jelly material called bone marrow. This where your blood cells are made.

Why are bones strong?
Their tough outer casing combines two materials—one that makes them flexible and another that makes them stiff. The flexible material is strong, stretchy strands called collagen. The stiff material is hard deposits of the minerals calcium and phosphate.

Why don't bones weigh you down?
Bones are incredibly light despite their strength because they are full of holes. Inside the casing is a crisscross honeycomb structure of struts called trabeculae.

What are joints?
Joints are places where two bones meet. A few joints, such as those in the skull, are completely rigid. But most joints allow the bones to move, and the end of each bone is shaped to allow it to move in a particular way. The knee is a hinge joint that lets the lower leg swing back and forward. The hip is a ball and socket joint that lets you rotate your leg all round.

What do muscles do?
Muscles make parts of your body move. They work by making themselves shorter, so that they pull things together. When the muscle on the front of your upper arm gets shorter, it pulls up your forearm.

Are there different kinds of muscle?
The outside of your skeleton is covered in muscles called skeletal muscles that you use to make your body move. But there are also muscles inside your body called involuntary muscles that move food through your guts and control your blood flow without you being aware of it. A third kind of muscle works your heart.

◄ **Skeleton**
Your skeleton is a tough, light framework of more than 200 bones.

Skull
Rib
Vertebrae or spine
Pelvis or hip
Patella or kneecap
Humerus
Radius
Ulna
Femur or thigh
Tibia or shin
Fibula or calf

Life all around: People

▼ Inside a muscle
A muscle is made of bundles of fibers, each made of strands called fibrils, which are in turn made up of myofibrils.

Muscle fiber
Fibril
Myofibril
Myosin filament
Actin filament

Why do muscles work in pairs?
Muscles work in pairs because they can only pull themselves shorter. They need a partner working the opposite way to pull them out again. On your upper arm, you have biceps muscles at the front, which shorten to lift your forearm. You have triceps muscles at the back to pull it lower again.

How do muscles work?
Muscles are made of bundles of tiny fibers that get thicker and shorter when the muscle is working. Each of the fibers is made of interlocking strands of two materials, actin and myosin. The myosin has little chemical hooks that twist and tug on the actin to make the muscle shorter.

How are bones and muscles attached?
Muscles are attached to bones by tough cords called tendons. Bones are bound together by tough cords called ligaments.

Different kinds of joint

Ball and socket joints like the shoulder and hip allow free movement in many directions.

The swivel joint between your skull and spine lets you turn your head to the left and right.

In your thumbs, two-saddle-shaped bone ends fit snugly to combine strength and free movement.

Hinge joints like those in the knee and elbow swing only two ways like a door, but are strong.

QUIZ

1. Your biggest muscle is in your buttocks: true or false?
2. How many muscles do you have a) 650 b) 860 c) 1,170?
3. What fuel do muscles run on a) glucose sugar b) hydrocarbons c) gas?
4. What are the muscles in the top of your chest called a) petrels b) pectorals c) dorsals?
5. Which is the longest bone in your body?
6. What mineral is good for your bones?
7. How many muscles has the average football player?

Answers
1. True; the gluteus maximus is your biggest muscle. 2. a) 3. a) 4. b) 5. Your thighbone or femur. 6. Calcium 7. 650, same as everyone

255

Seeing

How do you see things?

YOUR EYES ARE A LITTLE like tiny TV cameras. At the front is a lens called the cornea–the disk in the center of your eye. This projects a picture onto an array of light-sensitive cells called the retina lining the back of your eye. The retina then sends signals to your brain.

Why do we have two eyes?
Each eye gives a slightly different view of the same thing. The nearer a thing is, the greater the difference between the view. These slight differences combine in the brain to give us an impression of 3D depth and solidity, and allow you to judge easily just how far away things are.

How do you see when it's dark?
In order to see well in dim light, your pupils open wider to let in more light. In the dark, it gets up to 16 times bigger. The sensitivity of the retina increases too, by up to 100,000 times. But the retina becomes less sensitive and the pupil narrows in very bright light. Even so, very bright light can damage the eyes, which is why you should never look directly at the sun.

Optic nerve to the brain

Retina (light-sensitive layer)

Tear gland

Iris

Pupil

Cornea

Lens

Eyelash

▶ **Eyes**
Your eyes are two tough little balls filled with a jellylike substance. They are very sensitive to dirt, so you blink frequently to wipe away dust, and they are washed by tears.

Life all around: People

▶ **Color mix**
All the colors you see are contained in white daylight. If you spin this wheel of color, the colors would mix to look white.

What are rods and cones?
Rods and cones are the two kinds of light-sensitive cell in your retina. Rods tell you how bright light is. Cones tell you what color it is. Rods are much more sensitive than cones and work even in dim light. Cones don't work well in dim light, which is why colors look gray at night.

How do you see in color?
It was once thought that there are three kinds of cones in the eye—some sensitive to red light, some to green, and others to blue. So some scientists think you see colors simply as different mixtures of these three "primary" colors. Others think there are pairs of cones sensitive to blue and yellow, red and green, and the color you see depends on which half of the pair is stimulated most by the light.

What's in your eyeball?
Eyes are filled with a jellylike substance called vitreous humor, which is very clear to let you see well.

What are primary colors?
Primary colors are three basic colors that can be mixed in different proportions to make every other color. The primary colors of light are blue, green, and red. But when mixing paint you use three different primary colors—yellow, magenta (a kind of purply red), and cyan (a greeny blue).

What is short sight?
Not everyone sees equally well. Short sight is when your eyeball is slightly stretched out, so you can only see things nearby clearly without glasses or contact lenses. Long sight is when you only see distant things clearly.

What is your iris?
The iris is the ring around the dark center or pupil of your eye. It contracts or expands to open the pupil wider, or close it.

◀ **Flipped flower**
As rays of light focus through the cornea, they cross over. So the picture in your eye is flipped upside down, though your brain sees it as normal.

QUIZ

1. Which has the sharpest sight, in order: a) human b) fly c) eagle?

2. Astigmatism means: a) your eyes are different sizes b) you tend to blink frequently c) you see things magnified more in one direction than the other?

3. Everybody has a blind spot right in the middle of their eye: true or false?

4. Everyone has one strong eye and one weak: true or false?

5. Pupils get their name because the picture they give is small, like schoolchildren: true or false?

Answers
1. c), a), b) 2. c) 3. True 4. True 5. True

257

Hearing

How do you hear?

SOUND REACHES YOUR EAR AS VIBRATIONS in the air. Your ear flap funnels sound into a tube into your head called the ear canal. Inside, the sound hits a taut wall of thin skin called the eardrum and makes it vibrate like a drum. As the eardrum vibrates, it rattles three little bones called ossicles, which knock against the "cochlea," deep inside the ear. The cochlea is filled with fluid, and as it is knocked waves run through the fluid, and the waves waggle hairs attached to nerves. The waggling of the hairs tells your brain about the sound.

Why do you have two ears?
So that you can tell which direction a sound is coming from. You can pinpoint sound because a sound to the left of you is slightly louder in your left ear than in the right ear, and vice versa.

What is earwax?
Earwax is a yellow-brown waxy substance made in the glands lining the ear canal. Its purpose is to trap dirt and germs and prevent them getting into the inner ear. It is slowly eased out of the ear.

Why do ears pop?
When going up or down in a plane, the air pressure may change before the air inside your ears can adjust. The popping is when pressure evens out again.

▼ **Inside the ear**
The flap of skin on the side of your head is only the entrance to the real ear. Inside are all the complex mechanisms of the middle ear, designed to pick up the faintest vibrations in the air and amplify them enough for the hearing nerve to respond to.

- Semicircular canals
- Eardrum
- Auditory nerve to brain
- Cochlea
- Eustachian tube
- Ossicles
- Ear canal

Life all around: People

Inside the cochlea
The vibrations of a sound are amplified (made much bigger) by the time they reach the cochlea of the inner ear, but they are still very tiny. So inside the cochlea is a remarkably sensitive mechanism that picks up every slight movement of the fluid.

Flap that moves with waves in the cochlea

Nerve hairs that move with the flap

How is sound measured?
Sound is measured in decibels. Decibels go up geometrically—that is, three decibels is twice as loud as two and four twice as loud as three, and so on.

How loud is a pin dropping?
About ten decibels—just about the quietest sound you can hear. A whisper is about 20 decibels. Some animals hear even quieter sounds.

How loud is a jet?
Close up, a jet engine is about 140 decibels. This kind of noise is genuinely painful to the ears, and can do lasting damage. Indeed, any continuous sound over 90 decibels can be damaging.

How do your ears help you balance?
Next to the cochlea is a cluster of three fluid filled rings called semi-circular canals. These canals act like tiny spirit levels, telling you when you are tilting one way or the other, as the fluid moves inside the canal.

What are the ossicles?
The ossicles are three linked bones in the middle ear. They all have Latin names and a simple English equivalent: hammer or malleus, anvil or incus, stirrup or stapes.

Hammer

Anvil

Stirrup

▲ Ossicles
Sounds are transmitted through the middle ear by the tiny ossicle bones. The hammer bangs against the anvil like a blacksmith's hammer on his anvil. The stirrup gets its name because it is shaped like a rider's stirrup.

QUIZ

1. The cochlea is named after the snail: true or false?
2. The nerve hairs inside the cochlea are called a) the ear trumpet of Obi b) Copper's flute c) the organ of Corti?
3. Is the scientific name for your earflap: a) pinna b) sinna c) dinna?
4. Humans can hear much higher-pitched sounds than dogs: true or false?
5. Sound travels through the air in a) waves b) straight lines c) little lumps?
6. What is the loudest sound in space?
7. The pitch of a sound is measured in a) Hertz b) Akes c) Paynes?
8. Sound travels faster through water than air: true or false?
9. The ear is connected to the top of your throat: true or false?

Answers
1. True 2. c) 3. a) 4. False 5. a) 6. Nothing; there is no sound in a vacuum 7. a) 8. True 9. True

Taste, smell, and touch

How do you taste things?

YOU TASTE THINGS BOTH WITH taste buds on your tongue and also by using other senses. Your taste buds can only detect the difference between sweet food, salty food, sour food, and bitter food. But when you eat, other sensations—heat and cold, texture, and especially smell—also come into play. It is these extra sensations that help you tell the difference between a huge range of foods.

▲ **Taste bud**
The taste buds contain clusters of cells with hairs on the end. When these hairs are washed over by saliva, they react if the saliva contains the right taste.

▼ **Cheese tastes**
Taste buds can detect little real difference between all these cheeses. But other senses such as smell combine with taste to reveal the range of flavors.

What are taste buds?
Taste buds are clusters of special cells set in tiny wells in your tongue—so tiny that there are 10,000 of them altogether. As you chew, tiny particles of food dissolve in saliva and trickle down into the taste buds. Each taste bud reacts to a particular kind of taste—sweet, salty, sour, or bitter. If the food contains the right flavor, the taste bud is triggered and it immediately sends off a message down nerves to your brain.

Where do you taste sweet and sour things?
Your taste buds are hidden away inside tiny bumps on your tongue called papillae. Taste buds that respond to sweet tastes are on the tip of the tongue. Salty flavors are detected just behind on the sides of the tongue. Sour things set off taste buds on the sides of your tongue farther back. Really bitter tastes hit the back of your tongue.

How do you smell?
Smells are tiny particles in the air. As you breathe in, some of these particles travel up your nose and dissolve in the mucus. They then drift toward a small patch at the top inside called the olfactory epithelium. This tiny patch is packed with ten million smell receptors. These smell receptors react to chemicals dissolved in the mucus and send messages to your brain.

Life all around: People

How do you feel things?
You feel things touch your skin because your skin is packed with different kinds of receptors that can tell you whether things are hard or soft, hot or cold, rough or smooth to the touch.

Where can you feel things?
There are sense receptors in almost every part of your skin. But some places, like your hands and face, have lots of receptors and so are very sensitive. Other places on the body—the small of your back, for instance—have very few and so are not so sensitive.

How do you know how hard someone's pushing?
When someone touches you, the receptors in the skin send off signals to your brain. The harder the touch, the faster the nerves send signals.

Which parts of the body are most sensitive to heat?
Your elbows and feet are more sensitive to heat than many other parts of the body. This is why mothers sometimes test the bathwater for babies to make sure it isn't too hot by putting their elbow in the water.

The back of the tongue responds most strongly to bitter tastes

This part of the tongue detects sour tastes

This part of the tongue responds to salty tastes

The tip of the tongue detects sweet tastes strongly

▶ **Taste areas**
The taste buds are concentrated on certain parts of the tongue—and different areas of the tongue react to a different one of the four main tastes—sweet, salt, sour, or bitter.

QUIZ

1 Sometimes you can't taste things if your nose is blocked with a cold: true or false?

2 By the age of 20, you will have lost 20% of your sense of smell: true or false?

3 Dog's noses are a) 100 times more sensitive than humans b) 10,000 times c) 1 million times?

4 Babies have a better sense of smell: true or false?

5 It is possible to smell up to 100 feet (30m) underwater: true or false?

6 Sense receptors connect to which part of the brain: a) the midbrain b) the brain stem c) the cortex?

7 Taste buds last only a day: true or false?

Answers
1. True 2. True 3. b) 4. True 5. False; you can't smell underwater 6. c) 7. False; taste buds last a week before the body replaces them

261

Thinking

What is a brain?

YOUR BRAIN IS an amazing package of 100 billion tiny nerve cells, each connected with up to 25,000 others. This huge number of interconnecting nerve cells is what makes your brain clever-enabling it to do everything from analyzing all the signals coming from your senses to controlling your body-and thinking.

The cerebral cortex receives signals form the senses and sends signals to move parts of your body

The frontal lobe of the cerebrum is involved in thinking and planning.

Basal ganglia

Cerebellum

Hippocampus

Pituitary gland controls many important body hormones

Brain stem

▲ **Inside the brain**
All the brain looks quite similar to start with, but a closer look reveals a varied structure. It has two halves or hemispheres, left and right, linked by a bundle of nerves called the corpus callosum. In the center are a collection of different structures, each with its own task.

What goes on in the brain?

Different things happen in different parts of the brain. The center of the brain is right at the top of the neck where nerves from the spine join it. This is where body functions you don't have to think about—like breathing and heart rate—are controlled. Just behind this is the "cerebellum," which controls balance and coordination. Wrapped around the outside is the cerebrum where you think, and complex tasks such as speaking and actions you decide on are controlled.

What is the nervous system?

The nervous system is your body's hot line carrying messages from the brain to every organ and muscle in your body—and sending back a constant stream of information to your brain about the world both inside and outside your body. It is made from long strings of special nerve cells or neurons.

What is the central nervous system?

The brain and the spinal cord (the bundle of nerves that runs through the middle of your backbone) together make what is called the Central Nervous System, or CNS. All the body's nerves radiate out from the CNS in branches. This is why severe damage to the spine can make someone paralyzed.

Life all around: People

Where in your brain do you see things?
All your senses are received in a part of the brain called the cortex, which is like the brain's rind, the outer layer of the brain at the top. The part of your brain that registers what you see is called the "visual cortex." This is right at the back of the brain.

How does a brain appear?
It looks like a large, soggy, pinkish gray walnut on the outside. This is because the outer part of the brain is made of masses of nerves called gray matter, which are wrinkled up to get as much inside your head as possible.

▲ **Juggling**
Skills like juggling, which require tremendous coordination are gradually programmed into the cerebellum at the back of the brain.

What's the difference between the brain's two halves?
The left side of your brain controls the right side of your body; the right side controls the left. Most people are right-handed because the left side of the brain is dominant. In left-handed people, the right side of the brain is dominant. Since the part of the brain that controls speech is in the left of the brain, and the part of the brain that controls awareness of space is in the right, some people believe left-handed people are likely to be good at art and design.

◀ **Nerves in the body**
Nerves link your brain to every part of the body. Like branches on a tree, the nerves spread out from the Central Nervous System (the brain and spinal cord). Motor nerves control movement. Sensory nerves send signals back to the brain. Sensory and motor nerves are usually paired.

QUIZ

1. The small club-shaped part of the brain center that controls moods, willpower and learning is called the a) hippopotamus b) hippocampus c) cortex?

2. The brain is the only part of the body that can survive without oxygen: true or false?

3. Boys' brains are bigger in relation to their bodies than girls': true or false?

4. The tiny gaps between the ends of nerves are called a) gates b) prolapses c) synapses?

5. The brain goes to sleep when you do: true or false?

Answers
1. b) 2. False; even a few minutes without oxygen damages the brain 3. False; the reverse is true 4. c) 5. False

263

Growing

How do you grow bigger?

Y OUR BODY IS MADE UP FROM MILLIONS of tiny packets called cells, nearly all of them so tiny they can be seen only under a powerful microscope. You grow as these cells divide in two again and again to make new cells. This is called cell multiplication and happens most when you're young. You look young because most of your body is made from new cells.

What makes you grow?
You grow bigger mainly because the pituitary gland in your brain sends out a chemical in the blood called "growth hormone." When this hormone is released into the blood from time to time, it tells body cells to divide and multiply.

▼ **Body changes**
Most people in the richer parts of the world live until they are 70 or more, and some live until they are 100. During their lives, their body will have gone through many changes, gradually growing during childhood, then slowly deteriorating once they are adults.

You stop growing when you are and adult, and may have children of your own

At puberty, the body changes shape and sexual organs begin to mature

As people get older, they begin to slow down and get less fit and active

During childhood, legs and arms grow longer and adult teeth grow

Old people may become quite frail and their senses are weaker

A two-year old is about half the height it will be when an adult

Babies often learn to crawl before they take their first tottering steps

Life all around: People

What is puberty?
You are born with sexual or reproductive organs—the organs that enable you to have children when you are an adult. Puberty is the time of your life when they develop in the right way for you to have children. Puberty comes at different ages in different people. Girls typically reach puberty at 11 or 12. Boys reach it at 13 or so.

What happens at puberty?
Puberty is the time when your body begins to change from a child's into an adult's. A girl begins to grow breasts and her hips become wider, and she grows hair around her genitals. Eventually she starts her monthly periods of menstruation. A boy's testes begin to grow and produce sperm. He begins to grow hair on his chin and his voice deepens.

What happens when you grow old?
By the time you are 20 or so, you are fully grown. From then on, your body starts to slowly deteriorate. People age at different rates, but by the time you are 65 or so, you will be less fit, and less able to run and jump. Your hair will probably be gray or white. You may be bald if you are a man. Your skin will be wrinkled. You may stoop. You will certainly find all your senses less sharp. All the same, all body cells except for nerve cells are continually being renewed, even when you old.

1. Before cell division begins, each chromosome is copied, and the two copies coil up into dark rods that join to make an X-shaped pair

2. The pairs of chromosomes line up across the center of the cell. They stick on to tiny threads that grow across the cell

3. The threads begin tugging in opposite directions. The pairs split in half, and each half is pulled to the opposite end of the cell

4. A new nucleus starts to form around the cluster of chromosomes at each end of the thread. Each cluster of chromosomes is identical

5. A membrane grows around the two new nuclei, and eventually the old cell divides down the middle to create two brand new cells

▲ **How cells grow**
New human cells are made when old cells split in half. This is how your body grows when you are young, and how body cells that are worn out are replaced by new ones. The process of cell division is called mitosis, and ensures that each new cell is identical and gets a copy of the cell's instructions or chromosomes.

QUIZ

1. The part of your body that grows quickest until you are five is a) the brain b) the legs c) the tongue?

2. A doctor who specializes in treating children is called a a) neurologist b) pediatrician c) pedologist?

3. Your brain goes on growing all your life: true or false?

4. The rate at which you grow is controlled by a chemical released by the pituitary gland in your brain: true or false?

5. The tallest man who ever lived was nearly 9 feet (2.7m) tall: true or false?

6. What part of your body is almost as big when you are baby as it will be when you are an adult?

Answers
1. a) 2. b) 3. False 4. True 5. True 6. Your head

What's the biggest creature that
ever lived on land?

Where does sand
come from?

Was Australia ever
joined to Africa?

What is a wadi?

Do glaciers ever
melt?

How do we know
dinosaurs existed?

Could we ever visit the center of the Earth?

Was New York ever in the tropics?

Earth

How does frost break rock?

268 Earth's history
270 Fossils
272 Continental drift
274 Structure of the Earth
276 Mountain building
278 Volcanic eruptions
280 Earthquakes
282 Weathering
284 Rivers
286 Glaciers
288 Deserts
290 Coasts
292 Caves

How long do earthquakes last?

When did the first humans appear?

How hot is it in the Earth?

Earth's history

How old is the Earth?

THE EARTH IS ABOUT 4.6 BILLION YEARS OLD. Scientists know this from analyzing meteorites—lumps of rocky debris that have fallen to Earth from space and probably formed at the same time as the Earth. They can tell the age of a meteorite by studying atoms in it. When the meteorite formed, certain atoms in it began to break up at a constant rate. By analyzing just how far they have broken up scientists can tell exactly how old the meteorite is. This is called radioactive dating.

Earth formed 4.55 billion years ago

Archean

Precambrian   Proterozoic

How is Earth's history divided up?

Just as the day is divided into hours, minutes, and seconds, geologists divide the Earth's history into different time Periods. The longest are eons, which are hundreds of millions of years long. The shortest are Chrons, just a few thousand years long. In between come Eras, Periods, Epochs, and Ages.

What do we know about Earth's early history?

We know only a little about the first four billion years of Earth's history, called the Precambrian because fossils from that time are rare. But we know a great deal about the last 590 million years, since the beginning of the Cambrian Period, and this is split into 11 Periods.

How can you tell how old a rock is?

Many rocks form from mud and other sediments on seabeds and riverbeds. When living things die, their remains are sometimes preserved in sediments like these. Because different plants and animals lived at different Periods in Earth's history, geologists can tell how long ago the rocks formed from the fossils they contain.

When did the dinosaurs live?

The dinosaurs first appeared during the Triassic Period, about 220 million years ago. They became widespread over the next 150 million years, during the Jurassic and Cretaceous Periods. Then about 65 million years ago, they suddenly died out—perhaps because a huge asteroid struck the Earth and turned it cold.

Key:
1. Jellyfish
2. Trilobite
3. Acanthodian (jawed fish)
4. Cooksonia (early land plant)
5. Ichthyostega (early amphibian)
6. Dimetrodon (early mammal-like reptile)
7. Anteosaurus
8. Herrerasaurus (early dinosaur)
9. Pterandon (early flying reptile)
10. Cephalopod (squidlike shellfish)
11. Brachiosaurus (dinosaur)
12. Crusafontia (small mammal)
13. Merychippus (early horse)
14. Proconsul (great ape)
15. Homo sapiens (early man)

Physical World: Earth

QUIZ

▼ Earth's history

This illustration shows the major time Periods of Earth's history and some of the characteristic fossil creatures and plants that help geologists identify rocks from each of these different Periods.

Key to Periods:
Archean: 4,600-2,500 million years ago (mya)
Proterozoic 2,500-590 mya
Cambrian 590 mya
Ordovician 505 mya
Silurian 438 mya
Devonian 408 mya
Carboniferous 360 mya
Permian 286 mya
Triassic 284 mya
Jurassic 213 my.a
Cretaceous 144 mya
Tertiary 65 mya
Quaternary 2 mya

Cambrian Period
Ordovician Period
Silurian Period
Devonian Period
Carboniferous Period
Permian Period
Triassic Period
Jurassic Period
Cretaceous Period
Tertiary Period
Quaternary Period

Palaeozoic Era
Mesozoic Era
Cenozoic Era

1. Is a meteorite a a) ball of rock from space b) kind of ancient rock c) kind of dinosaur?
2. The Earth formed from the remains of an old star: true or false?
3. What was the first living thing on Earth?
4. What period in Earth's history did the swamps that gave us coal form in:
   a) Precambrian
   b) Carboniferous
   c) Quaternary?
5. How old is the oldest rock ever found a) 38,000 years b) 380 million years c) 3.8 billion years?
6. When did the first humans appear?

Answers
1. a) 2. True 3. Bacteria 4. b) 5. c) 6. 30,000 years ago

269

Fossils

What are fossils?

FOSSILS ARE THE RELICS of plants and animals that have been preserved for many thousands or millions of years, usually in stone. They may be the remains of living things—bones, shells, eggs, seeds, and so on. Or they may just be signs, such as footprints or scratchmarks, left behind.

▼ Fossils
There are many different ways in which once living things can be fossilized.
Key: 1. Spider in amber, the hardened resin of ancient trees
2. Leaves turned to carbon
3. Trace fossil: footprint preserved in hardened mud
4. Fossilized shark's teeth
5. Trilobite: ancient shellfish
6. Petrified (turned to stone) logs

What is the oldest fossil?
The oldest fossils, but for microscopic traces of bacteria, are "stromatolites." These are fossils of giant pizzalike mats, made by colonies of billions of microscopic cyanobacteria. Some of these date back more than 3 billion years!

How do fossils form?
When an animal dies, its soft parts rot away quickly, but if its bones or shell are buried quickly in mud, they may eventually turn to stone. When a shellfish dies and sinks to the seafloor, its old shell gets buried in mud. Over millions of years, water trickling through the mud dissolves away the shell, but minerals in the water fill its place, making a perfect cast.

How do scientists tell a fossil's age?
From the rock it is found in. They know how old rocks are relative to each other because layers of rock form on top of each other, so the lowest layers are oldest. Measuring the fossil's radioactivity gives a more precise date.

Physical World: Earth

▼ Big lizard
Iguanadon was one of the first dinosaurs identified, by the fossil hunter Gideon Mantell in the 1820s. Mantell found a fossilized claw of the iguanodon, and realized that it was very similar to that of a modern iguana (a kind of lizard)—only twenty times as big! Mantell thought it had four legs like an iguana. We now know it only had two.

Why do geologists study fossils?
The simplest way to tell the age of a rock is from the fossils it contains. Many species only lived at certain times during Earth's history. So if a rock contains a species that dates from a certain time, the rock must have formed at that time too. Useful fossil species for dating are called index fossils. These index fossils include certain ancient kinds of shellfish called trilobites, graptolites, brachiopods, crinoids, ammonites, and belemnites.

What do fossils tell us?
It is from the study of fossils that fossil scientists have learned how plants and animals evolved on Earth. They have found that most species only lived for a short time, before being superseded by another better adapted to the conditions of the time.

How do we know dinosaurs existed?
Because they left behind a huge number of their fossilized remains. No one knew what they were for a long time. In China, people thought they belonged to dragons. Then in the 1820s an English naturalist named William Buckland recognized them for what they were. Now hundreds of species of dinosaur have been identified from fossils, and recently, a clutch of dinosaur eggs was discovered with the babies inside.

What's the biggest creature that ever lived on land?
The largest dinosaurs were the plant-eating sauropods, which had long necks for browsing on trees. The biggest may have been the brachiosaurus, which was at least 46 feet (14m) tall and 80 feet (25m) long—four times as tall as an elephant and six times as long.

QUIZ

1. What was the biggest predatory dinosaur that ever lived?
2. There once were flying dinosaurs as big as airplanes: true or false?
3. There were creatures on land long before there were any in the sea: true or false?
4. Coal is the fossilized remains of swamp plants: true or false?
5. Woolly mammoths (large, hairy elephantlike creatures) were found preserved in a) sugar b) ice c) sand?
6. Which of these shelled creatures was related to squids: a) ammonite b) cockle c) brachiopod?

Answers
1. Tyrannosaurus Rex 2. True 3. False 4. True 5. b) 6. c)

271

Continental drift

Have the continents always been the same?

NO. THEY MAY LOOK VERY FIXED but the continents are moving slowly all the time. Sometimes they crunch together. Sometimes they break apart in the middle. But they are always drifting about the world, like ice floes on a pond. This is called continental drift.

How fast are the continents moving?

The speed continents move varies from place to place. North America is drifting away from Europe at about an inch (2.5cm) a year—the same rate a fingernail grows. This might seem slow but over millions of years, it can take continents thousands of miles.

Why could South America and Africa fit together like a jigsaw puzzle?

Because they were once joined together—along with all the other continents—in a giant supercontinent that geologists call Pangea. About 200 million years ago, Pangea began to break up, and the fragments have drifted apart to form today's continents.

What happens when continents crunch together?

The edge of one continent may well be crumpled up. These crumples or folds form high mountain ranges. The Himalayan Mountains were thrown up where India crashed into Asia. Indeed, the Himalayas are getting higher, because India is still pushing into Asia.

Is it just the continents that move?

No. The whole of the Earth's surface is broken into 20 or so giant fragments called tectonic plates, and all of these move around. The continents are simply carried on top of these moving plates, like cargo on a raft.

220 mya The continents were joined together as Pangea

▶ **Pangea**
The map of the world has been changing over time. 220 million years ago (mya), there was just one supercontinent, Pangea, and one giant ocean Panthalassa. By analyzing the alignment of magnetic particles in rocks (which set pointing North like compasses), geologists have traced how the continents have drifted since.

200 mya Pangea split into two landmasses, Gondwanaland in the south and Laurasia in the north

135 mya The South Atlantic opened between South America and Africa. India broke off and drifted toward Asia

Physical World: Earth

▶ Ice cover in the Ice Age
At times during Earth's history, in cold periods called Ice Ages, many parts of the world have been covered in thick ice. Because continents have drifted, even the Sahara was once glaciated!

Was New York ever in the tropics?
Yes. 250 million years ago, the place where New York is now was on the equator, and it was a boiling hot desert. It was in this hot desert that the sandstone formed that gave New York its famous brownstone houses. 300 million years ago, New York was a steamy swamp.

40 mya Europe split from North America, and the continents began to drift to their current positions

Why do the continents move?
Probably because they are carried on by moving currents of molten rock in the Earth's interior. Just as bubbles rise to the surface in boiling soup, so giant streams of molten rock rise up through the Earth's hot interior. When they come up beneath the surface, these "convection currents" spread out sideways, carrying the continents with them.

Was Australia ever joined to Africa?
Yes, about 200 million years ago the north coast of Australia was joined to the south east coast of Africa.

The future The Pacific will shrink and the Atlantic will get wider. Africa will split along the Great Rift Valley in the east

QUIZ

1 Million of years ago you could have walked from Spain to Newfoundland in a few hours: true or false?

2 What continent was once attached to the south coast of Australia?

3 Which two continents crashed together to form the Alps?

4 The San Andreas fault in California is the gap between two tectonic plates: true or false?

5 Tides in the sea occur because the continents are moving: true or false?

6 There were once dinosaurs in Antarctica: true or false?

7 Was the Sahara always a desert?

Answers
1. True 2. Antarctica 3. Europe and Africa 4. True 5. False 6. True 7. No

Structure of the Earth

What's inside the Earth?

THE HARDY, ROCKY SURFACE OF THE EARTH, called the crust, is just a thin shell. Inside, the Earth gets hotter and hotter until at the very center the temperature reaches 12,600°F (7,000°C)–hotter than the surface of the Sun. So just beneath the crust, there is an ocean of half-molten rock thousands of miles deep called the mantle. Beneath this, in the Earth's center is an outer core of molten iron and nickel. In the inner core, pressure is so intense that the metal cannot melt despite the heat.

Inner core of solid iron at 12,600°F (7,000°C)

Outer core of molten nickel and iron

Mantle of hot semi-molten rock

Thin crust of solid rock

▲ **Inside the Earth**
Beneath the thin shell called the crust, the Earth churns and bubbles like soup, and at the boundary of the Earth's core there may be continents and oceans like those on the surface.

How big is the Earth's crust?
The Earth's crust is surprisingly thin. Proportionally it is not much thicker than the skin on an apple. It is thickest beneath the continents. But even here it is no more than 40 miles (68km) thick at most. It is thinnest beneath the oceans, often less than 5 miles (8km) thick.

How do we know what the Earth is like inside?
From the vibrations of earthquakes. Long after the ground stops shaking, the reverberations from earthquakes shudder through the Earth. Sensitive detectors pick them on the far side of the world. Just as you can hear the difference between metal and wood if you tap them with a spoon, so scientists can "hear" the Earth's interior from the pattern of earthquake waves (page 106).

Could we ever visit the center of the Earth?
No one has ever managed to drill more than 7 miles (12km) down. Even at this depth, pressures are so great and rock so hot and soft that drill bores close up as fast as they are drilled. It seems unlikely then that anyone will ever get through the thin crust to the mantle, let alone down to the core.

What's the mantle made of?
The mantle is made of rock, like the crust. But the most common minerals are minerals that are rare on the surface, like perivskovite and olivine.

Lithosphere

Physical World: Earth

Where does the crust end?
The crust meets the mantle along a boundary called the Mohorovicic discontinuity. Chemically, this is a distinct break. But the top of the mantle is just as rigid as the crust. So scientists often group the top of the mantle together with the crust and call it the lithosphere. "Litho" means stone. Beneath the lithosphere is a layer that flows like very, very, sticky treacle called the asthenosphere.

▼ Crack in the Earth
The Earth's surface is cracked in many places. One of the biggest cracks is under the middle of the oceans. Here the tectonic plates that form the Earth's rigid shell or lithosphere are pulling apart. As they do, molten rock from the mantle oozes up, cools, and solidifies, forming a long ridge of rock.

Mantle

Are there any gaps in the crust?
Yes, the crust—or rather the lithosphere (see left)—is actually broken into 20 or so giant bits called tectonic plates. Molten material from the mantle oozes up along the cracks, creating volcanoes—especially where they are pulling apart.

How hot is it in the Earth?
In the lithosphere, the temperature climbs 63°F (35°C) every 3,300 feet (1,000m) you go down. The core reaches 12,600°F (7,000°C).

Molten rock oozes up between the plates

The solidified magma forms a mid-ocean ridge

QUIZ

1. How thick is the Earth's mantle a) 186 miles (300km) b) 1,860 miles (3,000km) c) 18,600 miles (30,000 km)?
2. In 1864, the famous book 'Journey to the Center of the Earth' was written by a) Nathaniel Hawthorne b) Charles Dickens c) Jules Verne?
3. There are continents on the Earth's core: true or false?
4. Most of the water in the oceans came from inside the Earth: true or false?
5. What have the Earth beneath the crust and old cloaks in common?
6. Some caves reach right down into the mantle: true or false?
7. Which one is lightest (least dense): a) the Earth's crust b) its mantle c) its core?
8. The world's deepest borehole in the Kola Peninsula in Russia goes down: a) 2 miles (3km) b) 7 miles (12km) c) 50 miles (80km)?

Answers
1. b) 2. c) 3. True 4. True 5. Both are called mantles 6. False 7. a) 8. b)

275

Mountain building

What are the world's highest mountains?

THE WORLD'S HIGHEST MOUNTAINS are the Himalayan mountains in Asia to the north of India. Here are all the world's ten tallest mountains, including Mount Everest, the very highest mountain of all, 29,021 feet (8,848m) high. But each continent has its high mountain range. There are the Andes in South America where there are many peaks over 20,000 feet (6,100m), the Rocky Mountains in North America, and the Alps in Europe.

▲ **The Himalayas**
The Himalayas include such soaring peaks as K2 (28,244 feet/8,611m), Kanchenjunga (28,201 feet/8,598m) and Lhotse (27,916 feet/8,511m) as well as Mt. Everest.

▼ **Folding mountains**
Whether they are made from sediments settling on the seabed or from volcanic plateaus, most rocks form in flat layers. But as the plates of the Earth's crust move together, folds form as the layers are squeezed horizontally.

Have mountains always been there?

New mountains are being created all the time—although it takes many millions of years. Most of the world's highest mountains were formed quite recently in Earth's history. The Himalayan mountains, for instance, have been built up within the last 40 million years—and they are still growing even today.

How are mountains made?

Some mountains are created by volcanic eruptions, but most mountains are thrown up by the tremendous power of the Earth's crust moving. Some mountains are huge slabs called fault blocks or "horst" that are thrown up by powerful earthquakes. The biggest ranges, though, are created by the crumpling of rocks as the great plates that make up the Earth's crust squash together. Mountains that form like this are called fold mountains. The Alps, Himalayas, and the Andes are all fold mountains.

As plates of the Earth's crust push together, layers of rocks get pushed up in folds

If the plates go on pushing, the layers may overturn and snap

Eventually the layers may begin to snap altogether, creating a "nappe"

276

Physical World: Earth

Where do mountains form?
Fold mountains are usually thrown up where the edge of a continent is crumpled as it collides with another tectonic plate. The Andes, for example, were crumpled up right along the edge of South America, as the plate beneath the Pacific ocean crunched into it. When two continents collide, the mountains may be huge. The Himalayas are being thrown up where the Indian plate is driving into Asia.

▼ Block mountains
The movement of tectonic plates can put rocks under such strain that they fracture, creating cracks called faults in the rock. Large faulted blocks of rock may then be thrown up to create mountains.

Will mountains always be there?
No, each mountain range is slowly worn down by the weather, and by rivers and moving ice, over millions of years. Scotland's Caledonian mountains and North America's Appalachians were once among the world's highest, but are gradually being worn flat. Other parts of the world that are now completely flat were once mountainous.

When did mountains form?
Fold mountains are usually created in fairly short mountain-building phases. By short, geologists mean a few tens of millions of years, rather than hundreds. In different parts of the world, geologists identify different phases from the past. In North America, there are phases called the Huronian, Nevadian, and Pasadenian. In Europe, there were the Caledonian, Hercynian, and Alpine. Most of today's major mountain ranges were formed in the last 50 million years.

Why are some mountains snow-capped?
Air gets colder as you get higher. Above a certain level, called the snowline, it is always too cold for snow to melt, so it stays all year round. The snowline is 16,500 feet (5,000m) up in the tropics, 8,900 feet (2,710m) in the Alps, and at sea level at the Poles.

QUIZ

1. What is the highest mountain in North America?
2. How high is the Vinson Massif in Antarctica: a) 4,070 feet (1241m) b) 11,683 feet (3,562m) c) 16,859 feet (5,140m)?
3. Mt. Everest is gaining height: true or false?
4. The Black Forest in Germany was originally volcanoes: true or false?
5. Which continent has no mountains over 16,400 feet (5,000m)?
6. A syncline is a) a steep slope b) a downfold in rock c) a bad habit?
7. How did Japan's highest mountain form?

Answers
1. Mt. McKinlay (20,316 feet/6,194m) 2. c) 3. True 4. False; it is made from fault block mountains 5. Australasia 6. b) 7. Mt. Fujiyama is a volcano

277

Volcanic eruptions

What are volcanoes?

VOLCANOES ARE PLACES where molten rock from the Earth's hot interior comes up through the ground. The molten rock is called magma, and sometimes it just oozes slowly onto the surface as a red hot stream called lava. Sometimes, though, the magma builds up underground then bursts through in a huge explosion called an eruption. When this happens, steam and ash are thrown high into the air, ash and hot cinders rain down far around, the volcano, and streams of lava gush from the neck of the volcano.

▲ **Crater**
Around the top of a volcano's vent, there is usually a wide mouth called a crater. Occasionally, the entire top of the volcano collapses into the magma chamber to form a huge crater called a caldera.

▼ **Types of volcano**
No volcano is quite the same. Each has its own shape and way of erupting—and each eruption is slightly different. But there are three main kinds of volcano: shield volcanoes, cone volcanoes, and composite volcanoes.

How does the magma get out through the ground?
Before it emerges, magma builds up in a space underground called the magma chamber. The pressure of magma bubbling up underneath builds until it pushes magma up to the surface—either through a pipe called a vent, or a crack called a fissure.

Are all volcanoes made of lava?
No, some are made of ash, and some are made of alternate layers of lava and ash.

Are all volcanoes the same?
No. There are many different kinds. The kind of volcano depends mainly on the nature of the magma. When magma is low in silica, it is very runny. It gushes out from cracks in the ground and flows out over wide areas and hardens to form what are called shield volcanoes, because they are shaped like shields. When magma is high in silica, it piles up around the vent. A tall cone is built up in successive eruptions. It is these cones which make the most distinctive volcanoes, like Mt. Fuji in Japan, and Kilimanjaro in Kenya.

Shield volcanoes are formed by gentle eruptions of runny lava

Cone volcanoes are built up by successive eruptions of sticky, acidic lava

Physical World: Earth

Quiz

▶ **Lava stream**
The red hot stream of molten rock called lava looks frightening, but it is rarely lava that kills people in a volcano eruption. The real killers are usually the clouds of choking ash that bury the landscape far around—or worse still, high-speed flows of mud or glowing ash called nuée ardenté.

Where are volcanoes found?

Volcanos are found mainly along the boundaries between the great tectonic plates that make up the Earth's surface—and in particular, a ring around the Pacific Ocean called the Ring of Fire. They are also found on "hot spots"—places where columns of hot rock bubble up under the crust and burn through.

What is a dormant volcano?

Some active volcanoes erupt almost continuously, but others go quiet for periods and so are said to be dormant. If they never erupt, they are extinct.

Why do some volcanoes erupt explosively?

When the magma is very thick and sticky, it can clog up a volcano's vent. When it finally bursts through, it is like popping the cork of a champagne bottle. Steam and carbon dioxide gas dissolved under pressure in the magma boil and bubble violently as the pressure is released, and these bubbles drive the magma in an explosive froth up through the vent. The old clog is shattered to smithereens by the explosion, forming ash, and cinder that are hurled for miles around the volcano.

Composite volcanoes are built up from alternate layers of lava and ash

In each eruption the ash falls slowly to settle on top of the lava flow

1 Which is the tallest volcano in Japan?

2 What volcano erupted and buried the Ancient Roman town of Pompeii in Italy
a) Etna b) Stromboli c) Vesuvius?

3 Edinburgh Castle is built on an extinct volcano: true or false?

4 Most of the world's active volcanoes are on land: true or false?

5 Can volcanoes change the world's weather?

6 Vulcanologists try to predict eruptions by looking for a slight swelling in a volcano: true or false?

Answers
1. Fujiyama 2. c) 3. True 4. False; most are under the sea 5. Yes 6. True

279

Earthquakes

What are earthquakes?

EARTHQUAKES ARE A SHAKING of the ground. Some are so slight they can barely rock a cradle. But some are so violent they can shake down mountains and destroy cities. All kinds of things can set off small earthquakes, from the rumbling of heavy traffic to the eruption of a volcano. But the biggest earthquakes are set off by the shuddering of the vast tectonic plates that make up the Earth's surface as they grind slowly together underground.

What sets off an earthquake?
Tectonic plates are sliding past each other all the time but sometimes they jam. Then the rock bends and stretches for a while until the strain gets so much that it snaps and the plates lurch on again. The snapping of the rock and sudden jolting of the plates sends shock waves out in all directions. When these waves reach the surface, they create earthquakes.

Where do earthquakes start?
The starting point of an earthquake underground is called the hypocenter or focus. The epicentre is the point on the surface above the hypocenter. Earthquakes are strongest at the epicenter, and get gradually weaker farther away.

Crust

P waves are waves that alternately stretch and squeeze the rock

The Earth in cross-section: P waves

Mantle

Outer core

P waves are refracted as they pass through the Earth's liquid core

Inner core

S waves are waves that move the ground from side to side or up and down

S waves are deflected altogether by the liquid core

The Earth in cross-section: S waves

▶ **P and S waves**
Earthquake body waves can travel right through the world. Some, called P waves, can reach the other side in barely an hour and register on seismometers far from the earthquake. S waves take only a little longer. Comparing readouts from two or three stations pinpoints the earthquake's epicentre. The way the different kinds of waves are refracted or bent through the Earth reveals a great deal about its interior.

Physical World: Earth

QUIZ

▲ **Earthquake zones**
Earthquakes tend to occur mostly along the boundaries of tectonic plates. Places like Japan and Mexico are particularly prone to quakes.

What are earthquake zones?
Earthquake zones are places particularly prone to earthquakes. Most of these lie on or near the edges of tectonic plates. Many major cities, such as Los Angeles, Tokyo, and Mexico City, lie in earthquake zones.

How long do earthquakes last?
Most earthquakes are over quickly, lasting less than a minute. The longest, which hit Alaska in March 1964, lasted just four minutes.

How are quakes measured?
With a device called a seismometer, which responds to vibrations and records them on a computer display.

What are earthquake waves?
Earthquake or "seismic" waves are the vibrations from earthquakes. There are two main kinds. Body waves travel underground at huge speeds, and can vibrate all around the world. Surface waves travel out along the surface from the epicenter and are much slower, but it is these which do the real damage in an earthquake. Surface waves called Q waves shake the ground from side to side, bringing down tall buildings. Surface waves called Rayleigh waves shake the ground up and down, and seem to roll through sandy or muddy ground like waves in the sea.

What is the Richter scale?
The Richter scale shows an earthquake's magnitude—that is, how strong the waves are on a seismometer. Each point indicates a tenfold increase in size. A really big earthquake is at least 6 on the Richter scale.

1. Which Japanese city was devastated by an earthquake in 1995: a) Kobe b) Nagasaki c) Tokyo?
2. What is the name of the fault that sets off earthquakes in California?
3. Which year was San Francisco burned to the ground after an earthquake: a) 1854 b) 1906 c) 1937?
4. Giant waves called tsunami are set off by a) tidal movements b) volcanoes c) undersea earthquakes?
5. The ancient Chinese detected earthquakes with brass frogs: true or false?
6. Earthquakes can make rock rise and fall like tides in the sea: true or false?

Answers
1. a) 2. San Andreas 3. b) 4. b) and c) 5. True 6. False

Weathering

▲ **Grand Canyon.**
The Grand Canyon was carved by the Colorado river as it cut down through the Colorado Plateau, which was lifted up thousands of feet in a massive movement of the Earth's crust.

How do hills wear down?

HILLS AND MOUNTAINS are all worn flat eventually. It takes many thousands or even millions of years, but the combined attack of the weather, chemicals in rainwater, running water, wind, glaciers and various other "agents of erosion" will wear them flatter and flatter. Valleys will get broader, hilltops will get lower, ridges will get narrower until at last an entire mountain range is turned into a lowland plain.

What is weathering?
Although rock is hard, the assault of the weather will turn even the hardest granite into soft clay over time. The weather breaks down rocks through the attack of moisture, heat and cold and chemicals in rainwater. Usually only rocks near the surface are affected, but water trickling down through the ground can weather rocks far underground. The more extreme the climate, the faster rock weathers.

How does frost break rock?
When water freezes it expands by almost a tenth. So when it freezes inside cracks, it can push them apart. This expansion can exert a pressure of 6,600 pounds (3,000kg) on an area of rock the size of a postage stamp. As water freezes and thaws repeatedly inside cracks, this pressure can shatter rocks.

What is scree?
Scree is the huge piles of angular rock you often see littering mountain slopes. As the rock shatters, the chunks fall off and build up at the bottom of the slope.

Limestone scenery

What is karst?
Streams and rainwater absorb carbon dioxide gas from the soil and air, and so become a weak acid called carbonic acid. Most things are unaffected by this acidity, but limestone is very easily corroded by this acid. So when limestone is near the surface, water trickling down through the rock can dissolve huge holes in it. This can create a spectacular landscape of gorges, caves and jagged rock called karst, after the Karst region of Bosnia.

◀ **Uluru**
Uluru or Ayers Rock is a dome of sandstone in the middle of the Australian bush. Deep furrows down its side testify to the erosive power of running water even in this dry place.

Physical World: Earth

Quiz

1 In China there is a spectacular range of pointed limestone hills made of eroded limestone. What are they called?

2 The corroded grooves in limestone are a) tongue and groove b) brett and pull c) clint and gryke?

3 The flaking of rock on the Yosemite dome in California is caused by the removal of the weight of rock above: true or false?

4 Rabbits make rock vulnerable to erosion by their burrowing: true or false?

5 What's the main erosive force on mountaintops?

▲ **Wave rock**
This fantastically curved rock was carved by floods of water in much wetter times. A dry climate has preserved its shape since.

What is exfoliation?
In dry areas, rocks often flake off in leaves at the surface. This is called exfoliation. It was once thought this was due to extremes of heat and cold. Now scientists think it is caused by the growth of salt crystals in water that seeps into the rock.

What are tors?
Tors are outcrops of rock often seen on the tops of hills on granite moors, such as Dartmoor in England. The tor began as bedrock beneath a hilltop, but as water trickled into cracks, it rotted away below the ground—except where there were massive block with few cracks. These massive blocks were left standing out above the ground as the rotted rock around was worn away.

What happens to weathered rock?
Fragments of weathered rock roll downslope to be washed away by rivers, creep down slowly, or get gradually worn finer and form the basis for soil.

◀ **Shattered peak**
Thousands of years of frost have shattered the peaks of high mountains like the Matterhorn, creating sharp, craggy, broken ridges and a jagged rock summit.

Answers
1. Guilin Hills 2. c) 3. True 4. True 5. Frost shattering

283

Rivers

What makes rivers run?

RIVERS ARE KEPT RUNNING BY RAINFALL. The rain does not always run off the land directly into rivers. Sometimes it sinks into the ground on hilltops and emerges lower down through holes called springs. Sometimes it is frozen into ice and snow for a while and does not reach the river until it melts. But without rain every river will stop running eventually. The more it rains, the fuller the river will be. Floods usually occur a little while after heavy rainstorms, or after winter snows melt in spring.

High in the hills, a small stream tumbles over rocks in a narrow V-shaped valley

Farther downstream rivers flow in smooth channels made of their own deposited material.

Oxbow lake formed by a cut-off meander

Toward the sea, the river may flow across the broad plains of silt it has washed down

As tributaries join, the river grows bigger

Lower down, the river may wind across the valley floor in broad meanders

▶ **Changing river**
Near its start, high in the hills, streams simply tumble this way and that over rocks in steep valleys. But as they become broad rivers farther down, they begin to flow in smooth channels made entirely of fine material worn away higher up and washed down by the river.

Physical World: Earth

Why do rivers wind?
All rivers tend to wind, especially as they near the sea, where they often wind in horseshoe shape bends called meanders. The biggest meanders occur where the river flows wide and smooth through soft muddy banks. They form partly because of the way water in the river spirals, and partly because of the way the river wears away its bed and banks in some places, and deposits grains of mud and sand in others.

Where do rivers start and end?
Rivers start off as small streams high in the hills. As they flow downhill, they are joined by other streams, called tributaries. They grow bigger and bigger, and at last flow into a sea or lake.

How do rivers shape the land?
Over many thousands of years, rivers can wear away the land. First, they carve downwards to create deep V-shaped valleys. Then they swing sideways to widen the valleys, eventually, into broad plains. They may also bury the valley floor or plain in fine silt.

As it nears the sea and slows down, the river may drop its sediment load and split into branches

What is a waterfall?
A waterfall is a place where a river plunges straight over a ledge of rock. Typically, they occur where the river flows across a band of hard rock. The river wears away the soft material, leaving the hard rock barely touched. The highest waterfall is the Angel Falls in Venezuela, which plunges 3,211 feet (979m).

What is a delta?
Deltas are areas of sediment—sand, silt, and mud—piled up in a river's mouth, as the river hits the sea, or a lake, and slows down. Often the river splits up into many smaller branches called distributaries.

How do rivers move silt and sand?
Rivers carry their "load" of sediment in three ways. Big stones are rolled along the riverbed. Smaller grains are bounced along the bed. The finest grains float in the water.

What is an oxbow lake?
An oxbow lake is a small lake formed where a river meander has been cut off. The river wears away the outside bend of the meander, making its neck narrower and narrower, until the river cuts through, cutting off the meander.

QUIZ

1. The Mississippi River forms a delta as it enters the Gulf of Mexico: true or false?
2. River flow reaches its peak a) just before a rain storm b) during a rain storm c) just after a rainstorm?
3. What is the world's longest river?
4. Is river braiding a) where rivers branch b) where rivers wear their banks away c) raised river banks?
5. The River Orinoco, a tributary of the Amazon, flows uphill: true or false?

Answers
1. True 2. c) 3. The River Nile in Egypt (4,151 miles/6,695km) 4. a) 5. True

285

Glaciers

What are glaciers?

GLACIERS ARE RIVERS OF SLOWLY moving ice that form when it is too cold for snow to melt. Nowadays, they form only in high mountains and towards the North and South Poles. But in the past, during cold periods called Ice Ages, glaciers were far more widespread. Huge areas of North America and Europe were under ice, and the ice left dramatic marks on the landscape.

How do glaciers form

Glaciers form when new snow, which scientists call névé, falls on top of old snow. The weight of the new snow compacts the old snow into denser snow, which the scientists call firn. In firn, all the air is squeezed out, so it looks less like fluffy snow and more like white ice. Over time, the ice is compacted more and more until it turns into thick white glacier ice and begins to flow, very slowly, downhill.

Névé

Moraine—rock debris

Cirque where glacier begins

Crevasses

▶ **Alpine glacier**
Glaciers are great rivers of ice that flow down through mountain valleys, creeping lower and lower until they melt. The ice in glaciers is not clear, but opaque like packed snowballs, and it is filled with dirt and debris. Bands of dirt fallen from the mountain slopes above streak the surface, and cracks appear where the ice bends over bumps in the valley floor.

Snout

Physical World: Earth

How do glaciers shape the land?
Glaciers move very slowly but their sheer weight and size gives them enormous power to carve out the landscape. They carve out huge U-shaped valleys, gouge out great bowls in hills called cirques, and truncate (slice away) entire hills and valleys. They can also move huge amounts of rock debris then drop it in large distinctive piles called moraine.

Do glaciers ever melt?
Yes, they are melting all the time. As they flow downhill into warmer air, the end, or "snout" of the glacier melts. But snow falling up in the mountains replenishes the top of the glacier and keeps it from shrinking—unless the climate begins to warm.

What are fjords?
Fjords are very deep inlets in the coasts of Norway, New Zealand, and Canada. They were carved out by glaciers in the last Ice Age, then flooded by the sea.

▲ **Icebergs**
Icebergs are large floating chunks of ice that break off the end of ice sheets, icecaps, and glaciers and float out to sea.

When was the Ice Age?
There is not just one Ice Age. There have been four in the last billion years, and each of these has many colder periods called glacials and warmer ones called interglacials. There have been 17 glacials in the last 1.6 million years, and the last ended just 10,000 years ago.

Why do Ice Ages happen?
They are probably caused by regular wobbles of the Earth's axis, called Milankovitch cycles.

QUIZ

1. Where is the world's longest glacier?
2. Glaciers take how long to flow 6 feet (1.8m) a) a year b) a day c) a second?
3. What did the ship *Titanic* hit before it sank?
4. The largest iceberg ever was almost as big as Denmark: true or false?
5. In 1913 an iceberg was seen floating past the Statue of Liberty: true or false?
6. The landscape of Cape Cod in Massachusetts was shaped by ice: true or false?
7. What continent has the biggest area of ice?
8. What are the cracks in glaciers called?

Answers
1. Antarctica 2. b) 3. An iceberg 4. True 5. False 6. True 7. Antarctica 8. Crevasses

287

Deserts

What are deserts?

DESERTS ARE VERY DRY PLACES where it hardly ever rains. Some deserts are very hot, like the Sahara desert in northern Africa. Some are very cold, like Antarctica. In hot deserts, what little rain there is quickly evaporates, so there is little water available for plants. So plants are very scarce in the desert. Indeed, most deserts are bare rock, rubble, or sand, with no soil.

▼ **Desert landforms**
The bare, dry landscape of the desert has its own distinctive range of landforms. With no water to round hills, the landscape is jagged, and filled with odd-shaped rocks sculpted by the wind, as well as seas of sand dunes.

Key:
1. Mushroom rock
2. Sand dunes
3. Sand ripples
4. Deflation hollow (blown out by wind)
5. Oasis

Where do deserts occur?

Many deserts occur in the subtropics—that is, just outside the tropics. The natural circulation of air around the world means air is very calm, clear and dry. The Sahara and the Great Australian desert are subtropical deserts. Some deserts, like Chile's Atacama, occur in the lee of mountain ranges that act as a barrier to rain-bearing winds. A few deserts are near seacoasts and are dry because cool ocean currents dry the air.

How hot are deserts?

Hot deserts can be the hottest places in the world, because there is no moisture in the air to block the sun's rays. Summer temperatures in the Sudan desert in Africa can soar to 133°F (56°C), hotter than anywhere else in the world. But even here it can get cold at night, because the heat escapes through the clear skies.

Are all deserts sandy?

No. Deserts that are vast seas of sand are actually quite rare. Just as many deserts are pebbly or rocky.

Are there any rivers in the desert?

Some rivers, like Egypt's River Nile, start in wet regions outside the desert and flow right through it and out the other side. Others flow only when it rains, leaving a dry riverbed most of the year round. Rivers like these are called ephemeral.

Physical World: Earth

Mushroom rock

Barchan

Wind

▲ **Wind action**
Wind plays an important part in shaping the desert landscape. Wind bouncing sand along the ground can undercut rocks to create distinctive mushroom-shaped rocks.

What is a wadi?
A wadi is a gorge cut by rivers in the desert when it rains. Most of the time it is completely dry, but after a rain storm it can fill suddenly with water in a flash flood.

How is the desert landscape shaped?
Since desert sand is very dry, it is easily blown up by the wind, and the desert has its own range of landforms sculpted from sand hurled by the wind. The high temperatures mean that rocks can easily be corroded by salts as well—or even baked to breaking point.

What is a sand dune?
A dune is sand blown into a mound by the wind. Dunes come in many different shapes and sizes, including stars, long ridges (called seifs) and crescents (barchans). It all depends on how sandy it is, and where the wind blows from. Barchans are moved along gradually as sand is blown up one side and rolls down the other.

QUIZ

1. How much of the world's land surface is covered by desert: a) a tenth b) a fifth c) one half?
2. What is the world's biggest desert?
3. Vast areas of central Asia and China are covered in a thick layer of yellow dust: true or false?
4. What is an oasis?
5. Buttes are a) sheer-sided rocks b) deep dry gorges c) the end of a valley?
6. The technical name for wind action is a) alluvial b) aeolian c) ventilation?
7. Where is Uluru, or Ayers Rock?
8. There used to be snow in the Sahara desert: true or false?

Answers
1. b) 2. The Sahara in Africa 3. True; the dust called loess was blown by winds in the Ice Age 4. A moist area in the desert 5. a) 6. b) 7. Australia 8. True

289

Coasts

How do waves shape coasts?

ON EXPOSED COASTS, the pounding of waves can wear away solid rock, undercutting hills to create sheer cliffs. As the cliffs are worn back farther, they leave behind a wide ledge of rock at sea level called a wavecut platform, or upstanding remnants of the cliff called stacks. On sheltered coasts, however, waves can build up the coast, washing in sand to create beaches.

▼ Coastal landforms
Constant battering by waves and sea water gives coasts their own range of landforms. In exposed places such as headlands, the coast is rocky, with steep cliffs, wavecut rock platforms, stacks, and even natural rock arches. In sheltered places, sand worn away from the headlands piles up as beaches.

Where does sand come from?
Sand is what is left after material broken off cliffs and rocky coasts has been battered this way and that in the sea for many years.

What is shingle?
Shingle is like sand, but with much bigger grains, the size of small peas, rather than sugar. Water sorts different grades of grain out, so that some beaches are pebbly, some are shingly, some are sandy.

Sand piles up as beaches in bays

Waves wear exposed headlands into cliffs and stacks

Physical World: Earth

▲ Blowhole
Sometimes, the sheer pressure of water from a breaking wave may force water up through a crack to burst through the top of a cliff like a fountain. This is called a blowhole.

▲ Rock arch
As waves wear away the base of a cliff over the years, they may eventually wear right through a headland, creating a natural rock arch, if the rock higher up stays intact.

▲ Stack
As the waves go on wearing away at the base of the cliff, the rock arch gets wider and eventually is so weak that it collapses, leaving just a column called a stack.

In places on low coasts, salty lagoons form

How are waves made?
Waves begin as wind blowing across the open sea whips the surface into ripples. If the wind is strong enough and blows far enough over the water, the ripples build into waves. The stronger the wind and the farther it blows (called the fetch), the bigger the waves are. In big oceans like the Atlantic and Pacific, the fetch is so big that huge "swells" build up.

How do waves move?
Waves move like a relay race. The water in them barely moves, but simply goes round in a circle, like the roller on a conveyor belt.

What are tides?
Tides are the slight rising and falling of the sea—usually twice a day—as the Earth turns round. They are caused by the pull of the Moon's gravity on the waters of the oceans.

Why do waves break?
Waves break when the water becomes so shallow that the water cannot complete a circle. Instead, water rolling round the top of the wave spills forward onto the beach, then falls back.

QUIZ

1. Groynes on a beach are a) barriers of rock b) sand bars c) fences put up to to stop sand being washed along the beach?
2. What is a bight?
3. Sand moves along a beach when waves hit the beach at an angle: true or false?
4. A coast with lots of islands and inlets is called a) an archipelago b) an insular coast c) an escarpment?
5. What is an ebb tide?
6. Spring tides are a) tides that happen only in spring b) tides that race up and down c) the most extreme tides each month?
7. What is a long, narrow continental size inlet?

Answers
1. c) 2. A very large bay 3. True; this is called longshore drift 4. a) 5. A falling tide 6. c) 7. A gulf

291

Caves

What are caves?

CAVES ARE LARGE NATURAL HOLES UNDERGROUND. Some are little bigger than a closet. Others are bigger than a cathedral. The biggest caves are called caverns. Some are single caves. Others are huge networks of chambers linked by long passageways through the rock.

How do caves form?

Caves form in many ways. Some are the old pipes that lava flowed through in volcanoes. Some are created when earthquakes crack the rock. Some are opened up by the sea. But the biggest and most extensive caves are usually in limestone. Streams and rainwater absorb carbon dioxide gas from the soil and air, turning it into a weak acid. Limestone has plenty of cracks called joints. As the acid water trickles down through these joints into limestone, it gradually dissolves away the rock underground. As more and more of the rock around a joint is dissolved away, it forms a cavern.

▲ **Stalagmites and stalactites**
Hanging needles and pillars formed by dripping water can turn limestone caverns into natural cathedrals.

What is a pothole?

Because limestone rock has so many cracks or joints, most streams quickly disappear into the ground. The hole down which a stream runs into the ground is called a swallowhole. Over time, mild acids dissolved in the water may corrode the crack in the rock into a deep vertical shaft. This is a pothole. Sometimes streams plunge into them as spectacular waterfalls.

▶ **Limestone underground**
Slightly acidic water trickling down through cracks in limestone gradually eats away the rock underground, opening up caverns and potholes. Below a certain level, called the water table, the rock is completely saturated with water, and the caverns are flooded.

Old cavern

Stalactite

Stalagmite

Physical World: Earth

What are stalagmites and stalactites?

Stalagmites and stalactites are formations made by water dripping through the ceiling of a limestone cavern. Calcium carbonate dissolved in the water forms long, icicle-shaped deposits that hang from the ceiling. These are called stalactites. As water drips from a stalactite onto the cavern floor, calcium carbonate is also deposited on the floor, piling up in a narrow pinnacle called a stalagmite. Eventually, the stalagmite and stalactite may actually meet to form a pillar from floor to ceiling.

Do caves last forever?

No. Although some are very old, most are gradually corroded away. As more and more of the roof rots away, it gets weaker and may eventually collapse, leaving just a large hole in the ground, called a polje. If an entire interlinked string of caverns collapses, it may create a long cliff-walled valley called a gorge, though gorges may also form in other ways.

What are gallery caves?

Gallery caves are long, dry tunnel-like caves originally formed by an underground stream, but left dry when the water table (the level of water) in the rock dropped.

Swallowhole   Pothole or ponor   Cavern   Joint

QUIZ

1 The world's longest cave network is Mammoth Cave in Kentucky. It is a) 12 miles (20km) long b) 120 miles (200km) long c) 350 miles (560km) long?

2 The world's biggest single cave is the Sarawak Chamber in Sarawak. It is big enough to hold a) a house b) the Louisiana Superdome c) the city of New York?

3 What is the technical name for an expert on caves?

4 There are huge caves under the ocean, created by waves: true or false?

5 Stalagmites and stalactites are covered in material that makes them shine in the dark: true or false?

Answers
1. c) 2. b) 3. A speleologist 4. False 5. True

293

Why does the Moon shine?

How hot is the Sun?

How many stars are there in the sky?

Who were the first men on the Moon?

How do rockets work in space?

How do satellites stay up?

Is there life on Mars?

Why do stars twinkle?

How did the Universe begin?

Space

296 The Earth
298 The Moon
300 The Sun
302 The night sky
304 Space travel
306 Satellites
308 Inner planets
310 Outer planets
312 Stars
314 The life of a star
316 Galaxies
318 Distant objects
320 The Big Bang

Why is Venus pink?

The Earth

What is the Earth?

THE EARTH IS ONE OF THE NINE PLANETS that continually circle the Sun, making up the solar system. It is the third planet out from the Sun, between Venus and Mars, and like them and Mercury, the planet nearest the Sun, it is a ball made largely of rock. What makes it special is the fact that its surface is two thirds covered by water. It is also the only planet with oxygen in its atmosphere. Without water and oxygen, there would be no life.

How was the Earth formed?

No one is absolutely sure how the Earth began. But most astronomers think that about five billion years ago there was just a vast cloud of hot gas and dust circling around the newly formed Sun. Then gradually, parts of this cloud began to clump together, pulled together by gravity. These clumps grew to form the planets.

▶ **The formation of the Earth**
Around four and a half billion years ago, the vast dark hot cloud of gases and dust around the Sun began to cool and the gas condensed into trillions of droplets. Slowly the droplets were pulled into clumps by gravity, and carried on clumping until the planets, including Earth, formed. Earth was just a fiery ball to start with, but it gradually cooled and a hard crust formed, and then an atmosphere.

Earth was born from hot gases and dust spiraling round the newborn Sun

As more and more droplets and grains of dust clumped together, the newborn Earth congealed into a red hot ball

The early Earth was a fiery ball of molten rock, but as it cooled lumps formed on the surface

Volcanoes poured steam and gases onto the surface to form the atmosphere and oceans

As the Earth cooled, the surface hardened to a crust

What shape is the Earth?

The Earth is round, but it is not quite a perfect sphere. Because it spins faster at the equator than at the Poles, the Earth is flung out a little at the equator and so bulges here. Scientists describe the Earth's shape as "geoid," which simply means Earth-shaped.

Physical World: Space

How far is Earth from the Sun?

About 93 million miles (150 million km) on average, but it varies according to the time of year. Its closest, on January 3, is called the perihelion. The farthest point, on July 4, is called the aphelion.

The crust cooled to form continents

How long does the Earth take to turn?

The Earth turns around in 24 hours, which is why days are 24 hours long. Actually, it takes 23 hours, 56 minutes and 4.09 seconds to turn around, but because the Earth moves round the Sun as well as turning, it takes exactly 24 hours for the Sun to return to the same place in the sky.

Why do we have leap years?

It takes the Earth just over 365 days to go round, which is why a year is 365 days. The journey actually takes 365.242 days, not 365. To make up for the 0.242 days and keep the calendar in step with the Earth, we add an extra day to February every fourth year, the leap year. Even this doesn't make it quite right, so a leap year is left out at the end of three centuries out of four.

Does the Earth tilt over?

Yes. It spins round on a line between the Poles called its axis. The axis is tilted over at 23.5° in relation to the Sun.

◀ **Seasons**

We get seasons because the Earth is always tilted over in the same direction. So when the Earth is on one side of the Sun, the northern hemisphere (the world north of the equator) is tilted toward the Sun, bringing summer here. When the Earth is on the other side of the Sun, the northern hemisphere is tilted away, bringing winter. The seasons are reversed in the south.

QUIZ

1. How old is the Earth:
   a) 46,000 years
   b) 4.6 million years
   c) 4.6 billion years?

2. It is shorter to go from pole to pole then back than to go around the equator: true or false?

3. The astronomer who first realized Earth goes round the Sun was a) Ptolemy b) Copernicus c) Hubble?

4. The Earth is moving round the Sun at 50,000 mph (80,000km/h): true or false?

5. The Earth is spinning at over 25,000 mph (40,000km/hour): true or false?

Answers
1. c) 2. False 3. b) Nicolaus Copernicus (1473-1543) 4. True 5. False; it takes 24 hours to spin 25,000 miles (40,000km)

297

The Moon

What is the Moon?

THE MOON IS A BALL OF ROCK, about a quarter of the size of the Earth. The Moon is held close to the Earth, like a ball on a string, by the mutual pull of the Moon and Earth's gravity. It circles continually around the Earth, taking about a month to go round, and as it goes round it also turns slowly on its axis, taking exactly the same time to go round–nearly 30 times slower than the Earth, which spins round in 24 hours.

◀ **Inside the Moon**
The Moon has a very thick crust of solid rock (about 90 miles/150km thick), a very cool mantle of softer rock beneath, and a tiny metal core.

▼ **Changing Moon**
As the Moon circles the Earth over the course of a month, we see different amounts of its bright, sunlit side, so it appears to change shape. The changes are called the phases of the Moon. The phases are, from left to right: New Moon, Half Moon, Gibbous Moon, Full Moon, Gibbous Moon, Half Moon, Old Moon. When it is growing bigger it is said to be waxing; when it is growing smaller it is said to be waning.

Why does the Moon shine?
The Moon is by far the brightest thing in the night sky. Indeed, it is so bright that you can often see it in the sky during the day too. But it does not have any light of its own. Moonlight is simply the Sun's light reflected off the white dust on the Moon's surface.

What are the Moon's seas?
The large dark patches on the Moon that look like seas are, in fact, ancient lava flows from volcanoes.

Physical World: Space

▶ Solar circle
When the Moon swings in between the Sun and the Earth, it blocks off the Sun from a small region on Earth for a few minutes. This is a solar eclipse.

Why does the Moon change shape?
It doesn't, but looks as if it does because as it circles the Earth we see its bright sunny side from different angles. At New Moon, it is between the Sun and the Earth, and we catch just a crescent-shaped glimpse of its bright side. Over the first two weeks, we see more and more of its bright side until at Full Moon, we see all of it. Over the next two weeks, we see less and less until we get back to a sliver, the Old Moon.

How long is a month?
It takes the Moon 27.3 days to circle the Earth, but 29.53 days from one Full Moon to the next, because the Earth moves as well. This 29.53 day cycle is a lunar month. Calendar months are entirely artificial.

What is an eclipse?
As the Moon goes round the Earth, it sometimes passes right into Earth's shadow, where the Sun's light is blocked off. This is called a lunar eclipse. Sometimes, the Moon passes between the Sun and the Earth and blocks off the Sun's light from a bit of the Earth. This is called a solar eclipse.

Who were the first men on the Moon?
The first men on the Moon were Neil Armstrong and Buzz Aldrin of the US Apollo 11 mission. The Apollo's lunar module landed Armstrong and Aldrin on the Moon on the July 21, 1969.

QUIZ

1. Why does the Moon look the same size as the Sun?
2. Why does the Moon look like cheese?
3. There is water on the Moon: true or false?
4. A harvest moon is a) a golden moon b) a kind of cheese c) the bright full moon of harvest time?
5. The footprints left by the astronauts on the Moon in the 1960s are still there: true or false?
6. The terminator is a) Arnold Schwarzenegger b) the boundary between the Moon's dark and bright sides c) The dark side of the Moon?

Answers
1. Because the Moon is much, much nearer. 2. Because its surface is pitted with craters 3. True 4. c) 5. True 6. a) and b)!

The Sun

What is the Sun?

THE SUN IS A STAR, just like all the others you see in the night sky. The only difference is that it is just 93 million miles (150 million km) away, not many billions. It formed about 5 billion years ago after an earlier, much bigger star blew up, and now, in middle age, burns yellow and fairly steadily, giving the Earth daylight at remarkably constant temperatures. It will probably burn for another five billion years before burning out.

Above the chromosphere is the Sun's halolike crowning ring, called the corona

The chromosphere is a thin layer through which dart tongues called spicules, making it look like a flaming forest

Core where the Sun fuses hydrogen nuclei to create enormous heat

Convection currents in the Sun's mantle

The photosphere is a sea of boiling gas, and gives us the heat and light we get on Earth

▶ Inside the Sun

The Sun is not just a flaming ball. Although it is made almost entirely of hydrogen and helium, its structure is complicated. Like the Earth, it has a core, and this is where most of the heat is produced, taking 10 million years to reach the surface. Above that are a number of different layers, including (in order outward): the photosphere, the Sun's visible surface; the chromosphere; and the corona, its glowing white hot atmosphere.

Sunspot

Physical World: Space

▲ **Solar prominences**
Solar prominences are giant flame-like tongues of hot hydrogen that loop well over 100,000km out into space — as far as the Moon from the Earth.

High above the chromosphere are prominences

How hot is the Sun?
The surface of the Sun is a phenomenal 10,800°F (6,000°C). But its core is much, much hotter, at over 27 million°F (16 million°C)!

Why is the Sun hot?
The Sun gets its heat because pressures deep in its core are enormous. Pressures are so great that the nuclei (centres) of hydrogen atoms are fused together as helium atoms. This nuclear fusion reaction—the same reaction that makes atomic bombs explode—releases a huge amount of heat.

How big is the Sun?
The Sun is medium-sized for a star, but it is more than 170 times as big as the Earth. It is 863,000 miles (1,392,000km) across.

What is the solar wind?
The solar wind is the stream of radioactive particles that is blowing out from the Sun all the time at hundreds of miles a second. These particles are so dangerous that life on Earth would be destroyed if the Earth were not protected from the wind by its magnetic field. A little of the wind creeps in through the clefts above the Poles, creating the light displays in the sky known as aurorae.

What are sunspots?
Sunspots are dark blotches that can be seen on the Sun's surface with special instruments. They are dark because they are about 3,600°F (2,000°C) cooler than the rest of the the surface. They usually appear in groups and move across the Sun's face as it rotates— in about 37 days at the equator and 26 days nearer the Poles. The average number varies, reaching a maximum every 11 years, and may be linked to storm spells on Earth.

What are solar flares?
Flares are eruptions from the Sun's surface that spout into space every now and then. They last about five minutes but they have the energy of one million atom bombs.

QUIZ

1. A postage stamp size area of the Sun's surface shines with the power of a) 1000 candles b) 150,000 candles c) 1,500,000 candles?

2. The smallest sunspots are a) as big as Africa b) 50 times as big as Africa c) 50 million times as big as Africa?

3. We get day and night because the Sun's output is continually fluctuating: true or false?

4. The solar wind escapes through holes in the corona: true or false?

5. The corona is all you see of the Sun in a solar eclipse: true or false?

Answers
1. c) 2. b) 3. False 4. True 5. True

The night sky

How many stars are there in the sky?

WITHOUT A TELESCOPE, you can probably see almost two thousand stars in the sky at night if your eyesight is reasonably good. With the most powerful telescopes of all, it is possible to see many millions. But even this is just a tiny fraction of all the stars in the Universe. Astronomers guess that there are perhaps 200 billion billion altogether, most of them as big or bigger than our Sun.

▼ Observatory
Because the world is turning, observatory telescopes have to turn too to follow the pattern of stars. So the telescope here is mounted on a turntable, and the roof turns with it. The dish to the right is a radio telescope.

What is an observatory?
An observatory is a place where astronomers study the night sky. Although some are located near cities for convenience, the air near cities is dirty and the light from cities makes night viewing hard. So most observatories are situated high on mountaintops, far away from cities, to give as clear a view as possible.

What can you see in the night sky?
The biggest and brightest thing is the Moon. Everything else is just pinpoints of light to the naked eye. Most are stars. But you can also see five of the planets—Mercury, Venus, Mars, Jupiter, and Saturn—if you look at the right time. Occasionally, you may see comets and meteors shooting through the sky. The pale band across the middle of the sky called the Milky Way is actually a concentration of the stars of our own local Galaxy.

How powerful are astronomers' telescopes?
In the last century, the most distant objects astronomers could see were about 15,000 light years away. Now powerful telescopes enable them to see galaxies 13 billion light years away. If it could focus on nearby things, a telescope this powerful would enable you to read this book from well over 300 feet (90m) away.

How do astronomers study the night sky?
In the past, they would stare at it for hours on end through a telescope, recording where every pinpoint of light was. Nowadays, the view through the telescope is usually recorded electronically, and astronomers study the electronic image on a computer screen.

Physical World: Space

January

July

◀ **Night sky**
The pattern of stars in the night sky is fixed, and has hardly changed since prehistoric times. But as the Earth moves, so we see a changing view of the pattern. So the pattern of stars gradually arcs through the sky during every night as the Earth turns. Each night, the pattern begins slightly further on. Only after a year, when the Earth has completed its journey, does the pattern start in the same place again.

What are radio telescopes?

The stars are beaming a range of radiation at us. Some, called visible light, is the light we can see. Most is invisible, with wavelengths too long or too short for our eyes. But though we can't see them, special telescopes can pick them up and so see much more of the stars than we could by visible light alone. Radio telescopes are telescopes that respond to radio waves. They use dishes to focus the rays rather than lenses, and the dishes are often 100s of yards across. Other telescopes respond to radiation bands such as microwaves and X-rays.

What are space telescopes?

Looking at the night sky through our atmosphere is like looking through frosted glass. So astronomers send up electronic telescopes on satellites to get a clear view into space. The most famous is the Hubble Space Telescope, launched in 1990.

Can you see other planets?

Until recently the only planets known were those around our Sun, but astronomers have now observed a few very big planets circling around other stars too.

▼ **Gazing at the sky**
A small telescope enables amateur astronomers to see much dimmer stars.

QUIZ

1 What is light pollution?
2 The SOHO space telescope is targeted on a) the Moon b) Uranus c) the Sun?
3 Which famous scientist was the first to look at the night sky through a telescope?
4 With a powerful telescope, you can see the equipment left behind on the Moon by the Apollo missions: true or false?
5 A light year is the distance light travels in a year: true or false?
6 Where is the largest telescope in the world being built?

Answers
1. The light from cities that makes it hard to see the night sky 2. c) 3. Galileo 4. False 5. True 6. Paranal in northern Chile

303

Space travel

Why do you need a rocket to go into space?

TO ESCAPE FROM THE PULL OF EARTH'S GRAVITY demands the power that only a rocket can provide. But traveling through the emptiness of space doesn't. So spacecraft are usually boosted into space by powerful launch vehicles–rockets designed to fall away in stages when the spacecraft is on its way.

How do rockets work in space?
There is nothing to push on in space, but rockets move forward because the burning gas swells inside the rocket burners. As it swells, the gas pushes the rocket forward.

▼ **Lunar module**
The lunar module was the small part of the Apollo 11 spacecraft that detached to carry astronauts Neil Armstrong and Buzz Aldrin down to the Moon's surface for the first Moon landing in 1969.

When was the first space flight?
The first space flight was made in October 1957 by Russia's *Sputnik 1*. The second, a month later, launched a dog called Laika into space in *Sputnik 2*. Sadly, Laika never came back.

What is the space shuttle?
Early spacecraft were used for one flight only. The space shuttle is a reusable spacecraft. It is launched on the back of rockets like all spacecraft, but glides back to Earth and lands just like an aeroplane, and so can be used for missions again and again.

▶ **Rocket power**
Some rockets such as boosters burn a solid rubbery fuel, but most are powered by liquid fuel. Since this only burns with oxygen, the rocket also carries a tank of liquid oxygen. The fuel and the oxygen mix in a combustion chamber, then an igniter sets them alight.

The payload—the satellite or crew—are in just a tiny section on top of the rocket

The second stage of the rocket will come into action when the first falls away

The liquid fuel and the liquid oxygen are stored in separate tanks

Fuel and liquid oxygen mix in the combustion chamber and swell ferociously as they burn, giving the rocket thrust

Physical World: Space

▶ **Men on the Moon**
Astronaut Neil Armstrong waves during the Moon landing of July 21, 1969—the first manned landing on another world.

▼ **Space shuttle in action**
The space shuttle can be used for anything from ferrying scientists to space labs, to repairing satellites.

Why are things weightless in space?
Astronauts orbiting the Earth float around as if they are weightless. In fact, they are not, but the spacecraft is hurtling around the Earth so fast it counteracts the effect of gravity. It is as if the astronauts were in a lift falling so fast they float off the ground.

Where can astronauts go?
Except for the manned missions to the Moon, all the spacecraft that have been sent off to explore the planets are robot craft, guided automatically by computer, and by radio signals from Earth. They have to be automatic, because it is very hard to bring them back to Earth. The farthest humans are likely to go is Mars.

How many planets have spacecraft been to?
The first successful planetary spacecraft was *Mariner 2*, which flew past Venus in 1962. *Mariner 10* reached Mercury in 1974. The *Vikings 1* and *2* landed on Mars in 1976. The *Voyager* spacecraft flew past Jupiter (1979), Saturn (1980-81), Uranus (1986), and Neptune (1989) before heading out of the solar system. So only Pluto has not been visited.

What are space stations?
Space stations are bases in space where astronauts can live and work. The Russian *Mir* has been orbiting the Earth since 1986, and the crew is replaced every two or three months. The giant ISS (International Space Station) is being built now and should be launched in 2002.

How do satellites stay up?
By circling the Earth so fast that they never come down—like a ball thrown very hard. The closer they are to Earth, the faster they have to go.

QUIZ

1 Who was the first man in space?
2 What did Neil Armstrong say when he stepped onto the Moon?
3 You can see TV pictures from Mars live over the Internet: true or false?
4 To escape Earth's gravity, spacecraft need to travel at least: a) 240 mph (400km/h) b) 2,400 mph (4,000km/h) c) 24,000 mph (40,000km/h)?
5 There is a Russian space station orbiting Venus: true or false?
6 How many manned missions to the Moon were there a) 1 b) 6 c) 22?
7 Who was the first man to walk in space?

Answers
1. Yuri Gagarin in 1961
2. "One small step for a man; one giant leap for mankind"
3. True 4. c) 5. False 6. b)
7. Alexei Leonov in 1965

305

Satellites

What are satellites?

SATELLITES ARE OBJECTS that orbit (circle) around planets. There are natural satellites, like our Moon, and the moons that orbit planets such as Jupiter and Saturn. But in the past few decades, we have launched more and more man-made satellites. These tiny spacecraft are designed to stay in space orbiting the Earth to perform all kinds of tasks, from land use surveys to speeding up worldwide telephone communications.

▶ Satellite
Most satellites get their power from panels of solar cells that turn sunlight into electricity. The panels are hinged to ensure they always face the Sun. Many satellites also have little gas jets to turn the satellite around and ensure it is positioned exactly right.

When were the first satellites launched?
The first artificial satellite was the *Sputnik 1* launched by the Soviet Union in 1957. Three years later, the *Tiros 1*, the first weather satellite was launched. Then in 1962, the *Telstar* satellite beamed the first live television pictures across the Atlantic.

How do satellites stay up?
The Earth's gravity stops satellites flying off into space, but they stay up because they are moving too fast through space to fall back to Earth. To stay in orbit, the satellite must fly fast enough not to fall but not so fast that it whizzes off into space. Gravity gets weaker further from the Earth, so the higher the orbit, the slower the satellite needs to fly to stay up.

Are all satellite orbits the same?
No. The orbit chosen for a satellite depends on its purpose. Many satellites are launched into what is called a low orbit, about 180 miles (300km) above the Earth. A low orbit satellite circles the Earth in about 90 minutes. Low-orbit satellites cost the least to launch, since it requires a low power rocket to get them up. To get a satellite into a high orbit—above 18,000 miles (30,000km)—the satellite has to be launched first into a high orbit with one set of rockets. A second set then fires to steer it into the correct orbit.

Why do they bother with high orbits?
It costs a lot to launch a satellite into a high orbit. But an orbit 22,187 miles (35,786km) above the Earth takes exactly 24 hours. If a satellite in this orbit is above the equator, it always stays above the same place on the ground. This "geostationary" orbit is used for many weather and communications satellites.

Physical World: Space

◀ **Orbiting satellite**
There are now hundreds of observation satellites in space designed to look back down on Earth, for anything from science to spying. Cameras on board spy satellites can now give such high resolution that they can pick out individual buildings and even people.

▶ **Land and sea**
Most satellite photos are in artificial colors to penetrate the atmosphere better.

What's a polar orbit?
Polar orbiting satellites circle the Earth from Pole to Pole about 530 miles (850km) above the ground, covering a different strip of the surface each time around. So eventually, the satellite scans the entire surface in detail.

How are satellites launched?
Satellites are launched into space either by rockets, or carried up by the space shuttle. The shuttle can only reach heights of a few hundred miles, so can only place satellites in low orbit. But some satellites have little rockets to move them up to a higher orbit.

What is a communications satellite?
Communications satellites transmit around the world anything from TV pictures to telephone calls. Each word of a telephone call from, say, New York to Australia is bounced around the world off the satellite on a beam of microwaves.

What's the GPS?
The GPS is the Global Positioning System. This is a network of satellites in space that allows people with a GPS device on land, on sea, or in the air to fix their position accurately to within a few feet.

QUIZ

1 About how many satellites are launched every year: a) 10 b) 30 c) 100?

2 Satellite measurements have shown that there are hills and valleys on the ocean surface: true or false?

3 You can see some satellites in space with the naked eye: true or false?

4 How many satellites are there in space: a) 170 b) 550 c) more than 1,500?

5 The Pentagon (in Washington) knows exactly where every single satellite is all the time: true or false?

6 What is the launch path of a satellite called?

7 What kind of orbit do TV satellites have?

Answers
1. c) 2. True 3. True 4. c) 5. True 6. Trajectory 7. Geostationary

307

Inner planets

What is the solar system?

THE SOLAR SYSTEM is the Sun and all the planets and other bits and pieces that circle around it. There are nine planets altogether–four rocky inner planets near the Sun including the Earth, and five farther out away from the Sun. The bits and pieces include comets, tiny lumps called asteroids, and meteors.

◀ **Mercury**
Mercury hurtles around the Sun in just 88 days (compared to 365 for the Earth). But it takes 59 days to turn once on its axis. This means the Sun comes up only once a year. But once it's up it stays up for 176 days!

What are the inner planets?

The inner planets are, in order away from the Sun: Mercury, Venus, Earth, and Mars. All four are quite small compared with some of the outer planets such as Jupiter, and all four are made mostly of rock. Because they are made of rock, they have a hard surface on which a spacecraft could land, and are sometimes called the "terrestrial" (earthlike) planets. Space probes have landed on both Venus and Mars.

How hot is Mercury?

Mercury is so near the Sun that daytime temperatures soar to 800°F (430°C), more than enough to melt lead. But its atmosphere is so thin that it loses all this heat at night, when temperatures plunge to -290°F (-180°C)!

Swirls of carbon dioxide and sulfuric acid

The thick atmosphere boosts surface pressure to 90 times that of Earth's

▶ **Venus**
Venus turns very slowly indeed compared to Earth. It takes 225 days to go around the Sun, yet 243 days to turn once around. So a day on Venus is longer than its year.

The atmosphere is made from fumes of gases from volcanoes

308

Physical World: Space

Why is Venus pink?
Venus is pink because it has an atmosphere so thick we can never see the surface of the planet. The atmosphere is made of white fumes of carbon dioxide and pink clouds of sulfuric acid, so it would be deadly for humans. The atmosphere is so deep that the pressure on the ground would be enough to crush a car to foil.

Why is Venus so hot?
Venus is the hottest planet in the solar system, with surface temperatures of 890°F (470°C). The build up of carbon dioxide gas in its atmosphere has created a runaway "greenhouse effect," trapping the heat from the Sun like the panes of glass in a greenhouse.

Why is Venus called the evening star?
Venus's thick atmosphere reflects light so well it shines like a star. But because it is quite close to the Sun, we can only see it in the evening, just after the Sun sets. By midnight, it has disappeared. But it may become visible again just before sunrise.

What volcano is three times as high as Mt. Everest?
The surface of Mars is much more stable than Earth's and there is no rain or running water to wear down the landscape. So mountains can be very high. One volcano, called Olympus Mons, is 15 miles (24km) high—three times as high as Mt. Everest!

Is there life on Mars?
When the Viking space probes landed on Mars in the 1970s, they found it completely lifeless. But in 1996, microscopic fossils of what might be miniviruses were found in a meteor from Mars. Future space probes may reveal microlife beneath the surface.

▼ **Mars**
Mars is sometimes called the red planet because it is rusty. The surface has a lot of iron dust which has been oxidized (rusted) by the carbon dioxide in its atmosphere.

Mars has small polar ice caps

Markings on Mars's surface were once thought to be signs of civilization—but they are purely geological

QUIZ

1. Venus turns backward (the opposite way to its orbit): true or false?
2. There are ancient pyramids on Mars: true or false?
3. For a few hours during Mercury's day the Sun goes backward through the sky: true or false?
4. What is the name of the space probe that landed on Mars in 1997?
5. Which of the inner planets have moons?
6. Mercury has ice caps of yellow acid: true or false?
7. Which planet is closest to Earth?
8. Which planet has the shortest year?
9. Are there volcanoes on Venus?

Answers
1. True 2. False 3. True 4. Mars Pathfinder 5. Mars and Earth 6. True 7. Venus 8. Mercury (88 days) 9. Yes

Outer planets

What are the outer planets?

THE OUTER PLANETS BEYOND MARS are, in order away from the Sun: Jupiter, Saturn, Uranus, Neptune, and Pluto. Of these, all but Pluto are very, very big—much bigger than the inner planets such as Earth and Mars. They are also made mostly of liquid gas rather than rock. So spacecraft could never land on them.

Which is the biggest planet?

Jupiter is 88,650 miles (142,984km) across, 450,000km around and twice as heavy as all the planets put together. It is 1,300 times as big as the Earth, but only 318 times as heavy, because it is made largely of liquid hydrogen and helium.

▼ **Saturn**
Saturn is the most beautiful of all the planets, with its shimmering pale butterscotch atmosphere and its halo of rings.

▶ **Uranus**
Uranus is the seventh planet out from the Sun, and rolls around it almost on its side.

Like Saturn, Uranus has rings, but much smaller

Saturn's rings occur in broad bands, labeled with the letters A to G outward

Great Red Spot

◀ **Jupiter**
High-speed winds—six times faster than hurricanes on Earth—whir through Jupiter's atmosphere, creating bands of curling clouds on the surface—including a whirlpool called the Great Red Spot or GRS, which has been there at least 300 years.

What are Saturn's rings?

Saturn's rings are the planet's shining halo, first noticed in 1659 by Dutch scientist Christiaan Huygens (1629-1695). They are made of countless billions of tiny chips of ice and dust—most the size of ice cubes. The rings are incredibly thin—no more than 150 feet (45m) deep—yet they stretch more than 46,000 miles (74,200km) out into space.

Physical World: Space

▼ Neptune
Neptune is the eighth planet out from the Sun—up to 2.5 billion miles (4 billion km). It is so far away from the Sun that it takes 164.79 years to go around—its year is 164.79 Earth years.

Neptune receives so little solar heat that the surface is -346°F (-210°C)

Winds of hydrogen and helium roar round at over 2,000kmh

How many moons have the outer planets?
All the outer planets except Pluto have lots of moons. Jupiter has 16, Saturn at least 19, Uranus 17, and Neptune 8. Some of them are almost as big as the planet Mercury. Saturn's moon Titan is exciting astronomers because it has an atmosphere—the only moon in the solar system with one—so may have some form of life.

When were Uranus and Neptune discovered?
Unlike the planets farther in, Uranus and Neptune were completely unknown to ancient astronomers. They are so far away from us and so faint that they can only be seen through powerful telescopes. Uranus was discovered only in 1781, and Neptune in 1846. They were both visited by the *Voyager* space probe between 1986 and 1989.

▶ Pluto and Charon
Pluto is five times smaller than Earth, and its moon Charon is almost half its size. It is so far away that it was only spotted for the first time in 1930.

Why is Neptune turquoise?
Neptune and Uranus are both bluey turquoise in color because their surfaces are completely covered in deep oceans of liquid methane (the same gas you burn in ovens).

How cold is it on Pluto?
Pluto is so far from the Sun, the Sun looks just like a star in the sky, and temperatures plunge to -364°F (-220°C). Each day on Pluto lasts 6.39 Earth days—but a year lasts 248.54 Earth years, during which time Pluto travels more than 9 billion miles (15 billion km).

QUIZ

1 Which planet is farthest from the Sun?
2 Comets are made mostly of ice: true or false?
3 Saturn would float if you could find a bath big enough: true or false?
4 Which planet is named after the Roman god of the underworld?
5 The surface of Jupiter spins at 28,000 mph (45,000 km/h): true or false?
6 Saturn's moon Enceladus is made mainly of sugar: true or false?
7 On Uranus in spring, the Sun rises and sets backward: true or false?
8 Which planet has the most moons?
9 Jupiter glows like a big light bulb: true or false?

Answers
1. Pluto 2. True 3. True 4. Pluto 5. True 6. False 7. True 8. Saturn 9. True

Stars

What are stars?

STARS ARE HUGE FIERY BALLS OF GAS. They shine because they are burning. Deep inside, hydrogen atoms fuse together to form helium as they are squeezed by the star's gravity. This nuclear reaction unleashes so much energy that the core of the star reaches millions of degrees and makes the surface glow—sending out light, heat, radio waves, and many other kinds of radiation.

How big are stars?
Our Sun is an average sized star. There are "red giant" stars 20 to 100 times as big. Supergiants such as Betelgeuse are 500 times as big and 420 million miles (700 million km) across. There are also smaller stars too, such as white dwarfs smaller than the Earth and neutron stars just 9 miles (15km) across. These remnants of old stars have collapsed under their own gravity.

Stars begin life when clumps of gas and dust in nebulae are pulled together by gravity

As gravity squeezes the clumps, they begin to get hot

Only big enough clumps get hot enough to start the fusion reaction

Nuclear fusion begins as hydrogen atoms fuse together to make helium. The heat makes the star glow

▶ **Star life**
Stars are born when clumps of gas in space are drawn together by their own gravity, and the middle of the clump is squeezed so hard that temperatures reach 18 million°F (10 million°C)—enough to start the nuclear fusion reaction that makes stars glow. All this happens inside vast clouds of dust and gas called nebulae.

Physical World: Space

What is a constellation?
Constellations are patterns made by stars that astronomers use to find their way around the night sky. There is no link at all between the stars in a constellation; it simply looks that way. They were given names like the Great Bear and Orion by astronomers long ago. There are now 88 recognized.

Why do stars twinkle?
They twinkle because the Earth's atmosphere is never still, and starlight twinkles as the air wavers. Light from the nearby planets is not distorted as much, so they don't twinkle.

How hot are stars?
The surface temperature of stars ranges from 6,300°F (3,500°C) to more than 72,000° (40,000°C).

What is the brightest star?
The nearer a star is, the brighter it appears. So some of the biggest brightest stars in the Universe appear quite dim simply because they are far away. The star that seems the brightest from Earth is Sirius the Dog Star, which is 26 times brighter than the Sun. But the hypergiant Cygnus OB2 No. 12 is 810,000 times brighter than our Sun but is almost 6 billion light years away, so seems quite dim.

What is the nearest star?
Apart from our Sun, the nearest star is the faint Proxima Centauri just over 4 light years away. The nearest visible to the naked eye is Alpha Centauri, 4.35 light years away.

If the heat made in the core pushes out as hard as gravity pulls in, the star stabilizes and burns steadily for billions of years

QUIZ

1 What constellation is named after a fish?

2 What star shines at the dead center of the northern sky?

3 The constellation Pleiades is named after a) three sisters b) seven sisters c) twelve sisters?

4 The group of stars called the Big Dipper in the USA is called in Europe a) the Plow b) the Panhandle c) the Scythe?

5 The constellation Cygnus is named after a god who became a swan to seduce a girl: true or false?

6 The Dog Star has a companion star called the Pup Star: true or false?

7 Betelgeuse gets its name because it is the color of beetle blood: true or false?

Answers
1. Pisces 2. Polaris, the Pole star 3. b) 4. a) 5. True 6. True 7. False

313

The life of a star

How long do stars live?

THE BIGGEST, BRIGHTEST STARS are the shortest-lived, many surviving less than ten million years. Medium-sized stars like our Sun last much longer—ten billion years or more. Small stars may last much, much longer.

▼ The end of a star
Toward the end of a star's life, its hydrogen is burned up and it shrinks to burn helium. When the helium runs out, the outer layers cool and it swells to become a red giant. The biggest stars go on swelling to become supergiants with cores so pressurized that carbon and silicon fuse to make iron.

Why do stars die?
Stars die when they have exhausted their vast supplies of nuclear fuel. When the hydrogen runs out, they switch to helium. When helium runs out, they quickly exhaust any remaining nuclear fuel then either blow up, shrink or go cold.

What is a supernova?
A supernova is a gigantic explosion that finishes off a supergiant star. For just a brief moment, the supernova flashes out with the brilliance of billions of suns. They are rare and short-lived, but there is always one somewhere in the Universe.

What are the oldest stars?
The oldest stars are not stars at all but look like them because they are so far away. Some of these "quasi-stellar radio objects" or quasars, are so far away, the light we see left them 13 billion years ago.

Once iron forms in its core, the star does not release energy but absorbs it

Physical World: Space

What are nebulae?

Nebulae are giant clouds of gas and dust spread throughout the galaxies. Some of them can be seen through telescopes because they shine faintly as they reflect starlight. Others, called dark nebulae, can only be seen because they hide the stars behind with an inky black patch. It is in these dark nebulae that stars are born.

The collapse of a supergiant star triggers an explosion like a gigantic nuclear bomb called a supernova

As it absorbs energy, the star suddenly and catastrophically collapses in a few seconds to little bigger than a planet

What is a white dwarf?

White dwarfs are the small white stars formed as stars smaller than our Sun lose their surface gas altogether and shrink. Yet they are much bigger than neutron stars, which are all that is left of a supergiant star after a supernova explosion. Neutron stars are unimaginably dense.

QUIZ

1 Supernova can send out more energy in a few seconds than our Sun in 200 million years: true or false?

2 Stars called pulsars which beam out regular radio signals are called LGMs. LGM stands for: a) Little Green Man b) Low Gas Matter c) Light Generating Masses?

3 A teaspoonful of neutron star weighs a) 10 tons b) ten million tons c) ten billion tons?

4 Red dwarf stars glow red because they are made of coal: true or false?

5 Astronomers have discovered alcohol in the clouds called nebulae: true or false?

Answers
1. True 2. a), because the signals are so regular, it was once thought they might be aliens 3. c) 4. False 5. True

Galaxies

What are galaxies?

OUR SUN IS JUST ONE of a vast concentration of more than 100 billion stars, arranged in a shape like a fried egg, more than 100,000 light-years across. This huge star city is called the Milky Way or the Galaxy because we see it as a pale band across the night sky–the word "galaxy" comes from the Greek for milky. But earlier this century, astronomers realized that the Galaxy is not the only star city in the universe. In fact, there are billions of similar star groups scattered throughout space. These are also called galaxies (with a small "g").

▼ **The Milky Way**
The Milky Way is the pale, blotchy white band that stretches right across the night sky. A powerful telescope reveals that is made of countless stars. It is actually an edge on view of our Galaxy.

The trailing arms of stars are embedded in a ball of dark matter

Why is the Milky Way just a band across the sky?
Because we are seeing it edge on. We are out on one edge, looking in toward the center and the Milky Way in the sky is the narrow layer of stars stretching away from us. If we could travel millions of light years out at right angles to the Milky Way, we would see that it is indeed spiral.

Where is the Earth?
The Earth and the solar system are on one of the Galaxy's spiral arms, about 30,000 light years out from the center.

The Galaxy is sweeping the Sun and other stars around at 60 million mph (100 million km/h)

There is a concentration of stars at the heart of the Galaxy

Physical World: Space

Barred spiral galaxy

Irregular galaxy

Spiral galaxy

Elliptical galaxy

▶ **Galactic shapes**
There are four main kinds of galaxy, but the distinction between them is not always completely clear.

Is the Galaxy turning?
Yes, it is whirling round so fast it sweeps us along at 60 million mph (100 million km/h)! We go once round the Galaxy, a journey of almost 100,000 light years in just 200 million years. But we are so much a part of the Galaxy we only know we are moving by watching distant galaxies.

The Sun is just one of the stars in the Galaxy, located on an arm 30,000 light-years out

What is a spiral galaxy?
A spiral galaxy is one of the four kinds of galaxy. It has spiraling arms of stars like a giant Catherine wheel. They trail because the galaxy is rotating rapidly. Our Galaxy is a spiral galaxy.

Where is the next galaxy?
The Galaxy's nearest neighbor is the only other galaxy you can see with the naked eye, the Andromeda galaxy, which is about 2.9 million light years away. But there are 30 or so galaxies in our own neighborhood, called the Local Group, which is itself part of a cluster of 3,000 galaxies.

Is there anything else but stars in a galaxy?
The Milky Way and other spiral galaxies look flat like a fried egg. In fact, they may be shaped more like burgers—and all we are seeing is the meat in the burger. The bread is mysterious stuff called Dark Matter, because it can't be seen or detected in any way. We only know it is there because of the way it's gravity affects the stars. It may be that more than 90 percent of the mass of the Universe is dark matter.

QUIZ

1 Every now and then galaxies crash into one another: true or false?

2 The Large Magellanic Cloud is a) a nebula b) a kind of thundercloud c) a galaxy?

3 What creatures dominated the Earth the last time our spiral arm of the Galaxy was in the same place?

4 The biggest structure in the Universe is the Great Wall of galaxies. It is a) 4,000 b) 4 million c) 500 million light-years thick?

5 Which astronomer first showed there were galaxies beyond our own a) Copernicus b) Herschel c) Hubble?

Answers
1. True 2. c) 3. Dinosaurs 4. c) 5. c) Edwin Hubble (1889-1953), along with other astronomers in the 1920s

Distant objects

▲ **Candle power**
The farther away a candle is, the more dim it looks. The same is true of stars—and this is how astronomers measure how far away the stars are.

How big is the Universe?

BIGGER THAN YOU CAN possibly imagine. Venus, the nearest planet, is 25 million miles (40 million km) away at its nearest. The planet Pluto is 3.7 billion miles (6 billion km) away. The nearest galaxy beyond our own is 19 quadrillion miles (30,000 trillion km) away. The farthest object astronomers can see is 400,000 times farther away still—and the Universe must stretch way beyond that, and is getting bigger by the second.

How are distances given in space?

Distances are so great in space that they can't be measured in miles or kilometers. Instead, they are measured in light-years and parsecs. A parsec is 3.26 light-years.

A black hole is a place where gravity is so strong it sucks everything in, even light

What's a light year?

Light is the fastest thing in the Universe, travelling at almost 186,000 miles (300,000km) a second. It gets to the Moon in the blink of an eye. It takes eight minutes for light to reach us from the Sun and four YEARS to reach us from the nearest star. A light-year is the distance light travels in a year, which is about 600 billion miles (one trillion km)!

Black holes form when a star or galaxy gets so dense that it collapses under the pull of its own gravity

▶ **Quasar**
Quasars are so bright we can see them billions of light years away. Their energy may come from gas being sucked into a black hole in their midst.

Physical World: Space

◀ **Miles or light-years**
Distances within the solar system can be given in millions of miles, but distances to the stars and beyond are given in light-years or parsecs.

What's the farthest object?
The farthest things are quasars (page 140), many of which are 10 billion light-years away. This means we are seeing them as they were 10 billion years ago—more than five billion years before the Earth was formed, and shortly after the dawn of the Universe.

How do they measure how far a star is?
Distances to nearby stars can be measured by the parallax method. As the Earth circles the Sun, a nearby star seems to shift a little compared to stars farther away, as our viewpoint changes slightly. By measuring how much it shifts, we can work out how far off it is.

How do they measure how far to more distant stars?
The further away a star is, the dimmer it looks. But some stars burn brightly while others glimmer. So it's hard to tell if a dim star is far away or just feeble. But the color of a star shows how bright it really is. If you know how bright a star really is from its color, you can work out how far away it is by comparing this with how bright it looks.

How far away are galaxies?
Beyond about 30,000 light-years, stars are too indistinct to work out the color accurately. So for objects at this distance, we look for "standard candles"—that is, a star whose brightness we know. The dimmer it looks compared to how bright it should look, the farther away it must be. Standard candles include supernova and fluctuating stars called cepheid variables.

What is red shift?
When a galaxy is moving rapidly away from us, the waves of light from it become stretched out—that is, they become redder. The greater this red shift, the faster the galaxy must be moving away from us.

Are the galaxies moving?
Studying red shifts has shown that every galaxy is moving away from us. The farther away it is, the faster it is receding. The most distant galaxies are receding at almost the speed of light.

QUIZ

1. At its nearest, the Moon is 100,000 miles (160,000km) away: true or false?
2. The distance to the Moon is measured with laser beams bounced off mirrors left on the surface by space probes: true or false?
3. The sun is about 93 million miles (150 million km) away: true or false?
4. How many light-years away is Andromeda?
5. The star Deneb is 3,200 light-years away. Who was ruling in Egypt at the same time as we see it?
6. How soon could you get to the Sun and back at the speed of light?

Answers
1. False: 220,974 miles (356,410km) 2. True 3. True 4. About three million 5. Tutankhamun 6. 16 minutes

319

The Big Bang

How did the Universe begin?

THE UNIVERSE began with the biggest explosion of all time, called the Big Bang. One moment there was just an unimaginably small, incredibly hot little ball. A moment later, the Universe burst into existence with a gigantic explosion. Within a split second, all the forces that shape the Universe were created and so too was all the matter. The explosion was so big that material is still hurtling away from it in all directions at astonishing speeds.

What was the early Universe like?

The early Universe was very small, but it contained all the matter and energy in the Universe today. It was a dense and chaotic soup of tiny particles and forces—and instead of the four forces scientists know today, there was just one superforce. But this original Universe lasted only a moment. After just three trillionths of a trillionth of a trillionth of a second, the superforce split to create the separate forces we know today.

Physical World: Space

Can you see the Big Bang?
Astronomers can see the galaxies hurtling away from us in all directions. They can also see the afterglow of the Big Bang—as low level microwave radiation coming toward us from all over space. This is called microwave background radiation. In 1992, the Cosmic Background Explorer (COBE) made a complete map of the background.

When did the galaxies and stars form?
Galaxies and stars probably began to form about 300 million years after the Big Bang, from curdled lumps of hydrogen and helium gas. Some astronomers think they formed as large clumps and broke into smaller clumps. Others think they formed as clumps packed tighter and tighter.

What will happen in the future?
No one knows if the Universe will go on growing. It all depends on how much matter it contains. If there is more than the "critical density," gravity will put a brake in its expansion, and it may soon begin to contract again to end in a Big Crunch. If there is about the same, it may already be in a "steady state" neither expanding nor contracting. If there is much less than the critical density, it will go on expanding forever. This is called the Open Universe.

How old is the Universe?
We know that the Universe is getting bigger at a certain rate by observing how fast distant galaxies are moving. By working out how long it took everything to expand to where it is now, we can wind back the clock to the time when the Universe was very small. This suggests the Universe began somewhere between 13 and 15 billion years ago. However, studies of globular clusters of stars suggest some stars in our galaxy may be 18 billion years old.

What was there before the Universe began?
No one has the remotest idea. Some people think there was a weird ocean, beyond space and time, full of potential universes continually bursting into life. Ours was one of the successful ones. There may be others.

How do scientists know what the early Universe was like?
They don't for certain, but they can get a good idea from mathematical calculations based on laws of physics today, and from experiments with huge machines called colliders and particle accelerators. These recreate conditions in the early Universe by using magnets to accelerate particles to astonishing speeds in a special tunnel, then smashing them all together.

QUIZ

1. What was the first chemical element to form?
2. Which scientist wrote a book called "A Brief History of Time"?
3. How old is the Earth?
4. The Universe is getting bigger, but only the space between the galaxies is stretching: true or false?
5. Which formed first: the Milky Way or the Sun?
6. Two of the four basic forces in the Universe hold the nuclei of atoms together. What are the other two?
7. Is the Andromeda galaxy getting nearer to us or farther away?
8. Astronomers can detect sounds from the far side of the Universe: true or false?

Answers
1. Hydrogen 2. Stephen Hawking 3. 4.6 billion years 4. True 5. The Milky Way 6. Gravity and electromagnetism 7. Farther, like all galaxies 8. False, there are no sounds in space

What substance has the highest melting point?

What did Newton learn from an apple?

How big are atoms?

Why are racing bicycles made of light materials?

Why don't lakes freeze solid?

What frog makes Indian arrows deadly?

Why is laser light special?

Science

324 Matter
326 Atoms
328 Chemicals
330 Heat and energy
332 Forces
334 Movement
336 Water
338 Electricity
340 Electronics
342 Light
344 Sound
346 Magnetism
348 Nuclear power

Can sound travel in a vacuum?

Why does hair go frizzy?

What is virtual reality?

Matter

▲ **Freezing**
When a liquid cools, the molecules slow down enough for regular bonds to grow between them. When water freezes to snowflakes, beautiful crystals form.

▼ **Water cycle**
Water is the only substance to exist naturally on Earth in all three states—solid ice, liquid water, and the gas water vapor. Water is called water vapor when it is a gas; steam is actually lots of tiny drops of water.

What is matter?

MATTER IS EVERY SUBSTANCE in the universe—everything that is not simply empty space. There are three different forms or "states" of matter—solid like a brick, liquid like water, and gas like air. Every substance can change from one state to another and back again, providing the temperature and pressure are right.

What is a solid?
When a substance is solid, it has strength and a definite shape. Every substance is made from minute bits called molecules, much, much too small to see. In a solid, the molecules are bonded together firmly in a regular structure. Like all molecules, they are moving all the time, but in a solid molecules simply vibrate on the spot. The hotter it gets, the more they vibrate.

What is a liquid?
A liquid is substance in a state like water, which flows and takes the shape of any container it is poured into. It does this because although bonds hold its molecules together, the bonds are loose enough for molecules to roll over each other like dry sand.

Water falls from clouds as a solid (snow) or a liquid (rain), either on to land or back into the sea

Ice and snow melts and runs into rivers

Rainwater and snow runs back into the sea in rivers

Physical World: Science

Solid

▲ Loosening bonds
It is the bonds between the molecules it is made from that make a substance solid, liquid, or gas. As the temperature rises, the molecules move more and the bonds get looser.

Liquid   Gas

What is a gas?
A gas is when a substance is in a state like air. It does not have any strength, shape, or volume. The molecules move so fast that they break any bonds that might hold them together.

What happens when things melt or boil?
When a solid melts, it turns to liquid because heat makes the molecules vibrate so much that they break the bonds that hold them together. If it gets even hotter, the molecules zoom all over the place, and some move so fast they break away from the surface of the liquid altogether, turning to gas.

As seawater is warmed by the sun, some of it evaporates (turns to vapor) and begins to rise up through the air on warm air currents

As it rises through the air and cools, water vapor condenses (turns to liquid), and forms clouds

QUIZ

1 Water boils at a) 122°F (50°C) b) 212°F (100°C) c) 1,832°F (1,000°C)?

2 Helium has the lowest freezing point of any substance. Is it a) -458°F (-272.2°C) b) -9.5°F (12.5°C) c) 30°F (-1.1°C)?

3 Iron has the highest melting point of any metal: true or false?

4 What substance has the highest melting point?

5 What is condensation?

6 What is melting point?

7 Which metal is liquid at normal temperatures?

8 Clouds contain water in which states of matter?

Answers
1. b) 2. a) 3. False; tungsten at 6,188°F (3,420°C) 4. Carbon 5. The change from gas to liquid 6. The temperature at which a substance changes from a solid to a liquid 7. Mercury 8. All three

325

Atoms

What is an atom?

ATOMS ARE THE TINY BITS OR "PARTICLES" of which every substance is made. They are far too small to see. Two billion of them would fit on the dot on the top of this "i." Scientists once thought they were the smallest things in the universe—and that they were tiny hard balls that could never be split or destroyed. Now they know atoms are more like clouds of energy, and are mostly empty space, dotted with even tinier "subatomic" particles.

▲ **Helium nucleus**
The nucleus of an atom of helium is one of the smallest—though not as small as hydrogen. It combines two protons with two neutrons.

What's inside an atom?
Right in the center of every atom, like a pea in a basketball, is a dense core or "nucleus" containing two kinds of tiny particle—protons and neutrons. Around the nucleus are even tinier particles called electrons, whizzing round at the speed of light.

How big are atoms?
They are about a ten millionth of a millimeter across and weigh 100 trillionths of a trillionth of a gram. The smallest atoms of all are hydrogen atoms.

Electrons behave as if they were stacked around the nucleus in different levels, like layers of an onion. The levels are called shells

The particles of the nucleus are held together by a force called the strong nuclear force

Electrons are held to the nucleus by electrical charge—because they have an opposite electrical charge to the protons in the nucleus

The nucleus is made from particles called protons and neutrons, which are made, in turn, of even smaller particles called quarks

▶ **Inside an atom**
Atoms don't really look this, but it is a good way to think of them. Most of an atom is empty space, but right in the center is a nucleus of protons and neutrons, held together by special nuclear forces. Around the outside whizz electrons, held in place by the opposite electrical charge on the protons.

There is only room for a certain number of electrons in each shell

326

Physical World: Science

◀ Ionic bond
Atoms are only stable if they have a full set of electrons in their outer shells. They can get this by bonding with other atoms to make molecules. In "ionic" bonds one atom donates an electron to the other and becomes negatively charged. The atoms are then bonded by mutual electrical attraction. This is how sodium atoms bond with chlorine atoms to make salt molecules.

Sodium atom gives up an electron
Mutual electric attraction
Chlorine atom gains an electron

What is an electrical charge?
Protons have a "positive" electrical charge, which just means they attract electrons. Electrons have a "negative" electrical charge, which means they attract protons. Neutrons have no charge. Most atoms have the same number of protons and electrons, so their charges balance out. The charge on electrons drives them apart. If they were not attracted to the protons, the electrons on an atom would fly off.

What is an ion?
An ion is an atom that has either lost one or more electrons, making it positively charged (cation) or gained a few, making it negatively charged (anion).

▶ Covalent bond
Atoms are only stable when they have a full set of electrons in their outer shell. Atoms which have too many or too few can get a full set by sharing electrons with other atoms. This makes a "covalent" bond.

What are molecules?
Some atoms cannot exist by themselves, and so join up with others—either of the same kind, or with others to form chemical compounds. A molecule is the smallest particle of a substance that can exist on its own.

How many kinds of sub-atomic particle are there?
At least 200, besides electrons, protons and neutrons. But most are created in special conditions and last only a split second.

What are the smallest particles?
Protons are made of tiny particles called quarks. Electrons are also tiny. But the smallest of all are neutrinos.

Shared electrons
Electrons in their shells
Atomic nucleus

QUIZ

1. The smallest atom is hydrogen, which has one proton in its nucleus. Meitnerium is the biggest. It has a) 30 protons b) 40 protons c) more than 100 protons?

2. Who first split an atomic nucleus in 1919 a) Newton b) Dalton c) Rutherford?

3. Scientists think quarks are stuck together by gluons: true or false?

4. All particles are either quarks or leptons: true or false?

5. An atom with a full outer shell of electrons, like argon, does not react with others: true or false?

6. A new chemical element is made when an atom gains a proton: true or false?

Answers
1. c) 2. c) 3. True 4. True 5. True 6. True

Chemicals

What are chemical elements?

CHEMICAL ELEMENTS ARE substances that cannot be split up into other substances. Gold is an element because it cannot be split. Water is not, because it can be split into the elements hydrogen and oxygen. What makes each element different are the atoms it is made from. Each element is made from atoms with a certain number of protons in their nucleus. Atoms of gold have 79 protons in their nucleus; atoms of hydrogen have 1.

How many elements?

85 or so occur naturally. But scientists have found a further 25 or so, bringing the total so far identified to 112.

What is the periodic table?

Devised by the chemist John Dalton (1766-1844) the Periodic Table is a chart on which all the elements can be arranged according to the number of protons in the nucleus. Columns are called Groups, rows are called Periods. Each Period contains elements with atoms which have the same number of electron shells. In each Period, the number of protons (and so the number of electrons) in the atom goes up one by one. Elements in the same Group have the same number of electrons in the outer shell of their atoms, and so have similar properties.

▶ **The Periodic Table**
The Periodic Table arranges all the elements in Periods (rows) and Groups (columns). The colors show some of the major kinds of element, including metals and transition elements.

What are the noble gases?

Noble gases are the elements in Group 0, on the far right of the Table. Their outer electron shells have a full complement of electrons. This means they rarely react with other substances. This is why they are sometimes also called inert gases. The noble gases argon and xenon are often used in light bulbs, because the light bulb's filament will get hot in them without burning.

Hydrogen has the lightest and simplest atoms, with just one proton, one neutron and one electron

Metals are "electropositive" elements, which means they lose negatively charged electrons easily—which is why they conduct electricity well

Group 1 are metal elements with just one electron in their outer shells — so are very reactive

The actinides are 15 radioactive elements like radium and plutonium that get their name from actinium

Physical World: Science

Why are some elements reactive?

Elements are reactive if they readily gain or lose electrons. The farther to the left in the Table they are, the more reactive they are. Group 1 metals such as sodium and potassium are very reactive.

What is a metal?

Metals are hard, dense, and shiny substances that ring when you hit them with another metal. They also conduct heat and electricity well.

Group 5 is nonmetals such as nitrogen at the top, but gets more and more metallic lower down with antimony and bismuth

Group 4 includes silicon and carbon, which form more compounds than any other elements

What is a compound?

Compounds are substances made from two or more elements joined together. Every molecule (smallest particle) in a compound is made from the same combination of atoms. Molecules of sodium chloride, for instance, are one sodium atom joined to one chlorine. Compounds have different properties to the elements that make them up. Sodium spits when put in water; chlorine is a thick green gas. Yet sodium chloride is table salt.

Group 7 is the halogens—nonmetals such as chlorine and iodine

Group 0 is the noble gases such as neon, which have full outer electron shells and are unreactive

QUIZ

1. Which two elements is water made from?
2. Is table salt an element?
3. Who discovered the element radium?
4. Diamonds, coal, lead pencils, and racing cars are made from the same element. Which is it?
5. What is the main element in the air besides oxygen?
6. What is the second lightest element?
7. Which has the most protons in its atoms: gold or lead?
8. Krypton is a highly reactive gas: true or false?
9. Chemists can try out new molecules on computer screens: true or false?

Answers
1. Hydrogen & oxygen 2. No, a compound 3. Marie Curie 4. Carbon 5. Nitrogen 6. Helium 7. Lead 8. False 9. True

329

Heat and energy

What is heat?

HEAT IS A FORM OF ENERGY–the energy of molecules moving. The faster they move, the hotter it is. When you put your hand over a heater, the warmth you feel is actually an assault by billions of fast-moving air molecules, spurred along by even faster moving molecules in the heater. We measure how hot something is by its temperature. But temperature is not the same as heat. Heat is the combined energy of all the moving molecules. Temperature is simply a measure of how fast the molecules are moving.

◀ **Thermometer**
In a thermometer like this, the temperature is shown by how far the liquid in the bulb at the bottom expands and rises up the tube.

▼ **Fire**
Fire is a chemical reaction in which one substance gets so hot that it combines with oxygen in the air. The reaction releases so much energy that the atoms send out rays of light, making bright, dancing flames.

How does heat move?

Heat moves in three ways: conduction, convection and radiation. Conduction involves heat spreading from hot areas to cold areas by direct contact, as moving particles knock into one another. Convection is when warm air or water rises as it expands and gets lighter. Radiation is heat rays—invisible rays of infrared light.

How is temperature measured?

Temperature is measured with a thermometer. Some thermometers have a metal strip that bends according to how hot it is. Most hold a liquid, such as mercury, in a tube. As the air warms, the liquid expands, and its level rises in the tube. The level of the liquid indicates the temperature.

What are Centigrade and Fahrenheit?

These are two scales for measuring temperature. Centigrade is also called Celsius. Water freezes at 32°F (Fahrenheit) and 0°C (Centigrade). It boils at 212°F and 100°C. To convert from °F to °C, first subtract 32 and divide by nine then multiply by five. To change °C to °F, divide by five and multiply by nine, then add 32.

Physical World: Science

◀ **Energy stored as coal**
Most of the energy we use comes from the sun via plants—either directly as food, or indirectly as the fossil fuels which our machines run on.

When the plants died, the stored energy in the fibres was squeezed into coal as fibres were buried beneath thick layers of sediment

The creation of fossil fuels began millions of years ago as plants used the sun's energy to grow new fibres

What is energy?
Energy is the capacity to make things happen or, as scientists put it, "work." It takes many forms. Heat energy boils water. Chemical energy fuels cars and airplanes. Electrical energy drives all kinds of small machines and keeps lights glowing. Most of our energy comes from the sun, mostly indirectly either from plants or as fossil fuels (see page 21).

What happens to energy?
Energy can neither be created nor destroyed. When you use energy, you simply convert it from one form to another. When you run, you simply change the chemical energy of your muscles into heat energy, which is lost from the body. When energy is converted, there is always the same amount of energy after as before.

What's absolute zero?
Absolute zero is the coldest possible temperature—at which atoms and molecules stop moving altogether. This is -459°F or -273.15°C, or 0 on the Kelvin scale.

◀ **Movement to electricity**
Hydroelectric power stations convert the energy of moving water into electrical energy.

QUIZ

1. The highest temperature ever measured, in a nuclear fusion experiment, is
   a) 54,000°F (30,000°C)
   b) 900,000°F (500,000°C)
   c) 72 million°F (40 million°C)?

2. The highest air temperature recorded, in Libya, is 199°F (92°C): true or false?

3. The lowest air temperature ever recorded, -127°F (-88°C), was in Alaska: true or false?

4. What do solar cells do?

5. Energy is a form of mass: true or false?

6. On the Kelvin scale used by scientists water freezes at 273.15 K: true or false?

7. How much of the world's energy comes from coal a) 12% b) 27% c) 45%?

Answers
1. c) 2. False; 136°F (58°C) 3. False; 136°F (58°C) in Antarctica 4. Convert sunlight into electricity 5. True 6. True 7. b)

331

Forces

What is a force?

A FORCE IS JUST A PUSH OR A PULL. Some forces are invisible, like gravity, which holds us to the ground. Some are visible, like a kick. But they all work by making something go faster, slow down or change shape.

▲ **Isaac Newton**
Isaac Newton (1643-1727) was the great scientist who developed the idea of gravity and other forces.

What did Newton learn from an apple?

According to the great 17th-century scientist Sir Isaac Newton, his ideas about the force of gravity came to him as he was sitting under an apple tree. When he saw an apple fall, it occurred to him that the apple was not simply falling, but being pulled to the ground by an invisible force, which he called gravity.

What is gravity?

Gravity is the invisible force of attraction between every bit of matter in the universe. Its strength depends on the mass of the objects involved and just how far they are apart.

Are mass and weight the same?

No. Mass is the amount of matter in an object. It is the same wherever you measure it. Weight is the force of gravity on an object. It varies with where you measure it.

Are there other forces?

Wherever there is movement there is a force involved, but there are four basic forces which work right down to the level of atoms. These are gravity, electromagnetism, and two "nuclear" forces—forces that act only in the nuclei of atoms.

Tailwings provide a down force to help keep the car stable

Thrust is developed as hot gas expands between the rocket housing and the air

The shape is smooth and streamlined to cut friction with the air—air resistance

Rocket motors provide huge forward thrust

▲ **Land speed record breaker**
The main obstacle to traveling fast is friction—friction with the ground, friction with the air, and friction between moving parts. To beat the world land speed record, Thrust II needed huge rocket motors to develop enough thrust to overcome this force.

Physical World: Science

▶ **Strike force**
When a batsman strikes a cricket ball, the ball shoots off somewhere between the direction of the force of the ball's momentum and the direction of the force of the bat. Just where in between depends on the force of the ball's momentum and the force of the strike. The ball's new direction is called the "resultant" by scientists studying forces.

What force holds things together?
Nuclear forces hold atomic nuclei together, but electromagnetism holds atoms together, binds atoms to make molecules and binds molecules to make different substances. When it binds molecules, it is called an intermolecular force.

What is friction?
Friction is the force between two things rubbing together, which may be brake pads on a bicycle wheel or air against an airplane. It tends to slow things down, making them hot as momentum is changed to heat. It is caused by the intermolecular force between the molecules of the two things rubbing.

▶ **Take off**
Airplanes stay up because their wings provide a lift force to counteract the force of gravity. The lift comes from the air that is forced to flow over the wings as the plane flies forward. To take off, the plane must accelerate until it is going fast enough for the wings give the lift to beat gravity.

What is a force field?
A force field is the region over which forces like gravity and electromagnetism have an effect. They are invisible, and the only way of knowing they exist is by the way they move things coming within range. Force fields are often shown as lines with arrows to show the direction and strength of the movement.

How is force measured?
Force is measured in newtons, in honour of Sir Isaac Newton. A newton is the force needed to accelerate 1kg by 1m per second in a second.

QUIZ

1 What is the force that holds you on the ground?

2 How fast does gravity make things accelerate a) 1 inch (2.5 cm) per second^2 b) 32 feet (9.8m) per second^2 c) 2,500 miles (4,032km) per second^2?

3 What is the force that makes compass needles point North?

4 What force does a train have to overcome to move fast?

5 All forces act in straight lines: true or false?

6 Who dropped different balls from the Leaning Tower of Pisa to show they fall at the same rate?

7 Air resistance gets less the faster a car goes: true or false?

Answers
1. Gravity 2. b) 3. Magnetism 4. Friction 5. True 6. Galileo 7. False

Movement

How do things start to move?

THINGS ONLY MOVE IF FORCED TO MOVE. This is called inertia. The heavier something is the more inertia it has and the harder it is to start moving. So when something starts to move, there must be a force involved—whether it is visible, like someone pushing, or invisible, like gravity—and the force must be large enough to overcome the inertia. Once things are moving at the same speed and in the same direction, they keep on doing so until another force (typically friction) slows or turns them.

What's the difference between inertia and momentum?

Inertia is the tendency of things to stay still unless forced to move. Momentum is the tendency of moving things to keep moving, unless forced to stop or slow. This is Newton's First Law of Motion.

What is acceleration?

Acceleration is how fast something gains speed. The larger the force and the lighter the object, the greater the acceleration. This is Newton's Second Law of Motion.

The four-stroke sequence

1. Inlet valve opens to let in a dose of fuel drawn in by the descending piston

2. The valve closes and the piston rises, squeezing the fuel as it does

3. The spark ignites the fuel, which swells and thrusts the piston down

4. The piston rises again, pushing burned gases out of the exhaust

- Inlet valves which open to let in fresh fuel-air mix
- Spark plugs ignite the fuel-air mix
- Exhaust valve opens to let out burned gases
- Combustion chamber, where the mix is burned
- Piston, which slides up and down the cylinder
- This engine has four cylinders
- Crankshaft turned by the piston as it is pushed down

▶ **Four-stroke car engine**
In car engines, power is created as a mix of fuel and air is ignited by an electric spark. It swells as it burns, pushing a piston down a tube called a cylinder. As the piston is thrust down, it turns a rod called a crank, and the turning is transmitted by shafts to the wheels.

Physical World: Science

◀ **Hydraulic bore**
The arms are raised and lowered on this drill by pumping fluid in and out of the tubes that support them. The drill is driven hydraulically too, to ensure a smooth action.

What is a four-stroke engine?

Most car engines are four-stroke engines. This means that each of the pistons goes up and down four times for each power stroke—that is, for every time the piston is thrust down by the burning gases. Most car engines also have at least four cylinders, and each fires in succession, so that one is on its power stroke while the rest are on their idle strokes.

What is hydraulic power?

Fluids like water cannot be squashed. So if you push fluid through a pipe, it will push out the other end. Hydraulic power uses fluid-filled pipes working like this to drive things smoothly. Hydraulic means water, but most hydraulic systems use oil to avoid rusting.

What is Newton's Third Law of Motion?

That for every action, there is an equal and opposite reaction. This means that whenever something moves, there is a balance of forces pushing the other way. So when you push your feet on the bicycle pedals, the pedals are actually pushing back just as hard.

How do engines work?

Most engines work by burning fuel to make gases that expand rapidly as they get hot. In cars and trains, the hot gases swell inside a chamber called the combustion chamber and push against a piston or a turbine (a kind of fan). In jets and rockets, the burning gases swell and push against the whole engine as they shoot out the back.

▶ **Jet engine**
A plane's jet engines suck in air through the front to burn with aviation fuel. As it is burned with aviation fuel, it swells so rapidly from the back of the engine that the plane is thrust forward.

QUIZ

1 Why are racing bicycles made of very light materials?

2 How many Laws of Motion did Isaac Newton find?

3 What are the two major fuels used by car engines?

4 What is the gas that combines with fuel as it burns in a car engine?

5 Why do heavy trucks take longer to stop than cars?

6 Which two scientists invented jet engines?

7 What is the force that slows cars down?

8 Cars are powered by dead shellfish: true or false?

9 What is the world's fastest train?

Answers
1. To cut inertia to a minimum 2. Three 3. Gasoline & diesel 4. Oxygen 5. They've more momentum 6. Frank Whittle & Pabst von Ohain. 7. Friction 8. True 9. The French TGV

335

Water

Why is water special?

THERE ARE MANY REASONS why water is a remarkable substance. But there are two that stand out. First of all, it is the only substance that can be solid, liquid, and gas at everyday temperatures. Second, it has a remarkable capacity for making mild solutions with other substances, so that it can be used to transfer everything from sugar to salt. These two properties above all make water perhaps the most important material of all for life–and make Earth, the only planet blessed with an abundance of water, so special.

▲ **Floating ship**
Ships made of heavy metal float because they trap air inside their hulls. They float at the point where the weight of the ship and air exactly matches the weight of water displaced (pushed out of the way).

▼ **How submarines work**
Submarines rise to the surface by pumping water out of their buoyancy tanks to lighten it enough to float to the surface. To dive again, it pumps water into the buoyancy tanks to increase its weight enough to sink.

What is water made of?
Water is made of molecules which are built from two atoms of hydrogen and one of oxygen, bound in a Y-shaped. This is why its chemical formula is H_2O. This molecule is said to be "polar," because the oxygen side is a little more negatively charged electrically.

Why is water liquid?
Water is liquid until 212°F (100°C) because its polar molecules form strong bonds with each other, as the positively charged end of one molecule is drawn to the negative end of another. These bonds are called hydrogen bonds.

To surface, the submarine pumps water out of the tanks

At the surface, the submarine's buoyancy tanks are empty

To dive, the submarine pumps water into the tanks

Physical World: Science

▶ **Tidal boom**
The rising and falling of tides in the sea can generate electricity as it waggles floating booms like these to and fro.

Why don't lakes freeze solid?
Uniquely, ice is less dense than cold water, so it floats on top, acting as a blanket and stopping cold water below from freezing. Water is at its densest at 39°F (4°C). It actually expands when it freezes, which is why water pipes can burst in cold winters, and how water splits rock.

What is water pressure?
Water pressure is the combined push of moving molecules of water. The deeper the water, the greater the pressure.

What is a solution?
When a substance is added to a liquid, various things can happen. If the substance does not mix in at all, and lumps of it float in the liquid, it is a "suspension." If the atoms, ions and molecules of the substance break up and intermingle with the liquid it forms a new liquid called a solution. When you dissolve coffee powder in water, you make a solution. Water here is the "solvent" and coffee powder the "solute."

What is a saturated solution?
As you dissolve more of a solid, the solution becomes stronger and stronger until no more will dissolve. The solution is then said to be saturated. If you heat a solution, more will dissolve before it becomes saturated. But if a saturated solution cools down, or is left to evaporate, solute molecules may begin to link and grow into solid crystals.

◀ **Sugar solution**
Count how many spoons of sugar you can dissolve in cold water or tea. Then count how many you can dissolve in warm water.

QUIZ

1. So much water flows through the Amazon river that it could fill London's St. Paul's Cathedral in a) 1 second b) 1 minute c) 1 hour ?

2. How much of the world's surface is covered by water: a) 25% b) 55% c) 70%?

3. How much of the world's water is frozen: a) 2% b) 5% c) 12%?

4. Things float better in salty seawater than fresh water: true or false?

5. Which famous scientist shouted 'Eureka!' when he worked out how things float?

Answers
1. a) 2. c) 3. a)
4. True
5. The Ancient Greek thinker Archimedes (287–212 BC)

337

Electricity

Why does hair go frizzy?

WHEN YOU COMB DRY HAIR tiny electrons are knocked off the atoms in the comb as it rubs past. The effect is that your hair is coated with these tiny negative electrical charges and so is attracted to anything that has the normal amount of electrons, or less. An electrical charge built up like this is called "static" because it does not move. You could try rubbing a balloon on your sweater to create a static charge on the balloon to stick it to a wall.

What is electric current?

Static electricity does not move. Current electricity does. It is a continuous stream of electrical charge. It only happens when there is a complete, unbroken "circuit" for the current to flow through—typically a loop of copper wire.

What makes lightning flash?

Lightning flashes produce millions of volts of static electricity. Lightning is created when raindrops and ice crystals inside a thundercloud are flung together by strong air currents. They become electrically charged as they gain or lose electrons. Negatively charged particles build up at the base of the cloud. When this charge has built up enough, it discharges as lightning, either flashing within the cloud or forking between the cloud and ground.

▶ **Lightning flashes**
Lightning flashes are sparked by the build up of huge differences in static electrical charge between the top and bottom of a thundercloud. The flash is the sudden jump of electrons from one place to another to bring the charge back to normal. This can happen within the cloud (sheet lightning), or between the cloud and ground (fork lightning).

Negative charges build up in the base of the cloud

Lightning neutralizes the charge difference

The flash heats air so suddenly that it creates a sonic boom: thunder

The ground is naturally positively charged

Fork lightning

338

Physical World: Science

▲ Simple battery
Acid contains both positive and negative particles. When copper and zinc plates are dipped in and connected, pluses are drawn to one, minuses to the other.

How does current flow?
The charge in an electric current is electrons that have broken free from their atoms. None of them moves very far, but the current is passed on as they bang into each other like rows of marbles.

How do batteries work?
Batteries work because when certain substances are placed next to each other, there is a difference in charge between them. In the simplest cells, the materials are copper and zinc plates dipped in acid. When a wire between the plates completes the circuit, current flows.

▶ Flashlight
In a flashlight the electrical power comes from the charge difference between chemicals in the batteries—typically zinc and carbon. One end of the batteries touches the casing. The other touches the bulb to complete the circuit. The bulb glows because the current meets resistance in the bulb's thin filament.

▲ Electric current
Electric current in a wire is passed on by free electrons (tiny blue dots). The electrons are drawn to the positive nuclei of atoms (red).

What is resistance?
Not all substances conduct electric currents equally well. Resistance is a substance's tendency to block the flow of current. A narrow place in the circuit can also be a resistance and the wire here can get very hot. In light bulbs, a thin section of wire or "filament" is what glows. A fuse is a thin bit of wire that burns through and breaks the circuit if it gets overloaded.

Carbon rod
Zinc casing
Carbon and manganese oxide paste to control the discharge of current

QUIZ

1 The electric current that supplies your house switches direction several times a second: true or false?
2 What two metals are the best conductors of electricity?
3 A volt is a measure of
 a) electrical resistance
 b) a difference in charge
 c) the speed of the current
4 Who invented the battery
 a) Volta b) Faraday
 c) Maxwell?
5 Which American statesman discovered the electrical nature of lightning?
6 A battery that uses paste rather than acid is called a dry cell: true or false?
7 A good place to stand in a thunderstorm is under a tall tree: true or false?
8 Who discovered the link between electricity and magnetism?

Answers
1. True 2. Copper and silver 3. b) 4. a) 5. Benjamin Franklin 6. True 7. False; trees attract lightning 8. Michael Faraday

339

Electronics

What are electronics?

ELECTRONICS ARE SYSTEMS that control things by switching on and off tiny electrical circuits. The switches are not like light switches on the wall, but work automatically. The simplest are transistors; the most complex are linked together in integrated circuits, silicon chips and microprocessors. These are the clever systems that control everything from cookers to guided missiles.

▲ **Aircraft flight deck**
The flight deck of a modern aircraft flight deck is almost entirely "glass," which means it is full of electronic control screens and displays.

How do electronic systems work?

Inside every electronic device, from TVs to air traffic control systems, there are scores or even millions of tiny electric circuits continually switching on and off. The operation of the device depends on which circuits are on and which are off. In a computer, each bit of data is directed through a different combination of circuits.

What are transistors?

Transistors are tiny switches made from materials called semiconductors, including germanium and silicon. What makes them special is that their ability to conduct electricity changes quickly as they warm up. Transistors can be used to control an electric current in several ways, including amplifying it (making it bigger) and switching it on and off.

What is a silicon chip?

Dozens or even thousands of tiny transistors can be joined together in a single "integrated circuit." This can be printed onto a tiny sliver of silicon, called a silicon chip. They can be anything from simple circuits for a clock to complex microprocessors for controlling computers.

Internet   Computer   Radio mast   Radio   Satellite dish
TV   Telephone   Satellite

What are bits in computers?

Since electronic circuits can only be on or off, computers work by using a "binary" system. This codes all data as either 1s or 0s, "ons" or "offs." Each is called a "bit," and bits are grouped together in bytes. This is why a computer's ability to handle data is measured in bytes.

Physical World: Science

How do computers remember?
Some computer memory is printed into microcircuits when it is made. This is ROM (Read-only memory). RAM (Random-access memory) circuits take new data and instructions. Data is also stored in magnetic patterns on removable discs or in the laser-guided bumps on CDs.

What is a fractal?
In improving computers, scientists have learned much about numbers. Fractals are beautiful patterns generated by the computer from simple repeated mathematical calculations. Since they seem to mimic natural shapes like trees, some believe such shapes were created in a similar way, step by step.

What is virtual reality?
Virtual reality (VR) systems build a picture electronically to give you the illusion of reality. Special eyepieces show a slightly different view to each eye, giving the impression of a real, 3D space. As the view in each changes, it seems you are moving through a real space. Special gloves and other devices to control movement enhance the illusion. VR devices are now used for a wide range of tasks, as well as games. With VR, people can operate a computer-guided device in places where it is far too dangerous or difficult to work themselves, including in wrecks under the sea, inside the body and many other places.

▼ **Telecommunications**
The telecommunications systems that now allow virtually instant communication around the world would not be possible without tiny electronic control devices and circuits.

QUIZ

1. What does CAD stand for: a) Computer-aided Design b) Calculating Arithmetical Device c) Continually-activated Diode?
2. The first computer was built by Charles Babbage in the 1830s: true or false?
3. Electronic devices can be grown by bacteria: true or false?
4. The internet was first developed by the American military: true or false?
5. What is the artificial environment created by computers called?
6. Robot is a Czech word for forced labour: true or false?

Answers
1. a) 2. True 3. False 4. True 5. Cyberspace 6. True

Light

What is light?

LIGHT IS WHAT YOU SEE THINGS BY. It is a radiation sent out by atoms in light sources such as the sun, stars, and electric lights. There are other kinds of radiation, but light is the only kind your eyes can see. Light always moves in straight lines, and so people talk about light rays, but rays are just the straight path taken by the light.

▲ Splitting colors
Daylight and most other lights contain a whole mixture of different wavelengths—different colors—of light. Daylight can be split into a full range of colors, or spectrum, with a triangular chunk of glass called a prism. The prism bends each color of light to a different extent, so each emerges from the prism in a different place.

▼ Electromagnetic spectrum
Light is just a small part of a huge range of radiation sent out by atoms. At one end are radio waves and microwaves, and infrared heat radiation. At the other are ultraviolet light (which we can't see), and X-rays and gamma rays.

Does light travel in waves?
In the last century, most scientists thought light did travel in tiny waves fractions of a millimeter long, rather than in bulletlike particles. Now they agree it can be both, and it is best to think of light as vibrating packets of energy.

What are photons?
Photons are almost infinitesimally small particles of light. They have no mass and there are billions of them in a single light beam.

What is a shadow?
Since light travels in straight lines, its path is blocked whenever it meets an obstacle. The shadow is the dark space behind the obstacle.

What happens when light hits things?
When light rays hit a surface, some bounce off. This is called reflection. Some are absorbed by atoms in the surface, warming it very slightly. If the surface is transparent, like glass, some will pass straight through.

Does light change when it hits a surface?
Each kind of atom absorbs a particular wavelength (color) of light. The color of a surface depends on the atoms it contains and so which wavelengths are absorbed and which reflected. A leaf is green because the leaf's atoms soak up all colors but green from sunlight, and you see only the reflected green light.

| Radio waves | Microwaves | Infrared | Visible light |

Physical World: Science

◀ **Perfect reflection**
Mirrors give a clear reflection because light bounces off them at exactly the same angle that it hits them.

▶ **Laser reading**
The perfect precision of laser light means it can be used to pick up the tiny pits on the surface of a CD that store the memory of the music. The laser light is bounced into them and the head picks up the reflections from the pits.

How is light bent?
The bending of light rays is called refraction. This happens when they strike a transparent material like glass or water at an angle. The different materials slow the light waves down, so that they bend around, like car wheels driving onto sand.

How do mirrors work?
Most mirrors are made of glass, but the back is coated with a shiny metal (called silvering) that perfectly reflects all the light that hits it, at exactly the same angle.

Why is laser light special?
Most light contains a jumbled mix of different wavelengths. Laser light contains only a single wavelength—and what's more, all the waves are traveling perfectly in step. This means the beam can deliver a very concentrated but small burst of energy.

How do fiber-optics bend light?
They don't; they simply bounce it again and again down the shiny insides of the long, thin glass fibers they are made from.

Ultraviolet   X-rays   Gamma rays

QUIZ

1 A frosted glass window is
   a) opaque b) transparent
   c) translucent?

2 Where do the colours of the rainbow come from?

3 Many birds can see ultraviolet light: true or false?

4 The angle that light strikes a mirror is called
   a) the angle of reflection
   b) the angle of incidence
   c) the light angle?

5 Things are the same colour in the dark as they are in daylight: true or false?

6 A light bulb works because the pressure of the electric current through its thin filament makes it glow: true or false?

Answers
1. c) 2. Sunlight 3. True 4. b) 5. False; they have no colour at all in the dark 6. True

343

Sound

What is sound?

SOUND IS VIBRATIONS IN THE AIR. Sometimes you can see the vibration; sometimes you cannot. If you pluck a taut rubber band, you can see the band twang. If you clap your hands, you see nothing. Vibration is there all the same. But it is not only the band or your hands that move. You hear the sound because the air moves too. As the source of the sound moves, it sets the air molecules moving to, and so the vibration is transmitted through the air to your ears.

▲ **Doppler effect**
The sound of a car's engine drops in pitch as it zooms away from you because the sound waves are stretched out behind it.

Can sound travel in a vacuum?

No. Sound can travel through solids and liquids as well as air. In fact, it can travel faster through solids and liquids than air, because their molecules are more closely packed. But there is always complete silence in a vacuum because there is nothing to vibrate.

What are sound waves?

Sound waves are not like waves in the sea, which go up and down. Sound waves move by alternately stretching and squeezing. When a sound is made, air molecules near the sound are squeezed together. They, in turn, jostle up against the molecules next to them—and then are pulled back into place by the molecules behind.

How do you hear sounds?

You hear because your ears pick up the tiny vibrations in the air made by sounds. Inside the ear is a taut, thin window of skin called the eardrum, which vibrates with the air and rattles three tiny bones called ossicles. The last of them, called the stirrup, rattles farther than the first and amplifies the sound. The stirrup shakes another thin skin, sending waves through a fluid filled tube called the cochlea, deep inside your head. Ripples in the cochlea trigger sensitive nerve receptors to send signals to your brain.

What is an echo?

An echo is sound bouncing back. You don't often hear echoes, because sound only bounces back clearly off smooth, hard surfaces, and in confined spaces. Even in a confined space, the wall must be at least 56 feet (17m) away— which is why you usually hear echoes only in large empty halls.

Cassette tape

Driving wheel

Recording head

Erase head to wipe out previous recordings

The recording head is a tiny electromagnet that switches on and off

◀ **Recording tape**
In a tape recorder, the recording head sends out electrical pulses in the same pattern as the sound. These arrange tiny magnetic particles on the tape and so record the sound.

Physical World: Science

▼ The sound barrier
The sound barrier was broken for the first time in 1947 by American test pilot, Chuck Yeager flying the specially built Bell X-1.

What is the sound barrier?
When a plane starts to fly faster than sound, it breaks the sound barrier. There is no real barrier to break. But as the aircraft travels faster and faster it squashes the air in front of it, generating a shock wave that is heard as a loud explosive sound called a sonic boom.

What's the speed of sound?
In air, sound travels about 1,115 feet (340m) per second. It travels faster on a hot day.

What is sound frequency?
Some sounds like squealing brakes are high-pitched. Others like thunder, are low-pitched. The difference is in how frequently the sound waves follow each other. If the waves come in quick succession, the sound is high-pitched. If they are widely separated, the sound is low-pitched. A low sound is 20 Hz, or waves per second. A high sound is 20,000 Hz.

▶ Squeezing the air
When a loudspeaker vibrates with a sound, the vibrations travel out through the air in a series of waves that alternately squeeze the air molecules together and stretch them apart.

QUIZ

1 What is the study of the way sound behaves called?
2 What scale is the loudness of a sound measured on?
3 The highest frequency a human can hear is
   a) 5,000 Hz b) 20,000 Hz c) 50,000 Hz?
4 Which does sound travel fastest in: a) air b) water c) metal?
5 The longest strings in a piano produce the highest notes: true or false?
6 Ultrasound is sounds too high for humans to hear: true or false?
7 Bats locate prey in the dark by sending out beams of ultrasound: true or false?

Answers
1. Acoustics 2. Decibel 3. b) 4. metal 5. False 6. True 7. True

Magnetism

What is magnetism?

MAGNETISM IS AN INVISIBLE FORCE, which acts between iron, steel, and a few other metals. Each magnet has an area around it where it exerts its force power, called its magnetic field. This field gets weaker farther away from the magnet. But if another magnetic material comes closer, the magnet either pulls it closer or pushes it away.

What is a magnetic pole?

Magnetic force is especially strong at the end of each magnet. These two ends are called the poles. One is called the north (or north-seeking) pole, because if the magnet is suspended freely, this pole swings round until it points north. The other is called the south pole. If the opposite poles of two magnets come close, they will be drawn together. If the same poles meet, they will push each other apart.

What is a lodestone?

Long before people learned how to make steel magnets, they found that certain rocks attract or repel each other, and bits of iron. These rocks are called lodestones, and contain iron oxide, which makes them naturally magnetic.

▶ **Magnetic field**
This illustration shows the magnetic field around a simple bar magnet. The lines indicate the direction in which the force works—from turning magnetic materials toward its poles.

Why is the Earth magnetic?

As the Earth spins, the swirling of its iron nickel core turns it into a giant magnet. Like a bar magnet, Earth has two poles, North and South. It is because the Earth is a magnet that small magnets point the same way if left to swivel freely.

How big is Earth's field?

Earth's magnetic field extends far out into space, forming a plum-shaped barrier called the magnetosphere. On the side facing the Sun it stretches out 37,000 miles (60,000km). On the far side it is blown out four times this far by the solar wind.

Concentration of lines of magnetic force on the pole

North pole

Lines of magnetic force, indicating direction in which magnetism acts

South pole

Physical World: Science

◄ **Electromagnet**
When an electric current is switched on, it creates a magnetic field around the wire. The arrows indicate the direction of the field.

What is electromagnetism?
Electricity and magnetism are deeply linked. Every electric current creates a magnetic field around it, and moving a magnet past an electric wire will induce (create) an electric current in it. An electromagnet is a coil of copper wire, which creates a very strong magnetic field when a current is switched through it.

What are the northern lights?
The northern lights, or Aurora Borealis, are spectacular curtains of light that shimmer in the night sky over the North pole. They occur because there is a cleft in the magnetosphere above the pole, where lines of magnetic force funnel in. Every now and then, charged particles from the Sun stream in here and cannon into air molecules, making them glow brightly.

▼ **The Northern Lights**
The interaction of solar radiation with the Earth's magnetic field creates spectacular light shows or auroras over the North and South Poles.

Quiz

1. What did sailors use magnets for?
2. Iron loses its magnetism above 1400°F: true or false?
3. Every magnet has two poles, no matter what its shape: true or false?
4. The effects of magnetic attraction are not transmitted between objects: true or false?
5. Aluminium is magnetic: true or false?
6. The Earth's magnetic North Pole is hundreds of miles from the North Pole: true or false?
7. What is the aurora over the South Pole called?

Answers
1. To make compasses to find north 2. True 3. True 4. False 5. False 6. True 7. Aurora Australis

Nuclear power

Why is nuclear power huge?

THE ENERGY THAT BINDS TOGETHER the nucleus of an atom is huge, even though the nucleus is minute. In fact, as Einstein showed in 1905 with his theory of Special Relativity, the particles of the atom can be regarded as pure energy. It is releasing some of this energy from millions of atomic nuclei that allow nuclear power stations to generate so much power from just a few tons of nuclear fuel. It also gives nuclear bombs their terrifying destructive power.

What is nuclear fusion?

Nuclear fusion is when nuclear energy is released by fusing or joining together small atoms like those of deuterium (a form of hydrogen). Nuclear fusion is the reaction that keeps stars glowing and provides the energy for H-bombs (see *What is an atomic bomb?*) Scientists hope to find a way of harnessing it for power.

▼ A nuclear power station

Inside a nuclear reactor there are fuel rods made from pellets of uranium oxide, separated by spacers. When the station goes on-line, a nuclear fission chain reaction is set up in the fuel rods. This is slowed down by control rods, which absorb the neutrons so that heat is produced steadily to make the steam that drives the turbines that generate electricity.

Superheated water in the primary loop boils water in the secondary loop into high pressure steam

High pressure steam spins the turbine blades

The turning of the turbines turns the electricity generator

Steam condenses into liquid water

Pumps keep the water moving around the circuits

In the reactor vessel, nuclear fission releases huge amounts of heat energy

Hot water comes out of the reactor

Cool water returns to the reactor

A containment building houses the reactor vessel, keeping in heat, radioactivity, and other energy

The nuclear reactions take place in fuel rods in the reactor core

Physical World: Science

▶ **Nuclear fission**
Nuclear fission involves firing a neutron (yellow ball) at a nucleus of uranium or plutonium. When the nuclei splits, it fires out more neutrons, which split more nuclei, creating a chain reaction.

What is nuclear fission?
Nuclear fission releases energy by splitting large nuclei such as uranium and plutonium. To split the nuclei, neutrons are fired at it. As they crash into it, they split off more neutrons, which bombard other nuclei, setting off a chain reaction.

What is an atomic bomb?
An atomic bomb or A-bomb is one of the two main kinds of nuclear weapon. An A-bomb relies on the explosive nuclear fission of uranium-235 or plutonium-239. Hydrogen bombs, also called H-bombs or thermonuclear weapons, rely on the fusion of hydrogen atoms to create explosions a thousand times bigger.

Who invented the A-bomb?
The first A-bombs were developed in the USA toward the end of World War II by a team led by Robert Oppenheimer (1904-1967). Their first bombs were dropped on Hiroshima and Nagasaki in Japan in 1945 with devastating effect.

What is radioactivity?
The atoms of an element often come in several different forms or isotopes. Each form has a different number of neutrons in its nucleus, indicated in the name, as in carbon-12 and carbon-14. The nuclei of some of these isotopes—the ones scientists call radioisotopes—are unstable, and decay (break up). As they break up, they release radiation, consisting of streams of particles called alpha, beta, and gamma rays. This is radioactivity.

What is half-life?
No one can predict when the atomic nucleus will decay. But scientists can predict how long it will take for half the particles in a substance to decay. This is its half-life. Strontium-90 has a half-life of just nine minutes. Uranium-235, on the other hand, has a half-life of four and a half billion years. Most fall somewhere in between.

QUIZ

1 Exposure to high levels of radioactivity can be fatal: true or false?

2 Which two countries have the biggest stockpile of nuclear weapons?

3 Nuclear power stations do not burn fuel: true or false?

4 Where in the Ukraine was there a major accident at a nuclear power station?

5 What is the most devastating accident that can happen to a nuclear reactor?

6 The age of many ancient remains can be dated by their radioactivity: true or false?

7 What do the stars and H-bombs have in common?

Answers
1. True 2. The USA and the Russian Federation 3. False 4. Chernobyl 5. Meltdown 6. True 7. Nuclear fusion

349

Key facts: Science

Milestones

- 300 BC: Greek mathematician Euclid lays down the principles of geometry still used today.
- 250 BC: Archimedes lays down the basic principles of physics.
- 1665-1686: Isaac Newton introduces his theory of gravity and his three laws of motion.
- 1683: Anton van Leeuwenhoek discovers bacteria.
- 1789: Antoine Lavoisier makes the first list of chemical elements.
- 1804: Richard Trevithick builds the first steam loco.
- 1808: John Dalton proposes the atomic theory of matter.
- 1820: Hans Oersted finds that electricity creates a magnetic field.
- 1830: Joseph Henry and Michael Faraday find how electricity can be generated by a magnetic field.
- 1858 Charles Darwin and Alfred Wallace suggest the theory of the evolution of species by natural selection.
- 1860s: Étienne Lenoir builds the first gasoline engine car.
- 1865: James Clerk Maxwell suggests the idea of electromagnetic fields.
- 1869: Dmitri Mendeléev creates the Periodic Table of the elements.
- 1897: J. J. Thomson discovers the electron.
- 1900: Max Planck invents quantum theory.
- 1903: Orville and Wilbur Wright make the first powered human aircraft flight.
- 1905: Albert Einstein invents the theory of Relativity.
- 1911: Ernest Rutherford discovers the atomic nucleus.
- 1945: The first atomic bomb.
- 1953: Francis Crick and James Watson find the structure of the DNA molecule in every living cell.

Conversions

Conversion factors
To convert, multiply by the number shown

Length
- in. to cm   2.54
- ft. to m   0.3048
- yd. to m   0.9144
- miles to km   1.6093
- cm to in.   0.3937
- m to ft.   3.2808
- m to yd.   1.0936
- km to miles   0.6214

Weight
- oz. to g   28.3495
- lb. to kg   0.4536
- tons to tonnes   0.9058
- g to oz   0.0352
- kg to lb   2.2046
- tonnes to tons   1.104

Volume
- in.^{3} to cm^3 (cc)   16.3871
- ft.^{3} to litres   28.3169
- yd.^{3} to m^3 0.7646
- fl. oz. to m^3 28.4131
- pints to liters   0.4507
- gallons to liters   3.606
- cm^3 to in.^{3} 0.0610
- liters to ft.^{3} 0.0353
- liters to pints   2.2187
- liters to gallons   0.2773

Science

Fast, slow

Fast phenomena
- Light — 185,871,324 miles per second
- Lightning — up to 31,248 miles per second
- Earth's orbit — 66,470 mph
- Speed of sound in water — 4,724ft per second
- Speed of sound in air — 1122ft per second at 64°F
- Skydiver — 620 mph
- Jet stream — up to 435 mph
- Tornado — 280 mph
- Surface wind — 230 mph

Fast machines
- Fastest steam locomotive — 126 mph by the *Mallard* in 1934.
- Fastest train — 320 mph by French TGV in 1990.
- Fastest road car — 217 mph by Jaguar XJ220 in 1992.
- Fastest speed on land — 763 mph by *Thrust SSC* in 1997.
- Fastest jet plane — 2242 mph by Lockheed SR-71A in 1990.
- Fastest airliner — 1608 mph by Russian Tupolev Tu-144.
- Fastest human flight — 24792 mph by crew of *Apollo 10* spacecraft in 1969.

Dead slow
- Fingernails grow at around 0.02 inch a week.
- Toenails grow at about 0.004 inch a week.
- Continents move at around 16 inches a year.
- Snails move at up to 0.005 mph.
- A tortoise moves at 0.17 mph.
- Glaciers flow at 0.0003 mph.
- Lichen grows at 0.00000000006 mph.

Loud, soft

Loud noises
- Supernova explosion — 210 decibels
- Rocket launch — 180 db
- Toy guns — 170 db
- Jet taking off at 30m — 140 db
- Rock concert — 130 db
- Loud scream — 128 db
- Racing car — 125 db
- Dance club — 117 db
- Car horn — 110 db
- Chainsaw — 100 db
- Thunder — 90 db

Quiet sounds
- Ant breathing — less than 0 db
- The quietest we can hear — 0 db
- Rustling leaves — 10 db
- Quiet whisper — 12 db
- Average whisper — 20 db
- Conversation — 40 db
- Empty theater — 45 db
- Loud conversation — 60 db
- Niagara Falls — 85 db
- Loud snore — 87 db
- Heavy traffic — 90 db

Key facts: Science

Number power

Large and small numbers

- Large numbers can have a huge number of digits. There are 17,000,000,000,000,000,000 water molecules in a single drop of water. So scientists often express large numbers in terms of "powers" of 10. This is the number of times you have to multiply 10 by 10 to give the number. So 100 is 10 to the power to 2, which is written 10^2. One thousand is 10 to the power 3, written 10^3, and so on.
- Tiny fractions can be written in the same way—as the number of times you have to divide 10 by 10 to give the fraction. So a hundredth is 10^{-2}. A thousandth is 10^{-3}, and so on.

Millions

- One million is 10 to the power 6 or 10^6.
- Ten million is 10 to the power 7 or 10^7.
- Seven million or 7×10^6 people live in New York.
- The Sun is 9.3×10^7 miles away.
- There are just over 31 million or 3.1×10^7 seconds in a year.

Billions

- One billion is 10 to the power 9 or 10^9.
- There are 6 billion or 6×10^9 people in the world.
- There are 100 billion or 1×10^{11} brain cells in your brain.

Trillions

- One trillion is 10 to the power 12 or 10^{12}.
- Your body contains 25 trillion or 2.5×10^{13} red blood cells.
- A swarm of 12.5 trillion or 1.25×10^{13} locusts invaded Nebraska in 1875.

Quadrillions

- One quadrillion is 10 to the power 15 or 10^{15}.
- There are about one quadrillion or 10^{15} ants in the world.
- There are about 10 million quadrillion or 10^{21} molecules in a single apple.

Add-ons

These prefixes have number meanings, e.g. *kilo*watt and *mega*byte.

deca	10^1
hecto	10^2
kilo	10^3
mega	10^6
giga	10^9
tera	10^{12}
peta	10^{15}
exa	10^{18}
zetta	10^{21}
yotta	10^{24}

These prefixes mean different fractions, e.g. *milli*liter and *centi*meter.

deci	10^{-1}
centi	10^{-2}
milli	10^{-3}
micro	10^{-6}
nano	10^{-9}
pico	10^{-12}
femto	10^{-15}
atto	10^{-18}
zepto	10^{-21}
yocto	10^{-24}

Science

Cold, hot

Cold and hot points	°F	°C	K
Coldest possible temperature (atoms stop moving)	-459.67	-273.15	0
Coldest temperature achieved in a laboratory	-459.399	-272.999	2
Helium melts	-458	-272.2	3
Outer space	-457	-270	4
Helium boils	-452	-268.9	5
Nitrogen melts	-344	-209.86	67
Coldest weather recorded on Earth	-128.6	-89.2	183.8
Water freezes	32	0	273.15
Butter melts	90	30	300
Human body temperature	98.6	37	310
Hottest weather recorded on Earth	136.4	58	331
Water boils	212	100	373.15
Surface of Venus	890	480	750
Coal fire burns	1,500	800	1,100
Iron melts	2,795	1,535	1,808
Gas flame burns	3,000	1,600	1,900
Molten lava	3,200	1,700	2,000
Carbon melts	6,422	3,550	3820
Surface of the Sun	10,000	6,000	6,000
Centre of the Earth	30,000	16,000	16,000
Lightning	54,000	30,000	30,000
Centre of a star	180 mill	100 mill	100 mill
Centre of an H-bomb	700 mill	400 mill	400 mill

Tiny, big

Atomic nucleus	0.39 quadrillionth in.
Hydrogen atom	100 millionth in.
Living cells	3.9 hundreth in.
Dust	0.039 in.
Fly	0.2 in.
Human	6.5 ft.
The Earth	7,457 miles
Jupiter	88,859 miles
The Sun	0.87 million miles
The Milky Way	587,833 quadrillion miles
The Universe	186 million quadrillion km

Light, heavy

Photon	11.7×10^{-63} lb
Oxygen atom	6.6×10^{-26} lb
Ant	2.2×10^{-5} lb
Human	2.2×10^{2} lb
Elephant	2.2×10^{4} lb
Blue whale	2.2×10^{5} lb
Oil tanker	2.2×10^{8} lb
The Earth	13.2×10^{24} lb
The Sun	4.4×10^{30} lb
The Galaxy	4.4×10^{41} lb
The Universe	2.2×10^{51} lb

Key facts: Space

The planets

Planet	Diameter (miles)	Av. distance from Sun (million miles)	Rotation period	Length of year	Tilt of axis	Mass, if Earth =1	Brightness
Mercury	3,031	35.98	58.65 days	87.97 dys	2°	0.055	-1.9
Venus	7,520	67.2	243.01 dys	224.7 dys	177.3°	0.815	-4.4
Earth	7,926	93	23.93 hours	365.26 dys	23.45°	1	
Mars	4,217	141.6	24.62 hrs	686.98 dys	25.19°	0.107	-2.0
Jupiter	88,849	483.6	9.84 hrs	11.86 years	3.1°	317.94	-2.7
Saturn	74,900	886	10.23 hrs	29.46 yrs	26.7°	95.18	+0.7
Uranus	31,764	1,784	17.9 hrs	84.01 yrs	98°	14.53	+5.5
Neptune	30,776	2,794	19.2 hrs	164.79 yrs	29.6°	17.14	+7.8
Pluto	1,429	3675	6.39 hrs	248.54 yrs	122.5°	0.002	+15.1

Milestones

- AD 140: Ptolemy devises his model of the motion of the planets and stars.
- 1543: Nicolaus Copernicus shows that the planets revolve around the Sun, not the Earth.
- 1610: Galileo uses a telescope to see things such as the phases of Venus and the Moons of Jupiter.
- 1659: Christiaan Huygens discovers the rings of Saturn.
- 1781: William Herschel discovers the planet Uranus.
- 1801: Giuseppi Piazzi discovers Ceres, the first asteroid.
- 1846: John Galle discovers the planet Neptune.
- 1929: Edwin Hubble shows that there are other galaxies beyond our own and that the Universe is expanding.
- 1930: Clyde Tombaugh discovers the planet Pluto.
- 1978: James Christy finds Pluto's moon Charon.
- 1995: Michael Mayer and Didier Queloz spot a planet circling the star 51 Pegasi.

The Constellations

Andromeda
Antlia, the Air Pump
Apus, the Bird of Paradise
Aquarius, the Water Bearer
Aquila, the Eagle
Ara, the Altar
Aries, the Ram
Auriga, the Charioteer
Boötes, the Herdsman
Caelum, the Graving Tool
Camelopardalis, the Giraffe
Cancer, the Crab
Canes Venatici, the Hunting Dogs
Canis Major, the Great Dog
Canis Minor, the Little Dog
Capricornus, the Sea Goat
Carina, the Keel
Cassiopeia
Centaurus, the Centaur
Cepheus
Cetus, the Whale
Chamaeleon, the Chameleon
Circinus, the Compasses
Columba, the Dove
Coma Berenices, Berenice's Hair
Corona Australis, Southern Crown
Corona Borealis, the Northern Crown
Corvus, the Crow
Crater, the Cup
Crux, the Southern Cross
Cygnus, the Swan
Delphinius, the Dolphin
Dorado, the Swordfish
Draco, the Dragon
Equuleus, the Foal
Eridanus
Fornax, the Furnace
Gemini, the Twins
Grus. the Crane
Hercules
Horologium, the Clock
Hydra, the Water Snake
Hydrus, the Little Snake
Indus, the Indian
Lacerta, the Lizard
Leo, the Lion
Leo Minor, the Little Lion
Lepus, the Hair
Libra, the Scales of Justice
Lupus, the Wolf
Lynx, the Lynx
Lyra, the Lyre
Mensa, the Table
Microscopium, the Microscope
Monoceros, the Unicorn
Musca, the Fly
Norma, the Rule
Octans, the Octant
Ophiuchus, the Serpent Bearer
Orion
Pavo, the Peacock
Pegasus, the Flying Horse
Perseus
Phoenix, the Phoenix
Pictor, the Painter
Pisces, the Fishes
Piscis Austrinus, the Southern Fish
Puppis, the Poop
Pyxis, the Compass
Reticulum, the Net
Sagitta, the Arrow
Sagittarius, the Archer
Scorpius, the Scorpion
Sculptor, the Sculptor
Scutum, the Shield
Serpens, the Serpent
Sextans, the Sextant
Taurus, the Bull
Telescopium, the Telescope
Triangulum, the Triangle
Triangulum Australe, the Southern Triangle
Tucana, the Toucan
Ursa Major, the Great Bear
Ursa Minor, the Little Bear
Vela, the Sails
Virgo, the Virgin
Volans, the Flying Fish
Vulpecula, the Fox

Key facts: Space

Planets' moons

Earth's moon
- The Moon

Mars's moons
- Phobos
- Deimos

Jupiter's moons
- Metis
- Adastrea
- Amalthea
- Thebe
- Io
- Europa
- Ganymede
- Callisto
- Leda
- Himalia
- Lysithea
- Elara
- Ananke
- Carme
- Pasiphae
- Sinope
- Phoebe

Saturn's moons
- Unnamed
- Pan
- Atlas
- Prometheus
- Pandora
- Janus
- Epimetheus
- Mimas
- Enceladus
- Tethys
- Telesto
- Calypso
- Dione
- Helene
- Rhea
- Titan
- Hyperion
- Iapetus
- Phoebe

Uranus's moons
- Cordelia
- Ophelia
- Bianca
- Cressida
- Desdemona
- Juliet
- Portia
- Rosalind
- Belinda
- Puck
- Ariel
- Umbriel
- Titania
- Oberon

Neptune's moons
- Naiad
- Thalassa
- Despina
- Galatea
- Larissa
- Proteus
- Triton
- Neraid

Pluto's moon
- Charon

Saturn, with 19 moons, has more moons than any other planet in our Solar System.

Nearest and brightest stars

Nearest stars
- Sun (0.0 light-years away from Earth)
- Proxima Centauri (4.2)
- Alpha Centauri A (4.3)
- Alpha Centauri B (4.3)
- Barnard's star (5.9)
- Wolf 359 (7.6)
- Lalance 21185 (8.1)
- Sirius A (8.6)
- Sirius B (8.6)
- UV Ceti A (8.9)

Brightest stars
- Sun (0.0-light years away from Earth)
- Sirius A (8.6)
- Canopus (200)
- Alpha Centauri (4.3)
- Arcturus (36)
- Vega (26)
- Capella (42)
- Rigel (910)
- Procyon (11)
- Achernar (85)

Space exploration

- **1926** The American engineer Robert Goddard designed and launched the first liquid fuel rocket.
- **1942** Wernher von Braun developed the V2 rocket in Nazi Germany.
- **1957** The world's first artificial satellite, the USSR's *Sputnik 1*, was launched.
- **1957** The Russian dog Laika became the first living creature in space aboard *Sputnik 2*.
- **1961** The Soviet cosmonaut Yuri Gagarin became the first man in space aboard *Vostok 1*.
- **1963** The Soviet cosmonaut Valentina Tereshkova became the first woman in space.
- **1966** The USSR's unmanned probe *Lunar 9* landed on the Moon.
- **1969** US astronauts Neil Armstrong and Edwin Aldrin were the first men to walk on the Moon.
- **1972** *Apollo 17* was the sixth and last US manned mission to the Moon.
- **1973** First US space station *Skylab* launched.
- **1980** The US *Voyager 1* took the first detailed photos of Saturn's ring systems and discovered six additional moons.
- **1981** The US space shuttle *Columbia*, the world's first reusable spacecraft, was launched.
- **1982** The Soviet probe *Venera 13* sent back colour photos of the surface of Venus.
- **1986** The shuttle program was halted for several years after the shuttle *Challenger* exploded, killing its crew of seven.
- **1990** The Hubble space telescope was launched.
- **1996** US scientists found evidence in meteor fragments that microbes may have existed on Mars.

Key facts: Earth

Highest waterfalls

Angel Falls (Venezuela)		3,212ft
Yosemite Falls (USA)		2,425ft
Mardalsfossen (S)(Norway)		2,425ft
Tugela Falls (S. Africa)		2,011ft
Cuquenan Falls (Venez.)		2,001ft
Sutherland Falls (NZ)		1,903ft
Ribbon Falls (USA)		1,611ft
Great Falls (Guyana)		1,601ft
Mardalsfossen (N)		1,535ft
Della Falls (Canada)		1,444ft
Gavarnie Falls (France)		1,385ft
Skjeggedal Falls (N'way)		1,378ft
Glass Falls (Brazil)		1,325ft
Krimml Falls (Austria)		1,312ft
Trummelbach Falls (Switz)		1,312ft
Takakkaw Falls (Canada)		1,200ft
Silver Strand Falls (USA)		1171ft
Wallaman Falls (Aus)		1138ft
Wollomombi Falls (Australia)		1099ft

Cities

The world's biggest cities

Mexico City	14,987,051
Cairo	13,000,000
Shangai	12,760,000
Bombay	12,571,720
Tokyo	11,718,720
Seoul	10,920,000
Calcutta	10,916,272
Beijing	10,860,000
São Paulo	9,480,427
Paris	9,318,800
Moscow	8,700,000
Delhi	8,375,188
Jakarta	7,885,519
New York	7,322,564
Istanbul	7,309,190
Karachi	7,183,000
London	6,934,500

Continents

Asia
Area	17,048,000 sq miles
Population	3,112,700,000
Population density (People per sq km)	113

Africa
Area	11,647,000 sq miles
Population	642,111,000
Population density	21

Antarctica
Area	5,477,000 sq miles

North America
Area	15,069,000 sq km
Population	427,226,000
Population density	13

South America
Area	11,060,000 sq miles
Population	296,716,000
Population density	17

Europe
Area	6,524,000 sq km
Population	498,371,000
Population density	96

Oceania
Area	3,281,000 sq km
Population	26,481,000
Population density	3

Population

The most populous countries

China	1,188,000,000
India	879,500,000
USA	255,200,000
Indonesia	191,200,000
Brazil	154,100,000
Russia	149,003,000
Pakistan	124,800,000
Japan	124,500,000
Bangladesh	119,300,000
Nigeria	115,700,000
Mexico	88,200,000
Germany	80,300,000
Vietnam	69,500,000
Philippines	65,200,000

Earth

Biggest lakes

Caspian Sea	143,240 sq miles	Lake Ontario	7,336 sq miles
Lake Superior	32,526 sq miles	Lake Balkhash	7,115 sq miles
Lake Victoria	26,820 sq miles	Lake Ladoga	6,835 sq miles
Aral Sea	24,904 sq miles	Lake Chad	6,300 sq miles
Lake Huron	24,361 sq miles	Lake Maracaibo	5,120 sq miles
Lake Michigan	22,300 sq miles	Patos	3,920 sq miles
Lake Tanganyika	12,650 sq miles	Lake Onega	3,710 sq miles
Lake Baikal	12,160 sq miles	Lake Eyre	3,598 sq miles
Great Bear Lake	12,095 sq miles	Lake Titicaca	3,200 sq miles
Lake Nyasa	11,150 sq miles	Lake Nicaragua	3,100 sq miles
Great Slave Lake	11,030 sq miles	Lake Mai-Ndombe	3,100 sq miles
Lake Erie	9,966 sq miles	Lake Athabasca	3,063 sq miles
Lake Winnipeg	9,416 sq miles		

Richest and poorest

The world's richest countries
GNP per head in the 90s $US

Switzerland	33,510
Liechtenstein	33,000
Luxembourg	31,080
Japan	26,920
Sweden	25,490
Finland	24,400
Norway	24,160
Denmark	23,660
Germany	23,650
Iceland	22,580
USA	22,560
Canada	21,260
France	20,600
Austria	20,380

The world's poorest countries
GNP per head in the 90s

Mozambique	60
Tanzania	110
Ethiopia	110
Somalia	150
Nepal	170
Sierra Leone	170
Uganda	170
Bhutan	180
Cambodia	200
Guinea-Bissau	210
Burundi	210
Malawi	210
Bangladesh	220
Chad	220
Zaîre	220

Mountains

The world's highest mountains

Asia
Everest	29,029ft.
K2	28,251ft.
Kanchenjunga	28,209ft.

South America
Aconcagua	22,834ft.
Ojos del Salado	22,664ft.
Bonete	22,546ft.

North America
McKinley	20,322ft.
Logan	19,524ft.
Citlaltépetl	18,406ft.

Africa
Kilimanjaro	19,341ft.
Kenya	17,060ft.
Margherita Peak	16,762ft.

Europe
Elbrus	18,510ft.
Dykh Tau	17,070ft.
Shkara	17,064ft.

Oceania
Wilhelm	14,793ft.
Cook	12,316ft.
Tasman	11,473ft.

Key facts: Earth

Major rivers of the world

Nile	4,147 miles
Amazon	4,083 miles
Yangtze	3,900 miles
Mississippi-Missouri-Red Rock	3,740 miles
Ob-Irtysh	3,362 miles
Yenesei-Angara	3,100 miles
Yellow	2,877 miles
Amur-Shilka	2,744 miles
Lena	2,734 miles
Congo	2,718 miles
Mackenzie-Peace-Finlay	2,635 miles
Mekong	2,597 miles
Missouri-Red Rock	2,563 miles
Niger	2,548 miles
Plate-Parana	2,450 miles
Mississippi	2,348 miles
Murray-Darling	2,331 miles
Missouri	2,315 miles
Volga	2,194 miles
Madeira	2,014 miles
Purus	1,995 miles
São Fransisco	1,989 miles
Yukon	1,979 miles
St Lawrence	1,900 miles
Rio Grande	1,883 miles
Tunguska, Lower	1,861 miles
Indus	1,800 miles
Danube	1,775 miles
Salween	1,770 miles
Brahmaputra	1,700 miles
Euphrates	1,700 miles
Para-Tocantins	1,677 miles
Zambezi	1,600 miles
Nelson-S.Saskatchewan-Bow	1,600 miles
Paraguay	1,584 miles
Amu Darya	1,579 miles
Kolyma	1,562 miles
Ganges	1,549 miles
Ural	1,508 miles

Islands

The world's biggest islands

Island	sq miles
Greenland	840,000
New Guinea	305,000
Borneo	290,000
Madagascar	226,657
Baffin (Canada)	195,927
Sumatra (Indonesia)	164,000
Honshu, Japan	87,805
Great Britain	84,200
Victoria, (Can)	83,896
Ellesmere (Can)	75,767
Sulawesi (Indo)	73,056
South Island (NZ)	58,384
Java (Indo)	48,842

Earthquake disasters

Date	Location	death toll
464BC	Sparta, Greece	20,000
856AD	Corinth, Greece	45,000
856	Damghan, Iran	200,000
893	Ardabil, Iran	150,000
1038	Chihli, China	100,000
1138	Aleppo, Syria	230,000
1293	Kamekura, Japan	30,000
1556	Shansi, China	800,000
1667	Shemaka, the Caucasus	80,000
1731	Peking, China	100,000
1737	Calcutta, India	300,000
1755	Lisbon, Portugal	100,000
1906	San Francisco, US	3,000
1908	Messina, Italy	160,000
1920	Kanshu, China	200,000
1923	Kwanto, Japan	144,000
1960	Southern Chile	5,700
1964	Anchorage, Alaska	131
1970	Ancash, Peru	66,000
1976	Tangshan, China	655,000
1985	Michoacán, Mexico	9,500
1994	Northridge, US	60
1995	Kobe, Japan	5,200

Earth

Sea deeps

The deepest sea trenches

	feet from sea level
Mariana	35,826
Tonga	35,433
Philippine	32,995
Kermadec	32,963
Izu-Ogasawara	32,087
Kuril	31,332
North New Hebrides	30,102
New Britain	29,331
Puerto Rico	28,232
Yap	27,976

Glaciers

The world's longest glaciers

Lambert-Fisher Ice Passage (Antarctica)	320 miles
Petermanns Glacier (Greenland)	124 miles
Hubbard Glacier (N.America)	98 miles
Siachen Glacier (Karakoram, Asia)	47 miles
Skeidarajokull (Iceland)	30 miles
Tasman (New Zealand)	18 miles
Aletsch Gletscher (European Alps)	15 miles

Oceans & seas

Oceans

Pacific	62,644 sq miles
Atlantic	31,830 sq miles
Indian	28,355 sq miles
Arctic	5,440 sq miles

Seas

South China	1,331 sq miles
Caribbean	1,711 sq miles
Mediterranean	967 sq miles
Gulf of Mexico	596 sq miles
Sea of Japan	389 sq miles
East China	290 sq miles
North	222 sq miles
Black	178 sq miles
Baltic	163 sq miles

Weather

The world's sunniest place is the Eastern Sahara, with sunshine for over 90% of all daylight hours.

The world's hottest place is Dallol, Ethiopia, with an average temperature of 34°C in the shade.

The world's driest place is the Atacama Desert in Chile, with an annual average of just 0.51mm of rain.

The world's coldest place is Vostok in Antarctica, where it averages -57.8°C.

The world's major deserts

	square miles
Sahara	3,500,000
Arabian	899,614
Gobi	500,000
Patagonian	259,846
Rub al-Khali	250,000
Kalahari	225,019
Chihuahuan	173,745
Taklimakan	140,000
Kara Kum	135,135
Great Sandy	130,695
Great Victoria	130,694
Gibson	120,000
Thar	100,000
Atacama	70,000
Sonoran	70,000
Simpson	40,000
An Nafud	40,000
Mojave	15,019
Death Valley	3,012
Namib	498

Key facts: Animals

Kingdoms

1. **Monerans**
Simple single-cell organisms with no nucleus, e.g. bacteria.
2. **Protista**
Mostly single-cell organisms with a nucleus, e.g. amebas.
3. **Fungi**
Multicelled organisms that feed on living or dead organic matter, e.g. molds.
4. **Plantae**
Multicelled organisms such as trees, plants, and grasses.
5. **Animalia**
Animals—multicelled organisms that must find food and can move around.

The animal kingdom:
- Vertebrates
  - Mammals
  - Birds
  - Amphibians
  - Reptiles
  - Jawless fish
  - Sea squirts
  - Sharks and rays
  - Bony fish
- Invertebrates
  - Echinoderms
  - Arthropods
  - Velvetworms, lampshells etc.
  - Worms of all kinds
  - Sponges
  - Cnidaria
  - Mollusks

Animal classification

Classification of a lion:

Kingdom
Animalia
Multicelled organisms that cannot make their own food.
Phylum
Chordate
Animals that have a single nerve cord at some stage during their life.
Class
Mammal
Animals that suckle their young on milk and have hair or fur.
Order
Carnivore
Land mammals adapted to hunting.
Family
Cats
Have sharp, retractable front claws.
Genus
Big cats
Includes five species—lions, tigers, leopards, snow leopards, and jaguars.
Species
Lion

Males, females, and babies

Animal	Male	Female	Young
Antelope	Buck	Doe	Kid
Bobcat	Tom	Lioness	Kitten
Buffalo	Bull	Cow	Calf
Camel	Bull	Cow	Calf
Caribou	Stag	Doe	Fawn
Duck	Drake	Duck	Duckling
Fish	Cock	Hen	Fry
Goat	Billygoat	Nannygoat	Kid
Goose	Gander	Goose	Gosling
Seal	Bull	Cow	Pup
Swan	Cob	Pen	Cygnet
Weasel	Boar	Cow	Kit

Animals

Animal habitats

Freshwater lakes
- otter, water vole, harvest mouse
- reed warbler, heron, kingfisher, marsh harrier, coot
- frogs, toads, newts
- dragonfly, pondskater, waterboatman, mayfly
- stickleback, trench, pike, perch

Tundra and Arctic
- polar bear, Arctic fox, Arctic hare, gray wolf, vole, ermine, lemming, musk ox, caribou
- eagles, grouse, plover, goose, snowy owl
- mosquito

Mountains
- ibex, chamois deer, yak, llama, vicuna, puma, snow leopard, lynx, chinchilla, marmot
- eagles, condor, lammergeier
- ice worm

Tropical grasslands
- giraffe, zebra, antelope, lion, leopard, cheetah, elephant, water buffalo, mongoose, hyena, jackal
- ostrich, marabou stork, oxpecker, weaver bird, secretary bird, vulture
- Eastern brown snakes, red-bellied snakes
- dung beetle, termite, locust

Temperate grasslands
- saiga antelope, pronghorn antelope, bison, prairie dog, mole rat, coyote, fox
- rhea, guanaco, buzzard
- grass snakes, lizards
- grasshoppers, flies

Tropical forests
- monkeys, leopard, shrew, sloth, coati, opossum, okapi, tamandua, jaguar
- macaws, parrots, toucans, hummingbirds, jacamars
- viper, anaconda, python, tree frogs, iguana, crocodiles, turtles
- morpho butterfly, hunting spider, ants

Temperate forests
- squirrel, skunk, badger, mouse, raccoon, hedgehog, chipmunk, beaver, rabbit, fox, deer, bear, wolf, wild boar
- warbler, tits, woodpeckers, woodcock, jay, owl
- salamanders, slugs
- ants, purple emperor butterfly, moths, beetles, earthworm, snails, centipede

Deserts
- camels, addax, fennec fox, long-eared jackrabbit, kangaroo rat, gundi, jerboa
- roadrunner, hummingbird, vultures, nighthawk, burrowing owl, sand grouse
- spiny lizard, gila monster, rattlesnake, gecko, thorny devil, toroises
- scorpion, antlion, spiders

Seashore
- anenomes, barnacles, mussels, starfish, crabs, sea cucumber, cockles, lugworm, sea urchin, scallop, limpets
- gulls, tern, gannet, pelican

Oceans
- Surface waters: seal, porpoise, shark, mackerel, jellyfish, turtle, seahorse
- Midocean: squid, octopus, swordfish, hatchet fish, lanternfish, flatfish
- Deep sea: ray, gulper eel, angler fish, giant squid, sperm whale

363

Key facts: Animals

Birds

- **The biggest bird**
  The biggest bird is the ostrich, which can grow up to 9 feet tall.
- **The smallest bird**
  The smallest bird is the bee hummingbird, which is just 2.2 inches long.
- **The biggest flying bird**
  The biggest flying bird is the Kori bustard, which can weigh up to 40 pounds.
- **The biggest bird of prey**
  The Andean condor can weigh 24 pounds or more.
- **The fastest flier**
  The fastest flier is the peregrine falcon, which can fly up to 210mph.
- **The oldest bird**
  Cocky the cockatoo of London Zoo was more than 80 when he died in 1982.
- **The longest journey**
  An Arctic tern flew 13,970 miles from Russia down through the Atlantic over Africa and the Indian Ocean to Australia.
- **The most time in the air**
  No bird spends more time flying than the sooty tern, which can remain in the air for 3-10 years.
- **The biggest egg**
  The biggest egg is the ostrich, which can grow up to 8 inches across.
- **The highest flier**
  The highest flight was by a Ruppell's vulture, which hit a plane at 36,989 feet.
- **The fastest swimmer**
  A gentoo penguin gets to 17mph.

Sea creatures

- **The smallest fish**
  The smallest fish is the Marshall Islands goby, which is only 0.6 inch long.
- **The largest fish**
  The largest crab is the Whale shark, which can grow more than 40 feet long.
- **The fastest fish**
  The fastest fish is the sailfish, which can travel at up to 68mph.
- **The oldest fish**
  The Whale shark can live to more than 70 years.
- **The deadliest jellyfish**
  The deadly Australian Sea Wasp can kill a man in just one minute.
- **The noisiest animal**
  The noisiest animal is the Blue whale. Its sounds can be detected from 500 miles away.
- **The smallest crab**
  The smallest crab is the pea crab, which really is as small as a pea.
- **The largest turtle**
  The largest turtle is the Pacific leatherback, which grows up to 7 feet long.
- **The longest journey**
  European eels travel 4,650 miles on their spawning migration from the Baltic to the Sargasso Sea.

Animals

Mammals

- **The biggest mammal**
  The biggest mammal is the Blue whale which can grow up to 110 feet long and weigh up to 210 tons.
- **The biggest land mammal**
  The biggest land mammal is the African bush elephant, which can grow up 13 feet tall and weigh up to 13 tons
- **The tallest mammal**
  The tallest mammal is the giraffe, which can grow more than 20 feet tall.
- **The smallest mammal**
  The smallest mammal is the bumblebee bat of Thailand, which weighs less than 0.1 ounce.
- **The smallest land mammal**
  The smallest land mammal is the Etruscan shrew, which is less than 2 inches long.
- **The fastest sprinting land mammal**
  The fastest land mammal is the cheetah, which can reach 60mph for short bursts.
- **The fastest running land mammal**
  The fastest running land mammal over a sustained distance is the North American pronghorn antelope, which can keep up 35mph for more than 4 miles.
- **The fastest marine mammal**
  The fastest swimming mammal is the killer whale, which can reach 35 mph.
- **The highest jumper**
  The highest jumping animals are pumas and leopards, which can jump more than 16 feet.
- **The oldest mammal**
  The oldest mammal (apart from humans, of course) is the elephant, which can live more than 70 years.

Reptiles

- **The largest reptile**
  The largest reptiles are the crocodiles of SE Asia, which can grow up to 16 feet in length.
- **The biggest lizard**
  The biggest lizard is the komodo dragon which grows more than 10 feet and has been said to grow to 30 feet.
- **The biggest amphibian**
  The biggest amphibian is the Chinese giant salamander which is more than 3 feet long.
- **The longest snake**
  The longest snake may be the reticulated python at more than 30 feet long.
- **The most poisonous snake**
  The most poisonous snake is the Marine Cobra of the western Pacific.

Insects

- **The heaviest insects**
  The heaviest flying insects are the Goliath beetles of Africa, at up to 3.6 ounces.
- **The longest insect**
  The longest insects are stick insects, which can grow up to 16 inches long.
- **The fastest flier**
  The Australian dragonfly reaches 36 mph.
- **The largest butterfly**
  The Queen Alexandra's birdwing of Papua New Guinea can be up to 10 inches across.
- **The loudest insect**
  Male cicadas (like crickets) rub their abdomens so loud they can be heard at 1,300 feet.

Key facts: Plants

Plant records

- **The smallest plant**
  The smallest plant is the duckweed Wolffia arrhiza, which has fronds less than 0.04 inch across.
- **The biggest plant**
  The biggest plant is the Giant Sequioa tree called General Sherman in California which is 272 feet tall.
- **The oldest plant**
  The oldest plant is a lichen in Antarctica thought to be more than 10,000 years old.
- **The tallest tree**
  A eucalyptus in Victoria, Australia, is 469 feet tall.
- **The biggest flower**
  The biggest flower is the Rafflesia of Indonesia, which has blooms more than 6 feet across.
- **The biggest water plant**
  The biggest water plant is the Amazon water lily, which has leaves more than 6 feet across.
- **The biggest leaves**
  The biggest leaves belong to the raffia palm, which can grow up to 60 feet long.
- **The deepest roots**
  The deepest roots belong to a fig tree growing in South Africa, which has roots down more than 120m.
- **The biggest seed**
  The biggest seed is the coco de mer coconut, which weighs up to 40 pounds.
- **The fastest growing plant**
  The fastest growing plant is the bamboo, which can grow 3 feet in a single day.

Plants

1. Flowering plants or angiosperms
   Monocotyledons
   (one leaf sprout, eg. grasses, cereals, tulips and daffodils)
   Dicotyledons
   (two leaf sprout, eg. most deciduous trees, vegetables and fruits)
2. Gymnosperms
   Conifers
   (eg. spruces, firs, pines and larches)
   Cycads
   Gingkos
3. Ferns
4. Clubmosses
5. Horsetails
6. Mosses and liverworts
7. Algae
   Red
   Green
   Brown

Fungi

1. Rusts and mildews
2. Molds
3. Sac fungi
4. Club fungi
5. Imperfect fungi
6. Slime molds

Plant environments

Temperate woodlands
Deciduous
- trees such as beeches, birches, hickories, maples, oaks, poplars, and walnuts
- shrubs such as brambles, hawthorn, and honeysuckle
- woodland flowers such as bluebells, primroses, foxgloves, willowherbs, and anenomes

Coniferous
- trees such as redwoods, giant sequoias, Douglas firs, cedars, and pines
- small trees such as rowan and hazel
- ferns
- bilberries

Grasslands
- grasses such as tussock, marram, meadow, blue and rye
- trees and shrubs such as acacia, thorn, baobab, and rokerboom
- flowers such as vetches, trefoils, orchids, blazing star, worts, and coneflowers

Tropical forests
- trees such as mahoganies, teaks, banyans, and palms
- lichens
- vines and lianas
- epiphytes such as orchids, ferns, tree ferns, and bromeliads
- carnivorous plants such as Venus fly traps and pitcher plants

Lakes and rivers
- reeds, rushes, and papyrus
- sedges
- worts such as bladderwort and fanwort
- water crowfoot
- waterlilies and irises
- water hyacinths

Deserts
- cacti
- creosote bushes, thorn trees, quiver trees, Joshua trees, sagebrush, yuccas, and prickly pear
- window plants and pebble plants
- palm trees
- evening primrose

High mountains
- rowan and dwarf willow, crowberries and bilberries
- wild flowers such as alpine bluebells, mountain avens, gentian, edelweiss, snowbells, saxifrage, and saussurea
- grasses and mosses

Key facts: Body

People: tallest, shortest, oldest, youngest

- The tallest man ever was the American Robert Wadlow (b. 1918) who reached 8 feet, 11 inches tall.
- The shortest man ever was American "General Tom Thumb" who was just 3 feet, 5 inches tall when he died in 1885.
- The fattest man ever was American Jon Minnoch, who weighed 1,400 pounds when he died in 1983.
- The lightest human adult ever was the Mexican girl Lucia Xarate who weighed just 4.7 pounds when she was 17 in 1889.

- There is a woman in Africa who is thought to be 150 years old, but no one can prove it.
- In 1997, Frenchwoman Jeanne Calment died aged 122 years and 164 days.
- In 1986, Japanese Shigechiyo Izumi died aged 120 years and 237 days.
- The most children born at once were decaplets—2 boys and 8 girls born in 1946 in Bacacy in Brazil.
- Mr. and Mrs. Vassileyev, who lived near Moscow in 1782 had 69 of their own children.

Inside the body

- There are more than 600 billion cells in your body.
- There are more than 200 types of cell in your body.
- There are 100 billion nerve cells in your brain.
- 14% of your body weight is bone; 40% is muscle.
- You have 213 bones in your body.
- Babies have 300 bones.
- There are 22 bones in your skull.
- There are 33 bones or vertebrae in your spine.

- You have 7 pairs of true ribs. 3 false ribs and 2 floating ribs.
- There are 27 bones in your hand.
- The longest bone is the femur or thighbone.
- You have 640 muscles in your body.
- The longest muscle is the sartorius on the inside of the thigh.
- The biggest muscle in your body is the gluteus maximus or buttock.

Body

Breath facts

- You will probably take about 600 million breaths if you live to the age of 75.
- Every minute you are alive, you breathe in more than 200 fluid ounces of air.
- A normal breath takes in about 14 fluid ounces of air.
- On average, you breathe about 13-17 times a minute.
- If you run hard, you may have to breathe up to 80 times a minute.
- Newborn babies breathe about 40 times a minute.
- There are about 300 million little air sacs or alveoli in your body.
- Opened out and laid flat your lungs would cover an area about the size of a tennis court.
- There are more than 1,500 miles of airways in your lungs.

Blood count

- Your heart beats 30 million times each year.
- The chambers of the heart each hold about 2.5 fluid ounces of blood.
- Pulse rates average 60 to 100 beats a minute.
- Blood travels through the capillaries at 3 feet a second.
- There are 36,000 miles of capillary in your body.
- Capillaries may be just a thousandth of an inch thick.
- Someone who weighs 165 pounds has about 11 pints of blood.
- Someone who weighs 165 pounds and lives on the high Andes has about 13 pints of blood.
- A microliter of blood holds 4-6 million red blood cells.
- A microliter of blood holds 5-10,000 white blood cells.
- A microliter of blood holds 150,000-500,000 platelets.
- Blood is 60% plasma.
- Plasma is 90% water.
- There are 13 blood clotting factors, numbers I-XIII.
- There are 4 blood groups: A, O, N, and ABO.
- 85% belong to the blood type Rhesus positive.

Milestones

- 1543: Vesalius created his book *De Humani Corporis Fabrica*—which became the basis of modern anatomy.
- 1550: Gabriel Fallopio's close study of the body revealed tiny structures.
- 1590: Santorio Sanctorius created the science of physiology. He also showed how to measure pulse and temperature.
- 1628: William Harvey revealed how the heart circulates blood.
- 1661: Using a microscope, Marcello Malphigi saw tiny blood vessels called capillaries.
- 1798: Edward Jenner showed people could be vaccinated against infectious diseases.
- 1840s: Rudolf Virchow and Jakob Henle found that the body is built up from tissues made from tiny cells.
- 1900: Karl Landsteiner showed that people's blood belongs to different groups.

INDEX

A

aba 248
abdomen 66-67
absolute date 136
Absolute Magnitude 112
Absolute Zero 171, 331
abyssal plain 151
acacia tree 203
acanthodian 137, 268
acceleration 167, 334
acid 339, 179
Aconcagua 147
acorn 79, 81, 189
acoustics 345
actin 18-19, 255
actinides 328
acupuncture 37
Adams, John Couch 109
addax 226
aeolian 289
Africa 273
Afro-Caribbeans 242
Ages 136, 268
AIDS 33
air 128-129
air plants 198
albatross 218
Albizia falcata 79
alcohol 171
Aldrin, Buzz 101, 121, 299, 304
Aleppo, Syria 144
algae 88-89, 184, 209, 222
algal bloom 89
alginate 89
alimentary canal 28-29, 250
Alkali metals 176
Alkaline-Earth Group 176
alkalis 179
allergy 33
alligator 63, 222
Alpha Centauri 313
alpha particles 160
alpha stars 113
Alpine 277
alpine flowers 206-207

Alps 146-147, 206-207, 273, 276-277
alveoli 16
alveolus 252
amanitine 87
Amazon 149, 337
Amazon water lily 95
amber 270
Amboseli, Kenya 220
amethyst 140
amino acids 30
ammonia 106-107
ammonites 271
amniotic fluid 27
amphibians 64-65, 233
Ancient Egypt 244, 248
Andes 146, 276
Andromeda 114-115, 118
Andromeda galaxy 317, 319, 321
anenome 229
anesthetic 38
Angel Falls, Venezuela 149, 285
angiosperm 71, 74, 185
anion 327
annuals 75, 77
anoraks 249
Antarctica 209, 219, 273, 287-288, 331
Antares 113
antelope 47, 220, 226, 234
antennae 66
anteosaurus 137, 268
anther 186
anthracite 139
antibiotics 36, 86
antibodies 32-33, 37, 89
anticlines 146
anticyclone 132
antigen 33
antlers 215
ants 66-67
anus 32, 250
anvil (see incus)
aorta 253
apes 32, 48-49
aphelion 127, 297

Apollo 11 299, 304
Appalachian mountains 277
appendicular skeleton (see skeleton)
appendix 29, 250
aquatic plants 200-201
Archean 136, 268
Archimedes 337
archipelago 291
Arctic 208-209, 218-219
Arctic fox 218-219
Arctic poppy 208-209
Arctic tern 218
argon 155, 176-177
Armstrong, Neil 101, 121, 299, 304-305
arteries 14-15
arterioles 14
artery 252-253
artiodactyls 235
ash 142-143, 278-279
aspergillus 86
aspirin 93, 179, 192
asteroid 110, 308
asthenosphere 275
astigmatism 257
astronauts 101, 119, 305
astronomers 118-119, 122, 302-303, 311-312, 321
Atacama desert 205, 288
Atlantic 135
atmosphere 100, 102, 104-108, 110, 128-129, 134-135, 296, 308-311
atom 160, 163, 174-175, 178-179
atomic mass 176
Atomic Number 176
atoms 268, 326-7, 348-9
atrium 252-253
Aurora Borealis 157, 347
aurorae 301
Australia 230-231, 273
Australopithecus 240
axis 297
axolotl 65

370

axon 25
Ayers Rock (see Uluru)

B

Babbage, Charles 341
baboon 48
babylon 247
bacteria 32, 36, 136, 270
badgers 42, 214-215
baleen 52
bamboo 70
bandicoots 231
baobab 187, 202
barchan 289
bark 78, 188
barley 91
barometer 129
basal ganglia 262
basalt 138
basil 92-93
bats 345
battery 155, 339
battery hens 57
Battle of Hastings 111
beach 150
beaches 290
bears 50-51, 216-217
beavers 43, 217
Bedouins 242
bees 66-67
beet 72
begonias 73
belemnites 271
bell-heather 76
berry 79
beta 113
Betelgeuse 312-313
Bethlehem 111
biceps 255
biennials 77
Big Bang 122-123, 320-321
big cats 46-47
Big Crunch 321
Big Dipper 313
bight 291
bile duct 250
bill 59
billabong 174

binary system 159, 340
binoculars 162
biostratigraphy 136
birds 58-61
birdsfoot trefoil 76
birth canal 27
bismuth 141
bison 235
Black Forest 277
black hole 116-117, 318
bladder 28
bladderwort 201
blight 90
blind spot 257
blood 14-15, 21, 28, 34, 252-253
blowhole 52, 291
blubber 52, 218
Blue whale 219, 221, 236
bluebell 76-77, 80
boiling point 172, 325
bolus 29
bombs 349
bone marrow 254
bones 20-21, 254-255
boreal forest 82
bottlebrush 185
bowel 29
Boyle's Law 171
brachiopods 271
brachiosaurus 137, 268, 271
bracket fungus 87 brain 24-5
brain 262-263, 265
brain stem 262
bream 233
breathing 16-17, 252-253
bromeliads 198-199
bronchiole 16-17
Bronze Age 241, 245
browser 45
bryophytes 85
Buckland, William 271
bud 75
buffalo 44, 235
bulb (light) 72-73, 77, 328, 339, 343
buoyancy tanks 336
bush 202
buttercup 76

butterfly 66
buttes 289
byte 159, 340

C

cacao tree 191
cacti 94, 204-205
caimans 222
calcium 20-21, 31, 141, 254-255
calcium carbonate 293
caldera 278
Caledonian 277
Caledonian mountains, Scotland 277
calendar 127
calf bone (see bones)
cambium 74
Cambrian Period 137, 268-269
camel 45, 225-227
canopy (forest) 199
canopy 80
Cape Cod 113
capillaries 14-15, 253
carapace 63
carbohydrates 30-31, 250-251
carbon 176-177, 270, 341, 329
carbon dioxide 14-16, 71, 105, 142, 169, 185, 279, 282, 292, 308-309
carbonic acid 282
Carboniferous Period 84, 137, 139, 269
caribou 217
carnation 76
carnivore 45, 50
carrots 72
cartenoids 222
cartilage 20
cassowary 235
Catal Hüyük, Turkey 246
caterpillar 66
cation 340
catkin 79
cats 46-47, 54-55
cattle 45, 56
Caucasian 242
Caucasus 146
cavern 292-293

371

caves 292-3
CD 341, 343
cedar (see trees)
celanides 76
Celestial Police 110
cell division (see mitosis)
cell multiplication 264
cellulose 71
Celsius 341
Centaur 118
cephalopod 137, 268
cepheid variable 119, 319
cereal 90-91, 190
cerebellum 24, 262-263
cerebral cortex 262
cerebrum 24, 42, 262
Ceres 110
Cernan, Eugene 101
cervix 27
cetacean 52
chador (see aba)
chalcopyrite 141
Challenger Deep 151
chameleon 212
chamois 225
Charles's Law 171
Charon 108-109, 311
cheese 260
cheetah 221, 234
chemicals 178-179, 328-9
chemistry 175
cherry 74
chicken 57
chimpanzee 49
chip (see silicon chip)
chitin 67
chlorine 178, 327
chlorophyll 71, 81, 185, 188
chloroplasts 71
chocolate 190
chopines 249
chromosome 265
chromosphere 102, 300-301
Chrons 136, 268
chrysalis 66
chrysanthemum 76-77
chyme 29
cinammon 93
circuit (electric) 340

circulation 14, 104, 252-3
cirque 286-287
cities 246-247
civilization 246-7
cliffs 290-291
clothes 248
cloud 132, 131, 324-5, 338
clover 76
CNS (Central Nervous System) 25, 262-3
coal 139, 168-169, 195, 269, 271, 331
coasts 150, 290-291
COBE 321
coca plant 193
cochlea 23259, 344
coconuts 186
cocoon 66
codpieces 249
coffee 92
cold front (see fronts)
cold-blooded 42, 62
collagen 20-21, 254
colliders 321
collie 54
colon 29
color 163
combustion chamber 335
comet 110-111, 308, 311
communications satellites 306-307
compass 156-157, 333
compounds 178-179, 328-9
computer 158-159, 340-341
conception 27
condensation 173, 325
condors 224
conduction 170, 330
conductor 155
cone (eye) 22
cone (pine) 79, 82-83
cones 257
conifer 79, 82-83, 184-185, 188, 194
coniferous forest 82
constellation 113, 313
continental drift 272-273
continental shelf 151
continents 134-135, 272-273

convection 170, 330
convection currents 273, 300
conventional medicine 37
cooksonia 137, 268
coordination 24, 263
copaiba tree 195
Copernicus, Nicolaus 297
copper 141, 155, 177
coppice 197
coppicing 81
core, Earth's 99
cork 195
corm 72-73
corn 90, 190
cornea 22, 256-257
corona 102-103, 300-301
corpus callosum 262
cosmetics 248
cosmic microwave background radiation 122
costumes 248-249
cotton 194
covalent bond 178, 327
cow 56-57
coypu 233
CPU 159
crabs 228-229
cranium (see bones)
crater 100, 110, 278
cretaceans 236
Cretaceous Period 268-269
crevasses 286-287
crinoids 271
crinoline 249
crocodile 62-63, 222-223
crocuses 73
crops 90-91, 190-191, 244
Crunch 122
crusafontia 137, 268
crust (Earth) 99, 274, 276, 279-280
crustaceans 236
crystal 138, 140, 175
crystallization 175
crystallography 175
cud 56
Culpeper, Nicholas 193
culture 33
cuneiform 247

Curie, Marie 329
Curie, Pierre 157
current, electric 154-155
cursor 159
cyan 163, 257
cyanobacteria 270
cyberspace 175, 341
cycad 82-83, 184
cyclone 132
Cygnus 313

D

Dallol, Ethiopia 131
Dalton, John 328
Danube 149
dark 122
Dark Matter 317
Dartmoor, England 283
date palm 187
dating 136
daylight 257, 342
deadly nightshade 193
Death Valley, California 205, 226
decibels 259, 345
deciduous forests 81
deciduous trees 80-81, 188
deer 215
delphinium 77
delta 149, 285
dendrite 25
Deneb 113, 319
denim 249
dentine 251
depressions 130, 132
desert 204-205, 226-227, 288-289
desert hedgehog 227
Devonian Period 137, 269
dew point 128
diamond 140, 173, 175
diaphragm 17
dicotyledons 185
digestion 28-29
digestive system 29, 250
digitalis 93, 192, 197
dimetrodon 137, 268
dingo 230
dinosaur 222, 241, 268, 271, 273, 317
dip 146
diphtheria 36-37
disease 15, 31, 32-33
distributaries 285
DNA 179
doe 215
Dog Star (see Sirius)
dogs 50-51, 54-55
dolphin 52-3, 236-237
domains 157
Doppler effect 344
downs 202
dragonfly 67
drupe 74, 187, 197
duck 57, 60
duck-billed platypus 42, 231
ducks 232
dugong 53
duodenum 29
Dutch elm disease 81
dwarf star (see stars)
dwarf willow 78
dynamics 167

E

ear 23, 258-259
ear canal 258
eardrum 258
Earth 98-100, 102-103, 104-106, 116, 123, 126-127, 134-136, 156, 268-269, 274-275, 296-301, 304-311, 316, 319, 336, 346
earthquake 98, 134-135, 144-145
earthquake zones 144
earthquakes 274, 280-281
earwax 258
Easter Island 242
eating 250-251
ebb tide 291
echinoderms 236
echo 344
eclipse 99, 299
eddies 130
edelweiss 76, 206-207
Edinburgh Castle 279
Effort 164-165
egg (see ovum)
Einstein, Albert 102, 348
El'brus, Mt 147
elapid 62
electric charge 154-155
electric circuit 158
electricity 154-155, 168, 338-340, 348
electrode 155
electromagnet 347
electromagnetic radiation 160, 162, 170
electromagnetic spectrum 342-343
electromagnetism 154, 321
electron 154-155, 174-178
electronics 158-19, 340-341
electrons 326-329
elements 141, 176-177, 328-329
elephant 44, 220-221
elk 217
elliptical galaxy (see galaxies)
embryo 27
emergent layer (rain forest) 199
emmer 190, 244
Emperor penguins 219
emu 235
enamel 251
Enceladus 107, 311
Encke's comet 111
endothermic (see warm-blooded)
energy 168-169, 330-331
engine 334-335
enzyme 29, 86
Eon 136, 268
ephemerals 77
epicenter 144-145, 280
epiglottis 250
epiphytes 198
Epoch 136, 268
equator 98, 126-127, 296
Era 136
erosion 282
eruptions 142-143, 146
esophagus 199
estuary 150
Etruscan shrew 42

373

eucalyptus 189, 194
evaporation 173
evening primrose 205
Everest, Mt. 147
evergreen 188
exfoliation 283
exoskeleton 67
exosphere 129
extensor 18
eye 256-257

F

Fahrenhiet 171, 330
Fallopian tube 26
fallow 191
false fruit 74
false morel 87
Faraday, Michael 339
farm animals 56-57
farms 244-245
fast twitch red muscle 19
fat 30-31, 250-251
fault 144-145, 147, 277
feldspar 140
femur 254-255
fennec fox 227
ferns 82, 84-85, 184-185, 197-198
fertilizers 190-191
fetch 291
fever 33
feverfew 92-93, 192-193
fiber-optics 343
fibrils 255
fibula 254
filament (light bulb) 328, 339, 343
filament (plant) 186
fire 330
firn 286
fish 232-233
fission 160
fissure 278
fjords 287
flamingo 222
flare 103
flash flood 289
Flashlight 339

flexor 18
flight deck 340
floodplain 148
flour 90-91
flower 74-75, 76-77, 185
fluorine 141
fly agaric 86-87
Flying Horse, the (see Pegasus)
fetus 27
food 250-251
force 164-167, 332-334
force field 333
formic acid 66
formula (chemical) 177
fossil fuel 139, 169, 195, 331
fossils 268, 270-271, 309
four-stroke engine 334
fowl 57
fox 50, 214
foxglove 93, 192
fractals 341
freezing point 325
friction 333-334
frill-necked lizard (see lizard)
frog 64-65, 232
fronds 84-85
fronts (weather) 130-131
frost 130
frost 282-283
fruit 74, 90
fruits 185, 348
fulcrum 165
fungi 33, 71, 82, 86-87
fusion 160

G

Gagarin, Yuri 121, 305
Galapagos 63
galaxies 114-115, 117, 119, 122-123, 319-323, 321
Galaxy 114
Galilean moons 106
Galileo 121, 303, 333
Galle, John 109
gamma rays 160, 343
garlic 93
gas 324-325
gases 172-173

gastric juices 29
gaucho 203
gazelle (see antelopes)
gears 164
gecko 63
gems 140
General Sherman 79
generator 154
genetic engineering 37
gentian 206-207, 209
geodes 140
geoid 98, 296
geological column 136
geologists 136, 140, 271, 277
geostationary orbit 121, 306-307
germination 187
germs 32-33, 36-37
geyser 143
gharials 222
giant stars (see stars)
gibbon 49
gila monster 227
gills 237
ginger 93
gingkos 82
ginseng 193
giraffe 221
glacials 287
glaciers 286-7
glade 81, 197
glass 342
glucose 255
gluons 174, 327
gluteus maximus 18, 255
gnu (see wildebeest)
goat 56
gold 176-177, 328-329
goldfish 55
Gondwanaland 272
goose 232
gorge 293
gorse 76
GPS 307
grain 190
grains 138, 140
Grand Canyon 105, 148, 282
granite 138, 140
granules 103
graphite 155

graptolites 271
grass 72
grasslands 202-203, 234-235
gravity 101, 104-106, 112, 116, 166-167, 291, 296, 298, 304-306, 312-313, 318-319, 321, 332-333
gray matter 89
grazing animal 45
Great Australian desert 288
Great Bear 113, 313
Great Red Spot 106, 310
Great Rift Valley 273
Green Revolution 190
greenhouse effect 105, 309
Greenwich, England 126
groundsel 77, 207
Group 115, 176
growing 264-265
growth hormone 264
groyne 150, 291
Guilin Hills, China 283
guillemot 229
guinea pig 43
gulf 291
gull 229
gut (see alimentary canal)
guyots 151
gymnosperm 71, 82, 185
gyromitrin 87

H

half-life 349
Halley's comet 111
halogens 329
hammer (see malleus)
hamster 55
Handy Man 240
Hanuman langur 48
hardwood 79, 194
harvest moon 299
Hawking, Stephen 321
hearing 23, 258-259
heart 14-15, 252-253
heartwood 78, 188
heat 330-331
helium 102, 106, 108, 300-301, 310-312, 314, 321, 325-326, 330
hemisphere 127
hemoglobin 14, 253
herb 92-93
herbal medicine 37
herbivore 44-45, 235
Hercynian 277
heroin 192
herrerasaurus 137, 268
hertz 259
Herzsprung-Russell diagram 112
Himalayan Snowcock 224
Himalayas 146, 276
hip 254
hip bone (see bones)
hippocampus 262-263
hippopotamus 64-65, 221
Hiroshima 349
HIV 33
hominids 240-241
Homo Erectus 240-241
Homo sapiens 137, 268
Homo sapiens sapiens 241
Honda 168
horn 45
horse 44-45
Horsehead nebulae 114
horsetails 84
horst 147
hot spots 279
howler monkey 213
Hubble Space Telescope 121, 303
Hubble, Edwin 348
humerus 254
humidity 128
Huronian 277
hurricane 132-133
Huygens, Christiaan 310
hydraulic power 335
hydroelectric power 169
hydrochloric acid 29
hydrogen 102-3, 106, 108, 112, 175-179, 300-301, 310-312, 314, 321, 326-329, 336
hyphae 86-87
hypocenter 280
hypothalamus 24

I

Iapetus 107
ibex 225
ice 172
Ice Age 273, 286-287
iceberg 287
Iceland 138
ichthyostega 137, 268
igneous rock (see rocks)
iguana 63
illness 34
immune system 32-33, 36, 38
implant 39
incidence, angle of 162
incus 23
index fossils 271
India 144, 146
inert gases (see noble gases)
inertia 166, 334
inflame response 32
inflammation 33
inflation 123
infra red 342
injury 34
insects 66-67
insulin 36
integrated circuit 158
interglacials 287
intermolecular force 333
International Date Line 127
Internet 159, 341
intestine 29, 250
Inuits 249
Io 106, 116
iodine 31, 89
ion 174-175, 327
ionic bond 178, 327
iris 22, 73, 256-257
iron 31, 99, 134, 140, 156-157, 274, 311
iron Age 241, 245
iron oxide 346
irregular galaxy (see galaxies)
ISS 305
ivy 72

375

J

jackal 50
jaguar 213
jaguar 46-47
Jarmo, Iraq 244
jay 187
jelaba 248
jellyfish 137, 237, 268
jerboa 227
Jericho, Israel 246
jerkin 249
joey 231
joint (cave) 292-293
joints 254-255
juggling 263
Jupiter 106-107, 110, 116, 166, 302, 305-6, 308, 310-311
Jurassic Period 137, 268-269

K

K2 276
Kanchenjunga 276
kangaroo 230-231
kangaroo rat 226
karst 282
Karst region, Bosnia 282
Kelvin scale 171, 331
keratin 45
kernal 74
kidney 28
Kilimanjaro, Mt.; Africa 147
killer cell 32
kimono 243
kingfisher 232
kittiwakes 229
kneecap 254
koala 230-231
Kobe, Japan 144, 281
Kola Peninsular, Russia 275
kookaburra 231
Krakatoa 143
krill 52-53
krypton 177

L

lacunae 20

lagoons 291
Laika 100
Laika 304
lammergeier 224
langur 48
lanthanides 176-177, 329
lapilli 143
Large Magellanic Cloud 317
larynx 16
laser light 343
latitude 126
Laurasia 272
lava 100, 143-143, 278-279, 292, 298
Laws of Motion (see Newton, Isaac)
leap year 126, 297
leeches 223
legumes 74
lemur 48
lens 256, 162
Leonov, Alexei 121, 305
leopard 46-47
Lepidoptera 66
lepton 174, 327
leukemia 93
lever 164-165
LGM 315
Lhotse 276
lianas 198-199
lichen 71, 82, 88-89, 184, 209
light 117, 160, 162-163, 342-3
light bulb 177
light pollution 303
light year 118-119, 303, 316-9
lightning 155, 338
limbic system 24
limestone 138, 173, 282, 292-293
lint 194
lion 46-47, 220-1
liquid 324-325, 172-173
lithosphere 134-135, 274-275
litmus paper 179
live attenuated organisms 37
liver 250
liverwort 84-85, 184
lizard 62
Load 164-165

lobsters 229
Local Group 115, 317
lodestone 346
long sight 257
longitude 126
longshore drift 291
loudspeaker 345
lunar eclipse 299
lunar module 304
lungs 16-17, 252-253
lymph 32
lymphatic system 32
lymphocyte 14, 32
lyre bird 230

M

machine 164-165
macrophage 33
Madagascar 48
Magellanic Clouds 115
magenta 163, 257
magma 138, 142, 278-279
magma chamber 142, 278
magnet 154-157, 346
magnetic dip 156
magnetic field 106, 156, 301, 346
Magnetic North 156
magnetism 154-7, 333, 346-347
magnetosphere 156-7, 346
magnetron 161
Main Sequence stars (see stars)
malaria 193
malleus 23
mammal 42-43, 44-5, 52-3, 62
Mammoth Cave, Kentucky 293
mammoths 271
manatee 53
manganese 140
mantle (Earth) 99-100, 134-135, 274-5, 280
Maoris 242
maple 188-189
Marattia (see ferns)
marble 138
margay 47
Marianas trench 151
mariner 2,10 305

marrow 21
Mars 104-102, 110, 120, 296, 302, 305, 308-9
Mars Pathfinder 120, 309
marsupial mole 231
marsupials 230
Masai 242
mass 167, 332
matriarch 44
matter 172, 174-175, 324-325
Matterhorn 147, 225, 283
meander 148-149, 284-285
measles 37
Mechanical Advantage 164-165
medicine 92-93
medulla 24
megaphyllous leaves 85
Meissner's corpuscles 23
melting point 172, 325
memory 24
menstruation 26, 264
Mercalli scale 145
Mercury 104, 296, 302, 308-309
mercury 325, 330
meridians 126
Merino 57
Merkel's disks 23
merychippus 137, 268
mesolithic 241
Mesopotamia 245
mesosphere 129, 134
Mesozoic Era 137
mesquite 204
Messina, Italy 144
mestizos 243
metal 328-329
metallic bond 178
metals 177
metamorphic rock (see rocks)
metamorphosis 65
meteor 104, 110
meteor shower 110
meteorite 110-111, 268-269, 308
methane 108, 311
mica 140
mice 43
microprocessor 158
microsurgeon 39

microwaves 160-161, 303, 307, 342
mid-ocean spreading 135
Milankovitch cycles 287
mildew 86
milk 42, 52-53, 57
Milky Way 114, 302, 316-317, 321
millet 90
minerals 30, 140-141, 274
Mir space station 305
mirror 162
mirrors 343
Mississippi River 285
Mississippi-Missouri river 149
mistletoe 72, 197
mitosis 265
moa 235
Mohenjo-Daro 247
Mohorovicic discontinuity 134, 275
Mojave desert 205
mold 82
molecules 172-173, 174, 179, 324, 327
mollusk 229, 236
momentum 166, 333-334
Mongols 242
monocotyledons 185
monotreme 42, 231
monotreme
month 299
month, lunar 100
Moon 99-102, 118-119, 120-121, 150, 291, 298-299, 301-302, 304-306, 318-319
moonlight 298
moons 311
moose 217
moraine 286-287
morphine 93, 192
moss 84-85, 184-185
moth 66
motion 166-167
mountain 135, 138, 146-147
mountain goat 225
mountain hare 225
mountain plants 206-207
mountains 276-277, 282

mouse (computer) 159
mouth 29
movement 334-335
Mt. Everest 105, 276
Mt. Fujiyama 277-279
Mt. Kenya 207
Mt. Kilimanjaro 220, 278
Mt. McKinlay 147, 277
Mt. St Helens, Washington 143
Mt. Tamboro, Java 143
Mt. Toba, Sumatra 143
Mt. Vesuvius 143
Mt. Wilhelm 147
mucus 260
mudskipper 223
muscarine 87
muscle 18-19, 254-255
mushroom rock 288-289
mushrooms 86-87
myofibrils 18-19, 255
myosin 18-19, 255

N

nappe 146, 276
NASA 105
natural gas 139, 169
Neanderthal Man 240-241
nebulae 114, 312, 315
nectar 66, 75
needles 82
Neolithic 241
Neptune 108-109, 121, 305, 310-311
nerves 22-25, 263
nervous system 25, 262
neurons 25, 262
neurotransmitters 25
neutrinos 327
neutron 160, 174, 326-8, 349
neutrophils 14, 32
Nevadian 277
névé 286
New Forest 215
New World monkeys 48
New York 273
newt 64-65
Newton, Isaac 167, 332-335
newtons 333

nickel 134, 156, 274
Nile river 149
nitrogen 108, 176
nitrous oxides 169
noble gases 177, 328-329
nomads 242
North Pole 126, 347
northern lights (see Aurora Borealis)
nuclear
nuclear fission 348-9
nuclear fusion 348
nuclear fusion reaction 312
nuclear power 348-349
nuclear power station 348
nucleus 174, 177, 326, 348-349
nueé ardenté 279
nutmeg 93

O

oasis 205, 288-289
Oaxaca 243
oblate spheroid 98
observatory 102, 302
oceans 150-1
Ohain, Pabst von 335
oil 139, 169
Okavango Delta, Botswana 223
Old World monkeys 48
olfactory epithelium 260
olfactory nerve (see nerves)
olives 90
olivine 141
Olympus Mons 105, 309
onion 72-73
opaque 162
Open Universe 321
open universe idea 122
opium 93, 192
Oppenheimer, Robert 349
opthalmoscope 34
optic nerve 256
orangutan 49
orbit 104, 107, 108-109, 116, 121, 306-307
orchid 76
Ordovician Period 137, 269
oregano 89-93

organ of Corti 259
Orion 113-14, 313
ossicles 23, 258-259, 344
osteoclasts 21
osteocytes 20
osteons 21
ostrich 220-221, 235
otter 232
ovaries (human) 26
ovaries (plant) 74, 79, 186-187, 197
ovulation 27
ovules 74
ovum 27
Owen, Richard 235
owl 61
oxbow lake 284-5
oxygen 14-15, 16-17, 19, 175-176, 178-179, 237, 252-3, 296, 304, 348

P

P waves 280
pacemaker 39
paddy field 91
paddy fields 190-191
Paleolithic 241
paleomagnetism 156
Paleozoic Era 137
pampas 202-203
pancreas 29
panda 50-51
panels 168
Pangea 272
Panthalassa 272
paper 194
papillae 260
papyrus 200, 247
parallax method 118-119, 319
parasite 86, 185
parsec 118-119, 318-319
particle accelerator 123, 321
Pasadenian 277
patella 254
payload 304
peat 85, 139
pectorals 255
Pegasus Constellation 55, 113

pelvis 254
penguin 53, 219
penicillin 36
penis 26
pentagon 307
perennials 73, 77
perihelion 127, 297
Periodic Table 176-177
periodic table 328-9
Periodics (comets) 111
Periods 136, 176, 268-269
periosteum 21
peristalsis 29
periwinkle 93, 192
Permian Period 137, 269
pesticides 190
petal 186
petal 75
petiole 70
Petra, Jordan 247
pets 54-55
phalloidine 87
pharaohs 247
pharynx 16
phases 101
phloem 70, 285
phosphate 21, 254
phosphor 158
photon 163, 342
photosphere 102, 300
photosynthesis 71, 169, 185
phytoplankton 89
pig 45, 56
pike 233
pine martens 216
pinna 259
Pioneer II 121
pip 80
Pisces 313
pistils 186
piston 334
pituitary gland 262, 264-265
placenta 27
planets 104-109
plankton 70, 89, 237
plantation 79, 81, 90
plants 184-185
plasma 14
plastron 63

platelets 14
Pleiades 313
plow 245
plum 74
plume 142
Pluto 108-109, 118, 305, 310-311, 318
plutonium 174, 349
poison-arrow frog 212
polar bear 219
Polaris 313
Pole Star 113
poles 156-157
polio 37
polje 293
pollen 67, 75, 79, 83, 186-187
pollination 77
Pompeii 143
pons 24
poppy 74, 93, 192
porcupine 43
porphyra 89
porpoise 52
possum 231
potato 72-73
pothole 292
poultry 57
power station 154, 168-169
prairies 202-203
Precambrian 137
Precambrian 268
pregnancy 27
prehensile tail 48, 213
pressure 129, 132-133, 171
prickly pear 94, 191, 205
primary colours 257
Prime Meridian 126
primroses 196-197
prism 163, 342
probe 159, 166
proboscis 44
proboscis monkey 223
proconsul 137, 268
prominences 103
prosthetics 39
protein 30-31, 251
Proterozoic 137, 268
prothallus 84-85
Protoctista 88

proton 174-176, 326-7
Proxima Centauri 118, 313, 318
pterandon 137, 268
pteridophytes 84
puberty 26, 264-265
puffball 86
pufferfish 237
puffin 229
pulmonary circulation (see circulation)
pulp 251
pulsars 315
pulse 14
puma 46, 224-225
pupa 66
pupil 22, 256-257
pylon 154
pyloric sphincter 29
pyramids 247
pyroxene 141
python 213

Q

quark 174, 326-327
quartz 140-141
quasar 117-118, 314, 319
Quaternary Period 137, 269
quinine 93, 192-193
quiver tree 204

R

rabbit 43
raccoon 50, 216
radar beams 119
radiation 117, 160-161, 170, 303, 312, 321, 324
radio waves 160, 303, 312, 342
radioactive dating 268
radioactivity 136, 160, 270, 349
radius 254
Rafflesia 95, 198
ragged robin 76
rain 128-129
rainbow trout 233
rainforest 94, 198-199, 212-213
RAM 159, 341
rare earths (see lanthanides)

rat 43
Rayleigh waves 281
reaction 102
recording tape 344
rectum 29
recumbent 146
red giant 314
red setter 55
red shift 122, 319
redwood tree (see trees)
reeds 194
reflection 162, 342
reflection, angle of 162
refraction 162, 343
reindeer 88, 217
Relative Humidity 129
Relative Magnitude 112
reproductive organs 24
reptile 42, 62-63
resin 270
resistance (electrical) 155
resistance 339
respiration 17
resultant 333
retina 22, 256
rhinocerous 42, 44-45
rhizoids 85
rhizome 72-73
rib 254
rice 90-91
Richter scale 145, 281
rift valley 147
Ring of Fire 279
River Nile 285, 288
rivers 148-149, 284-285
robot 341
rock 270, 276-278, 288-289, 298, 308
rock arch 290-291
rock pool 228-229
rocket 120, 304, 306-307
rocks 136, 138-139
Rocky Mountains 79, 146, 276
rodent 43
rods 22, 257
rokerboom 202
ROM 159, 341
rookeries 53
root hairs 72

379

roots 72-73, 94
rose 76-77
rosemary 93
rubidium 136
runners (plant) 73

S

S waves 280
Saami 249
saffron 93
sage 93
saguaro 204-205
Sahara desert 205, 227, 242, 273, 288-289
salamander 64-65
saliva 250, 260
salmon 233
salt molecules 327
San Andreas fault 144, 273, 281
San Francisco 144
sand 290
sand cat 226
sand dunes 288-289
sandstone 140
saprophytes 86
sapwood 78, 188
Sarawak Chamber, Malaysia 293
sari 248
satellite 98, 116, 120-121, 133, 144, 159, 305-307
saturated solution 173
Saturn 106-108, 121, 302, 305-306, 310-311
sauropods 271
scabious 203
scan 25, 34-35, 161
scarlet pimpernel 76-77
scorpion 227
scree 147, 282
sea campion 76
sea cow 52-53
sea lion 219
sea lion 52-53
sea urchin 229
seal 42, 52-53, 218

seamounts 151
seashore 228-229
seasons 127, 297
seaweed 89, 184-185
sediment 276, 285, 331
sedimentary rock (see rocks)
seeds (plant) 185-187, 190, 197
seeds 74-75
seifs 289
seismic waves 145
seismologists 144
seismometer 145, 280-281
self-pollination 186
semen 26
semicircular canals 258-259
semiconductors 340
sense receptors 261
senses 22-23
sepal 75, 186
septum 15
sequoia 79, 83
sequoia tree 189
setts 214
shadow 342
shark 236-237
sheep 56-57
shingle 290
short sight 257
Siberia 83
sickle 245
sickness 32-33
sight (eye) 22
silage 91, 190
silica 138, 278
silicates 140-141
silicon 141, 314
silicon chip 340
silk 249
silt 284
Silurian Period 137, 269
silver 141
singularity 117
Sirius 113
Sirius, Dog Star 313
skeleton 20, 254

skin 23
skull 254
slate 138
sloth 213
slow-twitch red muscle 19
smallpox 37
smell 23 260-261
smoking 253
snake 62
snout (glacier) 286-287
snow 128, 130-131
snow leopard 225
snowline 207, 277
snowshoe hare 218
sodium 104, 178, 327
sodium chloride 329
softwood 79, 194
SOHO space telescope 303
soil 72
solar eclipse 103, 299, 301
solar flares 301
solar prominences 301
solar system 296, 308-309, 311, 316, 319
solar wind 299, 346
solenoid 154, 156
solid 324-325
solids 172-173
solute 337
solution 173, 336-337
solvent 337
sonic boom 345
sooty tern 229
sorghum 90-91
sori 84
sound 258-259, 344-345
sound barrier 345
space labs 305
space probe 119-120, 308
space shuttle 120, 304-305
space stations 305
space travel 120-121
spacecraft 120, 304-305, 308, 310
spawn 64-65, 233

speech 24
speed of sound 345
spenophytes 84
sperm 26-27, 264
spheres 129
spice 92-93
spinal cord 24-25
spine 254
spoonbill 223
sporangia 84-85
spore 84-85, 185
spring tide 291
springbok 204-205
springs 148, 284
Sputnik 1 and 2 120-121, 304, 306
spy satellites 307
squid 237
squirrel 43
St. Bernard 55
stack 150, 290-291
stalactite 173, 292-293
stalagmite 173, 292-293
stamens 186
standard candles 119, 319
stapes 23
star anise 93
stars 105, 112-113, 116-117, 123, 302-303, 312-316, 318-9, 321
static electricity 155, 338
statics 167
stem 24
steppes 202
sternum (see bones)
stethoscope 34
stigma 186
stomach 29, 250
stomata 71
Stone Age 241
stonefish 237
storm surge 132
storms 129, 132
stratosphere 129
strawberry plant 73
strike 146
stirrup (see bones, also stapes)

stromatolites 270
strontium 161
style 186
sub-atomic particles 174
subduction 135, 140
submarines 336
submillimeter 303
succulents 94, 205
suckers 73
Sudan desert 288
sugar 191
sugarcane 91
sulfur 106, 141, 175
sulfuric acid 105, 308-309
Sumer 247
Sumeria 248
Sun 102-103, 104, 108-109, 115, 118-119, 123, 130-131, 132, 136, 157, 168, 296-302, 308-312, 314, 316-319, 346-347
sunflower 90
sunspot 103, 300-301
supercells 133
superforce 320
supergiant stars 314-315
supernova 113, 119, 314-315, 319
superplumes 134
surgery 38-39
suspension (chemical) 337
swallowhole 292-293
swan 60
swells 291
swim bladder 237
synapse 25, 263
syncline 146, 277
system 105, 110-111, 120, 123

T

tadpole 232
tadpole 64-65
takin 45
taproot 72, 77
Tasmanian devil 230
taste 23, 260-261

taste bud 260-261
tea 92
teats 42
tectonic plate 135, 142, 144-14, 272, 275, 277, 279-281
teeth 251
telecommunications 240
telescope 302-303
television 158
Telstar 306
temperature 330
tephra 142
terminal velocity 167
terminator 299
termite 67
terrier 54
Tertiary Period 137, 269
testes 26
tetanus 36
Tethys 107
tetracycline 36
TGV 335
thalamus 24
thermometer 170-171, 330
thermosphere 129
thinking 262-263
thorax 66-67
thorny devil 231
thrift 76
Thrust II 332
thunder 130
Tibet 224
tidal boom 337
tides 150, 291
tiger 46
timber 194
timber line 206
timber wolf 225
time zones 127
Tiros 1 306
Titan 107
Titan 311
Titanic 287
titanium 39
toad 66-65
toadstools 86

381

togas 249
tongue 260-261
tor 283
Tornado Alley 133
tortoise 63
toucan 212-213
touch 260-261
trabeculae 254
trace fossil 270
trachea 16-17
trajectory 116, 307
transistor 158, 340
Transition metals 176-177
translucent 162
transparent 162
transplant 38
tree rings 188
trees 78-83, 184-185
tremors 145
Triassic Period 137, 268-269
tributaries 284
tributary 148
triceps 255
trilobite 137
trilobite 268, 270-271
Triton 108
Trojans, the 111
tropical plants 198-199
troposphere 129
trousers 249
trunk (elephant) 220
trunk 44
tsunami 281
tuber 72-73
tuberculosis 36
tulip 76-77
Tully-Fisher technique 119
tuna 237
tundra 209
tungsten 325
turban 248
turbine 154, 335, 348
turkey 57
turning effect 165
turtle 63, 236-237
tusks 44, 53

Tutankhamun 319
Tutunendo, Colombia 131
typhoon 132
Tyrannosaurus Rex 271

U

ulna 254
ultraviolet light 343
Uluru 282, 289
umbilical cord 27
understory (rain-forest) 199
ungulates 45, 235
Universe 118-119, 122-123, 320-321
uranium 136, 160-161, 169, 348-349
uranium oxide 141
Uranus 108-109, 305, 310-311
urea 28
ureter 28
urethra 28
urine 28
Ursa Major (see Great Bear)
uterus 26

V

vaccination 32, 36-37
vacuum 344
vagina 26-27
valency 178
Valles Marineris 105
valley 148
vegetative propagation 73
vein 252-253
veins 14-15, 140
veld 202
velocity ratio 165
velvet 215
vena cava 253
Venera 11, 121
vent 278-279
ventricle 15, 252-253
venules 14
Venus 104-105, 118, 120, 286, 292, 298-299, 318
Verne, Jules 275
Verrier, Urbain le 109
vertebrae 254
vertebrate 42
Vesta 110
vibration 344
Victoria Falls 149
Viking space probes 305, 309
vincristine 93
Vinson Massif, Antarctica 277
virtual reality 341
virus 33, 36
visible light 303
visual cortex 263
vitamin 30-31, 251
vitreous humor 22, 257
vixen 215
volcanic bomb 142-143
volcano 100, 105-106, 108, 116, 134-135, 138, 140-141, 275, 278-279, 292, 296, 298, 308-309
vomit 251
Vostok, Antarctica 131
Voyager space mission 109
Voyager space probe 305, 311
vulcanologists 142, 279
vultures 226-227

W

wadi 289
wallaby 231
wallflowers 77
walnut 79
walrus 52-53
waning 101
warm front (see fronts)
warm-blooded 42, 52

water 98, 172-173, 128, 185, 296, 324-5, 329, 336-337
water cycle 324-32
water hyacinth 200
water table 292

water vole 292
waterfall 149, 285, 292
wattle 57
wavelength 342-3
waves 291
waxing 101
waxwing 187
weasel 43
weather 128-9
weathering 282-283
weight 332
wetlands 222-223
whale 236-237, 42, 52-53
wheat 90-91, 190
wheel 245
white dwarfs 312, 315
Whittle, Frank 335
whooping cough 36-37
wildebeest 47, 221, 234
wildflowers 76-77
willow 192
wind 129, 132-133
window plant 205
winds 310
witch doctor 37
withies 81
wolf 50
wolves 217
womb 26-27
wombat 230
wood mice 215
wood sorrel 197
woodland 80, 196-197, 214-215
woodpecker 214
work 165
writing 247

X

X-ray 34-5, 100, 160-161, 175,
    303, 343
xylem 70, 185, 189

Y

yak 224

Yangtze River 149
Yeager, Chuck 345
yeast 86
Yosemite dome, California 286

Z

zebra 47, 221
ziggurat 247
zinc 155
zones 135, 142

Acknowledgments

All photographs from
Miles Kelly Archive